LEARNING TO BE AN
ANTHROPOLOGIST AND
REMAINING "NATIVE"

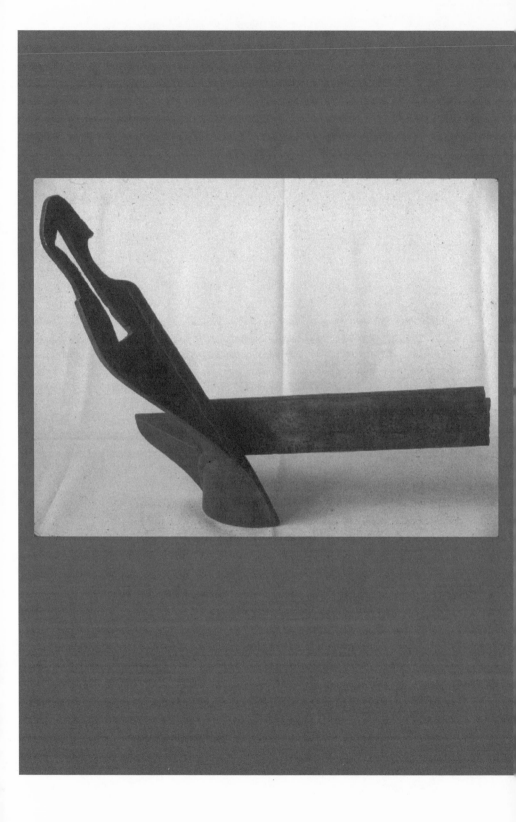

Learning to Be an Anthropologist and Remaining "Native"

Selected Writings

Dr. Beatrice Medicine

EDITED WITH SUE-ELLEN JACOBS

Forewords by Ted Garner and Faye V. Harrison

UNIVERSITY OF ILLINOIS PRESS

URBANA AND CHICAGO

© 2001 by the Board of Trustees
of the University of Illinois
Ted Garner retains the copyright to his
foreword and descriptions of his artworks
All rights reserved
Manufactured in the United States of America
1 2 3 4 5 C P 5 4 3 2 1
∞ This book is printed on acid-free paper.

Frontispiece: *Siouxish* ©1978 by Ted Garner (welded steel;
9.5 by 16 by 6 inches). (Courtesy of Ted Garner)

Library of Congress Cataloging-in-Publication Data
Medicine, Beatrice.
Learning to be an anthropologist and remaining "Native" :
selected writings / Beatrice Medicine ; edited with Sue-Ellen Jacobs ;
forewords by Ted Garner and Faye V. Harrison.
p.   cm.
Includes bibliographical references and index.
ISBN 0-252-02573-3 (cloth : acid-free paper)
ISBN 0-252-06979-x (pbk. : acid-free paper)
1. Indians of North America. 2. Dakota Indians. 3. Indian women—
North America. 4. Women anthropologists—United States.
5. Medicine, Beatrice. I. Jacobs, Sue-Ellen. II. Title.
E77.2.M43   2001
305.897—dc21   00–012722

CONTENTS

FOREWORD

Ted Garner

Growing up with both anthropology and Indianness, I was given the opportunity to view the world from both poles, so to speak. It is a very interesting contrast to observe, the intuitive and the cataloged, especially when the occupation and the avocation of the one is to attempt to describe the ineffable nature of the other.

Of course, my mother, Beatrice Medicine, is much more than just "Indian" and "anthro," but that contrast seemed, and in a way still seems, axiomatic, especially to me, with my feet (unfortunately, both usually the left) in each camp. In part, that is because this contrast captures both the unavoidable gulf and the welcoming comfort of fit between the group and the individual. And, like it or not, this is an eternal and omnipresent question for any mixed-blood individual—the question of belonging.

I learned to appreciate that truths appear in many diverse and sometimes contradictory manners, almost like the Heisenberg Principle of Uncertainty, which holds that one can know either the speed of an electron or its location, not both at the same time. The discovery is ruled and controlled by the methods of exploration, an early and important lesson in right-left brain activity and also in appropriate behavior between the two worlds. Not to imply that this knowledge occurred instantly, like Athena leaping full-grown out of Zeus' bad headache. Luckily, both of my parents instilled early in me a broad and catholic (small *c*) sense of the world that would help me use this dichotomy to understand my situation. To use some terminology of my adopted occupation, you have to paint like Andrew Wyeth and Franz Kline—both at the same time.

Similarly, my grandparents equipped my mother well and in the face of considerable obstacles. My grandfather, Martin Medicine, was born about nine months after Wounded Knee, and the cultural bias that allowed that horror dogged him his whole life. Given recent events in northern South Dakota, it is obvious that those tendencies have not faded, even with more time passed. Despite this, and having had to start work at a very young age because his fa-

ther was blind, he essentially educated himself and remained forever interested
in news and world affairs. Seeing action in World War I added to his interest in
the far-away and led to two later developments. First, he joined a largely (dis-
counting him, perhaps exclusively) white off-reservation veterans' post. To attempt to bridge the gap? To cultivate perceived opportunity? I never quite
figured it out. Second, he named his younger son after one of the battles he'd
been in, making Marne Medicine one of the few Sioux to be named after a river in France, I am sure.

I have always found naming your child for a war exploit earned in a khaki
Thirty-fifth Division uniform, complete with puttees, a curious mixture of tradition and modernity. It hearkens back to the warrior society of old in celebrat-
ing the new world of being American. My grandfather was always proud of
having been given the franchise in 1920 for his war service, four years before the
Indian population at large. At the same time, the changes the war was bringing
to the world as a whole, mechanization and increased communication, were
coming to Standing Rock to augment the massive changes already underway.

The 1920s and 1930s were not good times to be a Lakota, even before the Great
Depression, because of having to hide one's religion, which had just been officially outlawed, and being in the charge of "resident farmers" installed to su-
pervise the officially hoped for transition to being ranchers and dirt farmers.
That transition was an East Coast–Washington, D.C., plan doomed by gumbo
mud, fifteen-inch rainfall, and the strength of the concept of sharing among
tiyospaye (the extended family). The tiyospaye was itself under attack by regulations limiting travel, gathering, and dancing in the hope of "killing the Indian and saving the man."

Collier's Reorganization Act in 1934 helped, allowing some self-representa-
tion, but my grandfather found the same degree of interest among politicians
that his grandfather had found in 1872 when he went to Washington to protest
violations of the 1868 Fort Laramie Treaty. And we know how *that* wound up.

Despite all this, though, my grandparents, greats-, and other family members
instilled tradition and adaptability in my mother and her siblings, both biological and "temporary" (the fosters and cousins of that extended family)—sometimes clandestinely (my grandfather taking my mother to a still-forbidden Sun
Dance), sometimes by using the new institutions for his own aims. Others did
the same. This helps to explain the popularity of the Catholic Indian Congresses,
sanctioned opportunities to travel, gather, visit, and talk. All of which led to an
event in 1945 and a photograph that always had pride of place in my grandparents' home: my mother in gown and mortarboard between her parents in front
of the ivy-covered brick entrance to a building at South Dakota A&M (now
State) University.

That grounding in family gave my mother the strength to exploit opportunities offered by what I think of as the "second flowering of anthropology,"
fueled in part by the GI Bill and the restive returning veterans and in part by

the growing involvement of women in the discipline. It also gave her a sense of mentoring and ensuring continuity, the depth and strength of which I find her most admirable trait. She is bound to be encouraging students, children, and contemporaries almost any time you see her.

Her ability to both observe and partake in whatever solemnity or silliness is at hand has also always amazed me, whether she is giggling wildly in a tipi at some long-held yet freshly shared schoolgirl memories or fending off with good grace the subtle forays of a former cold warrior at a stately function. These skills have to do with being comfortable in one's skin and with one's own company.

Being a part of a history, an ethnicity, a culture, and a lineage that lives within oneself and yet can be transmitted to others—that is the art of life. The following pages will transmit some of that, but only a very, very small part. The remaining part belongs to those lucky enough to have known, loved, and been taught by Beatrice Medicine.

Pilamaye, Ina.

FOREWORD

Faye V. Harrison

MEDICINE WOMAN
Teacher
Social Worker
Counselor
Anthropologist

Poet
Humanist
Social Scientist
Applied Anthropologist

Neighbor
Kinswoman
Sacred Pipe Woman of the Sun Dance
Woman of Action and Activism
We esteem and honor you
And recognize the struggles and quests
That have led you down the path in which
You have walked and continue to walk
You do not travel alone
Your journey is part of a collective struggle
A movement forward to Freedom
A Freedom both creatively self-defined and
Gauged by the technical certainty of science
May your dream and vision of Freedom
Continue to inspire you
And those of us who dare
Seize the time Now for the Future
Of struggle and change in the New Millennium

Teacher
Sacred Pipe Woman of the Sun Dance
We sing our praises before the light of the Moon and Sun
Which illuminates empowering possibilities
For re-making the World.

In 1975–76, I began graduate school at Stanford University. Although I thought I had already decided that a career in anthropology was for me, I came much closer to a definite decision, not just in my mind but in my heart, when I arrived at Stanford and came across Bea Medicine, a visiting scholar there for only a year. Her presence struck me. There she was, a real, live, role model for students of color and for any perceptive, deeply thinking, and conscious student. I remember reflecting that if the "Indian"—especially the conventionally neglected "Indian woman"—as a historic object of the anthropological gaze could "seize the time" to constitute and assert the agency of critically thinking, challenging and demanding subjects, then certainly I, and other kindred spirits, could rightfully and righteously claim space and project a voice in response to the call to reinvent anthropology and apply its tools and gifts to this era of human social and cultural development. Little did I know then that I would be a witness to, and a participant in, this celebration and critical reflection in her honor.

In 1945 Bea Medicine graduated from South Dakota State University with a bachelor of science degree in the combined major of education and art history. Within less than a decade, she had earned a master's degree in anthropology and sociology. She has written that she, like the few other Native anthropologists before her, went into anthropology "to try and make living more fulfilling for Indians" (Medicine 1978c:196). Again, her goal reflected "a strong interest in the application of anthropological knowledge" (184). That approach was tied to "the native idea of education, no matter in what field, as a means of alleviating problems and providing self-help" (184). That Bea Medicine has been successful in meeting the goal she set for herself in 1945 is illustrated in one of the letters of commendation the Malinowski Award committee received. The author of the letter, Jane H. Kelley, wrote:

> I would like to begin by relating a fairly recent event that encapsulates one of Bea's unswerving commitments—namely that natives speak for themselves and deal with their own problems of contemporary life. The occasion was a session on the "Berdache" at the 1993 AAA meetings in Washington, at which Bea was one of two discussants. Most of the papers were given by native people, and there were many young native anthropologists and non-anthropologists in the audience. When Bea rose to speak, she received a standing ovation. My words of course fail to convey the strong emotion that was present in the room. If one hadn't known how important that woman is to native peoples, and, in this case, how important she has been in forwarding gender studies among

native peoples, this memorable reception would have been enough to impart such a message—even to someone who didn't know her work. (Oct. 26, 1995)

In many respects, Dr. Bea Medicine represents the quintessential outsider within a professional anthropology whose vision historically has been focused through the lenses of non-Native folk, who—however keenly perceptive, partially "objective," or well-intentioned—have dominated the privilege and authority to write, interpret, and theorize North American Indian culture. Nonetheless, to anthropology's advantage and benefit, Bea Medicine has dared to be an insider in the applied anthropology of Native communities and has served in the multiple capacities of educator, advocate, advisor, consultant, evaluator, planner, director, research coordinator, expert witness, public intellectual, and citizen. Because of her success and the support she has mobilized over the years in the United States and Canada, and more recently in Australia, New Zealand, Botswana, Russia, and elsewhere, she has brought anthropology's tools and perspectives to bear on problem-solving in the arenas of indigenous alcohol and drug treatment, community health and mental health, gender-cognizant multicultural education, language policy, criminal justice and law enforcement, religious revitalization and tolerance, and the organizational development of women's empowerment (Albers and Medicine, eds. 1983; Medicine 1975, 1976a, 1976b, 1978a, 1978b, 1978c, 1979a, 1979b, 1981a, 1981b, 1982, 1986, 1987a, 1987b, 1987c, 1987d, 1988, 1993, 1994; Medicine and Trimble 1976).

The many jokes about anthropologists being a dime a dozen on Indian reservations do not apply—at least not in the same way—to Bea Medicine or the kind of anthropological praxis in which she and her predecessors such as Ella Deloria, Francis LaFlesche, William Jones, and Ed Dozier have long engaged (see Medicine [1978b] and Sanjek [1993] for discussion on the ethnographic research of Native field assistants; see Finn [1993] for analysis of the ethnographic and experiential grounding of Deloria's novel, *Waterlily*). We need to ask ourselves about the kind of lessons Bea Medicine and the tradition of subaltern analysis that she represents can teach about recapturing, decolonizing, and transforming anthropology. Her perspective and experience as a Native intellectual and activist within, rather than "out there" as an informant in the field, enrich anthropological praxis in ways we are only beginning to understand and appreciate (cf. D'Amico-Samuels 1991; Harrison 1991; Rosaldo 1989).

Doctor Medicine has been an academic nomad for much of her professional life, which extends from the 1940s, when she began her distinguished career by teaching home economics and health education, to the present. She lives as a highly respected elder among her people, the Sihasapa Lakota Sioux, on the Standing Rock Reservation in Wakpala, South Dakota. The professional mobility she has experienced throughout her career is surely indicative of how much she is cherished by so many departments and programs in such universities as the University of Calgary, California State University at Northridge, the University of Toronto, the University of Wisconsin-Madison, the University of Washing-

xvi*Foreword by Faye V. Harrison*

ton-Seattle, San Francisco State University, Dartmouth College, and Stanford University. Her professional nomadism also reflects the responsibilities of leadership in the struggle for Native American or American Indian studies—both as a Native Americanist and an American Indian. Notwithstanding her deserved celebrity, Doctor Medicine's career trajectory—along with its hidden injuries and burdens—might also prompt us to interrogate (and seek to resolve) some of the contradictions within academia that make the retention and ambivalent hyperprivileging of minority scholars problematic (Dominguez 1994).

Awarded an honorary doctorate of humane letters from Northern Michigan University four years before she received a Ph.D. in anthropology from the University of Wisconsin-Madison in 1983, Bea Medicine's terminal degree was merely a rite of validation and intensification for one whose real initiation into the profession had occurred at least thirty years before and whose rise to national prominence had begun in the 1960s with publication of important articles on changes in the Dakota family and the status of Native Americans in modern society (Medicine 1969a, 1969b). Since that time, she has published extensively and become an authoritative voice in Native American studies, particularly in studies of Native American women, their struggles, and their needs. Over the past forty years, she has been an exemplary agent of praxis and change.

Note

Faye V. Harrison was chair of the Malinowski Award Committee in 1995–96. Her citation in honor of Beatrice Medicine, to whom that award was presented, is reproduced with minor editorial changes in this Foreword.

References

Albers, Patricia, and Beatrice Medicine, eds. 1983. *The Hidden Half: Studies of Plains Indian Women.* Washington: University Press of America.
D'Amico-Samuels, Deborah. 1991. "Undoing Fieldwork: Personal, Political, Theoretical and Methodological Implications." In *Decolonizing Anthropology,* ed. Faye V. Harrison, 68–87. Washington: American Anthropological Association.
Dominguez, Virginia. 1994. "A Taste for 'The Other': Intellectual Complicity in Racializing Practices." *Current Anthropology* 35(4): 333–48.
Finn, Janet L. 1993. "Ella Cara Deloria and Mourning Dove." *Critique of Anthropology* 13(4): 335–49.
Harrison, Faye V. 1991. "Anthropology as an Agent of Transformation." In *Decolonizing Anthropology,* ed. Faye V. Harrison, 1–14. Washington: American Anthropological Association.
Medicine, Beatrice. 1969a. "The American Indian in Modern Society." *South Dakota Review* 7(2): 189–91.
———. 1969b. "The Changing Dakota Family and the Stresses Therein." *Pine Ridge Research Bulletin* 9: 13–23.
———. 1975. "Self-Direction in Sioux Education." *Integrateducation* 78(Nov.–Dec.): 15–17.
———. 1976a. "Oral History as Truth: Validity of Recent Court Cases Involving Native Americans." *Folklore Forum,* Bibliographic and Special Series 9(15): 1–5.

———. 1976b. "The Schooling Process: Some Lakota (Sioux) Views." *The Anthropological Study of Education,* ed. Craig Calhoun and Francis A. J. Ianni, 283–91. The Hague: Mouton.

———. 1978a. "Higher Education: A New Arena for Native Americans." *Thresholds in Education* 4(2): 22–25.

———. 1978b. "Learning to Be an Anthropologist and Remaining 'Native.'" In *Applied Anthropology in America,* ed. Elizabeth M. Eddy and William L. Partridge, 182–96. New York: Columbia University Press.

———. 1978c. *Native American Women: A Perspective.* Las Cruces: ERIC/CRESS.

———. 1979a. "Bilingual Education and Public Policy: The Cases of the American Indian." In *Bilingual Education and Public Policy in the United States,* ed. Raymond V. Padilla, 395–407. Ypsilanti: Department of Foreign Languages and Bilingual Studies, Eastern Michigan University.

———. 1979b. "Native American Communication Patterns: The Case of Lakota-Speakers." In *The Handbook of Intercultural Communication,* ed. Molefi K. Asante, Eileen Newmark, and Cecil A. Blake, 378–81. Beverly Hills: Sage Publications.

———. 1981a. "American Indian Family: Cultural Change and Adaptive Strategies." *Journal of Ethnic Studies* 8(4): 13–23.

———. 1981b. "Native American Resistance to Integration: Contemporary Confrontations and Religious Revitalization." *Plains Anthropologist* 26(94): 277–86.

———. 1982. "Native American Women Look at Mental Health." *Plainswomen* 6(4): 7.

———. 1986. "Contemporary Cultural Revisitation: Bilingual and Bicultural Education." *Wicazo Sa Review Indian Studies Journal* 2(1): 31–35.

———. 1987a. "Understanding the Native Community." *Multicultural Education Journal* 5(4): 21–26.

———. 1987b. "The Role of Elders in Native Education." In *The Challenge,* vol. 2 of *Indian Education in Canada,* ed. Jean Barman, Yvonne Hébert, and Don McCaskill, 142–52. Vancouver: University of British Columbia Press.

———. 1987c. "Indian Women and the Renaissance of Traditional Religion." In *Sioux Indian Religion,* ed. Raymond J. De Mallie and Douglas R. Parks, 159–71. Norman: University of Oklahoma Press.

———. 1987d. "The Role of American Indian Women in Cultural Continuity and Transition." In *Women and Language in Transition,* ed. Joyce Penfield, 159–66. Albany: SUNY Press.

———. 1988. "Native American (Indian) Women: A Call for Research." *Anthropology and Education Quarterly* 19(2): 86–92.

———. 1993. "American Indian Women: Mental Health Issues which Relate to Drug Abuse." *Wicazo Sa Review Indian Studies Journal* 9(2): 85–90.

———. 1994. "North American Indigenous Women and Cultural Domination." *Cultural Survival Quarterly* 17(4): 66–69.

Medicine, Beatrice, and Joseph Trimble. 1976. "Development of Theoretical Models and Levels of Interpretation in Mental Health." In *Anthropology and Mental Health: Setting a New Course,* ed. Joseph Westermeyer, 161–200. The Hague: Mouton.

Rosaldo, Renato. 1989. *Culture and Truth: The Re-Making of Social Analysis.* Boston: Beacon Press.

Sanjek, Roger. 1993. "Anthropology's Hidden Colonialism: Assistants and Their Ethnographers." *Anthropology Today* 9(2): 13–18.

ACKNOWLEDGMENTS

As Sue-Ellen Jacobs and I have prepared this work, we have had wonderful assistance from students and staff in the Department of Women Studies at the University of Washington. We thank students Sarna Lapine (1997) and Kathryn R. Smith (1999–2000) and staff member Mary Saucier for data collection and entry, library searches, and devotion to the task of completing various phases of the manuscript's development. In addition, Carol Langdon facilitated the work of others. We are grateful to Alice Kehoe for a careful reading of the first collection of essays, and for making excellent suggestions for revisions of that draft manuscript, and to Elizabeth Dulany, our devoted editor at the University of Illinois Press, who has worked with us on several projects over the years. Mary Giles, our copy editor at the University of Illinois Press, provided close attention to detail and approached the task with an iron hand and a sense of humor. The result is the most thorough documentation of my work to date.

Kathryn Smith, a University of Washington graduate student in Slavic languages and literature, provided important attention to detail during the final correction of the manuscript, took on the responsibility of locating and corresponding with the original publishers of the essays presented here, and, when necessary, followed through with additional correspondence in order to secure their permission to republish the material.

Our deep appreciation and affection to Faye Harrison for graciously allowing the publication of her beautiful poem and complimentary introduction to the Malinowski Address included here. And last, but not least, we thank Ted Garner for writing the revealing Foreword and giving permission to reproduce photographs of his amazing sculpture: *Siouxish, Wešlekapi Teca, Deer Heart II, Babyneedsanewbonnett,* and *Ideadeer II.* The photographs taken by, and republished with permission of, C. E. Burke in chapter 17 are part of a series, "Quilt Parade," taken at the Bullhead Powwow Parade on Sunday, August 16, 1998. The other illustrations are from my private collection.

The image of Ted's sculpture *Siouxish* was chosen for the frontispiece of this volume because of an anecdote from his childhood. When he was about six, he asked a young playmate, "Have you heard about Jewish mothers?" When the playmate nodded, Ted said, "Siouxish mothers are worse."

Pilamaye, Kangi Iyotake.

* * *

Permission to republish the following chapters, with minor editorial alterations, has been granted by:

Chapter 1: "Learning to Be an Anthropologist and Remaining 'Native,'" reprinted with permission from *Applied Anthropology in America: Past Contributions and Future Directions*, edited by Elizabeth Eddy and William Partridge (New York: Columbia University Press, 1978), 182–96. Permission conveyed through the Copyright Clearance Center, Inc.

Chapter 2: "'Speaking Indian': Parameters of Language Use among American Indians," reprinted with permission from *Focus: National Clearinghouse for Bilingual Education* 6 (March 1981): 3–10.

Chapter 3: "Bilingual Education and Public Policy: The Cases of the American Indian," in *Ethnoperspectives in Bilingual Education Research Series*, edited by Raymond V. Padilla (Tempe: Bilingual Press, 1979), 1:395–407.

Chapter 4: "Contemporary Cultural Revisitation: Bilingual and Bicultural Education," reprinted with permission from *Wicazo Sa Review: A Journal of Native American Studies* 2 (Spring 1986): 31–35. University of Minnesota Press, Minneapolis.

Chapter 5: "'The Schooling Process': Some Lakota (Sioux) Views," reprinted with permission from *Anthropological Study of Education*, edited by Craig Calhoun and Francis A. J. Ianii (Hawthorne, N.Y.: Mouton Publishers, 1976), 283–91.

Chapter 6: "Self-Direction in Sioux Education," reprinted with permission from *Integrateducation* 12 (Nov.–Dec. 1975): 15–17.

Chapter 7: "My Elders Tell Me," reprinted with permission from *Indian Education in Canada*, vol. 2: *The Challenge*, edited by Jean Barman, Yvonne Hébert, and Don McCaskill (Vancouver: University of British Columbia Press, 1987), 142–52.

Chapter 8: "Higher Education: A New Arena for Native Americans," reprinted with permission from *Thresholds in Education* 4 (May) 1978: 22–25.

Chapter 9: "The Interaction of Culture and Sex Roles in the Schools," reprinted with permission from *Integrateducation, Special Issue: American Indian Education* 19 (Jan.–April 1981): 28–37 (published Jan. 1982).

Chapter 10: "Native American (Indian) Women: A Call for Research," reprinted with permission of the American Anthropological Association from *Anthropology and Education Quarterly* 19 (June 1988): 86–92, a special volume edited by Mary Anne Pitman and Margaret A. Eisenhart, not for further reproduction.

Chapter 11: "Changing Native American Roles in an Urban Context *and* Changing Native American Sex Roles in an Urban Context," reprinted from *Two-Spirit*

People: Native American Gender Identity, Sexuality, and Spirituality, edited by Sue-Ellen Jacobs, Wesley Thomas, and Sabine Lang (Urbana: Univeristy of Illinois Press, 1997), 145–55.

Chapter 12: "'Warrior Women'—Sex Role Alternatives for Plains Indian Women," reprinted with permission from *The Hidden Half: Studies of Plains Indian Women,* edited by Patricia Albers and Beatrice Medicine (Washington: University Press of America, 1983), 267–80.

Chapter 13: "Indian Women: Tribal Identity as Status Quo," reprinted with permission from Marian Lowe and Ruth Hubbard, *Women's Nature: Rationalizations of Inequality* (New York: Teachers College Press, 1983), 63–73. ©1983 by Teachers College, Columbia University. All rights reserved.

Chapter 14: "The Role of American Indian Women in Cultural Continuity and Transition," reprinted with permission from *Women and Language in Transition,* edited by Joyce Penfield (Albany: SUNY Press, 1987), 159–66.

Chapter 15: "North American Indigenous Women and Cultural Domination," reprinted with permission of the American Indian Studies Center, UCLA from *American Indian Culture and Research Journal* 17, no. 2 (1993): 121–30. ©Regents of the University of California.

Chapter 16: "Carrying the Culture: American Indian and Alaska Native Women Workers," reprinted with permission of Wider Opportunities for Women, Inc., from *Risks and Challenges: Women, Work and the Future* (1990): 53–60.

Chapter 17: "Lakota Star Quilts: Commodity, Ceremony and Economic Development," reprinted from the original article (without photographs) with permission of the Museum of New Mexico (Santa Fe) and Michigan State University Museum from *To Honor and to Comfort: Native Quilting Traditions,* edited by Marsha L. McDowell and C. Kurt Dewhurst (Santa Fe: University of New Mexico Press, 1997), 111–17.

Chapter 18: "Native American Resistance to Integration: Contemporary Confrontations and Religious Revitalization," reprinted with permission from *Plains Anthropologist* 26, pt. 1 (1981): 277–86.

Chapter 19: "American Indian Women: Spirituality and Status," reprinted with permission from *Bread and Roses* 2 (Autumn 1980): 15–18.

Chapter 20: "American Indian Women: Mental Health Issues which Relate to Drug Abuse," reprinted with permission from *Wicazo Sa Review: A Journal of Native American Studies* 9 (Fall 1993): 85–89. University of Minnesota Press, Minneapolis.

Chapter 21: "New Roads to Coping: Siouan Sobriety," reprinted with permission from *New Directions in Prevention among American Indian and Alaska Native Communities,* edited by Spero M. Manson (Portland: Oregon Health Sciences University, 1982), 189–213.

Chapter 22: "Alcohol and Aborigines: The North American Perspective," reprinted with permission from the Alcoholic Beverage Medical Research Foundation from *Alcoholic Beverage Medical Research Foundation Journal* 8, supplement no. 3 (Fall 1998): 7–11.

Chapter 23: "The Changing Dakota Family and the Stresses Therein," reprinted with permission from the *Pine Ridge Research Bulletin* 9 (1969): 13–23.

Chapter 24: "American Indian Family Cultural Change and Adaptive Strategies," reprinted with permission from the *Journal of Ethnic Studies* 8 (Winter 1981): 13–23.

Chapter 25: "Ella C. Deloria: The Emic Voice," reprinted with permission from *MELUS* [*Multi-Ethnic Literature in the U.S.*] 7 (Winter 1980): 23–30; "Ella Cara Deloria (1888–1971)," in *Women Anthropologists: A Biographical Dictionary*, edited by Ute Gacs, Aisha Khan, Jerry McIntyre, and Ruth Weinberg (New York: Greenwood Press, 1988), 45–50; and "Ella Cara Deloria: Early Lakota Ethnologist (Newly Discovered Novelist)," reprinted with permission from *The Americanist Tradition*, edited by Lisa Valentine and Regina Darnell (Toronto: University of Toronto Press, 1999), 259–67.

Chapter 27: "The Native American," reprinted with permission from *The Outsiders*, edited by D. Spiegel and P. K. Spiegel (New York: Holt, Rinehart and Winston, 1973), 391–407.

Chapter 28: "Oral History as Truth: Validity in Recent Court Cases Involving Native Americans," reprinted with permission from *Folklore Forum, Bibliographic and Special Series* 9, no. 15 (1976): 1–5.

Chapter 29: "Finders Keepers?" reprinted with permission from the American Association of Museums from *Museum News* 51 (March 1973): 20–26. ©1973 by the American Association of Museums. All rights reserved.

Chapter 30: "American Indians and Anthropologists: Issues of History, Empowerment, and Application," reprinted with permission from *Human Organization* 57, no. 3 (1998): 253–57.

We are also grateful that Sally at the *Indian Historian* informed us about the health of Jeannette Henry-Costo, who was unable to respond to our request for permission to republish chapter 26, "Anthropology as the Indian's Image Maker," which originally appeared in *Indian Historian* 4(3) 1971: 27–29.

INTRODUCTION

Beatrice Medicine, with Sue-Ellen Jacobs

We first met in 1965 (or thereabouts) in Omer Stewart's Tri-ethnic Project Office. I had come to Boulder to attend an American Indian meeting of some sort and had gone to visit Omer whom I had known for many years. Sue-Ellen Jacobs was Omer's graduate research assistant, and I was contemplating where to finish my graduate studies. In subsequent years, we met again and again at professional anthropology meetings, and found many common interests that led us to follow each other's paper presentations, writings, graduate careers, and other academic and activist work. We come to the compilation of this book because we have both encountered colleagues and friends who expressed a longing to see what Patricia Albers in 1999 called "a book which contains a collection of Bea's writings."

Sue-Ellen and I have selected writings that are intended to address three audiences: first, nonacademic indigenous people; second, academics in a wide range of disciplines (American Indian studies, anthropology, education, psychology, social work, women's studies, and related fields); and third, policymakers. Several themes appear repeatedly throughout this thirty-year corpus of my published and unpublished papers. We chose to concentrate on the themes of education, gender and cultural identities, beliefs and well-being, families, and the influence of anthropology in my own life and in the lives of other American Indians. We have not included my encyclopedia entries, articles that repeat content of these edited works, critical book reviews and essays, or speeches. My poetry and short stories will appear together in another book (a list of my publications and papers appears in the Appendix).

We selected only published works that we felt would form a cohesive collected work. Any redundancies that remain are the natural result of trying to cover a lifetime's work in a single volume. Seeming duplications among some articles reflect a continued desire to make my work relevant for diverse audiences and also reflect changes in orientation to issues that still remain of concern. Issues that are revisited regularly are of such lingering importance that they must be addressed repetitively because the problems have not been solved; in fact, many have become worse. A case in point concerns language loss and the further assimilation of indigenous people to larger societies surrounding them.

Part 1, "Biographical Essay," republishes a piece of work I was very reluctant to write. "Learning to Be an Anthropologist and Remaining 'Native'" presented seemingly insurmountable dilemmas that had to be addressed if I were to become an anthropologist. As a "student of my own culture," for example, how much could I write that would pass my own people's scrutiny without casting me (in their eyes) as an "informant" to anthropologists? Addressing that dilemma caused me to clarify my thinking and orientation to my life's work. The problem is common to those who have been subject to studies by European and Euro-American anthropologists for generations. I was persuaded to write the essay by Solon T. Kimball, my first professor in anthropology, who taught me that anthropology could be applied to benefit colonized people and also that what I had to say had meaning for others. I am grateful to Kimball and to Elizabeth Eddy and William Partridge for including the essay in their important edited collection *Applied Anthropology in America* (1978).

Part 2, "Education," contains nine essays that address issues in education in a way that broadens analysis of my own educational dilemmas: mandatory education, forced culture change, assimilation, language use, and a revisionist approach to bilingual education. In addition, the selections cover schools established for Indians by the dominant society, directions in education and self-determination, spurious and effective use of Indian elders in educational programs, Indian entrance into higher education, and how sex roles affect research parameters. They are also a call for more relevant research about Indian women.

Part 3, "Gender and Cultural Identities," presents analyses of diverse sex role changes and the ways that cultural identity shifts or remains intact as women, men, and two-spirited Indian people move to urban contexts. My research and other work with those who have gay and lesbian ("two-spirit") gender and cultural identities received recognition by the National Gay and Lesbian Task Force at the tenth annual Honoring Our Allies Ceremony on October 4, 1999, in Washington, D.C. The program notes for that ceremony read, "As a member of the Standing Rock Lakota Nation and an esteemed anthropologist, Beatrice Medicine has done groundbreaking work in support of gay Native people. She has lectured and published on the role of gender in historic and American Indian societies which redefined how Native two-spirited people have been perceived in the social sciences and among Native people." I was honored to be recognized for my work in this area.

Chapter 13, "Indian Women: Tribal Identity as Status Quo," deals with the legal restrictions placed on tribal membership. Tribal societies seldom had such stringent requirements for membership (i.e., blood quantum) as was forced on indigenous people by colonial governments. Such restrictions put women in particular quandaries in regard to selecting fathers for their children. There is also a discussion of the additional dilemmas women face as they successfully fulfill culture-broker roles and mitigate conflicting demands and expectations from Euro-American Lakota cultures. The problem is that women have moved into the traditional position of men, who had always dealt with outsiders, and that makes some men angry. Chapters 14, 15, and 16 offer differing viewpoints on how women and men maintain cultural continuity and participate in cultural transitions inspite of Euro-American cultural domination. Throughout North America, women carry on the culture while working to provide for their households (chapters 16 and 17). Unlike previous reports on Lakota quilting, my emphasis in "Lakota Star Quilts: Commodity, Ceremony, and Economic Development" (chapter 17) concerns the personal agency that Lakota women exhibit in their simultaneous ability to commodify quilts for economic development and yet maintain the sanctity of quilts for and in ceremonial events. The tradition grows directly from hide decoration and is true in other parts of the world where cloth has replaced skins for clothing and shelter. The decoration is merely transferred from one medium to the next.

In Part 4, "Beliefs and Well-Being," I confront the thorny issues of alcohol, sobriety, and wellness and deal with topics that need amplification, such as the emerging sobriety movement. Alcohol and drug use are dealt with in terms of aboriginal periods (before colonization); the conditions under which certain tribes used drugs for spiritual purposes; and the contemporary stresses that have led to a high incidence of alcoholism and drug abuse among indigenous people of North America.

Part 5, "Families," contains two essays on Indian families. The focus is on adaptive strategies and the dynamic character of contemporary Indian life.

In Part 6, "Anthropology," I begin by examining the Lakota ethnographer Ella C. Deloria and her contribution to the field. Often referred to as the first "Indian woman anthropologist," my studies of her writings indicate that she was unappreciated as a pioneer scholar by the discipline of anthropology. Only when she was later "discovered" by feminist searches for neglected women anthropologists did her story begin to draw attention. My three essays about her life, combined into chapter 25, in part demonstrate that although some may consider Deloria as a role model, for me she was merely a woman within my Lakota kinship nexus. Chapter 28, "Oral History as Truth: Validity in Recent Court Cases Involving Native Americans," is a critical appraisal of anthropologists' roles in the creation of stereotypes despite the early Native intellectuals in anthropology who wrote of their own cultures. That raises a question: Who speaks for Indians? Anthropologists were seen as *the* expert witnesses in land claims, federal recognition, and other judicial situations until oral history began to be perceived as expert testimony in court cases. In "Finders Keepers" (chapter 29) I describe how many early anthropologists (but later, more often archaeologists) acquired items of material culture and human remains from the ground, in many instances defiling sacred spaces. They also seldom asked people from as-

sociated cultures to interpret those things, which they called "artifacts." With
the Native American Graves Protection and Repatriation Act (NAGPRA) and
the National Museum of the American Indian (NMAI), we hope things have
changed for the better. The repatriation of human remains and material items
and the concern for intellectual property rights (including oral histories, language, traditional stories, songs, and dances) are well underway. Of course, some
applied anthropologists have been in the vanguard of this movement. In "American Indians and Anthropologists: Issues of History, Empowerment, and Application," my Malinowski Award address (chapter 30), I place the fragile relationship between Indians and anthropologists in historic perspective and note
the increase of anthropologists who are of Indian heritage.

PART 1

Biographical Essay

Learning to Be an Anthropologist and Remaining "Native"

I am a part of the people of my concern and research interests. Sometimes they teasingly sing Floyd Westerman's song "Here Come the Anthros" (1969) when I attend Indian conferences. The ambiguities inherent in these two roles of being an "anthro" while at the same time remaining a "Native" need amplification. They speak to the very heart of "being" and "doing" in anthropology. My desire to be an anthropologist has been my undoing and my rebirth in a very personal way, but that topic is outside the scope of this contribution.

Recently, many students—particularly Native Americans—have been dazzled by Vine Deloria, Jr.'s scathing attack on "anthros," as we are called by most Native Americans. His article, which first appeared in *Playboy* (Deloria 1969a), has since been reprinted in many anthropological works. Besides serving as a "sweat bath" to purge anthropologists of their guilt feelings, it has become a rallying cry for Indian militants and tribal people alike. Many Native people have articulated their discontent with the exploitative adventures of anthros in the American Indian field. (See, for example, the proceedings of a symposium entitled "Anthropology and the American Indian," held in San Diego at the 1970 annual meeting of the American Anthropological Association and published by the Indian Historian Press in 1973.) However, Native readers seemingly do not go beyond page 100 of Deloria's manifesto entitled *Custer Died for Your Sins*. Later, he states: "This book has been the hardest on those people in whom I place the greatest amount of hope for the future—Congress, the anthropologists, and the churches" (1969b:275). Because the churches and Congress have eroded my faith in the institutions of the dominant society, I shall focus on anthropology. It is, after all, the source of my livelihood.

Medicine (left) with other linguistics students at Indiana University, 1953. Seated in the center is Margaret (Bird Bear) Haven; to the right, Henrietta Pretty On Top. (Courtesy of Ray DeMallie, Indiana University)

"Anthropologist" as a role designation has been traditionally meaningful to American Indians or, as we have recently been glossed, "Native Americans." In the early days of American anthropology, we were seen as "vanishing Americans." Thus, students of Boas collected data on Plains Indian reservations and Northwest Coast villages in order to recapture "memory cultures" that reflected the "golden days" of Natives whose aboriginal culture was denigrated and whose future was seen as oblivion or civilization. Many felt that American anthropology was built upon the backs of Natives (DeLaguna 1960:792), but the contributions of American Indians to the discipline has never been fully assessed. Panday (1972), however, has detailed the interactions of anthros and Natives at Zuni pueblo.

Initially, it was Franz Boas's interest in folklore, linguistics, and other aspects of culture that led him to seek and train indigenous persons who seemed especially responsive to viewing their own cultures. Among the tribes of the American Midwest, there were persons such as Francis LaFlesche, an Omaha, and William Jones, a Mesquakie (Fox), who worked in the discipline. The latter died on a field trip to the Philippines while working among the Ilongots.

Nevertheless, the role of informant as anthropological reporter creates qualms among Natives who contemplate becoming anthropologists, and it is not surprising that early contributions by Native Americans were primarily in texts on the Native languages and in folklore and mythology. A pertinent observation was made by a black anthropologist: "In the same spirit that Boas encouraged Natives to become anthropologists, he also encouraged women because they could collect information on female behavior more easily than a male anthropologist. This attitude strongly implied that native and female anthropologists are seen as potential 'tools' to be used to provide important information to the 'real' white male anthropologist" (Jones 1970:252).

The late Ed Dozier, a Pueblo anthropologist, once commented that many Native Americans "went into anthropology as a means of helping their people" (summer 1948). This suggests strong interest in the application of anthropological knowledge and is tied to the Native idea of education, no matter in what field, as a means of alleviating problems and providing self-help among Native groups. It may also reflect the dominant white society's designation of *"the* Indian Problem." Moreover, anthropologists are the educated persons with whom most Indians are familiar, and they justify their data collection to us on the basis that "we want to write down your history and culture so that your grandchildren will know something about it."

The "personal communication" aspect of anthropological reporting upset me when I began reading interpretations and analyses of us (Lakota/Dakota: Sioux), based upon E. Deloria's "field notes," "personal communications," and "personal conversations," in such works as Mirsky (1961 [1937]) and Goldfrank (1943). Later, I realized that these and similar excellent studies based on others' field notes were common and acceptable in the discipline. Nevertheless, Native populations are wary of others' interpretations of their behavior, even when they are dealing with "one of their own." An added Native concern is that areas of living will be presented that they do not want revealed.

In all anthropological investigations, mutual trust and understanding must be built carefully and sensitively. As with any human relationship, reciprocity, responsiveness, and responsibility are essential. I learned this lesson early during an intensive year I spent in a southwestern pueblo noted for its conservatism. There I learned to eat hot, spicy foods and to leave the pueblo along with the non-Native teachers on special ceremonial occasions. I learned, too, that I would never write about this pueblo.

The pueblo experience affirmed the importance of segmentation for survival. An elder of the sacred and secret realm always spoke to me in his native language as he held my hand and put a turquoise ring on my finger during each visit to his home. Later, I saw him in his trader role in a southwestern city and heard him converse in excellent English. I rushed home to tell my son's father, "Mr. Z speaks English!" Little did I realize that I was being tested. Was I Native or white-oriented? Was I informer or friend?

While resident in the pueblo, my research interest in child-training methods was fulfilled. I established strong ties with the people and maintained visiting patterns and exchanges of gifts. However, my input into the village was minimal, only doing odd chores and interpreting educational policies. With respect to the last activity, this was my first experience in a Bureau of Indian Affairs "day school." It was my unhappy chore to explain to Pueblo parents why their kindergarten children could recite "Dick and Jane" stories by rote even though they did not understand a simple question in English. Theories of social change and social organization made my year tolerable as far as the school structure was concerned. I hope that I was a means of explaining the rigid educational system to the Pueblo people, who knew precisely what skills they wanted their children to have—mathematics and "enough English to get by." Their belief system, however, was a secret never to be divulged; I still heed this directive when a Pueblo student asks me not to discuss Pueblo religion in my classes.

Being a Native female delineated areas of investigation that were closed to me. This was aggravated by my prolonged infertility. Conversation or gossip about such matters as deviant sexual practices, abortions, and pregnancy taboos was immediately terminated when I appeared at female gatherings. It was only after ten years of marriage and producing a male child that I was included in "womanly" spheres. Until then, I was referred to as "Little Bea." The cultural constrictions of working within my own group caused me to reexamine value configurations, sex roles, Indian-white relationships, and socialization practices by spending most of my time with the children. Some persons in my *tiospaye* (extended kin group) said I "spoiled" (i.e., "catered to") children. But by treating children as people, I was only acting in the way I myself had been socialized.

In the contemporary era, the concepts of acculturation or culture change, cultural transmission, role-modeling, bicultural and bilingual education, cultural brokerage, and others are highlighted in anthropological research. For me, these concepts have become personal and concrete during the years of learning to be an anthropologist while remaining a native. My learning began in childhood and continues in the present.

Early Learning

Of significance to many of us Lakota people was Ella Deloria, a daughter of a Santee Dakota Episcopal missionary who worked among the Hunkpapa and Sihasapa (Blackfeet) bands of the Teton (Western) Sioux who were placed on the Standing Rock Reservation. She and other Native Americans and Canadians came within the orbit of Boas, with whom she coauthored a book on Dakota grammar (Boas and Deloria 1941). Her other work included linguistic, folklore, and kinship studies (Deloria 1944).

As a child, I observed Aunt Ella asking questions, taking notes and photographs, and, according to my mother, "finding out how the Indians lived." Even in those days, the divisions of intra-group polarities of "mixed-blood" and "full-blood" were operative. Because my father was a full-blood, he was a good source of linguistic and other information. Very often, questions were transferred through my mother. The division of Lakota souls into various Christian denominations, although arbitrarily assigned, could not obviate kin loyalties and expectancies. I am certain that Aunt Ella forgave "poor Anna" (my mother) for marrying a "full-blood" and a "Catholic."

Aunt Ella's participation in a world far removed from Standing Rock Reservation where she lectured "about Lakota" presented a model that I found attractive. Much later, I attended a lecture by a physical anthropologist (now deceased) who asked, "Will all the persons in the room who have shovel-shaped incisors please indicate?" This experience and being used as an informant (together with a Swedish student) in a "Personality and Culture" course raised many questions in my mind about becoming an anthropologist. Would it be possible to retain dignity as a Native while operating in roles other than informant? Would anthropological training alienate me from my people? Would it affect marriage? Aunt Ella had never married. Lakota ideals for women included marriage and children. I knew my father did not believe in what he later termed "cross-cultural" marriages.

In retrospect, I am pleased that my father was sufficiently farsighted to enroll his children as full-bloods. It has made my life and acceptance on reservations and reserves easier. I am also appreciative that my father took me to tribal council meetings when I was young. It was in this context that I was remembered and asked to translate for a Lakota male elder, a non-English-speaker, in the Wounded Knee trials of 1974. Such was socialization for modes of Lakota adaptation and persistence and the demanding and expected behavior of a Native (anthro—and female at that).

During my early life, I was cognizant of living in a society that was different from the one in which I would eventually interact. Many Natives have to learn to access cross-cultural cues and circumstances as techniques for accommodations and adaptations. Although we were trained for adaptation in the subordinate society, the ideals of expected behavior or responsibility and commitment of the Native society were constantly held before us. Being Lakota was seen as the most essential aspect of living. It was from this cultural base that strong individual autonomy was fostered and an equally strong orientation to the group's welfare and interest was instilled.

Early in my college experience, I was asked to read treaties and Bureau of Indian Affairs (BIA) policy directives and to write letters involving pony claims for elderly people on my reservation. Later, while doing fieldwork on Pine Ridge Reservation, I was asked to edit an elder Oglala male's collection of Lakota folktales that began with "And a Hearty *Hou Kola* (Hello, friend) to you all!" He was collecting these for a well-known female anthro. As I congratulated him on his excellent collection, he said, "I got them from a book put out by the Bureau of American Ethnology and changed them here and there." This raised issues of ethical consideration that were unimportant at the time, and it also indicated that many Native societies had access to previously published data.

At the time, I was not too concerned with his approach. I had already seen

RIGHT: Medicine and Mrs.
Fred Eggan at the D'Arcy
McNickle Center, Newberry
Library, Chicago, 1973.
(Courtesy of the McNickle
Center)

BELOW: D'Arcy McNickle
and Medicine at the
McNickle Center, 1973,
with Sylvester Brito (left)
and Anthony Michael.
(Courtesy of the McNickle
Center)

anthropologists offering old clothes to Natives in exchange for art objects, and
I had witnessed courting behavior on the part of male anthropologists and Indian women. On the other hand, I had seen the equally horrendous scene of a
large, aggressive Lakota woman forcing a thin, young, intimidated archeologist
to dance with her and buy beer in a border-town tavern.

My brother felt sorry for the archeologist and allowed his crew to camp in
our "front yard." In the Northern Plains, rapport between archeologists and the
local Indian group has been generally good. Many archeologists have maintained
contacts with the tribes. Their domain of investigation differs from that of ethnographers and social anthropologists, and they were more aware of my place
in the social system and did not use me as a source of information. They also
heeded the advice of my father (then a tribal council chairman), who, after feeding them buffalo steaks, said, "All we want from you guys is a good report." (It

is the lack of good reporting back to the tribes under investigation that has evoked the ire and discontent of so many.)

The same young archeologist witnessed border-town "justice" when one of my kinsmen was beaten by the police while in jail for intoxication. His attempt to intervene in the city court was negated as he was threatened with contempt of court. This need for intervention frequently presents itself to anthropologists as well. Working with powerless people has its heartaches and times of despair.

For me, these relatively common "advocate" involvements with the police made later appearances in court in support of Native women (one arrested for shooting her child's molester) somewhat less emotional. With increased articulation and age, by the time I testified in the case upholding our 1868 Sioux Treaty I was classified as an "expert witness" (Jacobs 1975). I thought I was upholding family tradition and honor. My great grandfather, Sitting Crow, was a signer for the Sihasapa (Blackfeet) band of the Teton. He had signed in good faith. My father had been involved in treaty rights and other government obligations and in tribal attempts to enforce them. Nonetheless, the Wounded Knee Legal Defense and Offense Committee, which was concerned with the dismissal of the occupiers of Wounded Knee hamlet, apparently expressed some hesitation over my court appearance. I was not seen as an overt supporter of the American Indian Movement (AIM).

Looking like a Native has been advantageous in my work. Although I have what Nancy Lurie, in a personal conversation in 1973, described as a "universal field face," which has often led me to be classified as northern Chinese, Japanese, and Filipino, my main research has been with the Natives of North America.

The Teacher Role

Early in my career, I was assigned the teacher role by the majority of the tribal people. Not having attended a Bureau of Indian Affairs or a parochial boarding school, my decision was to teach in one. I went with a baccalaureate degree to Haskell Institute, which Ed Dozier referred to as "the Harvard of the Indian Service." There I encountered bureaucracy more concentrated than on reservations and the complete institutionalization of Native students. To be fair, there is tremendous esprit de corps among graduates of this former business college, now a junior college. Haskell Clubs are common throughout the country. Many graduates feel sorry for those of us who never attended its hallowed halls.

At Haskell I first encountered differential evaluation. "For after all," I was told, "you did not spend ten years at an isolated school on some reservation but came here right from graduation." This merited me a rating of "good" rather than "excellent" teacher. I resigned. The teacher image still predominates, however, for the "professor role" is currently in the forefront of my activities.

Parents and others assume that I have information regarding aspects of career opportunities for students. They are continually reassured that educational activity on a post–high school level is not necessarily alienating when they see me participating in powwows and give-aways on Standing Rock and other reservations. My current role also involves advisement and support to Native and other minority students enrolled in colleges and universities.

A major request made of me is the distribution of anthropological sources to various tribes or Native organizations for specific, usually legal, cases. This is a continuing process, as is the dissemination of knowledge about private and governmental sources of funding that can be utilized by these groups. Monitoring proposals without jeopardizing one's position as a reader of them entails a constant weighing of benefits to both tribal groups and educational agencies. Extremely delicate situations are created when cousins and other relatives call for special considerations. Reliance on "old Lakota values" such as integrity is a healthy and understandable resolution for all concerned.

There are other requests of a general nature. These include Native persons seeking genealogical information and non-Native students writing at the request of their anthropology professors. Two examples from letters in my files are: "What we need is a list of Sitting Bull's nine wives and a list of his many sons and daughters," and "I want to work on an Indian reservation—preferably for money—this summer. Can you give me information?" There are constant requests for information about the treatment of foster or adopted Indian children, for example, "This child was fine until he went home to the reservation when he was thirteen. Now we can't do anything with him. Do you think his family gave him drugs—peyote—or something?" I am certain that requests of the kind described here are the lot of many Natives, not only in anthropology but in other professions as well. Fortunately, having worked as a psychiatric social worker with métis and Native persons in Canada, I am able to use my training in psychological anthropology in meeting them.

Work among Natives, however, is difficult when they view anthropological reports about their tribes as unreliable. Susie Yellow Tail (Crow) defines ethnographies as "Indian joke books." There is no noticeable reliance or reference to many of the earlier ethnographic sources, especially linguistics and ethnohistorical studies. Many tribes are writing their own tribal histories in an attempt to present their experiences from their own unique point of view. Native Americans often believe that most anthropologists already have a theoretical framework when they enter an indigenous social system and collect and report data in support of this prior formulation.

I have attempted a concerted effort to let people know the focus of my own investigations. Among the Lakota on Standing Rock, it is customary for "powwow committees" from various communities to ask visiting returnees to the reservation to address such gatherings of people. I have found this an ideal way to present interpretations of research in an acceptable manner. There is response and reaction to the speech-maker and members of my *tiospaye* (extended family). It is also an accepted means of conforming to tribal expectations. Many of us have been criticized by persons in governmental agencies, such as the United States Public Health Service and Bureau of Indian Affairs, who see our statements as ego-centered accounts of our activities in the "outside world." They fail to understand that this modern form of "coup-counting" is viewed by most community members as a means of modeling and enhancing Lakota values and conforming to expected behavior in contemporary reservation culture. It is a valuable outlet for letting the people know what will be written and for obtaining their assessment of it.

Many Native enclaves today are aware of the large amounts of money poured into the funding of research on such topics as Indian education. Statements such as "the Indian teachers, then, seem to be characterized as a group with close contacts to the Indian communities and firm Anglo orientations for themselves and in their view on the role of the school" (Fuchs and Havighurst 1972:197) cause Indian education committees of tribal and community councils to request that this and other studies—for example, *An Even Chance* (NAACP Legal Defense and Education Fund 1971)—be presented in terms they can more readily understand. In their minds, Natives involved as token researchers and validators tend to confirm their negative views of anthropological researchers. To explain without being patronizing is a skill to be learned, as is the need to be charmingly combative in certain anthropological arenas.

The translation of research terminology into an English vernacular that Native parents and students can comprehend is a formidable task that "target populations" take for granted. This is not to disparage the intellect of tribal people, but rather to acknowledge their estimate of anthropological research and indicate their preoccupation with the many daily tasks of reservation life. It speaks to the need for less jargon in anthropological reporting. The increasing number of Native college graduates who return to reservations or urban Indian centers and survival schools seldom utilize these studies at all. Their concern is the development of curricular materials that are more pertinent to their own and their students' needs.

One of the most successful educational endeavors in which I have worked was with the Sarcee [now T'suu Tina] tribe living on the outskirts of Calgary. I had already become involved in the social aspects—powwow and give-away events—before I began working there as a teacher-counselor. The aim of the Indian Affairs Branch of Canada was to enroll and keep Sarcee students in the public and parochial schools of Calgary, for there was the usual high dropout rate.

I visited every home on the reserve and became acquainted with the parents and grandparents. Fortunately for me, the chief was married to a Dakota female from Manitoba, and a pseudo-kin relationship was initiated by them. My goal was to enroll students in a kindergarten in the city and hire a local Native man to drive them there. This was accomplished, and the man now has a fleet of school buses that transport all Sarcee students to city schools. Although he says "I am still driving buses," he is also Band chief. Today, a Sarcee college graduate is also working in Native education, and many of the young people are involved in tribal affairs.

During this time, some of my white Canadian friends and I worked to establish an urban Indian center in Calgary. Some of these white friends have continued their work with urban groups, and one has received a degree in anthropology. Individuals who are both Native and Canadian are involved in national Indian educational associations in the United States. A truly binational interest on Native education and issues (the National Indian Education Association, North American Bilingual Education Association, and, more recently, the North American Indian Women's Association) seems to be emerging. Much of this involvement is attributable to the growing self-determination and articulation of Native people in North America. The thrust of commitment has gone beyond the mere networks of "powwow circuits" and kinship ties.

One aspect of concern and meaningful education for Native students has proven counterproductive to my own professional development. In addition, I cannot seem to cast off the indispensable mother role (I once overheard my son telling his friend, "You've heard of Jewish mothers; Siouxish mothers are worse"). Native pressure to take fellowships and jobs to ensure continued occupancy by Native people is great. Although I have, since 1969, spent two years in "my own area" of Montana and South Dakota, I have frequently moved to areas where Indian students have expressed interest or initiated action in hiring me. A common accusation, especially in California, is, "Why aren't you working with your own people?" This is an indication, it seems to me, of a growing tribalism with incipient and, in some cases, strong ethnocentrism. As far as moving so often is concerned, I jokingly refer to the former nomadism of my people. More recently, I have utilized a pan-Indian joke: "Sioux are just like empty beer cans, you find them everywhere."

Increasingly, Native students who have been in my classes are fulfilling my expectations. Many have entered into occupations with tribal groups and educational endeavors. They are, hopefully, negating my fears of untrained Indian educators replacing uncaring and, in some cases, badly trained white educators. A number of these students, who have absorbed anthropological theories and research methods, are working in areas of concern to our people. An interesting dilemma exists. Many tribal councils often "resolve" a problem with a statement: "We need a study on this." Yet it is in the areas of research and writing that the lack of skills is most evident in the training of Native college graduates. White ghostwriters are too prevalent.

Affirmative action policies in institutions of higher learning raise other problems. Administrators are seeking names of Native Americans to fill these slots. An onerous aspect of this recruitment is the validation of self-ascribed Natives, whom I have termed "woodwork Indians" who emerge to fill the slots of the momentarily "in" people ("Indians" and other minorities). This poses critical questions. How does one deal with a person who claims to be one-sixteenth or one-thirty-second Indian ancestry (usually Cherokee)? How does a cultural Native differ from a Native of convenience? We know that there are many blacks who, either through intermarriage or miscegenation, fit into a similar category. A more recent anomaly is the use of the gloss "Native American" by Samoans and Hawaiians in the quest for federal funds. These and related issues create real problems for the Native anthropologist. Does one set up a registry for "red bloods?"

Even more challenging dilemmas result from requests Native intellectuals make upon anthropologists. One example came from an Oglala (Sioux) law graduate who requested that I present evidence that Native Americans had originated in the New World. (What temptation for a Native American Piltdown "plant.") Concerns of this nature have even greater future repercussions because of the current rejection of the Bering Straits migration theory advocated by some tribal leaders. Many tribal people are as committed to their origin and creation statements as any other people. "What do you think of the story told by anthropologists that we all came across the Bering Straits?" was the question asked of me by a Navajo teenager in 1960.

Issues based on Indians' tribal sovereignty, water, and treaty rights will make the future interface of anthropologists and Natives a vital concern for those of us committed to a changing profession. This is especially evident in the use of the latter in the "contrived cultures" of Native militants.

"Traditionality" is often seen today as a selective mechanism that includes persons whose rhetorical "right-on-ness" negates the tribal heritage, oratorical wisdom, and concerted action that have sustained the Nativeness of the group. "Identity-questing" assumes a new perspective, and it reflects generations of superimposed policies of change. It is tragic to view some individuals who do not know their own unique tribal heritage amid the vast cultural heritages of Native North America. Thus, respect for elders is eroded in the exploitation of Native medicine men and the translation of Native prayers into slogans. However, a common denominator is that we Native Americans are varied hues in a bronzed and battered Native world and present uneven views of tribal traditions.

More important, our sheer survival has hinged upon a flexible ability to segment, synthesize, and act in changing situations. Although this should be understood and respected by anthropologists and others, a lack of sensitivity and perception has been a main tragedy of comprehending Native life. There is often a unidimensional aspect of power. The indigenous society is seen as a target population for manipulation and change, with little or no attempt to understand the textured and realigning configurations of persons and ideas, through time, that have allowed for Native persistence. For me, the categories of constituency are meaningless because my identity rests as a constituent of a viable Native group. Advocacy is constant and resides with powerless people. Involvement is ongoing, demanding, and debilitating emotionally, economically, and educationally.

To me, the most important aspect of applied work is the delineation of social forces that impinge upon indigenous societies and the ways that these affect each distinctive group. Social change, and how it is understood and acted upon by Native Americans, is the crux of anthropological understanding. It is through the role of cultural broker that the lack of insight and understanding of a more powerful social order may be mediated. The fact of living in social situations of administered human relations, where decisions affecting the present and future of Native Americans are controlled by external power components, is understandable and workable with anthropological concepts. In educational aspects especially, it has been imperative to reinterpret and flesh out the parameters of methods and techniques of change in terms that are meaningful to Native aggregates. Moreover, it is important that persons on both the receiving and applying levels understand the nature of factions in these societies. For Native societies, the labels "progressive" and "traditionalist" have many different meanings.

The "full-blood"/"breed" constellations have been correlated with both traditionalists and progressives in some Lakota reservations. This division of allegiances to old values and affinity toward "feathering one's own nest" at the expense of the other group are basic to understanding factions on contemporary reservations. Recently, the progressives (or "featherers") have begun to hearken back to "traditionality," which is operationally part of the reservation political arena.

The politics of social capital and power are elements that are forever present in Native social systems. They have served as vehicles for differential adjustment to the dominant culture. To an anthropologist from the Native enclave, kin affiliation is often within both spheres of social structure, necessitating a constant reassessment of power and emotional alliances. Surges of disaffection and disenchantment have to be isolated and put in proper perspective as a prelude to action.

Some events involve simple and fulfilling moments, such as sitting around a campfire and visiting with friends and kin, "waiting for the coffee to boil," or watching Lakota children "playing cowboy" in the bright moonlight. Listening to the Sioux National Anthem and then "dancing the drum out" in the cold dawn of a Northern Plains summer have become memories that sustain me in university settings, at meetings of governmental advisory boards, and during anthropological "tribal rites" (annual meetings) where we hear new interpretations and speculations about our Native life-styles. Being home and doing fieldwork recall Al Ortiz's significant statement: "I initially went into anthropology because it was one field in which I could read about and deal with Indians all of the time and still make a living" (1973:86).

I know I went into anthropology to try and make living more fulfilling for Indians and to deal with others in attempts of anthropological application meaningful to Indians and others.

References

Anthropology and the American Indian. 1973. San Francisco: Indian Historian Press.

Boas, Franz, and Ella Deloria. 1941. *Dakota Grammar.* Memoirs of the National Academy of Sciences, vol. 23. Washington: Government Printing Office.

DeLaguna, Frederica. 1960. "Method and Theory of Ethnology." In *Selected Papers from the American Anthropologist (1888–1920),* ed. Frederica DeLaguna, 792. Evanston: Row, Peterson.

Deloria, Ella. 1944. *Speaking of Indians.* New York: Friendship Press.

Deloria, Vine, Jr. 1969a. "Custer Died for Your Sins." *Playboy* 16(8): 131–32, 172–75.

———. 1969b. *Custer Died for Your Sins.* New York: MacMillan.

Dozier, Edward. 1948. Seminar associated with site survey by Florence Hawley Ellis. Albuquerque.

Fuchs, Estelle, and Robert J. Havighurst. 1972. *To Live on This Earth: American Indian Education.* Garden City: Doubleday.

Goldfrank, Esther. 1943. "Historic Change and Social Character: A Study of the Teton Dakota." *American Anthropologist* 45(1): 67–83.

Jacobs, Wilbur R. 1975. "Native American History: How It Illuminates Our Past." *American Historical Review* 80(3): 593.

Jones, Delmos J. 1970. "Towards a Native Anthropology." *Human Organization* 29(4): 251–59.

Mirsky, Jeanette. 1961 [1937]. "The Dakota." In *Cooperation and Competition among Primitive People,* ed. Margaret Mead, 382–427. Boston: Beacon Press.

NAACP Legal Defense and Education Fund. 1971. *An Even Chance.* New York: NAACP Legal Defense and Education Fund, with the cooperation of the Center for Law and Education, Harvard University.

Ortiz, Alfonso [discussant]. 1973. In *Anthropology and the American Indian,* 86. San Francisco: Indian Historian Press.

Panday, Triloki Nath. 1972. "Anthropologists at Zuñi." *Proceedings of the American Philosophical Society* 116(4): 321–36.

Westerman, Floyd. 1969. "Here Come the Anthros." On *Custer Died for Your Sins* (PLP-5 Perception).

PART 2

Education

CHAPTER 2

"Speaking Indian": Parameters of Language Use among American Indians

There is a pan-Indian joke heard in many American Indian (Native American) communities.[1] It involves an anthropologist who supposedly asked an Indian from the tribe, "Do you speak Indian?" This may be another put-down to make anthropologists look foolish (Deloria 1969); it may also be an attempt to build a rich folklore involving anthropologists. Strangely, linguists are not included in the anthropological joke. This may indicate a different perspective on linguists in Native communities.

Yet many of us have heard, and still hear, this very same question being asked *of* and *by* persons of Indian ancestry in reservation and off-reservation communities and in urban areas where Indians reside in increasing numbers. This essay seeks to address the broad parameters of language use and the effects and affects of speaking Native languages that are manifest in the lives of Native people.

Repression of Native languages among Indian tribes is a major aspect of cultural loss that is often brought up in conversations dealing with Indians. This usually follows the inflamed rhetoric of "You took our land away!" It is frequently mentioned to non-Indians as a guilt-inducing device, it seems.

Therefore, it may be imperative to examine the state of communicative and expressive elements operative in Native communities. Aspects of bilingualism and biculturalism need discussion to establish a benchmark for Indian educators and researchers attempting to formulate a state of the communicative arts. This examination should include an awareness of differential language use in contemporary Indian enclaves. The multicultural context of Native communities should be given greater exposure in an effort to eradicate images of a monolithic Indian Nation speaking one language.

The entire issue of Native language use is a very real one, which American Indians and Alaska Natives must confront. The bilingual ability and linguistic competence of persons involved in language programs usually are unknown factors. The affective environment composing the linguistic arena for Indians should form part of a sociology of education approach. The contextual background that involves many preferences and the politics of decision-making in regard to the use of ancestral languages begs to be formulated specifically for each tribal group. That sociolinguistic analyses based upon ethnohistorical evidence of language use in their communities should have high priority is seldom recognized by Native people. Indeed, many persons involved in language programs are seldom cognizant of work that might have bearing upon their speech communities (regarding Lakota-speakers, for example, see Leap 1977, 1978; Medicine 1979b; and Powers 1972).

Language Suppression and Adaptive Strategies

What was the Native viewpoint in learning the English language? There is little in the ethnographic literature that provides a broad database for comparative purposes. However, the poignant yet brave attempts of Native persons caught in this linguistic limbo give some insights into cultural deprivation of the first magnitude. The following selection speaks of language learning among the Omaha (Omaha is a Siouan language):

> From the earliest years the Omaha child was trained in the grammatical use of his native tongue. No slip was allowed to pass uncorrected, and as a result there was not child-talk such as obtains among English-speaking children— the only difference between the speech of old and young was in the pronunciation of words which the infant often failed to utter correctly, but this difficulty was soon overcome, and a boy of ten or twelve years was apt to speak as good Omaha as a man of mature years.

> Like the grown folks, we youngsters were fond of companionship and of talking. In making our gamesticks and in our play, we chattered incessantly of the things that occupied our minds, and we thought it a hardship when we were obliged to speak in low tones while older people were engaged in conversation. When we entered the Mission School, we experienced a greater hardship, for there we encountered a rule that prohibited the use of our own language, which rule was rigidly enforced with a hickory rod, so that the newcomer, however socially inclined, was obliged to go about like a little dummy until he learned to express himself in English.

> All the boys in our school were given English names, because their Indian names were difficult for the teachers to pronounce. Besides, the aboriginal names were considered by the missionaries as heathenish, and therefore should be obliterated. No less heathenish in their origin were the English substitutes, but the loss

of their original meanings and significance through long usage had rendered them fit to continue as appellations for civilized folk. And so, in place of Tae-noo-ga-wa-zhe, came Philip Sheridan; in that of Wa-pha'-dae, Ulysses S. Grant; that of Koo'-we-he-ge-ra, Alexander, and so on. Our sponsors went even further back in history, and thus we had our David and Jonathan, Gideon and Isaac, and, with the flood of these new names came Noah. It made little difference to us that we had to learn the significance of one more word as applied to ourselves, when the task before us was to make our way through an entire strange language. So we learned to call each other by our English names, and continued to do so even after we had left school and had grown to manhood.

In the talk of the boys I have striven to give a reproduction of the peculiar English spoken by them, which was composite, gathered from the imperfect comprehension of their books, the provincialisms of the teachers, and the slang and bad grammar picked up from uneducated white persons employed at the school or at the Government Agency. Oddities of speech, profanity, localisms, and slang were unknown in the Omaha language, so when such expressions fell upon the ears of these lads they innocently learned and used them without the slightest suspicion that there could be bad as well as good English.

The misconception of Indian life and character so common among the white people has been largely due to an ignorance of the Indian's language, or his mode of thought, his beliefs, his ideals, and his native institutions. Every aspect of the Indian and his manner of life has always been strange to the white man, and this strangeness has been magnified by the mists of prejudice and the conflict of interests between the two races. While these in time may disappear, no Native American can ever cease to regret that the utterances of his father have been constantly belittled when put into English, that their thoughts have frequently been travestied and their native dignity obscured. The average interpreter has generally picked up his knowledge of English in a random fashion, for very few have had the advantage of a thorough education, and all have had to deal with the difficulties that attend the translator. The beauty and picturesqueness, and euphonious playfulness, or the gravity of diction which I have heard among my own people, and other tribes as well, are all but impossible to be given literally in English. (LaFlesche 1963:xvi–xix)

One is able to glean similar statements from other Native writers (for example, Standing Bear, Ella Deloria, Charles Eastman, and others) for Lakota-speakers. One might also examine the ethnographic literature, specifically life history materials, for Native writers who have made statements about the learning experiences in their historic periods.

Prucha indicates (1976:286) that the most forceful promoter of English as a civilizing tool was J. D. C. Atkins, Indian commissioner from 1885 to 1888, who directed: "No textbooks in the vernacular will be allowed in any school where children are placed under contract, or where the Government contributes to the support of the school; no oral instruction in the vernacular will be allowed at such schools. The entire curriculum must be in the English language." This is but one example of the repressive policies that were rampant in the early educational process for all Indians. It is apparent, however, that this practice of cultural deprivation has continued. Metcalf states (1978:15), "Some of the instances of institutional abuse which were practiced against the Indian parents come under this definition. For example, several report that they were punished in boarding school when they were caught speaking their Native language by having their mouths washed out with soap."

Each tribe devised methods to circumvent the overarching stricture of language repression. It is by attempting to fathom this unique adaptation that the viabilities of Native language use will assume new dimensions and be fully comprehended in contemporary speech communities. The actual dynamics of language acquisition in schools that are not community-controlled need explication. The time for collecting such important data is fast diminishing. Many of the individuals who suffered physical and psychological abuse for speaking an Indian language while in boarding schools—Bureau of Indian Affairs (BIA) or parochial—are now elderly or have died. One must obtain information from these individuals to assess Native views of language learning—its loss or preservation.

More encouraging, however, is the compilation of information about the means by which Native languages and nonverbal communication skills were preserved. Some of these adaptive strategies are tribally unique. Others deal with the common experience in boarding schools, where a type of vernacular was developed to further communication between persons of different tribal and linguistic backgrounds and to exclude such change agents as teachers, disciplinarians, matrons, and other administrative personnel. It is only recently that such communicative codes have been examined (Basso 1970; Dumont 1972).

One outstanding source of information about the history of language suppression and the utilization of Native languages in new rituals may be obtained from Native clergy—especially after they have retired from their ministries. Among the Lakota-speakers, for example, Christianity provided a means by which the vernacular continued. Although it is common practice to indict Christian missionaries in the context of a new Indian ethic and a return to Native religions, one must recognize that the use of hymnals and prayer books in the Native languages and dialects was a strong factor in the retention of those languages. This was brought about through the development of an orthography reflecting the grammatical structure of the Native language. Among the Lakota, where the Native belief system—manifested in the Sun Dance—was prohibited, the value structure of a cultural whole was removed. Many persons used hymnals, prayer books, and Bibles and attended religious activities to continue language use under the guise of being civilized and Christianized. Native value systems, however, were astutely incorporated.

Contemporary Language Use

The influence that some of the religious writing systems exerted upon Native speakers persists. Lakota, for example, has many adherents to certain orthographic forms that are rooted in religious hymnals and prayer books. This has hindered attempts to utilize an agreed-upon orthography for bilingual programs on some Sioux reservations. The orientation of teacher aides or Native bilingual experts to a given writing system is seldom considered in assessing the effectiveness of bilingual bicultural programs.

The environments of affect and commitment that constitute Native speech communities must be comprehended to appreciate and appraise realistically subcultural and linguistic enclaves. Directives and their interpretations and implementations in emerging bilingual bicultural programs vary for different speakers of the residual languages extant in Native North America. Expectations of language use and communicative patterns have been set by various interpretations of policies constructed by decision-makers outside Native communities. How the policies are translated into action by Native participants in these communities is significant.

The most permeating and long-range effect of language suppression for all tribes, striking at the very basis for cultural continuity, is constantly evoked as a rationale for the uniqueness of linguistic programs for Indian tribes. The prohibition of Native language use has had great repercussions for the communicative skills of American Indians. It was aimed at the very matrix of the expressive elements of culture: language (vernacular and ritual), music, song, dance, art, and other emotion-laden aspects such as religion. This evidences the all-encompassing features of an educational policy that was pushed upon powerless people in a culture-change situation.

That languages have persisted attests to the great vigor of Native cultures and their members. It also indicates the value placed on Native languages by parents and parent surrogates (grandparents) who have continued to consciously teach their children a Native language. To them, language is critical in maintaining cultural continuity and Native identity.

Policies that impinge upon education for Indians are crucial. The period beginning in 1934 with the Indian Reorganization Act (IRA) evidenced a sympathetic policy that fostered the revitalization of languages, Native religions, and such aspects of expressive culture as dance, music, art, and folklore. This was an era of bilingual readers for Bureau of Indian Affairs day schools and boarding schools (Medicine 1979a). This unprecedented move, seen by some educators as a reversal of previous directives and a "return to the blanket," must have offered different interpretations to tribal people. Students of Indian affairs—anthropologists, historians, and others—are often too engrossed in the "golden age of past glories of Indian life" to be interested in the cultural rejuvenation that this era heralded. Among the Sioux, for example, the new trend reaffirmed the value of Native language and culture. Many students who did not attend government boarding schools at the insistence and sacrifice of parents nevertheless benefited from this new policy. In the spirit of the cultural mandate for generosity, kinfolk shared bilingual readers and biliteracy became the norm. Parents were teachers.

The utilization of several languages (Spanish, French, and English plus the ancestral language) in indigenous communities has also resulted in a wide range of adaptations. In the southwestern Pueblos, many Indian individuals are trilingual in Spanish, English, and a Native tongue—Keresan, for example. This is also true for many Navajo-speakers. In the Northeast, French, English, and a Native Indian language often describe the linguistic model. Thus, it is imperative that ethnohistorical approaches reflect the area and languages used there. This would grant a greater appreciation of functioning language use in the contemporary scene.

Nonetheless, there are few data deriving from contemporary Indian societies regarding the actual dimensions and idiosyncratic use of language among various communities on Indian reservations. Equally absent is information on the use of languages—ancestral or English—among Native residents in urban areas. There are a few studies concentrating upon the ethnography of speaking in Native American and Alaska Native communities (Basso 1970; Philips 1972, 1974). More dire is the lack of assessments of Native language vitality and strength in speaking styles and communicative skills in these communities.

In one of the rare studies dealing with Indians in public schools, Knack (1978:225) writes of the Southern Paiute in regard to the Mormon placement program that moves children to Mormon homes:

> By going away to school, they [parents] said, the children would no longer learn the Indian language and customs and would become whites. This argument was countered by other parents who said that staying in the community did not guarantee that children would grow up knowledgeable in their Indian heritage. They pointed out that today many of the young people who stayed home for schooling do not speak the language well or know the songs. They also pointed out that going away to school did not guarantee that the children would fail to speak Paiute fluently and participate in their culture or community. In general, it is up to the individual to make his choice and learn what he will, they said. It should be noted, and Paiutes usually do note this in such a discussion, that several of the most "traditional" leaders are those who were sent to BIA schools far away during their youth, often for long periods of time. They then consciously made the choice to return and learn their traditional ways and are now applying the skills they learned in school to the problems of leadership in the community today.

This excerpt shows the adaptive processes that are at work in many contemporary Indian communities. This published observation on one community's perception of language use and individual autonomy has great significance for Native language use as an ethnic marker and for other aspects of "Indianness" in current American Indian life.

In order to place language use in an overview, one must be aware of the scope of the issue. The final report of the American Indian Policy Review Commission, which is seen as the most recent consolidation of data involving tribal groups, indicates the universe: "A total of 289 tribes and bands live on 269 'federally recognized' reservations or otherwise defined 'trust areas' in 26 states" (1977–78:90). Of importance to issues of Indian vernaculars is that there are approximately 206 different languages and language dialects still spoken today among these Native people. Chafe (1962, 1965) gives a sense of language utilization when he estimates that forty-nine of these languages have fewer than ten speakers aged fifty or over, while six of these languages have more than ten thousand speakers in all generations representing language fluency. Fluency in the remaining 152 languages falls somewhere between the two extremes.

Bilingual Education and Indian-Controlled Schooling Policies

Because the final report of the American Indian Policy Review Commission may be viewed as the basis for policymaking, it is interesting to note that bilingual education was not specifically addressed except in some of the hearings that reflected an individualistic approach. However, in a statement submitted to the Policy Review Commission by the National Indian Education Association (NIEA), the National Congress of American Indians (NCAI) Education Committee, and the National Tribal Chairmen's Association (NTCA) Education Components, the following comments are significant:

ISSUE:
Bilingual and Multicultural Education Needs of Indians

Indian children speak approximately 252 languages. These children have been denied the right to obtain an education equal to the education offered English-speaking children.

The BIA's and OE's insistence in perpetuating the use of a monolingual [English] educational system cannot be sustained. Through the emphasis on existing monolingual curricula and the utilization of predominately English teachers, school systems promote a single-minded proficiency in English that would replace any "foreign" language. Indians do not receive adequate monies from the Bilingual Education Acts of 1968 and 1974.

RECOMMENDATIONS:
Title VII—The Bilingual Education Act should be amended to provide for the bilingual and bicultural education needs of American Indian children who speak 252 different languages. Tribes should be allowed to decide if curricula should be in both the tribal language and in the English language. Tribes, tribal

education divisions, and the family should also decide if teachers should acquire competencies in the tribal language before attempting to teach their children. Curriculum in Indian languages would be a priority of the Council of Indian Bilingual and Multicultural Education. (American Indian Policy Review Commission 1977–78:565–66)

Despite repeated concern, especially in congressional hearings (Lawrence 1978), for the need for bilingual bicultural education programs for Indian students, current research [as of 1970] has not yielded data that indicate the ranges and viability of bilingualism in Native American communities. Indeed, there are few articulated statements that would indicate the variables of language use in most communities. Perhaps the Navajo, with their population nearly monolingual in the Athapaskan language stock, have the most direct awareness of the use of Native language in their communities. This is evident in their bilingual programs (Holm 1964; Pfeiffer 1968) and those of others. The extent of bilingualism in Native American and Alaska Native communities can only be surmised.

As far as language programs are concerned, one prevailing caveat seems to indicate lack of agreement and inability to generalize on individual as well as tribal levels. Native language usage and the advocacy of bilingual bicultural programs have been given approval by most tribal groups. In many cases, however, the advocates of bilingual programs make a strong plea for cultural continuity without a full awareness and appreciation of language use in the Native community. Many groups are concerned that non-Indians might learn the ancestral language. Some tribes, such as certain Pueblo groups, tend to be conservative about language issues; other Pueblos, however, do have federally funded bilingual programs in their schools. John Wabaunsee feels that the increase in bilingual education is "a by-product of one major political event—the rise of Indian-controlled schools and schooling policies" (1977:66).

There seem to be several dilemmas, however. Implicitly, the need to expand the funding base for Indian education is a consideration. The pleas for more funding for bilingual bicultural programs and for community-controlled schools have been paramount in the thrust for any sort of language programs that may provide "monies," to use a prevailing English term. It may be noted in this context that needs assessments have been serendipitous and motivated by funding priorities that are often initiated by requests for proposals (RFPs). More significantly, needs often tend to be perceived and articulated by non-Indian researchers and proposal-writers.

A major finding based upon research conducted by the National Indian Training and Research Center, an Indian-operated firm, was that there was a wide discrepancy among educators in defining bilingual education and in interpreting bilingual education requirements. Congress directed the Department of the Interior to assess the bilingual education needs in schools operated by or receiving funds from the department. In response, questionnaires were sent to personnel in all BIA, contract, or public schools receiving Johnson O'Malley funds. It was found that only 33 percent of the federally funded schools had conducted needs assessments from which significant data could be utilized. The data suggested, nevertheless, that fewer parents actually did favor bilingual approaches to education. The study indicated that approximately one-third of the 169,482 Indian children in these schools evidenced bilingual education needs. Because, however, definitions of bilingual education were so discrepant among these educators, the need for more reality-based research seems essential.

Ancestral Language Use and Community Roles

Speaking an indigenous language is now a decided asset for any Indian or Alaska Native. For most persons who are able to understand and speak an ancestral language, the essence of being part of the group and thoroughly understanding the ramifications of the cultural base is often stated as a very positive situation. Speaking an ancestral language is often a key to ritual participation and other expressive elements of culture—the least of which is the lively humor that is so much a part of contemporary Indian life. Proficiency in the language can buttress one's tribal identity.

Not only does this expressive ability enhance a person's prestige within their own group, but it also gives a certain credence to their ability to provide more rounded interpretations of the group's needs to persons outside that domain. The role of interpreter of external decisions to the group, the opportunity to translate the tribe's needs to external groups, and a feeling of "in-group-ness" are assets that seem highly valued by those who are skilled in an ancestral language. If such persons maintain close ties with a natal community, the members of that enclave tend to view them as individuals who are not "stuck up" or "better then we are," to use Native expressions. They view such persons as uncoopted by education and participation in a dominant white superstructure. Essentially, feelings of trust and respect are accorded these persons. Conversely, an individual who is not able to speak an ancestral language is very often looked upon by speakers of that language as someone to be pitied. This person may be seen as outside the cohesive cultural group.

Although there are some isolated instances of individual resistance to outsiders learning a Native language, those persons—usually non-Natives working with a certain tribe—who attempt to learn the Native language are looked upon with respect, appreciation, and encouragement. This holds for most of the indigenous communities except the Pueblos, where, in most cases, attempts by outsiders to learn the languages are often rebuffed; aspects of religion and ritual are well guarded among these groups.

Again, however, one must look to each tribal group to ascertain the interplay of Native language and culture and the interface with the dominant society. In dealing with members of the dominant society, English is used by those interacting with non-Indians. Looking at Lakota-speakers, one can examine language use in the public sector, for example, at tribal council meetings, where the strength of language retention is extremely variable. In some council meetings, English is the sole means of communication. In others, both English and Lakota are used interchangeably. In some areas, the Native language is the sole means of interaction. In general, the outlying regions of reservations tend to be most conservative in ancestral language retention and use; there, many individuals are Indian-language monolinguals.

Ancestral language use appears to be tied very closely to a ceremonial or ritual structure. Among the Lakota Sioux, for example, distinctive factors involving language and culture are operative, and among many of the Lakota bands there is a decided effort to revitalize ceremonies. The Sun Dance is presently assuming intertribal dimensions and international participation. Because much of the ritual is conducted in Lakota, there is a concerted effort on the part of incipient religious practitioners (i.e., "medicine men") to learn the language. As "sun-dancing" and "piercing" assume qualities of ethnic markers, the ability to pray or sing in an ancestral language becomes highly valued. One would need to examine the dynamics of contemporary communities and rituals structures to assess the full implications of this asserted revival or revitalization for each group.

Even in such secular rituals as powwows, naming ceremonies, and give-aways, it is highly desirable that some of the events be conducted "in Indian." However, due to the intertribal character of the participation at larger powwows, the announcer uses English as the lingua franca. These generalizations have been confirmed by several persons of Native ancestry in the Northwest, Southwest, and Plains culture areas. What is necessary for comparative purposes is verification of these tentative statements regarding retention and revitalization of ancestral languages through research in areas of high ancestral language use.

Implications for the Future

These are a few dimensions of Nativeness, articulated by some indigenous people, which are based upon language use. Relating to a tribal language, however tenuous the tie might be, is one aspect of "being Native" that permeates much of the total identity question. Memory of linguistic ties that are evoked as ethnic markers is a prevalent theme. In addition, there is often a statement of an inextricable link between culture and language (Lawrence 1978). Contemporary reservation vernacular indicates an assessment of an individual's language competencies. Native linguistic descriptions that permeate discussions of language utilization are often stated in such glosses as "broken English," or "good Sioux," or "bad Lakota," or any other Native language (i.e., "Indian"). There are general consensus statements about what constitutes a "good speaker." What these qualifiers seem to indicate is an evaluatory appreciation of language use. Native language proficiency—"talking good" in an ancestral language—is valued in any tribe. This definitely affects one's use of language and the values that impinge upon Native languages.

The terminology of role models permeates much of the rhetoric in conferences pertaining to Native education. Thus, the view of parents is significant in terms of statements made historically and contemporarily. Some Indian parents ascribe to a widely held notion that "I don't want my children to have the hard time I did learning English when I went to school." This speaks to the degradation of spirit and intellect to which many parents and grandparents were exposed in the schooling process. In this era of enhanced Indian identity, it also places the parent or parental surrogate in an uncomfortable position in relation to the ability to "speak Indian" as an identity badge. What is important here is that the younger generation might feel robbed of a rich cultural heritage because significant others did not teach them their ancestral language(s). It must be remembered, however, that there are other factors involved, such as a long history of boarding school experience that led to many intertribal marriages. This fact certainly has some bearing upon language learning and use (Malancon and Malancon 1977).

There are other trends in the utilization of Native languages that need to be mentioned. Recently, there has been a proliferation of courses on Native languages in some linguistics departments but more commonly in Native American studies departments in universities and colleges throughout North America (Table 2.1 shows the range of languages taught in 1979). In addition to courses at universities, there are strong courses taught in Native cultures at the community colleges located on reservations. Examples of outstanding programs in bilingual and bicultural content are offerings at Navajo Community College and Sinte Gleska College on the Rosebud Sioux Reservation in South Dakota. These represent positive aspects of self-determination in higher education that will have implications for the future of Native languages (Medicine 1975, 1976). The rationale for the trend seems unclear at present. It might be part of the new Indian ethnicity and "identity-questing" for a cultural badge, or it may be part of an equity approach in some universities. One cannot speculate until one has data on whom these courses are serving. However, the teaching of Indian languages by Native persons in these departments may have implications for the future of ancestral languages. The impact of professorships for those of Native ancestry who serve as teachers (or informants) in these courses may have some implications for their roles in their home communities. Since the influx of Native studies departments in institutions of higher learning, the heretofore informants of the linguistic departments have achieved new status. Their continued influence upon their natal speech communities must be part of the concern for the direction of ancestral language use (Rood and Taylor 1978).

The impact of the non-Native students who have taken these language courses also presents some interesting implications. Many of these persons have entered

Table 2.1. Native Languages Taught at Universities and Colleges in North America

Language Taught	Number of Institutions	Places Taught
Eskimo (Inuit)	6	San Diego State University
		Bethel College and Seminary (St. Paul, Minn.)
		University of Alaska (Fairbanks)
		University of Western Ontario (London, Ont.)
		McGill University (Montreal, P.Q.)
		University of Saskatchewan (Saskatoon)
Navajo	6	Northern Arizona University (Flagstaff)
		University of California at Los Angeles
		San Diego State University
		Northwestern University (Evanston, Ill.)
		University of New Mexico (Albuquerque)
		Brigham Young University (Provo, Utah)
Cree	6	Cornell University (Ithaca, N.Y.)
		University of Calgary (Alberta)
		University of Saskatchewan (Saskatoon)
		Lakehead University (Thunder Bay, Ont.)
		University of Minnesota–Minneapolis
		University of Wisconsin–Milwaukee
Ojibwa	6	University of Michigan (Ann Arbor)
		University of Minnesota–Duluth
		McGill University (Montreal, P.Q.)
		Lakehead University (Thunder Bay, Ont.)
		University of Minnesota–Minneapolis
		University of Wisconsin–Milwaukee
Dakota	4	San Diego State University
		University of Minnesota–Minneapolis
		University of Manitoba (Winnipeg)
		York University (Toronto, Ont.)
Lakota	2	San Diego State University
		University of Colorado (Boulder)
Hopi	2	San Diego State University
		Northern Arizona University (Flagstaff)
Oneida	1	University of Wisconsin–Green Bay
Mohawk	1	State University of New York–Albany
Menominee	1	Cornell University (Ithaca, N.Y.)
Stoney	1	University of Calgary
Blackfoot	1	University of Calgary
Colville	1	University of Montana (Missoula)
Cherokee	1	University of Montana (Missoula)
Kashaya Pomo	1	Sonoma State University (Calif.)
Yakut	1	Indiana University (Bloomington)

In addition, there is a special program in American Indian linguistics at Massachusetts Institute of Technology (Cambridge). Other languages taught are Nahautl at California State University–Northridge; Quechua at UCLA, Indiana University (Bloomington), University of New Mexico (Albuquerque), and University of Wisconsin–Madison; Quechua-Maya at Stanford University (Palo Alto, Calif.) and SUNY-Albany; and Maya (Yucatec) at Stanford (Palo Alto, Calif.) and Yale University (New Haven, Conn.).

Source: Compiled from "Educational Sources for American Indian Languages," *Wassaja* (May 1979): 13. [*Editor's note:* All information contained within this table was accurate as of 1979, the date of the original publication.]

employment in Indian-related activities—that is, in Indian centers in urban areas, Indian associations, and institutions of higher education with a strong Indian component. Others have entered the proposal writing game for Indian and Alaska Native projects. Some have become proficient in expressive elements of Plains cultures as singers and dancers. Many of them have married Native persons. Their ultimate impact has yet to be seen.

Need for Research

This brief overview of the status of language in Native communities merely pinpoints the fact that there is very little information stemming from contemporary Indian societies regarding the actual dimensions and idiosyncrasies of language use among various communities on Indian reservations. This is mirrored by the absence of information regarding the use of ancestral languages among residents in urban areas. The existence of a decided network between reservation and urban conglomerates of tribal groups regarding social functions (powwows) and religious events (Native American Church and *Yuwipi* rituals) that involve the utilization of Native languages presents aspects for consideration in any appraisal of language function.

Historically and contemporarily, schools and the educational processes have been the most effective means by which Native people have become reoriented to a new life-way. We can see the effects of this secondary socialization process for individuals in bicultural and bilingual settings. Therefore, there is a decided need for the training of bilingual teachers in ethnographic methods for analyzing the experiences of persons in these settings. Besides the research suggestions interspersed throughout this presentation, there are immediately salient needs to be considered:

- There is little material regarding the Native language skills of those involved in language arts and bilingual programs where Native people reside.
- Speaking events, especially speeches at powwows on reservations and in urban centers and such other events as Native rituals or Christian church events and the many other ceremonies in which Indian people participate, would yield aspects of communicative skills that represent contemporary Native life.
- Mundane but critical analysis of speech patterns in domestic life would also focus upon the function of language use today.
- The use of Native languages in curing ceremonies and the increasing use of Native paraprofessional counselors in mental health and alcoholism programs are seldom examined areas.
- The utilization of Native language in the collection of folkloristic data such as legends, folktales, and oral history accounts as they might be

used in culturally relevant curricula can be examined as an index of ancestral language competence and function.

- In order to be effective, language components of education programs must contain culturally relevant materials for the tribes involved.

An appraisal of any of these programs would be helpful in coalescing research needs. The outstanding need for most tribal groups is a cogent examination of language use in the daily life of Indian communities. Studies of the extent of ancestral language use in relation to English and the code-switching involved would add much to our knowledge and policymaking acumen. The parent or parent surrogate and child dyad is another area that needs investigation. In general, knowledge of the processes of language learning would enhance understanding of linguistic usages in contemporary American Indian and Alaska Native communities.

This brief view of language use in current Indian life has indicated that in most instances the persistence of ancestral languages in Native culture has a significant and tenacious dynamism. This dynamic character has many dimensions—on both individual and tribal levels. The totality of the continuity of Native cultures and languages is important to comprehending the viability of life inherent in Indian communities and can be understood and dealt with only when the components are delineated. Languages are the key to understanding these qualities.

Note

1. *Native American,* the most recent gloss for North American aborigines, is now in disfavor with many tribal groups and individuals. Recent congressional hearings around the country have resulted in a "Definition of Indian Study" (National Tribal Chairmen's Association Education Components 1980) that will further cloud the issue. The powerful National Congress of American Indians entertained a resolution opposing the use of the term in 1978. Throughout the history of Indian–White relations, such terms as *Amerindian, Indian-American,* and *First American* have been stylish. This phenomenon also speaks to the effects of policy decisions as they relate to American tribal groups. In this essay, I shall use "Native American" and "American Indian" interchangeably. Most tribes have their own ethnic markers—for example, "Lakota," "Dakota," and "Nakota" for Sioux; "Dine" for Navajo; and so forth.

References

American Indian Policy Review Commission. 1977–78. *Meetings of the American Indian Policy Review Commission.* Washington: Government Printing Office.
Basso, Keith. 1970. "To Give Up on Words: Silence in Apache Culture." *Southwestern Journal of Anthropology* 26(3): 213–30.
Chafe, W. L. 1962. "Estimates Regarding the Present Speakers of North American Indian Languages." *International Journal of American Linguistics* 28(3): 162–71.

————. 1965. "Corrected Estimates." *International Journal of American Linguistics* 31(4): 345–46.

Deloria, Vine, Jr. 1969. *Custer Died for Your Sins.* New York: Macmillan.

Dumont, Robert V. 1972. "Learning English and How to Be Silent—Studies in Sioux and Cherokee Classrooms." In *Functions of Language in the Classroom,* ed. Courtney B. Cazden, Vera John, and Dell Hymes, 344–69. New York: Teachers College Press.

Holm, Wayne. 1964. "Let It Never Be Said. . . ." *Journal of American Indian Education* 4(1): 6–9.

Knack, Martha C. 1978. "Beyond the Differential: An Inquiry into Southern Paiute Indian Experience in Public Schools." *Anthropology and Education Quarterly* 9(3): 216–34.

LaFlesche, Francis. 1963. *The Middle Five.* Madison: University of Wisconsin Press.

Lawrence, Gay. 1978. "Indian Education: Why Bilingual-Bicultural?" *Education and Urban Society* 10(3): 305–20.

Leap, William T., ed. 1977. *Studies in Southwestern English.* San Antonio: Trinity University Press.

————. 1978. "American Indian English and Its Implication for Bilingual Education." In *International Dimensions of Bilingual Education,* ed. James E. Alatis, 657–69. Washington: Georgetown University Press.

Malancon, Richard, and Mary Jo Malancon. 1977. "Indian English at Haskell Institute, 1915." In *Studies in Southwestern English,* ed. William Leap, 143–53. San Antonio: Trinity University Press.

Medicine, Bea. 1975. "Self-Direction in Sioux Education." *Integrateducation* 78(Nov.–Dec.): 15–17.

————. 1976. "The Schooling Process: Some Lakota (Sioux) Views." In *The Anthropological Study of Education,* ed. Craig Calhoun and Francis A. J. Ianni, 283–91. The Hague: Mouton.

————. 1979a. "Bilingual Education and Public Policy: The Cases of the American Indian." In *Bilingual Education and Public Policy in the United States,* ed. Raymond V. Padilla, 395–407. Ypsilanti: Department of Foreign Languages and Bilingual Studies, Eastern Michigan University.

————. 1979b. "Native American Speech Patterns: The Case of the Lakota-Speakers." In *The Handbook of Intercultural Communication,* ed. Molefi K. Asante, Eileen Newmark, and Cecil A. Blake, 383–91. Beverly Hills: Sage Publications.

Metcalf, Ann. 1978. *A Model for Treatment on a Native American Family Service Center.* Oakland: Urban Indian Child Resource Center.

National Tribal Chairmen's Association Education Components. 1980. *Educational Components Newsletter* (June): 1.

Pfeiffer, Anita. 1968. "Educational Innovation." *Journal of American Indian Education* 7 (May): 24–31.

Philips, Susan. 1972. "Participant Structures and Communicative Competence: Warm Springs Children in Community and Classroom." In *Functions of Language in the Classroom,* ed. Courtney B. Cazden, Vera John, and Dell Hymes, 370–94. New York: Teachers College Press.

————. 1974. "Warm Springs 'Indian Time': How the Regulation of Participation Affects the Progression of Events." In *Explorations in the Ethnography of Speaking,* ed. Richard Bauman and Joel Sherzer, 92–109. New York: Cambridge University Press.

Powers, William K. 1972. "The Language of the Sioux." In *Language in American Indian Education,* ed. W. R. Slager, 1–21. Albuquerque: Indian Education Resource Center.

Prucha, Francis Paul. 1976. *American Indian Policy in Crisis: Christian Reformers and the Indian, 1865–1900*. Norman: University of Oklahoma Press.

Rood, David S., and Allan R. Taylor, eds. 1978. *Newsletter of Siouan and Caddoan Linguistics.* Boulder: University of Colorado Linguistics Department.

Wabaunsee, A. John. 1977. "Native American Viewpoint." *Bilingual Education: Current Perspectives—Law,* 65–70. Arlington: Center for Applied Linguistics.

CHAPTER 3

Bilingual Education and Public Policy: The Cases of the American Indian

As the name for the original inhabitants of this country has vacillated (Indian to American Indian, Indian-American to First Americans, and, presently, Native American), governmental policy as it relates to education and the very life-styles of these tribal people have evidenced the impingement of public sentiment and public pressure upon the policy decisions that have affected them for generations. Numbering fewer than a million persons, whatever the name applied to them, public policy has conveniently obscured the numerous tribal entities, and multifarious educational policies have been pressed upon powerless people. Historically and unilaterally, the thrust of all educational programs has been toward assimilation and eventual amalgamation into a larger, dominant, and mainly white society.

The final report of the American Indian Policy Review Commission notes that "a total of 289 tribes and bands live on 269 'federally recognized' reservations or otherwise defined 'trust areas' in 26 states" (1977:90). Of immediate significance for bilingual education is the fact that an estimated 206 different languages and language dialects are still spoken among these Native people. Wallace Chafe provides a sense of language utilization in Indian communities when he estimates that forty-nine of these languages have fewer than ten speakers aged fifty or over, while six of these languages have more than ten thousand speakers in all generations representing language fluency. Fluency in the remaining 152 languages falls somewhere within these polarities (Chafe 1962, 1965). Data of this nature points to the diverse need in terms of maintenance, transitional, or revitalization programs involving Native American groups.

Most Native American tribal aggregates view themselves as independent nations within a multicultural superstructure. Nationhood at the time of the signing of treaties has given most tribes a unique trust relationship with the federal government that is reflected in the requirements for education. Generally, Indians as tribal aggregates and as individuals hold that federal provision for their education is a treaty right for many of them and see it as an important aspect of a trust relationship. Each treaty is viewed as an important mandate for each tribe. When Congress halted treaty-making with tribes in 1871, Indian policies were determined unilaterally. This established a pervasive trend to generate and generalize public policy of overriding dimensions whatever the cultural background of the people involved.

This essay seeks to present an ethnohistorical overview to enhance awareness of these superimposed directives in the field of bilingual education as they relate to tribal people in the United States. It posits a nexus of policy and its implementation that should yield new insights into contemporary research needs and strategies for Native Americans.

Recent articulations by Indian militants, testimony-givers in countless congressional hearings on Indian "problems" across the country, and by members of innumerable "task forces" set up to deal with educational concerns have mentioned the loss of ancestral Indian languages. What scope and precision these losses have entailed are seldom articulated for tribally distinct groups. Language loss has been mainly verbalized in rhetoric, polemics, and possible guilt-inducing attempts for policy planners.

Most current studies on American Indians contain scattered references to the loss of Native languages and the inefficient use of English. Perspectives on the use of languages—ancestral and new—in specific tribes or communities are seldom delineated. A stringent analysis of language policy as intertwined with the entire process of education for a specific group of Natives is a research need of high priority. There are several reasons for this absence in the arena of language use and ethnicity. Historically, overarching governmental policy has not given credence to idiosyncratic reactions of tribes to the policy. Evaluative frames have not been applied in any equitable fashion. More recently, the deficit model as it has been applied to Indians has co-opted linguistic research into probing problems such as drop-out rates, reading difficulties, and insensitive teachers. Sociological and historical aspects in juxtaposition with the contours of speech communities must be perceived for Native American groups. Despite generations of propulsion to assimilation and concerted efforts for cultural change enacted via the educational process, each tribe has maintained some type of cultural base by virtue of ecological isolation (reservations), socioeconomic constraints (race and class), or by simple choice. Thus, despite superordinate governmental dictates and decision-making that has been external to the Native community, tribes have maintained some aspect of cultural and linguistic integrity. Therefore, in assessing public policy and tribal enactment of the rules and regulations, an ethnographic sophistication and an awareness of the interface between two different modes of social organization is essential.

Honoring dance for Bea Medicine, Stanford Powwow, 1980. (Courtesy of Susan Lobo, Community History Project, Intertribal Friendship House © 1980)

The wide range of cultural types exemplified by Native societies and the differential reaction to language policy may best be exemplified by cross-cultural comparisons. Indeed, if only a careful analysis of one tribe is done, it can show the dynamics of language use, retention, and change. Moreover, it can highlight the areas for current and future research.

The American Indian Policy Review Commission presented a report on one of the "five civilized tribes," the Cherokee:

In the 1820's [sic], that tribe established a peaceful, thriving, self-sustaining community whose governing elite actively promoted constitutionalism, commercial farming, education, and Christianity. The United States virtually denied the abundant evidence of Cherokee success, deliberately assaulted the administrative integrity of the Cherokee government, and fostered enduring tribal factions—all in a successful effort to secure a treaty for tribal lands in Appalachia.

Few tribes in the nineteenth century went as far as the Cherokees in trying to accommodate to the government's notion of civilization. But nearly all received their education for civilization in the context of an overall plan of action that deprived them of their most valuable resources, displaced them from their homes, attacked and subverted their chosen leaders, and denigrated their religious and ceremonial life, family relations, dress, *language,* and sexual division of labor. (1977–78:61, emphasis added)

The Cherokee had chosen accommodation and used the same criteria that the conquerors had. Indeed, they had become literate in their own Native language, using a syllabary said to have been developed by the Cherokee Sequoyah. Thus, most of the pinnacles of civilization had been achieved on Native terms. Yet in the forced displacement from the southeastern United States to Indian Territory (now Oklahoma), the more "full-blood" descendants of this Cherokee group are considered illiterate and "unacculturated."

Wahrhaftig and Thomas describe the Cherokee context in the Oklahoma area:

Prominent whites say with pride, "We're all a little bit Indian here." They maintain that real Cherokees are about "bred out." Few Cherokees are left who can speak their native tongue, whites insist, and fewer still are learning their language. In twenty years, according to white myth, the Cherokee language and with it the separate and distinctive community that speaks it will fade into memory.

Anthropologists visiting us in the field, men who thought their previous studies had taught them what a conservative tribe is like, were astonished by the Cherokees. Seldom had they seen people who speak so little English, who are so unshakably traditional in outlook. (1972:80–81)

Qualitative contours of this contemporary community are again illuminated by this excerpt from the same authors, Thomas (a Cherokee) and Wahrhaftig:

Before 1907, the entire area was part of the Cherokee nation. Today, 12,000 Cherokees live there, 9,500 of them in traditionally structured, small Cherokee-speaking settlements. The educational level of these Cherokee Indians is one of the lowest in the United States and their dropout rate is one of the highest. Of the adult Cherokees 40 percent are functionally illiterate in English. Approximately one in three heads of Cherokee households in country Cherokee settlements cannot speak English. Cherokees attended their own schools for half a century and the school system of the State of Oklahoma for sixty years thereafter. Even so, the Cherokee community of eastern Oklahoma is one of the least educated in our nation. (1971:231–32)

Recent effects of policy decisions that have affected this group have not yet been clarified—effective utilization of Title VII and other bilingual attempts are yet to be documented. One can state, however, that the Oklahoma Cherokee represent one example of the effects of forced relocation, cultural isolation, factionalism, loss of community control over schools, and educational policies to move a powerless people into a projected middle-class existence in an area that heretofore has been economically deprived. Recent emphasis upon the disadvantaged people of Appalachia in federal funding programs will also have implications.

Although many Native American individuals speak of treaty obligations, one finds that the younger generations seldom know the obligations of the federal government that are often outlined in the treaties and that form the basis for the relationships between tribe and federal government. To give the essence of "treaty talk," one famous agreement was examined for requirements on education. The 1868 Treaty with the Sioux, Brulé, Oglala, Miniconjou, Yanktonai, Hunkpapa, Blackfeet, Cuthead, Two Kettle, Sans Arc, and Santee bands (and Arapaho, an Algonkian-speaking Plains tribe) is quite explicit. (Parenthetically, in 1973 the Standing Rock Tribal Council published the text of all treaties pertaining to the Sioux for the tribal members.) The section delineating education is as follows:

> Article #7: In order to insure the civilization of the Indians entering into this treaty, the necessity of education is admitted, especially of such of them as are or may be settled on said agricultural reservation, and they therefore pledge themselves to compel their children, male and female, between the ages of six and sixteen years, to attend school; and it is hereby made the duty of the agent for said Indians to see that this stipulation is strictly complied with; and the United States agrees that for every thirty children between said ages who can be induced or compelled to attend school, a house shall be provided and a teacher competent to teach the elementary branches of an English education shall be furnished, who will reside among said Indians, and faithfully discharge his or her duties as a teacher. The provisions of this article to continue for not less than twenty years. (*Treaties and Agreements* 1973:94)

This directive is specific as to age, sex, type of education, provision of school house, and teacher for a stated number of pupils. Of significance is the equating of civilizing the Sioux Indians, a nomadic, warrior society, with an "English education." It also predicated a sedentary life with an agricultural base.

The following policy statement, although lengthy, gives a more detailed rationale for the linguistic education of Indian people and exemplifies the overarching formation of language policy:

> Longer and closer consideration of the subject has only deepened my [J. D. C. Atkins's] conviction that it is a matter not only of importance, but of necessity that the Indians acquire the English language as rapidly as possible. The government has entered upon the great work of educating and citizenizing the Indians and establishing them upon homesteads. The adults are expected to assume the role of citizens, and of course the rising generation will be expected and required more nearly to fill the measure of citizenship, and the main purpose of educating them is to enable them to read, write, and speak the English language and to transact business with English-speaking people. When

they take upon themselves the responsibilities and privileges of citizenship their vernacular will be of no advantage. Only through the medium of the English tongue can they acquire a knowledge of the Constitution of the country and their rights and duties thereunder. . . . Nothing so surely and perfectly stamps upon an individual a national characteristic as language. . . . Only English has been allowed to be taught in the public schools in the territory acquired by this country from Spain, Mexico, and Russia, although the native populations spoke another tongue . . .

Deeming it for the very best interest of the Indian, both as an individual and as an embryo citizen, to have this policy strictly enforced among the various schools on Indian reservations, orders have been issued accordingly to Indian agents . . .

It is believed that if any Indian vernacular is allowed to be taught by the missionaries in schools on Indian reservations, it will prejudice the youthful pupil as well as his untutored and uncivilized or semi-civilized parent against the English language, and, to some extent at least, against Government schools in which the English language exclusively has always been taught. To teach Indian school children their native tongue is practically to exclude English, and to prevent them from acquiring it. This language, which is good enough for a white man and a black man, ought to be good enough for the red man. It is also believed that teaching an Indian youth in his own barbarous dialect is a positive detriment to him. The first step to be taken toward civilization, toward teaching the Indians the mischief and folly of continuing their barbarous practices, is to teach them the English language. The impracticality, if not the impossibility, of civilizing the Indians of this country in any other tongue other than our own would seem to be obvious, especially in view of the fact that the number of Indian vernaculars is even greater than the number of tribes. Bands of the same tribes inhabiting different localities have different dialects, and sometimes can not communicate with each other except by sign language. If we expect to infuse into the rising generation the leaven of American citizenship, we must remove the stumbling blocks of hereditary customs and manners, and of these language is one of the most important elements. (House Executive Document no. 1, 50th Cong., 1st sess., serial 2542:19–21, reprinted in Prucha 1975:174–76)

This extract from the annual report of the commissioner of Indian affairs in 1887 indicates the official position of the department in viewing the English language as one of the chief modes of bringing civilization to the Indians. J. D. C. Atkins interprets this directive, which then could be reinterpreted down the bureaucratic ladder. The foregoing also brings into focus the extreme ethnocentrism and superior attitudes of those individuals dedicated to bringing a new life-style to Indian people. The tone and thrust of this policy formed the cornerstone of Indian education until the effects of the Collier administration were felt in the 1930s.

In an effort to give an epic view of this process of language repression, several statements from Siouan life histories are included. Throughout Indian country, from the Winnebago in Wisconsin (also a Siouan-speaking group) to the Makah (Wakashan-linguistic affiliation) in the Northwest on the Washington coast, a standard practice was to wash the mouth of the student who "reverted" back to speaking the Native tongue with "strong yellow laundry soap, you know, the kind that comes in bars" (quote from Pearl Warren [Makah], Medicine 1978). The trauma of this experience was still evident in this sixty-five-year-old woman as her eyes filled with tears. Most often in the history of language change, the recipients of the program's internalization of those superimposed policies are seldom considered.

Luther Standing Bear described his meeting with his father at Carlisle Indian School:

> When I got downstairs, my father was in the center of a large crowd of boys, who were all shaking hands with him. He was so glad to see me, and I was so delighted to see him. But our rules were not to speak the Indian language under any consideration. And here was my father, and he could not speak English!
>
> My first act was to write a note to Captain Pratt, asking if he would permit me to speak to my father in the Sioux tongue. I said, "My father is here. Please allow me to speak to him in Indian." Captain Pratt answered, "Yes, my boy; bring your father over to my house." (1928:149)

Later, Standing Bear noted, "He allowed the boys to talk to him in the Indian tongue, and that pleased the boys very much" (150). Luther Standing Bear, who entered Carlisle Indian School in 1897, recalled his father's conversation after Captain Pratt took the elder Standing Bear on a trip to Boston, New York, Baltimore, Philadelphia, and Washington.

> After he returned form the trip, he spoke to me in this wise: "My son, since I have seen all those cities, and the way the Long Knife people are doing, I begin to realize that our lands and our game are all gone. There is nothing but the Long Knives (or white people) everywhere I went, and they keep coming like flies. So we will have to learn their ways, in order that we may be able to live with them. You will have to learn all you can, and I will see that your brothers and sisters follow in the path you are making for them."
>
> This is the first time my father had ever spoken to me regarding acquiring a white man's education. He continued: "Some day I want to hear you speak like these Long Knife people, and work like them." This was spoken to me by my father in the Dakota tongue, but it meant so much to me. He was so serious in his conversation along this line that I felt quite "puffed up." I wanted to please him in everything—even to getting killed on the battlefield. Even that I was willing to endure. (151–52)

This statement is all the more remarkable because Luther volunteered to attend Carlisle without his father's permission, for he had heeded his admonishment "to die in battle, meeting the enemy." He viewed going to school in the East as "meeting the enemy," it seems. As Standing Bear had made an autonomous decision, his father agreed. Other data detailing the trauma of a forcible language-learning experience is given in the Appendix [47–48]. Noteworthy to mention at this time is the dearth of life history material for women. This is especially significant, for it reflects the male bias of early ethnographers and also indicates that—among the Sioux, for example—women were kept away from these investigators. It is possible to examine the roles of women in the socialization process by looking at life histories (Medicine 1978). This lack of data in language studies is especially crucial, because it is the mother and mother surrogate who is so important in the early language acquisition of children. The full effects of cultural genocide and the psychic toll on Native individuals have not been part of the investigative priorities of early researchers. Fragmentary references and anecdotal statements must be carefully honed out of the ethnographic record.

A cogent analysis of the numerous educational attempts forced upon the Indians, parochial and governmental, should be examined in the entire area of bilingual education for Indians. The translation of Native languages into religious items—Bibles, hymnals, and prayer books—is seldom acknowledged. These are important means by which many Native Americans, under the guise of Christianization, were able to retain their indigenous languages. Indigenous statements are forerunners and should be examined when reference is made to "Indian English" (Leap 1973) or when novelists (Hill 1979) speak of "archaic" Dakota languages and exploit Indian languages for profit.

The influence of John Collier in the New Deal era was enormous in charting new directions in Indian education. His thesis was that education should develop, rather than diminish, group loyalties and that the unique cultural backgrounds of the tribes be acknowledged, enhanced, and emphasized via the learning processes. His policy "insisted that Indians have religious and social freedom in all manners where such freedom was not directly contrary to public morals" (Philp 1972:69). After his appointment as commissioner of Indian affairs, he obtained, in June 1934, the passage of the Indian Reorganization Act. This act rejected the traditional policy of assimilation and "Americanization" of the Indians in favor of a policy of cultural pluralism.

As a part of cultural revitalization, bilingual reading books were developed for some tribes. The readers for the Sioux included such books as *Brave against the Enemy* (*T'oka wan itkop'ip ohitike kin he*) by Ann Nolan Clark. Thus the prolonged period when "the Indian Bureau tried to Americanize Native American children by sending them to boarding schools where they were taught to despise their culture" (Philip 1973:22) drew to a close. An element not sufficiently treated in historical analyses of Indian education is that of Native language use. Sociolinguistic studies of language use and retention and its utilization in Native communities are sadly lacking for this period. Basic to Collier's emphasis on cultural awareness via Native religious expression—the development of Indian arts, crafts, and music—was the seldom mentioned role of language as a medium by which religious ritual and expressive elements of Native cultures were fostered. A succinct statement must suffice for the period:

> There is also in press a series of books in Sioux and English. Here the problem is different. More of the Sioux speak English. They are more familiar with the world beyond the reservation. But their language is the one used in their own world. Owing to the labors of missionaries over many years, many of the Sioux are able to read and write their own language now. Here we need only take advantage of the work that has been done, and provide opportunities for its use. Our major departure has been to work in the dialect that has the greatest number of speakers—Teton—whereas most of the printed material used today is in the eastern dialects. Since they are all mutually intelligible, this is a matter of economy. (Kennard 1942:114)

The comparative stance here refers to the Navajo, who were, and are, the tribe evidencing the largest degree of monolingualism in their native language of the Athabaskan stock.

Forty-one years after the benchmark Meriam Report of 1928 that presaged the 1969 Senate committee report entitled *Indian Education: A National Tragedy, a National Challenge,* the subtle pressures toward cultural homogenization to white European language and values continued. Indians were still being victimized by an alien educational process. The well-funded study by Fuchs and Havighurst indicates the scope of bilingual education. Although they indicate no unanimous opinion regarding Native language use, they state, "The National Study found considerable support among Indian youths and their parents for instruction in the native languages themselves, as subjects of study, within the schools, both at the elementary and secondary level" (1972:213). Because the Bureau of Indian Affairs is now contracting its schools to tribal groups in an effort to sponsor community control and self-determination, the decisions regarding the impact of bicultural and bilingual education for Indians may have a new emphasis. Parent advisory councils that are mandated by proposal requirements, plus such Native organizations as the National Indian Education Association and the Coalition of Community Controlled Schools, are means of obtaining the much-overworked phrase "Indian input" into the curricula.

The negation of the ideal of a homogeneous American society plus the valuation of ethnicity in current contemporary American life-styles have in general given a new perspective to language use in most Native societies. The resiliency and adaptiveness of American Indians and Alaskan Natives, as the identity now goes, can be seen in efforts to strengthen the imperative that culture and language are wedded together and form a more positive identity. The enhanced aspects of being a Native in a white world will have some interesting connotations for future researchers. From a viewpoint of interaction in Native communities, the apparent interest seems to be increasing. We can, therefore, turn to recent public policies that have been responsible for this heightened interest.

The Indian Education Act of 1972 (P.L. 92–318) has authorized and given great impetus for innovative and compensatory programs in BIA, public, and community-controlled schools and in adult education and higher education programs. This legislation stresses the allocation of decision-making powers to Native tribes and groups. It also establishes an Office of Indian Education in the United States Office of Education under the supervision of the National Advisory Council on Indian Education appointed by the president. The council consists of fifteen Native Americans who are of varied tribal backgrounds. Local-level political systems were acknowledged with program review and veto powers given to Indian citizen groups. An outstanding feature of this legislation is a provision to serve all Native Americans whether or not they are affiliated with a federally recognized tribe.

The amendment of Title VII of the Elementary and Secondary Act of 1965, Bilingual Education (P.L. 93–380), passed on August 21, 1974, has added great impetus to the funding of bilingual programs for Native people.

William Demmert, first deputy commissioner of Indian Education and former director of Indian education in the Bureau of Indian Affairs has written: "It is absolutely imperative that Indian parents and communities participate in forming the cultural, psychological, physical, intellectual, and language base upon which schools must later build." He further indicates the scope of these acts: "In 1976, some 278,000 Indian students in over a thousand school districts are benefiting from Part A grants, which are supporting bicultural-bilingual enrichment activities that include the development of cultural awareness curriculums in reading and mathematics and such supportive services as guidance counseling and transportation" (1976:8).

What is empirical evidence of the need for bilingual education for Indian children? The National Indian Training and Research Center was contracted by the Bureau of Indian Affairs to conduct an assessment of the bilingual education needs of children (National Indian Training and Research Center 1975). Data were collected by use of questionnaires completed by officials at all BIA, contract, or public schools receiving Johnson-O'Malley funds. There were great variations in the ways in which bilingual education was defined and the regulations interpreted. Only 33 percent of the schools had conducted needs assessments to give data for program planning. Parents actually favoring the approach were not significant. The study indicated that of 169,482 Indian children enrolled in BIA schools, approximately one-third evidenced bilingual education needs, while almost one-fourth indicated need for this special program that at that time (1973) was not being met.

One report indicates that "before 1970 there would have been few bilingual programs to observe in Eskimo and Indian communities. Now there are more than thirty-five programs, some new and some that have been going on for several years, some in only certain grades in a single school, some in many schools in an area" (Bank Street College of Education 1976:253).

Recent discourse—academic, legalistic, and popular—has focused upon the larger populations of minority people involved in the bilingual education dilemma. The unique cases of the numerically smallest yet most culturally diverse of these groups had been ignored in recent research.

What then are the patterns of language use in the lives of contemporary Native Americans? In some areas, that is, the Pueblos in the Southwest, language has persisted and is closely tied to religious ritual and esoteric language. In many instances, the community people, especially the ritual leaders and religious practitioners, often resist bilingual education on the grounds that teaching a Native language in the school might reveal their religious beliefs and allow non-Pueblos to learn the Native tongue and gain access to cultural data. This rationale also has implications for utilization of cultural content in curricula. Santo Domingo Pueblo (a Keresan-speaking group) is an example.

However, among the numerous Navajo, there is a strong commitment to the use of the Native language, which is deemed essential for monolingual children or those who have little exposure to English to become bilingual with the least possible psychic stress to the individual. Many successful school situations, staffed by qualified Navajo educators who have a sound involvement with communities (i.e., Rough Rock), are exemplary experiments in bilingual education. The Navajo school at Rock Point is an excellent example of a language maintenance program where bilingual education is carried from kindergarten through the eighth grade. The enormous population growth of the Navajo seemingly coincided with more tolerant views regarding Indian education and a corollary training program for Navajo teachers. These factors may be credited for a more efficacious education program that is also attuned to the needs of this segment of the Indian population. The continued effectiveness of the Navajo language programs needs further evaluation.

An example of a retrieval-revival program is that of the Onieda (an Iroquoian-speaking group) in Wisconsin. This group is presently engaged in the revival of Native religion, the establishment of a tribal museum and archives, and increased interest in oral history. Much of this cultural revitalization may be tied to land claims.

The Makah (a Wakashan-speaking group) in northwestern Washington state have a large federal grant to revive their language. This nativistic movement is also to revive other expressive elements of culture as music, dance, and tribal dress.

Within the entire range of bilingual education programs for Native Americans there is a pervasive idiosyncratic expression of language use. Some parents and parental surrogates (grandparents) feel that the sooner the children learn English well, the easier it will be for them to adapt and function effectively in a predominantly English-speaking world. Others have stated, "I don't want my children to have the 'hard time' [difficulty] I had learning the English language" and will speak only "Indian English" to them. These individuals very often use a Native language in communicating with their aged cohorts and in community affairs. This attitude is typical in many Lakota Sioux communities, where the degree of bilingualism is difficult to determine. Language use in the Native vernacular may, in these and other Indian communities (i.e., Yakima), be seen as a means of adding "funding" to an educational base. In many contemporary Native communities, the parents and parental age-mates feel that education should begin in the child's first language with a gradual but effective transition to competence in English and the mastering of the school's curriculum. Others feel that a complete break with the community's language and culture is a prerequisite for adaptation in a white school and society.

A great majority of the current Indian population resides in cities or off-reservation communities. This group often holds their parents responsible for not teaching them their native language. The trend can possibly be reflected in the inclusion of the teaching of Native Indian and Inuit (Eskimo) languages in some universities and colleges.

The effects of the Bilingual Education Act (Title VII) undoubtedly will have some consequences for the future direction of education for American Indians and Alaskan natives. The Indian Self-Determination Act of 1977, with a clearly mandated issue of indigenous control, will present interesting directions in the field of language and culture. Presently, there have been few attempts to evaluate those bicultural and bilingual programs, which have been in operation since the funding base has been applied to Native communities.

The decisions made by a superordinate decision-making body in the execution of policy determining language use and the educational process have had dire effects upon the linguistic skills of contemporary Natives. Language policies have been tied to the civilization process based upon the destruction of Native language and life-styles.

The basic policies have been set and then reinterpreted by bureaucrats and decision-makers in the numerous federal and state agencies that impinge upon Native life. Thus, a certain capriciousness is evident in the ethnohistoric record, which can be seen in the idiosyncratic relationship of each tribe to its treaties and the Indian agent. More recently, this pattern of financial dependence is seen in the composition of advisory boards, interpreters of present language policy, and proposal readers.

At this juncture, several points can be made regarding contemporary programs. Most of the schools involved in bilingual education have been seen as "model" schools with the expectation that their continuity would be assured by the community. In most instances, due to monetary restrictions and dependence upon Title VII as the "funding" source, many of the bilingual programs have been abandoned after five years. In many communities, due to the historical restrictions on language use documented previously, many of the programs have assumed a cultural and language-retrieval aspect. In almost all communities, local-level politics entered the picture and oriented the programs. In many instances, the individuals most competent to teach Native languages and culture have been the most inept in the political machinations of school boards, parent advisory councils, and public school politics and were merely shunted aside for other more "acceptable" (from the administrative point of view) Native people.

What is evident in this brief essay is the fact of a super-subordinate situation in which language policy has, and is, being formulated at another level and being shifted upon the educational processes of powerless people of all tribes.

Appendix:

Francis LaFlesche gives an interesting view of language learning among the Omaha (also a Siouan language):

> From the earliest years the Omaha child was trained in the grammatical use of his native tongue. No slip was allowed to pass uncorrected, and as a result there was no child-talk such as obtains among English-speaking children, the only difference between the speech of old and young was in the pronunciation of words which the infant often failed to utter correctly, but this difficulty was soon overcome, and a boy of ten or twelve years was apt to speak as good Omaha as a man of mature years.
>
> Like the grown folks, we youngsters were fond of companionship and of talking. In making our gamesticks and in our play, we chattered incessantly of the things that occupied our minds, and we thought it a hardship when we were obliged to speak in low tones while older people were engaged in conversation. When we entered the Mission School, we experienced a greater hardship, for there we encountered a rule that prohibited the use of our own language, which rule was rigidly enforced with a hickory rod, so that the newcomer, however socially inclined, was oblige to go about like a little dummy until he learned to express himself in English.
>
> All the boys in our school were given English names, because their Indian names were difficult for the teachers to pronounce. Besides, the aboriginal names were considered by the missionaries as heathenish, and therefore should be obliterated. No less heathenish in their origin were the English substitutes, but the loss of their original meanings and significance through long usage had rendered them fit to continue as appellations for civilized folk. And so, in place of Tae-noo-ga-we-he came Philip Sheridan; in that of Wa-pah'-dae, Ulysses S. Grant; that of Koo'-we-he-ge-ra, Alexander, and so on. Our sponsors went further back in history, and thus we had our David and Jonathan, Gideon and Isaac, and with the flood of these new names came Noah. It made little difference to us that we had to learn the significance of one more word as applied to ourselves, when the task before us was to make our way through an entire

strange language. So we learned to call each other by our English names, and continued to do so even after we had left school and had grown to manhood.

Referring to his vignettes, LaFlesche continues:

In the talk of the boys I have striven to give a reproduction of the peculiar English spoken by them, which was composite, gathered from the imperfect comprehension of their books, the provincialisms of the teachers, and the slang and bad grammar picked up from uneducated white persons employed at the school or at the Government Agency. Oddities of speech, profanity, localisms, and slang were unknown in the Omaha language, so when such expressions fell upon the ears of these lads they innocently learned and used them without the slightest suspicion that there could be bad as well as good English.

The misconception of Indian life and character so common among the White people has been largely due to an ignorance of the Indian's language, or his mode of thought, his beliefs, his ideals, and his native institutions. Every aspect of the Indian and his manner of life has always been strange to the White man, and this strangeness had been magnified by the mists of prejudice and the conflict of interests between the two races. While these in time may disappear, no Native American can ever cease to regret that the utterances of his father have been constantly belittled when put into English, that their thoughts have frequently been travestied and their native dignity obscured. The average interpreter has generally picked up his knowledge of English in a random fashion, for very few have had the advantage of a thorough education, and all have had to deal with the difficulties that attend the translator. The beauty and picturesqueness, and euphonious playfulness, or the gravity of diction which I have heard among my own people, and other tribes as well, are all but impossible to be given literally in English. (LaFlesche 1963:xi–xv)

References

American Indian Policy Review Commission. 1977–78. *Meetings of the American Indian Policy Review Commission.* Washington: Government Printing Office.
Bank Street College of Education. 1976. *Young Native Americans and Their Families: Educational Needs Assessment and Recommendations.* Washington: United States Office of Indian Education Programs, Bureau of Indian Affairs.
Chafe, W. L. 1962. "Estimates Regarding the Present Speakers of North American Indian Languages." *International Journal of American Linguistics* 28(3): 162–71.
———. 1965. "Corrected Estimates." *International Journal of American Linguistics* 31(4): 345–46.
Clark, Ann, and Helen Post. 1944. *Brave against the Enemy (T'oka wan itkok'ip ohitike kin he).* Illustrated by Emil Afraid of Hawk. Lawrence: Haskell Institute Printing Department.
Demmert, William G., Jr. 1976. "Indian Education: Where and Whither?" *American Education* 112(7): 6–9.
Fuchs, Estelle, and Robert J. Havighurst. 1972. *To Live on This Earth: American Indian Education.* Garden City: Doubleday.

Hill, Ruth Beebe. 1979. *Hanta Yo.* Garden City: Doubleday.

Kennard, Edward A. 1942. "The Use of Native Languages and Cultures in Indian Education." In *The Changing Indian,* ed. Oliver LaFarge, 109–15. Norman: University of Oklahoma Press.

LaFlesche, Francis. 1963. *The Middle Five.* Madison: University of Wisconsin Press.

Leap, William. 1973. "Language Pluralism in a Southwestern Pueblo: The Evidence from Isleta." In *Bilingualism in the Southwest,* ed. Paul R. Turner, 274–94. Tucson: University of Arizona Press.

Medicine, Bea. 1978. *Native American Women: A Perspective.* Las Cruces: ERIC/CRESS.

Philp, Kenneth R. 1972. "John Collier and the American Indian, 1920–1945." In *Essays on Radicalism in Contemporary America,* ed. Leon B. Blair, 63–80. Austin: University of Texas Press.

———. 1973. "John Collier and the Crusade to Protect Indian Religious Freedom." *Journal of Ethnic Studies* 1(1): 22–38.

Prucha, Francis Paul, ed. 1975. *Documents of United States Indian Policy.* Lincoln: University of Nebraska Press.

Standing Bear, Luther. 1928. *My People, the Sioux.* Edited by E. A. Brininstool. Boston: Houghton Mifflin.

National Indian Training and Research Center. 1975. *Survey of Bilingual Education Needs of Indian Children.* Research and Evaluation Report, series no. 36. Albuquerque: Indian Education Resources Center, Bureau of Indian Affairs.

Thomas, Robert K., and Albert L. Wahrhaftig. 1971. "Indians, Hillbillies and the Education Problem." In *Anthropological Perspectives on Education,* ed. Murray L. Wax, Stanley Diamond, and Fred Gearing, 230–51. New York: Basic Books.

Treaties and Agreements and the Proceedings of the Treaties and Agreements of the Tribes and Bands of the Sioux Nation. 1973. Washington: Institute for the Development of Indian Law.

U.S. Congress, Senate Special Subcommittee on Indian Education. 1969. *Indian Education: A National Tragedy, a National Challenge.* Washington: Government Printing Office.

Wahrhaftig, Albert L., and Robert K. Thomas. 1972. "Renaissance and Repression: The Oklahoma Cherokee." In *Native Americans Today: Sociological Perspectives,* ed. Howard M. Bahr, Bruce A. Chadwick, and Robert C. Day, 80–89. New York: Harper and Row.

CHAPTER 4

Contemporary Cultural Revisitation: Bilingual and Bicultural Education

This essay will not deal with educational inequities and past programs of cultural genocide via schooling processes that were inflicted upon the indigenous populations of the United States. Rather, it will examine the many manifestations of self-determination and community control that have surfaced in Native communities since the enactment of the Indian Reorganization Act of 1934. Although many analyses of the "Collier years" have proliferated in historical journals (Philp 1972, among others), the Native viewpoint of these years had been largely neglected in the literature on Indian education. Growing up on Standing Rock Reservation in South Dakota during the initial enactment of the IRA, many of us involved in the politics of our parents asked each other, "Are you a 'New Dealer' or an 'Old Dealer'?" referring to the policies of the Roosevelt administration. More strikingly, many of the students in the public schools were astonished when we looked at bilingual readers written in our Native Siouan language, Lakota. Such books, "the Sioux series" by Ann Clark (1941, 1942a, 1942b, 1943a, 1943b, 1943c, 1944), were welcome additions to the Christian hymnals and Bibles that were often the main sources of our abilities to read our Native languages and learn some of the transformed value configurations that might have been lost if there were no written accounts of the underlying principles of our cultural beliefs and norms. Thus, the complete demolition of our cultural norms by missionaries had other unforeseen results. The Lakota norm of "sharing" also opened our horizons to bilingual readers. These bilingual readers, which were done in the Native languages of Navaho and Lakota, may be evaluated in the historic record as the initial impact of bilingual and bicultural education for but a segment of the Native population in the 1940s.

It was during this period, according to Margaret Szasz (1974), that revisionist educators in the U.S. Indian Service attempted to introduce "cross-cultural education" into the bureau's curricula. It appears that the subtle but perduring mode tended toward the acculturational model. Despite the rich and varied life-styles of the many different Indian tribes, the underlying premise of education was still oriented to the mode of adaptation to the dominant white society. This attitude seemed to reflect the actual practice rather than the policies of the Collier administration. Educational policies and their implementation are often at variance, and this dissonance still plagues many innovative programs today.

What were the parameters of bicultural and bilingual education? Some of the best sources for an assessment of these programs are found in the pamphlets published by the Education Division of the U.S. Indian Service and entitled *Indian Education* (Beatty 1953). By carefully perusing these, several saliencies emerge. Unfortunately, although the impact of parochial schools has been great upon the education of U.S. Natives, the culling of policies and practices is not as easy. The analysis of the impact of church schools upon the education of Indian people needs examination to give parity of processes.

However, under the guise of "progressive education" and the use of anthropologists in the teaching of cultural differences to Indian Service teachers during the early 1940s, this new trend to provide relevance to Natives in cross-cultural learning situations was initiated but not completely incorporated into the education of the indigenous people of the U.S. It was only in the 1960s when new orientations to old themes were instituted in Indian education. Whatever the evaluation of the Collier administration, the vision of an educational system that incorporated Native culture was perhaps too innovative for that time.

It behooves us at this juncture to examine some of the articulations of Native people in the educational realm. Edward Dozier, Santa Clara Pueblo anthropologist, noted that "high drop-out rates of Native students, as we go up the scale of grade levels, is largely the result of negative ratings attributed to Native-American culture" (Szasz 1974: 146). This succinct statement, I believe, correctly assesses factors that account for the supposed low self-image, the lack of motivation, and the general maladjustment to schooling processes that had no relevance to the Native student. It is apparent, however, that the continual denigration of one's natal culture and the superimposition of cultural values and norms that are without meaning have taken a toll in the self-actualization of indigenous people. However, the continued use of Native languages in homes in reservation, rural, and urban communities speaks to the value placed upon Native languages and stresses the viability of this form of cultural expression. We must not, however, forget the other aspects of culture, religion, beliefs, music, dance, and oral history, storytelling, worldview, and kinship systems that have been used as means of cultural and linguistic continuity. Although it is recognized that legislated policies have had a great effect on Indian learning systems, it is within the nexus of sociolinguistic manifestations in diverse Native communities that the essence of Native culture flourishes and exists despite generations of pressure to change. The very persistence of viable languages speaks immensely to the vitality of Native life in the United States. Rather than examine the imposed policies, it seems more profitable to look to sociolinguistic studies to comprehend the adaptive strategies utilized by Native people. Several studies (Dumont 1972; Phillips 1972) contain examples of adaptive strategies that Native students have evolved in communication styles. Studies of speech patterns in Native communities are not as evident. This is an area in which much research needs to be accomplished, for Native language use in community context will give new insights in cultural continuity.

Retrospectively, one must assess the decade of the 1960s in order to place bilingual and bicultural programs in proper perspective. This decade was a time of social unrest, with ethnic constituencies in various universities striking to make curricula more relevant to downtrodden blacks, Chicanos, Asians, and the newly designated "Native Americans." The thrust for significant change in Native education on the post-secondary level gained momentum with the occupation of Alcatraz (November 1969) by university students (and community members) in San Francisco. Student activism was essential in establishing ethnic studies programs that encompassed the American Indians as the smallest minority. Interestingly, this group presented the most distinctive aspects of cultural diversity and distinctiveness. Courses on Native culture and the teaching of Native languages, primarily Lakota (a Siouan language) and Navaho, representing the largest group in the U.S., were instituted at such places as the University of California-Berkeley, San Francisco State University, and other universities. An assessment of language use is outlined in "'Speaking Indian': Parameters of Language Use among American Indians" (Medicine 1981).

In some isolated cases, Native languages have been accepted as requirements for second (or foreign) language competency, for example, Eastern Montana College (Crow); the University of Washington (Salish); the University of Utah (Navajo); and the University of Minnesota (Ojibwa or Dakota). By far, the most important and tangible result of the 1960s was the establishment of Native American or American Indian studies programs at many institutions of higher education. Many of these programs provided consciousness-raising and positivism regarding Native cultures (Medicine 1971). Only recently has a program been established to grant M.A. degrees in Native American studies at the University of California, Los Angeles. The impact of these programs has been in the area of identity and ethnic pride. A final evaluation of the occupational achievement of students who have gone through an ethnic studies curriculum is still forthcoming. However, the impact upon universities has been sizable. The attendance of students in colleges and universities has increased tremendously since that era. Very often, enrollment in Native American studies programs has led students into other occupations, such as law, medicine, or the social sciences, with education still being the predominant choice of indigenous students. Concomitantly, there is evident a trend that many students, mainly urban, claim Native ancestry. This trend needs amplification for its impact upon enhanced Nativeness and self-image. Undoubtedly, the courses offered in such programs have engendered cultural awareness and heightened cross-cultural comparisons. This trend has been compatible with the emphasis on multicultural education in the dominant society.

Of direct impact upon Indian education have been the tribally controlled community colleges based on Indian reservations. As institutions based in communities, they are attuned to Native needs. One of the strong points of these indigenously controlled learning units is that they tend to attract drop-outs—or, as some persons state, "push-outs"—from high schools, take them through a general equivalency degree (GED), and attract more mature students into two years of college. At the present time, there is one community college, Sinte Gleska on the Rosebud Reservation in South Dakota, which has a four-year accreditation. Most of the colleges present courses on Native studies, and there is some evidence of Native languages being offered. Integration of Native cultural content throughout reservation learning institutions is not as readily apparent.

In some instances, the development of bilingual materials has been impeded by the lack of agreement on orthography and the effective design of curriculum materials. At present, there is a decided interest in the computerization of Native languages. The computerization of Navajo and the use of computers at Rock Point, New Mexico, presents new dimensions in language and culture for the Navajo. The Bad Wound School at the Pine Ridge Reservation also had computerized the Lakota language. Evaluations of these trends still remain to be accomplished.

Previous to this was the appearance of *Indian Education: A National Tragedy, a National Challenge* (U.S. Congress, Senate Special Subcommittee on Indian Education 1969), a landmark event. This government publication documented that "there are nearly three hundred Indian languages in use today. More than one-half of the Indian youth today between the ages of six and eighteen use their native language. Two-thirds of Indian children entering Bureau of Indian Affairs schools have little or no skills in English" (116). Certainly, although at this time approximately 60 percent of Native children were attending public schools, little mention was made of them except in the publication, *An Even Chance* (NAACP Legal Defense and Education Fund 1971). This pamphlet indicated that in all areas of education, "Indians do not get the educational benefits that they are entitled to receive" (2). The laws referred to are Impact Aid, Johnson-O'Malley (1934), and Title I (1965) of the Elementary and Secondary Education Act.

The document indicates that schools in the public system were not effective due to the lack of parental involvement (often because parents were left out of the decision-making processes on school boards), the racist nature of many communities in which Indians live, and the fact that curricula was oriented to main-streaming students.

Thus, the passage of the 1967 amendment of Title VII of the Elementary and Secondary Act of 1965 greatly stimulated interest in the bilingual education of Native children. Because language and culture are interwoven so intricately, this was a step forward in fostering cultural emphases in curricula. Although the funds allotted to Indian progress have been minimal, the aim of the amendment indicated that:

> This program can do much more than enable the child to learn English through use of his native language. It can emphasize the history and culture of the Indian, provide for native aides in the classroom and develop a system of home-school coordinators to improve the relationship between school and family. The bilingual education program offers opportunities to sensitize teachers to Indian Culture through in-service and pre-service programs. Programs can be provided to train students. One effort presently in operation provides for a curriculum guide for mothers of Cherokee children so that they can work with their children in understanding new language concepts. (U.S. Congress, Senate Special Subcommittee on Indian Education 1969:116)

As with most objectives set out in philosophical frames, the direction of programs depends upon the perception and implementation of policy directives. As much of the literature on successful programs indicates, Rough Rock Demonstration School has been touted as one of the most effective programs. Navajo is the language of instruction for beginning students, and cultural studies continue, with strong emphasis upon written Navajo, as the students progress. This has been possible because the ancestral language and culture are viable and functional in most Navajo communities. In addition, and more effective, the orthography developed by Oswald Werner for the Navajo language seems to have been accepted by most Navajo bilinguals. This has allowed for the development of cultural curricula as orthography has been standardized. In support of culturally relevant materials, the Navajo Curriculum Center has been producing materials that have fostered bilingual competence. The Navajo Community College Press at Tsaile, Arizona, has also developed oral histories, books, and classroom materials that have supported bilingual education. Besides having programs in elementary and secondary curricula, a strong and focused support system seems essential for effective bilingual and bicultural programs.

This commitment to a regularized orthography is a first step to realistic programs. Despite bilingual readers and materials for the Western Sioux, much time has been spent by Native educators in South Dakota to agree upon an orthography. There have been various commitments to different means of writing the Siouan language that have somewhat hindered bilingual development. Preferences for styles worked out by early missionaries have had their own proponents. Thus, the dynamics of Native communities in terms of bilingual and bicultural programs play an important part in the implementation of funded programs. As in most cases when new programs are introduced into Native communities, various political and practical interests come into play. Culturally relevant education programs have not been spared this evidence of local level politics. This fact has made the evaluation of the programs somewhat difficult. Again, it points to the problem of summative or cumulative evaluation procedures, for many of the bilingual programs have perhaps been the weakest aspect of programs funded by Title VII. Whatever the difficulties, it seems necessary at this time to emphasize the favorable aspects of these projects. The employment of Native persons who are experts in traditional language, history, and culture has given a new impetus to community input in schools. There has, however, been the ubiquitous problem of certification. The use of teacher aids in language programs has somewhat diminished the status of instructional hierarchy. Again, the quality of the program depends upon the interpersonal relationships of teacher, aid, and Native historians and language experts.

In general, the movement toward community control of schools (as with the Rocky Boy, Montana, Rock Point, New Mexico, and others) has given new hope to many American Indian parents. The Association of Community-Controlled Schools has trained school boards to manage their own institutions and has dovetailed with the movement for self-determination in Native institutions and the interface of school and community. This orientation has been fostered by the Indian Self-Determination Act of 1977. More recently, tribes such as the Papago and the Standing Rock Sioux have established tribal codes dealing with education in general and language maintenance in particular. As with other regulatory attempts, as the Indian Child Welfare Act, the enactment of realistic programs will depend upon enforcement of the codes.

But what has generations of language repression exerted upon Native communities in various tribal settings? Some speech communities have lost their ancestral languages entirely. Therefore, language retrieval programs have been part of the Title VII spectrum. The Onieda (an Iroquoian-speaking group) in Wisconsin have instituted a language revitalization project that has been tied to a cultural renaissance that has included the establishment of a tribal museum and archives and increased interest in Native religion and oral history. In general, the movement toward cultural revitalization is seen on many fronts in Native communities, both rural and urban, in the United States. The enactment of the Freedom of Religion Act of 1979 is evidence that Native cultural revitalization is a fact.

It seems apparent that a ground swell of revitalization is occurring in Native North America. Evidence of this nativistic orientation is also evident in Canadian Native communities. How can this ground swell be assessed in the area of language and culture? There is a paucity of evaluation studies. In one of the few assessments of a bilingual program funded by Title VII, Kenneth York (1979:35) documents the Choctaw Bilingual Education Program in Mississippi and concludes, "One of the unique characteristics of the Mississippi Choctaws has been their belief in true bilingual development utilizing both Choctaw and non-

Choctaw cultures and languages. The Choctaw parents wish for their children not only to be educated, but to be educated Choctaws."

What is needed in the literature of bilingual and bicultural programs, as evidenced in the educational institutions of Native communities, are assessments of programs and the interpretations of the results of the evaluations to community members. These additions to the literature should be done by Native researchers and shared with other language and culture programs. Cultural revitalization and restoration has resulted from education from a Native perspective. This has been one of the positive aspects of the educational emphasis upon Native language and culture, which has remained vibrant despite all efforts to change our institutions.

References

Beatty, Willard W. 1953. *Education for Cultural Change: Selected Articles from Indian Education, 1944–51.* Chilocco, Okla.: U.S. Department of the Interior, Bureau of Indian Affairs, Chilocco Indian Agricultural School Publications.

Clark, Ann. 1941. *The Pine Ridge Porcupine.* Illustrated by Andrew Standing Soldier. Lawrence: Haskell Institute Printing Department.

———. 1942a. *About the Slim Butte Raccoon.* Illustrated by Andrew Standing Soldier. [Washington]: Department of the Interior, Bureau of Indian Affairs, Branch of Education.

———. 1942b. *There Still Are Buffalo.* Illustrated by Andrew Standing Soldier. [Washington]: Department of the Interior, Bureau of Indian Affairs, Branch of Education.

———. 1943a. *About the Grass Mountain Mouse.* Illustrated by Andrew Standing Soldier. Lawrence: Haskell Institute Printing Department.

———. 1943b. *Bringer of the Mystery Dog.* Illustrated by Oscar Howe. [Lawrence]: Department of the Interior, Bureau of Indian Affairs.

———. 1943c. *The Hen of Wahpeton.* Illustrated by Andrew Standing Soldier. Lawrence: Haskell Institute Printing Department.

———. 1944. *Brave against the Enemy (T'oka wan itkok'ip ohitike kin he).* Lawrence: Haskell Institute Printing Department.

Dumont, Robert V. 1972. "Learning English and How to Be Silent: Studies in Sioux and Cherokee Classrooms." In *Functions of Language in the Classroom,* ed. Courtney G. Cazden, Vera P. John and Dell Hymes, 344–69. New York: Teachers College Press.

Medicine, Beatrice. 1971. "The Anthropologist and American Indian Studies Programs." *Indian Historian* 4(1): 15–18, 63.

———. 1981. "'Speaking Indian': Parameters of Language Use among American Indians." *Focus: National Clearinghouse for Bilingual Education* 6 (March): 3–10.

NAACP Legal Defense and Education Fund. 1971. *An Even Chance.* New York: NAACP Legal Defense and Education Fund, with the cooperation of the Center for Law and Education, Harvard University.

Phillips, Susan. 1972. "Participant Structures and Communicative Competence: Warm Springs Children in Community and Classroom." In *Functions of Language in the Classroom,* ed. Courtney B. Cazden, Vera John, and Dell Hymes, 370–94. New York: Teachers College Press.

Philp, Kenneth R. 1972. "John Collier and the American Indian, 1920–45." In *Essays on Radicalism in Contemporary America,* ed. Leon L. Blair, 63–80. Austin: University of Texas Press.

Szasz, Margaret Connell. 1974. *Education and the American Indian: The Road to Self-Deter-mination, 1928–1973.* Albuquerque: University of New Mexico Press.

U.S. Congress, Senate Special Subcommittee on Indian Education. 1969. *Indian Education: A National Tragedy, a National Challenge.* Washington: Government Printing Office.

York, Kenneth H. 1979. "Parent/Community Involvement in the Mississippi Choctaw Bilingual Education Program." In *Working with the Bilingual Community,* 29–35. Rosslyn, Va.: National Clearinghouse for Bilingual Education.

CHAPTER 5

"The Schooling Process":
Some Lakota (Sioux) Views

It is important to realize that with the increasing articulateness and sophistication evidenced among many Native American groups it is imperative that some consideration be given the viewpoints and attitudes that compose efforts for meaningful education for these indigenous populations.[1]

Increasingly, it should be apparent that it is impossible to speak of *the* American Indian. Therefore, a holistic view of "Indian education" is an impossibility. More significantly, a caveat exists that no one person—either Native or anthropologist—is able to speak authoritatively for Native Americans, relying on their expertise about "my people." This is a generally recognized rule in most tribal enclaves. Despite the trend toward pan-Indianism on some levels, tribalism is still a strong and vibrant force in contemporary Native American life. Tribalism can be tied in with regionalism in some instances, but such is not the case with the Teton or Western Sioux. There is a greater emphasis upon band membership based upon the older concept of the Seven Council Fires (Ocheti Sacowin). In such an atmosphere there is need for the presentation of statements and agreements that various persons of a specific tribe attempt in the wide area of education relevant to that group.

This essay will focus upon a meeting of Lakota (Sioux) persons who met at the tribally owned motel, the Land of Gall Inn, on the Standing Rock Indian Reservation in South Dakota in August 1973. The purpose of the meeting was to deal with curriculum development in "Lakota studies." The meeting was initiated by the director of one of the emerging Lakota community colleges in Pine Ridge, South Dakota. Besides the director, the group included two instructors of Lakota language, older women who were involved in tribal programs and had worked in the tribal governments from Cheyenne River and Standing Rock reservations. There were two younger Sioux men who had finished B.A. degrees in linguistics and education. One was teaching in Sinte Gleska (Spotted Tail) Community College, Rosebud Reservation, and the other was instructing at Lakota Higher Education Center (a community college on Pine Ridge Reservation).

The individuals so far delineated were actual residents of the reservations in the state of South Dakota and included all the bands of the Teton (Western) "Sioux" groups. A significant point regards language: The persons involved were all speakers of "Lakota," vernacularly called the "L dialect." It is one of the three dialects of the Siouan language group, which also includes Dakota and Nakota. More important, the individuals in attendance at this Native-initiated conference were from the so-called grass roots segments of the western Dakota reservations. The four reservations are Cheyenne River, Pine Ridge, Rosebud, and Standing Rock.

In addition, one Lakota person teaching in an institution of higher education but in another state, was invited as a resource person. Another, a female Sioux directing an Indian studies program at Black Hills State Teachers College, where the majority of Sioux students in the area attend, was also present. Her natal reservation is Standing Rock. One other female Sioux, originally from Pine

Beatrice Medicine, 1982.
(Courtesy of Garrett's Home of
Photography, Columbus, Ga.)

Ridge and with community college and university teaching experience in Washington State, was present. Because this person was from the *tiospaye* (extended kin group) of the tribal government allied against the urban militants represented by the American Indian Movement (AIM), there was a period of initial tension as the meeting began. It is critical to realize that the tiospaye is very closely tied to the factions that are current in contemporary reservation life. Extended kin, whether the kin still reside in off-reservation or urban centers, is an important factor in the total thrust of interpersonal relations on various reservations. Thus kinship affiliations are an important fact in Lakota Indian social and political life of the present day. The first question usually posed to a returning Dakota, whether he is returning for a visit, the summer powwow cycle, or permanent residence, is, "Who are you?" This is a necessary reference point to place one in proper kin behavior and also to assess the returnee's possible political orientations.

One non-Native person (white male) connected with a community college in an eastern, Dakota-speaking community was present. The writer, representing Lakota (Sioux) Indians and the discipline of anthropology in university teaching, taped the sessions. I live in Standing Rock, where I still maintain a home and vote in tribal elections. My main function was to listen to the discussion and attempt to relate the curriculum discussions to developments in other Native studies departments throughout North America and in general to comment on educational directions in other fields. This is significant not because I was invited, but because it indicates the increasing reliance upon indigenous people who have some credibility with local tribal people. It further points to the diminishing role of the "expert on Indians."

The two-day meeting opened with the question, "What is education?" It was agreed that it should be anything in which learning was involved—"not just school." The need was to "define and analyze the educational process as it pertains to Lakota people." Interestingly, much of the discussion was in the Siouan language, Lakota dialect. There was an easy flow from English to Lakota, with much of the discourse including the phrase "you know what I mean." This was not an effort to exclude the one non-Indian and one Native non-Lakota-speaking individual. It merely shows the ability to utilize both languages in the formulation of questions, ideas, and discussion. The use of nonverbal communication was evident and primarily indicated closure of topics and agreement. There was little disagreement on the points presented.

The discussion leader was the eldest man, affiliated with Lakota Higher Education Center as a Lakota language teacher. He made a chart—"Elders Are Wise People." This led to his statement:

> One of the most liberal educational philosophies that we have, and it should be rightfully pursued—is that what is taught at home must also be taught in the classroom, and what is being taught in the classroom must be taught at

home. It shouldn't be that when an Indian child comes from a home stepping into a classroom that it would be a different world—another world, and that he has to change himself, adjust himself to those situations and once he steps into his own home he would have to be another person—what his learning activities are should not change from one setting to another. That is the educational goal that we are promoting.

But on the other hand, BIA [Bureau of Indian Affairs] rules are guilty of this. Because they have wide recruitment programs, we get people from Texas, from Florida, from New York and all different places. These people have never seen an Indian, not knowing what he is like, not knowing his life, let alone knowing his life-style. They would step into the classroom and begin to promote and push their own values and expect the Indian people to accept them at face value or blindly, not respecting what they have learned at home. This is where the alienation process has come in, as some experts claim. The bureau doesn't seem to care too much, at least that I know of. Being a school board member, I'm trying to promote an orientation program of some type that these people— non-Indians—first entering into the Indian field must be oriented to conditions and situations on the reservations. The emphasis should be placed on respecting that child as a learner—as an Indian learner. In doing that, we wouldn't have so many "push-outs" as we have here. When I went to school— in reading John Artichoker's handbook [Artichoker and Palmer 1959], they had ninety-five Indian students pursuing four-year education programs. He interviewed them. Within one quarter he lost thirty-five of them. He only had a handful that he had to work with in order to complete the pamphlet that he was writing. We have a greater number of Indian people at this level [college]. Speaking of college centers and Indian studies programs—at Black Hills University—I think the atmosphere is a lot better than what we had to face at one time. The monies come by a lot easier than at that time [when this elder was going to college in the 1940s]. We had to borrow the money from the tribe, and we had to wait maybe six months before we could get to it, and this type of situation. Nowadays, they have the grant system. Money is no worry to them, at least in part. And yet, we still have a large percentage of people dropping out.

BM: Why do you think students are dropping out when money is easier to get?

SMD: I think it is through the use of words from the teacher to the scholars![2] You have to be able to communicate with the scholars. You must use the right words in order to do this. If you do this, you have the scholar's trust and he has confidence in you. The process of learning what you are trying to teach him is easier.

GOF: *Wasicus*[3] [white people] call this rapport.

SMD: I don't care what they call it!

This verbal exchange set the tone for the meeting, and the Lakota etiquette was met. After the long speech by the eldest man in which he covered a wide variety of points that he saw as important, I asked a question, showing my attentiveness and also establishing my prerogative to continue to ask questions. The oldest female (SMD) responded to my questions with her opinions. This allowed the director (GOF) to break into the discussion, utilizing our word for "whites" (wasicus) and one of their concepts, "rapport." This was done in a humorous fashion, to which she responded. The director had subtly entered the discussion, and the "give-take-and-ask" atmosphere was underway.

The director of the Dakota Higher Education Center then explained testing procedures used at Black Hills State College. He mentioned the results of a study he had conducted using the Vocational Inventory and the ACT scores from computer results. The implications of the tests were summarized: "Their preference was to work with things; they didn't want to have anything to do with people. The girls' emphasis was health. This was beyond the fiftieth percentile. The boys were taking forestry, range management and so on. . . . Indications were that being a teacher, an administrator, and those kinds of things were last on the inventory."

Obviously, teachers and administrators present negative models. Implicit in vocational tests are their biases toward vocations. As a result, he indicated that there were some attempts at restructuring some courses in industrial arts. He explained the ACT test: "One interesting phenomenon revealed that every year the freshmen were ranking on an equal basis with the seniors in college. The students coming in on the GED were only 2 percent behind." His interpretation: "On the college level, Indian students have very little difference in academic capabilities."

A younger male colleague stated, "I don't think we'll ever solve the problem until we [i.e., Lakota educators] get into high school." At this point the lone non-Indian made a strong plea for a "two-track system." He stated, "I don't care where you go to school, you're not going to get a diploma until you get academics. Students can get straight Fs and go down to the shops and be tremendous."

The same younger male countered, "Why can't we develop a suitable curriculum in elementary school to deal with what you're saying?" It is apparent that this individual is aware that pupil alienation has its roots earlier. He also pointed out the problems of the social setting in the classroom. He mentioned aspects of the "political rapport" between elementary school and secondary teachers. Of the "many lacks," he noted complete disregard of team teachers and teachers aides and the absence of "open-mindedness." He said, "I've never encountered anyone who was so good that he could sit down and listen—even though he's as smart as the kids." He stated that teachers were "balking" at his suggestions as a teaching intern, but "they have the prestige of having a degree and [are] in their first year of teaching." When queried as to who these teachers were, he answered, "Wasicup." Further, he said, "We *Lakotaki* should set up our own curricula." The non-Indian reemphasized, "Many kids couldn't get academics; they don't have it now." This shows great unawareness of the aims of the Lakota people.

After this, the Lakota director replied, "The situation is such that the Department of Public Instruction of South Dakota, Bulletin 99 or 95, restricted language 'that no ancient language be taught.' It took an act of the state legislature to modify that—to include our own native tongue. Teaching the Lakota language in elementary or high school classroom would be in violation of South Dakota law, and whoever is teaching it can lose his or her teaching certificate as a result." After this statement, the leader of the session produced the actual document and read it. This repeal provided the beginning of meaningful education for Lakota people. It also showed awareness of legal procedures that can be circumvented. The director again showed his respect for elders (and wisdom) by not producing the document himself.

The director resumed, "To sell this education business, we must deal with the community people. I think we should promote Indian studies, but we have to do a good job of selling. Otherwise, we can't do it."

A woman from Cheyenne River Reservation used the Johnson-O'Malley Act as an example. Lack of knowledge as to their proper share of federal funding is a real detriment to Indian education. She emphasized that in most cases, "bad feelings at school have to be overcome before involvement is begun, and this cannot be done overnight." She raised another critical issue: "There is a problem. When a new tribal council comes in, one administration throws everyone out, and school board members put in their own people. If we say, 'We are the people,' we must start from scratch."

Again, the director showed his astuteness in Lakota social organizational features, for he recognized that each community on these four reservations tends to be unique. He indicated the need for understanding the communities, but he was also calling to our attention the futility of high-level planning without community involvement. This allowed for the input of the other eldest woman, who referred to a well-documented issue of the misuse of federal funds for children in public schools (NAACP Legal Defense and Education Fund 1971). She also reminded the group of the power of the tribal councils and the quite prevalent practice of tribal councils or school boards who often reelect members of the same clique or faction on the reservations.

The leader of the conference attempted to summarize:

The inner core of the whole problem [will] have to dwell within the classroom—where factions and values are being staged, where the battles of the mind are taking place. The learner has to have confidence in the giver. In order to take his word or his word to be worth anything to the learner, that confidence will have to be gained. Many schools have failed to send their teachers out to their [students'] homes, and family visitations are to be acquainted with their students' homes. Once the learner knows that the teacher knows Mama and Papa, and Mama and Papa know the teacher, then this should improve his learning activity in the classroom. They see things on neutral grounds. They should have interests in common in the education of that child. All learning processes are hard. Learning in English alone, I couldn't pass first grade for three years. I guess I was pretty cute then, the teachers just kept me.

Again, we see verbalization ending on a note of lightness. The younger Lakota male then commented:

It is very difficult when you go into the classroom and get the *wasicu wicoyake* [the way to learn the English language and to live the white way] teaching concept. You got that in your mind, but at four o'clock you get on the bus and go home and start thinking Indian again. White learning deteriorates. You see where the stuff you learn leaves. All friends come over, and you go out playing "cowboys and Indians" or play cars in the dirt, maybe. Well, the next morning you go back to school and find yourself a "slow learner." As the semester goes on, you get further behind. So that has to be modified. The melting pot is no more than a myth because all it does is strengthen the middle-class values, and the lower economic level of people has never been reached by the American education system—public education system. The Negroes have become poorer, and they will be getting worse. While the American education system is growing and prospering, the parochial schools, in order to comply with state regulations, have been falling off.

This is a great statement that needed no explanation. As this speaker is only in his mid-twenties, it shows the longevity of meaningless education for the Lakota people in general.

Essentially, these Lakota educators—for this is their self-image—saw the educational process as an ongoing one. Ideally, they appeared to desire smooth transitions for Lakota individuals on all levels of the superimposed transfer points.

They seemed exceedingly aware of the structures of the agencies and institutions impinging on their lives and the lives of their children and grandchildren. The futility of trying to change the Bureau of Indian Affairs educational policy was implicit in their remarks. Therefore, they were looking to other areas for change, namely Lakota studies. Underpinning this attempt was the desire to reassess traditional values and incorporate them in a meaningful learning situation for future generations of Lakota people.

Perception of schools as social systems and institutions predominates as a general tendency. Therefore, these Lakota educators are knowledgeable about teacher cliques, institutions, and the need for restructuring the educational system. The crux of the problem lies in curriculum development. This was one area that needed precise and experimental approaches. To this end, they planned to have a special five-week session at one of the Lakota community colleges in the summer of 1974.

As a direct result of this meeting, a strong effort to enforce changes in the schools of education in all teacher-training institutions in the state was attempted. In order to be an accredited teacher in South Dakota, a mandate for a course in Lakota language and culture was placed before the state legislature. These were to be taught by Lakota people.

Notes

1. *Editor's note [from the original publication]*: It has become commonplace in recent years to hear students referred to as an "oppressed minority," and there may indeed be much truth in this judgment. Perhaps more remarkable is the extent to which the liberal American critics of education who make such judgments have been blind to the plight of those who are a double minority and who are often doubly oppressed. Occasionally, a tract has appeared on urban blacks, who are easily accessible to the slumming or more serious educationist, but few have had the vision or taken the effort to look at the problems of those minorities not so close at hand, much less to talk with them and give serious attention to their views. To be sure, anthropologists have now and then published comments on Native American education, but these have usually been attempts to reconstruct some indigenous system of cultural transmission, not deal with the reality of the current situation. The current situation includes schools, as well as traditions, and to understand it one must have the views of those who attend the schools, those who do not, and particularly those who are at the same time both members of the community and educators. These views must also be seen as valid, not merely as obstacles to be overcome. In this paper Bea Medicine, herself a Sioux as well as an anthropologist, provides a sensitive summary of the views expressed by a number of trained educators and members of the Lakota community on "the schooling process." We hope this will be part of an ever-growing movement to change the dominant conception of Native Americans from one in which they are the objects of anthropological study and government action to one where they are the subjects of their own lives. Sioux are educators as well as educated, they are to be listened to as well as talked about. Even more fundamentally, Native Americans must be able to control education and the rest of purposeful action in their communities to an extent similar to the rest of the nation. There is no reason why they, more than others, should have to ask before being able to do. We all make concessions to society, but we are by no means all equally enfranchised members.

2. In using the term *scholars,* the speaker indicates students. In this case, she is referring to Sioux Indian students on all educational levels.

3. It is interesting to note that the English plural *s* is added to a Native term. A Native variant might be *wasicukipi.* You will note "wasicup" used later in the discussion.

References

Artichoker, John, Jr., and Neil M. Palmer. 1959. *The Sioux Indian Goes to College.* [Vermillion]: Institute of Indian Studies and State Department of Public Instruction.

NAACP Legal Defense and Education Fund. 1971. *An Even Chance.* New York: NAACP Legal Defense and Education Fund, with the cooperation of the Center for Law and Education, Harvard University.

CHAPTER 6

Self-Direction in Sioux Education

For years, Navajo Community College has been held up as a model for innovative education for Native Americans on the post–high school level. This institution has indeed been praiseworthy in the field of self-direction in Indian education. However, there are other developments that must be presented to give a well-balanced view of Native education.

This essay will focus on another aspect in higher education: four community colleges in the Sioux Indian area. Lakota Higher Education Center at Pine Ridge and Sinte Gleska (Spotted Tail) College at Rosebud, which are in the Teton (western) Lakota area, are in South Dakota. Standing Rock Community College in North Dakota deals primarily with various bands also speaking the Lakota (western Siouan) dialect. There is one community college at Sisseton, South Dakota, in the area of the Dakota-speakers (eastern Siouan dialect).

Former President Nixon's proclamation of self-determination for Indians (July 8, 1970) appears to have been an assessment of forces already underway in Indian communities in the United States. Since the advent of Office of Economic Opportunity implementation of community action programs, there has been a tremendous upsurge in higher education for Indians of all tribes. The impact of the war on poverty and its cybernetic effect in propelling those Siouan individuals who served as paraprofessionals in community action programs into degreed programs has never been completely delineated. There are examples among the Lakota and Dakota (Sioux) groups in North and South Dakota that show a consistent movement from Head Start teachers and career development officers into higher educational arenas, chiefly counseling and guidance, education, and Indian studies. Many of these individuals are now in the lower echelons of academia.

Indians and Higher Education

In the eyes of the dominant society, the gloss of THE AMERICAN INDIAN has sufficiently screened the various and diverse notions of education held by Native Americans. It is quite clear that besides an individualized view of education, writ large and held by various tribal members, there is a tribal view of processes of education that distinguishes each tribe's commitment to education beyond grade twelve.

These views have taken different shapes in the post–high school plans of the education committees that were set up under the tribal charter of the Indian Reorganization Act of 1934. Each tribe's unique interpretation of the functions and roles of the tribal council and its component committees is pertinent here. The power and decision-making of these committees in tribal politics are also factors for consideration. Thus, in addition to the Bureau of Indian Affairs education officer, there is, on most reservations, an aspect of tribal control over the aspirations of Native American tribal youth. Counselors in government boarding schools and public schools alike have traditionally oriented Sioux students toward vocational and paraprofessional occupations. The notion that Indians have great manual dexterity and diminished ability to comprehend theoretical issues were/are prevailing attitudes. Indeed, one young Sioux male stated, "I can't go to college, I have a low I.Q."

However, a recent statement from National Indian Education Association officials indicates there are approximately thirty thousand Native Americans in higher education. This is largely the result of recruitment and involvement in Native American studies programs throughout the nation. Unfortunately, most of these programs in state universities and colleges have been funded by "soft money," and their continuation as ongoing programs is debatable in the present recession. Moreover, in many instances the quality of course offerings and teaching has led many professionals to equate Native American studies programs with black studies programs and to predict their diminution in university and college programs.

Little attention, however, has been given to a realistic assessment of significant education on the post-secondary level among various tribes. These are the community colleges operating on the Sioux Indian reservations in South Dakota and in other sections in "Indian Country."

Historically, much attention has been focused on the dismal failure of education for Lakota (Sioux) people. To cite only one example from many studies, Wax points out that on Pine Ridge, 87 percent of the children at the lowest economic level on the reservation had left high school (Wax 1967). Only 25 percent of the children at the upper economic level left school. In my recent perusal of BIA funding for higher education, I had a decided impression that much of the money went to children of BIA employees, community action employees, and U.S. Public Health Service families who are aware of scholarship aid. The result is a residue of "hard core" (in reservation vernacular meaning "unacculturated," or "drunks," or "unmotivated") Lakota without education or a means of making a living.

Most inequitably, this situation reflects the aspect of decision-making in most reservation enclaves, which results in those individuals who are the most astute manipulators of decision-makers (and usually the most acculturated) being the recipients of funding from tribal education committees, various private foundations, and other financial aid sources. It tends to perpetuate the disadvantaged and maintains nonmanipulative Natives in an unchanging mold and also accounts for a growing elite Native group. Kinship networks are also influential in most Native societies in deciding who should be educated. Those individuals who serve on tribal councils and education committees tend to allocate funds to the members of their *tiospaye* (extended family).

The Community Colleges

The conclusion is that the impoverished people on these reservations (and in most instances, they may be correlated with "full-bloods") are denied access to learning after grade six (Fuchs and Havighurst 1972). This is essentially the reason that many well-trained Lakota educators tenaciously uphold the community college approach. Moreover, their involvement indicates that in states such as North and South Dakota, where racist attitudes predominate, this approach to education may have long-range ameliatory effects. Essentially, I am positing that community colleges are attempting to remedy the situations on Sioux reservations that are basic to apathy, poverty, and political powerlessness. Most of the administrators and teachers are bilingual and bicultural and serve as role models for many of the full-blooded students. High school students and "pushouts" are now able to see educated Indians who are not regarded as *wasicu* (white persons).

One of the first community colleges was Lakota Higher Education Center at Pine Ridge, which was affiliated in the beginning with the University of Colorado and now with Black Hills State College, South Dakota. It offers traditional courses (English, mathematics, social sciences) that are accredited by Black Hills State College.

In addition, a strong emphasis is placed on Sioux language and culture. The latter courses were taught by older, "non-credentialed" Lakota individuals. But the fact that these keepers and perpetuators of Native culture are non-credentialed has been a problem in the development of significant Native American studies throughout North America. Rigid institutional requirements of M.A.

and Ph.D. degrees have raised obstacles of varying dimensions in Native elementary, secondary, and higher education programs, both rural and urban.

In 1970 a statute in the South Dakota Board of Education legal code restricting the teaching of any "foreign, ancient language" except Latin was overturned by Lakota leaders in the community college movement. This led them to pursue other legal avenues. Presently, there is a bill in the state legislature requiring that a course in Indian (Lakota/Dakota) culture be compulsory for students in all South Dakota teacher training institutions. Montana has successfully instituted this requirement, and Minnesota also has a requirement that teachers take a course in human relations (Beaulieu 1975).

The implications of the legal actions by these Native Sioux educators are great. They have relied heavily on Native American lawyers. Not only do these moves challenge the legal restrictions of racist practices, but they also open the doors to increased programs based upon traditional language and culture. Certainly, they have great importance for current programs initiated by the Department of Health, Education, and Welfare—such as Title VII, which is directly related to bilingual programs. The community college movement should have visibility in Title III, that is, a "strengthening developing institutions" program. But funding sections of the federal government, as well as of the private sector, seem unaware of these trends.

Sinte Gleska

Sinte Gleska (Spotted Tail) Community College at Rosebud, South Dakota, in the land of the Brulé Sioux will serve here as the main example of the community colleges. This does not mean that it is *the* model. Each community college has developed its offerings to meet the needs of the reservation communities it serves. This college was established in 1971. Its logo features four feathers, the circle, and a buffalo head, plus the Lakota words:

1. *Woohitika*—Courage
2. *Wowacintanka*—Great deeds
3. *Wacantognaka*—Understanding on a high level
4. *Wokape/Woksape*—Knowledge and/or wisdom

The board of directors are members of the communities within Rosebud Reservation. As in the other community colleges, they reflect the full gamut of educational levels of the residents. The number of members from each community varies in accordance with the total population of the respective communities. The board's input in decisions with regard to curriculum, fund-raising, and administrative policy is considerable. In reality, the board's control seems real, not "put on paper" for funding purposes. The commitment and interest of the board members are especially important.

The staffs of these colleges generally belong to the National Indian Education Association, which now has a membership of approximately five thousand. Sinte Gleska often has various board members accompany the "credentialed" faculty and staff to professional educators' meetings within and outside the state. This is a valuable way for community members to obtain new information and presupposes different perceptions of issues and problems within the total field of Indian education. It was encouraging to see the president and the chairman of the board of Sinte Gleska Community College attending sessions at the recent sixth annual National Indian Education meeting in Phoenix. Because both are completely bilingual, feedback into reservation communities seems assured. This aspect of communication needs appraisal.

Most community colleges in this area are chartered by their respective tribes through the tribal councils. There appears to be good rapport between the two bodies. There may be times, however, during tribal elections and preelection reservation political maneuvering when the college's situation may be precarious. During the Wounded Knee occupation on Pine Ridge, classes at Lakota Higher Education Center had to be discontinued.

Because political fervor during tribal elections is endemic to all Native American societies, there generally is a great turn-over of entrenched tribal persons when a new administration is installed. Changes in tribal government on all Sioux (and other) reservations have repercussions in most aspects of tribal life. This fact affects many educational programs and certainly is not true only of Native Americans. The "pork-barreling" aspects of politics is as prevalent on Lakota reservations as it is elsewhere in America.

Sinte Gleska is affiliated with Black Hills State College and the University of South Dakota. The courses in six areas that lead to an associate of arts degree are accredited by these institutions. The areas of instruction in the four community colleges vary and reflect the needs and requirements of each reservation. Even English, mathematics, art, Lakota studies, and social studies, which seem the most alike in all the colleges, vary in content orientation and teaching methods.

Planning by and for All

The basic tenet in all programs is that Lakota educators with degrees ranging from the baccalaureate to the doctorate are capable of supplying meaningful education to their tribal affiliates. Their mandate, as they see it, is to include Sioux people from all levels in planning, executing, and utilizing this educational facility. In order to reach a large majority of Sioux adults who are drop-outs or, as the Lakota more correctly state, "push-outs," many of the colleges carry a program in which high school equivalency work (GED) is offered.

Basic adult education as a form of upgrading is encouraged. This program has helped many Sioux who have dropped out of high school continue their schooling. Many studies on Indian education indicate that much of the secondary acculturational process for most Native Americans is characterized by poor counseling, unrelated curriculum, and prejudiced teachers.

The trend, at least at Sinte Gleska, is to take classes out to the people in what is called a "dispersal learning system." Fully aware that transportation and lack of money have hindered Lakota learning, instructors at this institution take their classes to outlying community centers in the 218-mile expanse of the reservation, guaranteeing an intense interaction between instructors and students of all ages. This program also keeps program directors and staff close to the grass roots and reduces the attrition of highly qualified Native educators.

An instructor at Sinte Gleska indicated that in the two years he had worked there he noted a definite trend toward a diversified age grouping. In outlying districts, many people in their sixties were enrolling. He also noted that high school students were becoming interested in supplementing their high school work by enrolling in the college.

I believe that the greatest strength of these colleges is their flexibility in enrollment requirements. Another strong feature is the area of cultural retrieval. After generations of suppressing the language, culture, and belief systems of the Lakota, the presentation of lectures by medicine men (and women) and the study of Native life as it was and is now are very positive forces in reservation life. The course variously entitled but centering on the "Native American in the Contemporary Society" deals with the role of Lakota in dual societies. There is a growing interest in the examination of Indian treaties. Many of the students are interviewing elders regarding early reservation life, traditions, and beliefs. The interest in oral history and folklore is great.

There is a great emphasis on traditional Sioux religion and curing ceremonies and a definite growth in attendance at such previously minor rituals as the *Yuwipi* cult and other ceremonies. This, I feel, will lead to an intelligent blending of tradition and change, not "contrived AIM [American Indian Movement]–type culture." The community colleges on all four reservations also belong to the American Indian Higher Education Consortium, which functions as an umbrella organization for funding and legal resources. This organization is staffed by Native Americans, and such foundations as Ford and Carnegie have contributed. Unfortunately, the constriction of funding from the private sector will have great repercussions in this area.

There is increased participation in the National Consortium of Indian-controlled school boards. Interestingly, although there may be a drastic change of personnel on school boards or education committees following a tribal election, there is a spin-off into other educational endeavors in reservation communities. As an example, we now have a sizable number of Sioux professors in state colleges and universities.

In sum, the educational picture for the "apathetic" Sioux looks hopeful. And being a Sioux chauvinist, I feel that educational repression on all levels is on its way out.

References

Beaulieu, David. 1975. Personal communication, Jan. 24.

Fuchs, Estelle, and Robert J. Havighurst. 1972. *To Live on This Earth: American Indian Education*. Garden City: Doubleday.

Wax, Rosalie H. 1967. "The Warrior Dropouts." *Trans-Action* 4(6): 40–46.

CHAPTER 7

My Elders Tell Me

This essay seeks to appraise the conceptual term *elders* in Indian education. This is difficult because the term *elder* has a diffuse and all-encompassing meaning, as used in contemporary Canadian Indian education from kindergarten through university.

This meaning, often articulated as "my elders tell me," is almost a slogan in contemporary Native society.[1] In this educational context, the term is variable and functionally different from anthropological studies in the role of the aged (Amoss and Harrel 1981:227–47; Cowgill 1986).

Elders are repositories of cultural and philosophical knowledge and are the transmitters of such information. This is succinctly noted by John Snow when referring to the revitalization of Native cultures, as evidenced in the annual Indian Ecumenical Conferences held at the Morley Reserve from 1970 to 1984. Snow states: "During these conferences, many Indian elders, medicine men and women taught us our basic beliefs and teachings, encouraging us to continue with our faith in the Great Spirit, the Creator" (1986:3).

These basic beliefs and teachings have continued throughout North America within the matrices of various Native Indian households, which tended to be more traditional in language use and participation in rituals and ceremonies grounded in the culture of a specific tribal or band group. The continuity of these cultural manifestations accounts for the viability and vibrancy of Indian cultures embedded in their elders. This unwritten tradition, expressed in rich recountings of legends, folk tales, and origin myths, were and are acted out in rituals and ceremonies. The expressive elements of cultural forms are powerful means of cultural transmission; they evoke respect and identity among Indians today. In those cases where Indian individuals have lost Indian cultural forms as a result of superimposed repressive systems mandated religiously or educationally, elders have assumed almost mythic and mystic proportions. This is often heard in statements of people, usually involved in educational programs, who reiterate "we involve elders" without specifying what the elders do indeed tell.

This assessment of the role of elders in Indian societies is necessarily impressionistic. The entire question of the status, configuration, and function of elders in educational contexts is extremely nebulous and imprecise. By using participant-observation, examining Indian education curriculum, and analyzing Indian publications, interviews, and a literature search, a view of elders' roles in the cultural transmission process begins to emerge, however tentatively. This chapter seeks to define the function of elders in the educational setting. It goes beyond standard treatises on enculturation and ethnographically oriented studies that essentially emphasize the roles of elders in naturalistic settings, embedded in an operational kinship nexus (Beck and Walters 1977; Morey 1970; Morey and Gilliam 1974:83–93). This examination indicates that the use of "elders" may be a strictly Canadian phenomenon, possibly rivaled only by the Navajo, where the Rough Rock Demonstration School and Navajo Community College have served as exemplary models for Native education in Canada (McKay and McKay 1987).

Conferences featuring elders, such as the ones at Brandon and Trent universities, tend to use them "to share experience, knowledge and wisdom" (*BIMISAY* May 1986). Besides opening the conference with a prayer, the contributions tend to include life histories and personal exhortations. These events also constitute consciousness-raising experiences for Natives and non-Natives.

What are the significant roles of elders in the educational context? More appropriately, how are elders' roles perceived? In constructing new pathways to culturally relevant curricula, the indigenous views need consideration. Elders can have an impact as sources of information, as transmitters of Native culture, and as mediators for cultural change.

Elders in the Political Realm and in Community

A chief in central Canada indicated at a conference held in November 1983 that "the AFN [Assembly of First Nations] has a very weak position for elders. They [elders] say something in Ottawa and are shouted down" (Ahenakew 1986). This may be contrasted with the interpretations of an individual working in tribal society and formulating "Native law," described as "tribal legal systems." Working with elders, this Native has also learned to speak Cree, of necessity to comprehend not only Native law and the nuances of the contextual characterizations of elders but also the indigenous categories that discretely assign certain efficiencies in the role of elder in Indian communities. In a first meeting of the researcher with the designation "elder," the community perception of qualifications emerged. An elder stated, "I'm not the one to talk to—so and so should be here. They know the rules" (Venne 1986). Then the Indian researcher "contacts the appropriate elder." This forthright statement demonstrates the fact, acknowledged in most Indian societies: Certain individuals, by virtue of qualifications and knowledge, are recognized by the Indian communities as the ultimately qualified reservoirs of aboriginal skills.

Expertness in other segments of indigenous Indian life are equally recognized in Indian communities, for example, herbalists, curers, and religious practitioners. Counselors of either sex are consulted when needs are to be met. Each category of competence is recognized by members of the community. The elders' skills are activated in contextual situations and to meet specific needs.

Elders as Transmitters of Culture

In the history of secondary enculturation of Indian people through the educational institutions of the larger society, elders and tribal historians were considered irrelevant in the education of Indian children. Indeed, in many instances these reservoirs of traditional knowledge were often considered by school personnel to be detrimental to the incorporation of Indian individuals into the mainstream of the dominant society. The removal of children into federal and residential schools in Canada and the United States broke intergenerational ties that guaranteed the cultural continuity of indigenous societies in the pre-contact period, when Indian cultures flourished in North America. This dispersal

At the Newberry Library, 1983. (Courtesy of the McNickle Center)

of members of an Indian family effectively eliminated Native forms and norms of the informal learning process (Barman, Hébert, and McCaskill 1987). As viewed by church personnel and teachers in government schools, this policy was undoubtedly the most effective way of propelling Indians into a new life-style that attempted to eliminate all vestiges of Indianness.

Recent studies on Native education do not concentrate upon the contemporary familial structures that might be significant in the learning processes of children and adolescents on reserves or in urban settings. Therefore, studies of the cultural relevance of older people remain to be written. Moreover, because a palliative approach is so evident in Indian educational research, recognition of the strengths of Indian kinship units as adaptive mechanisms is lacking (Medicine 1981).

Contemporary Indian Views of Elders

Few examples from the literature on Native Canadians are available to postulate or formulate comparative materials; however, on current-day kinship affiliations it is possible to elicit emic viewpoints. A view of the roles of elders emerges from a careful scrutiny of information that presents an indigenous articulation.

In the film *I Am an Indian: The Circle of Leadership,* one poignant statement emerges: "Sometimes I get scared—scared for the children. Language takes my children away from me, that is why I am scared. They do not hear my words. When he throws his language away, that is when it starts. He makes fun of his father and mother, his grandfather and grandmother. Nobody really listens to the elders anymore, the elders are being ignored" (Spiller 1984; see also Patrick n.d.). When discussing elders with a young Native male after viewing this film, his [Tralnner's] observations indicated that "elders were more inspirational than practical, but philosophical statements were important for younger Natives" (Tralnner 1986). Aware of cycles of life, the boy felt that maturation was part of this process. He considered himself impatient, and he felt that he was becoming calmer and more introspective as he matured. Conscious of cycles of information from generation to generation, he perceived a transition that came with age, maturity, and wisdom.

By a careful reading of statements made by elders, one can find beautiful examples of images of elders, as indicated by David Elliot (Saanich):

> As children we learned from the very beginning, by teaching and discipline, and later on through lecturing, and also by example. You saw how your elders lived, how respectful they were of one another, and how they loved each other. I used to see old people when they would meet after not seeing each other and tears would roll down their cheeks. It was one of the finest qualities of life . . .
>
> The training went on as a child grew older, became more severe, harder, tougher. Girls were taught to keep busy all the time, even when sitting their hands had to be going. It became a habit to live in a sane, sensible, and intel-

ligent way. Discipline took a step up when a girl was turning into a woman and the same with a young man. And on up through marriage. In the old days not only your own elders would discipline you, but also an outsider would come in and lecture the young. This could happen anytime, just happen naturally. (Elliot 1983:18)

Dorothy Sandridge (Mowachaht) presents a feminine perspective:

It wasn't hard to learn things because we listened and from that we learned. We learned at an early age. That is the way it was. That's what I always tell my grandchildren—when I get after them, you know. I have to scold them once in a while. But they have to be told, "If I didn't care for you, I'd let you do it. In a few years, you'd dislike me, you'd hate me, because I never got after you. Today you think I don't like you because I get after you, but I do it because our grandparents got after us. That's the way we were taught." (Sandridge 1983:43)

Involvement with contemporary groups yields a statement from a Blackfoot elder pertinent to the perceptions of the aged among some Indians. Asked to be on an elder committee for a local chapter of the Alberta Native Women's Association (ANWA), she stated, "What is the role of elders? Are we taken off the shelf just to give the opening prayer at some meeting?" (Waterchief 1985). In the same group, a Native appraisal emerged of the criteria that determine the concept of an elder. An older person was referred to as "our resident elder," yet an elder commented that this person "is really not an elder because she is only fifty-five" (Lavallee 1985). Thus, it can be seen that in certain current contexts some Indian people in Canada are expressing their concerns about an elder's contribution to contemporary life. Fulfillment of expectations in the dominant society may be difficult for Indian elders.

Defining the Concept of Eldership

In a study examining this specialized role among a specific tribe, Roderick Mark explicates his definition of an elder: "A point of reference: those people who have earned the respect of their own community and who are looked upon as elders in their own society" (Mark 1985). Furthermore, in his view, "We have misused the role of elder through our ignorance and failure to see that not all elders are teachers, not all elders are spiritual leaders and not all old people are elders" (Mark 1985:2). This definition can be juxtaposed with a characterization from an earlier study: "The elders, comprising the accumulation of tribal wisdom and experience, have always been a vital group in opinion-making, if not in actual decision-making. Many, if not all, of the political leaders depend on 'their elders' for advice in decision-making. Some are, in fact, members of the Band Council and perform the role of adding the cultural perceptions to the decision-making process" (*Selected Indian Perceptions* 16).

More interesting is a statement stemming from the consciousness of Indian people of their need to develop new approaches to their existence in a bicultural situation, expressed in a statement by elders at the Alberta Indian Language Seminar in February 1974:

> In order to survive in the twentieth century, we must come to grips with the white man's culture and with the white man's ways. We must stop lamenting the past. The white man has many good things . . . for example, his technology. We must take these things and discover and establish the harmonies with basic values the Indian way, they thereby forge a new and stronger sense of identity. To be fully Indian today, we must become bilingual and bicultural. *We have never had to do this before!* We will thus survive, for we have always survived! Our history tells us so! (*Selected Indian Perceptions* 3)

This statement clearly indicates a view, widely held by Indian people, that this is a time of transition and that the assistance of the dominant society is needed. To provide this assistance, it is necessary to develop a set of operative guidelines in consultation with all the communities concerned.

School Views of Elders

The non-Native principal of John D'or Prairie School, which is in a northern area, has a more compartmentalized version of an elder's role in the educational process. This woman indicates that, at least in the Cree community with which she is familiar, the roles divide into (1) source of information; (2) source of strength; (3) source of responsibility; and (4) source of direction (Goldsmith 1985). This is a concrete categorization that describes the participation of elders implicit in such generalized statements as that of September 30, 1985 from a Mr. Humbre, principal of the Morley School: "The program must be flexible to allow the inclusion of information of Native educators and elders as is appropriate." Statements such as these often color the function of elders, for "appropriate" is often defined by school personnel. It would appear that the input of elders is often determined by the tasks that are assigned to them. At the Plains Indian Cultural Survival School in Calgary, the elder program includes such tasks as "involvement in Legends, History, Personal Counseling, Old Medicine, Hand Sign Language, Indian religious values, Indian customs, Hand games, and other topics requested by students" (*Handbook* n.d.). A more precise contribution of the elder is presented in the curriculum developed by the Sacred Circle Project in Edmonton. In the grade 3 curriculum guide for the topic "Lifestyles in Culturally Distinctive Communities," these definitions are given:

> *The elder:* Not all older or elderly people are considered as elders. An elder is a person that has accumulated a great deal of wisdom and knowledge throughout his or her lifetime, especially in the tradition and customs of the group.

Elders emphasized listening and not asking WHY. There isn't any word in the Cree language for "why." A learner must sit quietly and patiently while the elder passe[s] on his wisdom. Listening is considered to be very important. Questions were not encouraged. Asking questions was considered rude. Clarification of a certain point or comments was considered okay.

Learners were also encouraged to watch and listen to what was happening around them. Eventually with enough patience and enough time the answer would come to the learner. When this happened, the learning was truly his own. (*Tipahaskan* 1986:104–5)

The elders' syndrome has permeated aboriginal organizational structures. The Indian Association of Alberta has held a bimonthly conference of elders since 1985. There is no agenda of specific topics. When someone says "put me on the agenda," the leaders call upon the requester. Speakers may raise several topics, including treaty concerns, self-determination, and educational issues. The configuration emanating from these speeches centers upon the fact that elders never had formal educational opportunities and stresses that band leaders should push younger people to further their education. The elders speak in their own language, translated into English by an interpreter. Discussions assume saliency and focus upon different interpretations that are discussed with the elders. Cultural ceremonies occur in the morning and evening as part of the meetings (McDougal 1986).

The role of elders in postsecondary education has been acknowledged by the hosting of two conferences. One, held at Brandon University on September 19, 1985, consisted largely of the contributions of a variety of older people speaking about their experiences as participants in various aboriginal cultures. The other, held at Trent University in 1986, was a conference of "elders and traditional people" (*BIMISAY* May 1986). Topics discussed included "Native-Way Education," "Treaties and True Self-Government," "The Drum, Women and the Pipe," "Native Inmate and His Culture," "Midewiwin Teaching," "The Counseling Wheel," and "Dene Traditional Culture." Feasting, traditional singing, drumming, and dancing pointed up ways in which elders could contribute to university life. In general, both conferences demonstrated an increased awareness of and focus on the need to reexamine aboriginal cultures.

Although the literature on anthropological studies is rich in the examination of the status of the aged in various non-Western societies, the research does not focus on the utilization of Indian elders in educational systems. The only American study deals with the use of elders among the Lakota (Sioux) of the Rosebud Reservation in South Dakota and examines the viability of elders in cultural transmission in very general anthropological terms. Noting the intergenerational learning that occurs in family and community contexts, one example specifically mentions the use of oral history: "Oral history is an excellent tool for incorporating societies' elders into the formal educational setting" (Kincheloe 1984:126).

In her anthropological study of aging among the Ojibwa of Manitoulin Island, Rosamond Vanderburgh mentions the use of elders in the educational program of the Ojibwa Cultural Foundation. She states:

> The Foundation has developed an impressive number of programs, three of which have involved the elders. These are:
>
> 1. The Language Program in the schools.
> 2. The Elder's Program.
> 3. The Art Program.
>
> To date, the Language Program in the schools has made only a limited use of the elders' knowledge of the Ojibwa language, and a few elders are involved in teaching the language in the school as well as in assembling curriculum material, especially oral narrative. (Vanderburgh 1982:11).

Vanderburgh indicates that for the last several years, the concentration has been mainly upon the retrieval of information relating to healing and the use of elders in counseling. She notes that the knowledge is being collected largely from males. Of special interest is the fact that the "emphasis of the O.C.F.'s approach to the elders is upon what the elders can do for the community, rather than what the community should be doing for the elders" (1982:11). This observation raises issues of equity along gender lines; more important, it raises issues of recompense for the services of elders, a subject that often meets opposition in the educational institutions of the dominant society. More significantly, it behooves educational administrators and teachers to evaluate the use of elders. Are they exploited as informants? Are they used without consultation? Are their duties explained previous to their entrance into an educational institution? Is their cultural mandate understood? In the latter case, asking an elder to bestow a name upon non-Natives or to offer prayers delves into delicate cultural norms. Merely asking elders from some bands puts them in a state of compliance to any request. In many aboriginal societies, there are specific ways of asking elders to participate in both a private and public domain. Only by comprehending the cultural background of contemporary Indian communities in which the school is embedded as a social system can all the actors in the "Indian World" be effectively contextualized.

A seasoned Blackfoot educator delineates an ideal world: "People responsible for the hiring of older Indians as resource people make the mistake of merely putting them in a classroom with young children. The elders want to tell stories as they used to do but children are either too impatient to listen, or perhaps do not understand. An alternative would be for the elders to teach the teachers, not the children. The elders have valuable knowledge to pass on and have a lot to contribute to education. They should be as adequately paid as other teachers" (Ayoungman 1975:36). In this interpretation of the roles of elders in the educational enterprise, it is apparent that contextual behaviors are functionally and situationally defined. Besides the sporadic and often idealistic state-ments made by some introspective elders, it is difficult at this juncture to as-certain how they have internalized this public and private vision of assigned roles.

A more efficacious implementation of the role of the elderly Indian in the education of Natives and non-Natives in Canadian educational systems might be to utilize the private and public domains as discrete entities. The conscious-ness-raising of Native communities is apparent in the following editorial:

> The message is clear. We must honor the elders and benefit from their wisdom. That message has been received loud and clear at Ben Calf Robe School, where elders were honored at the school's Fifth Annual Powwow. Elders also have an important role in the school's spiritual and cultural activities.
>
> That message is also being received and acted on in numerous Native communities, and in preventive and rehabilitative programs dealing with the serious personal and social problems facing Native people.
>
> The return of elders to prominence in the lives of Native people, and in their communities and organizations, is evidence in itself of their power and their importance. It is only through them that the traditions have survived at all in the face of heavy efforts over many years to destroy those traditions and mem-ory of them.
>
> For many years, they maintained their language while others tried to destroy it by forbidding the Native children in residential schools to speak it.
>
> For many years, they preserved rituals and traditions in secrecy in the face of suppression and oppression, and against the confiscation of sacred objects, many of which later appeared in museums and private collections.
>
> Now, the elders can speak freely, the language is being restored, the ancient rituals and traditions have been revived.
>
> Now, the elders speak.
>
> Let us honor them by listening to them and learning from their wisdom. (Buehler 1986:6)

All individuals involved with Native education will benefit by effectively using elders metaphorically as bridges between two cultural domains.

Note

1. In this essay, the terms *Indian* and *Native* are used interchangeably, as is the customary usage by indigenous people themselves.

References

Ahenakew, David. 1986. Indian/Native Studies Symposium, Saskatchewan Indian Federated College, Regina. Jan. 29.
Amoss, Pamela T., and Stevan Harrel, eds., 1981. *Other Ways of Growing Old.* Stanford: Stan-ford University Press, 1981.

Ayoungman, Vivian. 1975. In Jean Goodwill, *Speaking Tomorrow*. Ottawa: Secretary of State.

Barman, Jean, Yvonne Hébert, and Don McCaskill, eds. 1987. *Indian Education in Canada:* vol. 1, *The Legacy*. Vancouver: University of British Columbia Press.

Beck, Peggy V., and Anna L. Walters. 1977. *The Sacred*. Tsaile, Ariz.: Navajo Community College Press.

BIMISAY. May 1986. Peterborough, Ont.: Department of Native Studies, Trent University.

Buehler, Clint. 1986. "Honor the Elders." *Windspeaker*. May 16.

Cowgill, Donald O. 1986. *Aging around the World: Anthropological Perspectives*. Belmont: Wadsworth Publishers, 1986.

Elliot, David. 1983. In Dorothy Haegert, *Children of the First People*. Vancouver: Tillicum Library.

Goldsmith, Claire. 1985. Personal communication. Dec.

Handbook. n.d. Calgary: Plains Indian Cultural Survival School, Calgary Public Board of Education.

Kincheloe, Tersa Scott. 1984. "The Wisdom of the Elders: Cross-cultural Perspectives," *Journal of Thought* 19 (Fall): 121–27.

Lavallee, Carole. 1985. Alberta Native Women's Association meeting, Calgary. Aug. 17.

Mark, Roderick. 1985. "The Role of Elders in Contemporary Native Education" (manuscript). University of Calgary.

McDougal, Wilf. 1986. Personal communication. April 8.

McKay, Alvin, and Bert McKay. 1987. "Education as a Total Way of Life: The Nisga'a Experience." In *Indian Education in Canada:* vol. 2, *The Challenge*, ed. Jean Barman, Yvonne Hébert, and Don McCaskill, 64–85. Vancouver: University of British Columbia Press.

Medicine, Beatrice. 1981. "American Indian Family Cultural Change and Adaptive Strategies," *Journal of Ethnic Studies* 8(4): 13–23.

Morey, Sylvester M. 1970. *Can the Red Man Help with White Man?* New York: Gilbert Church.

Morey, Sylvester M., and Olivia L. Gilliam. 1974. *Respect for Life: Report of a Conference at Harper's Ferry, West Virginia, on the Traditional Upbringing of American Indian Children*. Garden City: Waldorf Press.

Patrick, Miken. n.d. *Role of Elders in a Northern Native Society*. 16-minute film for grades 4–6. Timmins, Ont.: Ojibway Cree Cultural Center.

Sandridge, Dorothy. 1983. In Dorothy Haegert, *Children of the First People*. Vancouver: Tillicum Library.

Selected Indian Perceptions of Human Resource Development on the Stoney Indian Reserve at Morley and the Cree Four-Band Reserve at Hobbema 1975. Calgary: New Man Associates, Office of Educational Development, Native Student Services.

Snow, John. 1986. *Bear Hills Native Voice*. March 27.

Spiller, Aiden. 1984. *I Am an Indian: The Circle of Leadership*. Winnipeg: Aiden Spiller Associates.

Tipahaskan. 1986. Edmonton: Sacred Circle Native Education Program, Instructional Services Division, Edmonton Public Schools.

Tralnner, Ken. 1986. Personal communication. March 20.

Vanderburgh, Rosamond M. 1982. "When Legends Fall Silent Our Ways Are Lost: Some Dimensions of the Study of Aging among Native Canadians." *Culture* 2(1): 11.

Venne, Sharon. 1986. Untitled presentation, Conference on Community-Based Research, Walpole Island Research Institute, Wallaceburg, Ont. Nov. 16.

Waterchief, Margaret. 1985. Alberta Native Women's Association meeting, Calgary. Aug. 17.

CHAPTER 8

Higher Education:
A New Arena for
Native Americans

A recent U.S. Department of Health, Education and Welfare report (1977) indicates that there are approximately thirty-three thousand Native
Americans in higher education. Higher education in the context of this report
means enrollment in community colleges, junior colleges, and colleges and universities. This presents a strong contrast to the one or two isolated tribal members scattered in colleges and universities throughout the United States just two
decades ago. This figure also marks great strides in a funding base available to
prospective students. Previously, one was required, for economic reasons, to
borrow money from the Bureau of Indian Affairs Education Division. Counselors in this division often determined the occupational choices for the student
by emphasizing "practical" courses. Presently, many Native American recruit-
ers from colleges and universities attend such conferences as the National Congress of American Indians and the National Indian Education Association to
entice students to their institutions. More significantly, the Bureau of Indian
Affairs funds programs such as those at Dartmouth College and Harvard University—institutions that were founded originally to educate the aborigines of
America. Another eastern university that is benefiting from bureau funds is
Pennsylvania State University. The entire scope of higher education for Indians has achieved new dimensions and possibilities.

It behooves us then to realize the effects of this fact upon Native Americans
as individuals and as members of tribal collectives. The impact upon Native
Americans as persons should begin, perhaps, with some semblance of self-
assessment and growing awareness. Most of us hold to a nebulous ideal of
"wanting to help our people." By that, do we mean ourselves, our individual
tribe, or the larger conglomerate of more than two hundred tribes? (More new

tribal groups and members seem to be evident every day.) When we hear this utterance of benevolence, is it an echo of an often-articulated caveat of the expectations of members of the larger society, or do we truly believe that this is the most basic motivating factor in our lives? If by the statement "wanting to help our people" we mean our own tribe, and if this motivation is an underpinning of a philosophical stance, what do we know about the contemporary situation and needs of that reference group? This may be reflecting a mere ethnocentric attitude, and we may be evidencing a "new ethnocentrism" based upon unique tribalism and tribal chauvinism that seems to be endemic in some areas in the Indian education realm. This salient tribal rivalry appears to have deleterious effects upon the education of young Indian students, and it seems to be intensifying at this time.

Another common folk-saying is that Indian professionals should be "working with their own people." This is commonly heard in many parts of the country, notably California but more recently in New Mexico. This may be related to the chauvinism that often assumes tribal and gender dimensions.

As a matter of fact, most of us are living away from our natal reservations. This is often by necessity rather than choice. In many instances, the nature of tribal councils and their unwritten mandate is to hire their own consanguinal and affinal kin. This reaffirms one fact that we as Natives already know—the bonds of kinship are very strong. Nepotism is a fact of life on most Indian reservations. More symptomatic of the current situation is that many Native Americans with an Ed.D. or a Ph.D. degree find it virtually impossible to obtain employment with tribal groups.

Moreover, it may be difficult to obtain appointments in colleges and universities (despite affirmative action policies) in states with high Indian populations, because many "Indian programs" are based upon transitory federal funding and not built into state funding of such programs in their higher education institutions. The role occupancy of the Native American professor is usually tied to his ability to obtain federal funds. Seldom understood is the subtle role of "white expertise," which often limits the invasion of the domains of education, history, or special education departments where such expertise resides. Startlingly, many tenure-track positions in these departments seem to be occupied by professors who claim a minuscule amount of Indian ancestry. Thus, the colleges and universities meet affirmative action requirements. Surprisingly, anthropology departments, despite their "rip-off" image in Native American communities, appear more amenable to tenure-track positions for minority professors of either gender.

Native American studies departments still offer the only academic arena in which Indian heritage is a valued and saleable commodity. There are, however, some doubts as to the academic quality of such departments (Washburn 1975). There are few such departments staffed with persons holding a doctoral degree and having significant publication records. The University of California at

Berkeley and Los Angeles, the University of Minnesota, University of Arizona, and Arizona State University at Tempe are the exceptions to this statement.

Many Native Americans in higher education are often labeled "academics" by persons in our own tribal groups, especially by non-Native members on re-view panels where we often participate. This posits the idea that by being in an academic setting we are no longer "tribal" or "community" people. It seems impossible for some of our white colleagues to comprehend the nature of be-ing Indian in the twentieth century. Many of us still maintain a home on our reservations; participate in political, ceremonial, and religious activities; and interact in a migratory pattern, moving from residential place of occupation to natal home (Kemnitzer n.d.). Others of us have completely severed ties with our tribal communities. And some of us have chosen to relocate, either voluntarily or via the relocation program of the Bureau of Indian Affairs.

Whatever the case, there are now Indian faculty of all degrees of blood quan-tum and phenotype in the academic setting. Indian faculty may sometimes fall into the category of "showpieces." They are seldom judged on their teaching ability, the acumen of their research results, or the desires of their constituen-cies but upon the prevailing criteria of their disciplines. There have been two Native male professors whose publication records were evaluated as being not of academic quality, for they had published mainly in Indian-operated journals. This places the Native academic in double jeopardy. Most Indian professors are pressured by Native groups to write articles or do research to meet crises and the immediate needs of communities—urban, rural, and reservation. Moreover, advocacy work involving testimony in legal cases, proposal writing and read-ing, and responding to requests for information often hinders the writing of papers that meet the criteria of academic peers. Frequently, however, this indi-cated in a sub rosa manner that the writing of Native candidates for university positions "does not meet the standards of academic excellence."

Indian faculty are seldom part of the regular administrative budgets but are more likely expected to rely upon their "grants-personship" abilities. Perhaps they share this with other ethnic or minority faculty. We do know that involve-ment in "community work" of other minority faculty is also not considered in selection for tenure-track positions. Publications in scholarly journals of their respective disciplines is the main criteria for assessing a Native intellectual's worth. This is understood by many of us. However, more devastating is that frequently our advocacy faculty of white friends and colleagues is often accused of doing "welfare work" if they are involved with us or in helping Native Amer-ican students. As I have written elsewhere:

I shall address my remarks to Higher Education as that is my field. The future of Higher Education for Indians is not as healthy as I had hoped. In the gen-eral retrenchment in universities, and despite affirmative action policies, there are still pitifully few native educators in tenure-track positions in colleges and universities in those states with large Indian populations. It appears that our commitments are not attuned to university expectations. We have not done what our "White" counterparts traditionally do. That is, we have not utilized the "buddy system" and the selective choosing of our favorite graduate students as our replacements. Thusly, there are too few Indian professors who are able to provide viable and significant models to the upcoming generations of our young adults. Moreover, the siphoning off of our creative and committed college instructors into lucrative "funded-but-softly" Indian programs presents a bleak picture for our future college students. Thus, I see a continued high drop-out rate of our college students. (Medicine 1977:8)

One area in the higher education realm that needs to be addressed is the role of the "white ghostwriter." At this time, the legacy of the "poverty pimp," who wrote proposals for tribal groups in the days of the Great Society war on poverty, seems continuous in some areas. This, of course, is a very delicate area. This is evident, however, in some writings by Native American professionals and bilingual education proposals. It is also discernible in the writings of some Native educators. This is a worrisome practice and negates the presentation of "felt needs" by Native American groups. It also strikes at the very fabric of self-determination. Therefore, it was upsetting to learn that the report of the American Indian Policy Review Committee's segment on cultural aspects had mainly white input. This brings into perspective the entire ideal of integrity in higher education and the roles of Native academicians in various fields. At this juncture, it is hoped that we do not reflect the corruption we see in the dominant society but look to our own personal and tribal ethics and values and enact them.

In general, it would appear that the nature of higher education institutions in the United States has not changed appreciably in response to minority protests of the late 1960s. Many of us who have worked in the system prior to the 1960s hoped for more change. We possibly have stayed within the higher education realm because we find that it is more predictive than the emergent systems of indigenous power struggles and ego-gratifying maneuvers of Native systems of education and Indian organizations. A few of us have been affiliated with universities that have allowed, if not sanctioned, advocacy in action cases and have been attuned to judgments on teaching, research, and writing expectations. On the other hand, some Native professors have been penalized for activism. Moreover, the appeal of academic freedom is strong in that it allows one to express research concerns and results.

The Native American student composition of most higher education institutions consists of students directly from reservation or rural Native communities in various degrees of isolation from mainstream society. Others are from urban areas. The impact of the Relocation Program (now called Employment Assistance Program) of the BIA upon the deculturalization of Indian youth is not evident in the research literature. One can, however, point to many of these college students who were enrolled in the 1960s in urban universities and whose knowledge of their own tribal heritage, much less an overview of Native Americans in general, was extremely limited. In this era, one must acknowledge campus unrest, with the resultant establishment of ethnic studies departments, including Native American studies departments, with their latent "Indian culture-building" mechanisms. These programs did much to meet the needs of Native students on "identity-questing" endeavors (Medicine 1971). The long-range effects of "Indian awareness" weeks, "Native expert" lecture circuits, and the "inter-tribal pow-wow" may all have contributed to a "contrived culture" that is almost devoid of distinctive tribal values, ethos, and ethics. In retrospect, some of us fostered a curricula that examined distinctive socialization practices and values clarification based upon unique tribal valences and philosophical systems. It may be possible, however, that the need for Native identity was too overpowering for students. Even today, we are faced with Native students of all tribes participating in the Siouan Sun Dance at Pine Ridge.

Students as well as academics apparently view reservations as residual reservoirs of Native culture. These social systems need to be examined periodically. Certainly, the analysis of "reservation culture" and processes of Indian urbanization could form basic data for theory construction and methodological development in Native American studies departments. This dual experience could fit under courses entitled "Contemporary Issues" in Native American studies curricula. Thornton indicates that "a final grouping [of courses] pertains to contemporary American Indians in rural, reservation, and urban areas. Topics here range from contemporary legal considerations, educational issues, Indian organizations and social movements, intergroup relations, migration to urban areas, and pan-Indianism to tribal, political and economic development on reservations" (1977:3). This statement seems sufficiently comprehensive, but one questions how much can be covered comprehensively in a quarter-system university calendar.

After spending six months on a reservation in the Northern Plains, I consider several research needs to stand out in sharp focus. A foremost need is a study of tribal councils as Native elitist bureaucracies. The composition of tribal councils varies for each reservation and election period (interestingly, two tribal chairmen on the Teton Lakota reservations are former BIA employees). Aspects of power and decision-making are features that are seldom researched. Aspects of staff incentive payments (at Standing Rock, $100 was paid to certain tribal employees prior to the election) and the role of the tribal chairman's inaugural ceremony, with its give-away, need clarification. Unfortunately, funding agencies in the public and private sector rely completely upon the approval of tribal councils. It is important that this lack of knowledge about the realities of reservation life be placed within the comprehension of proposal-readers as well as whites and blacks in federal bureaucracies.

The sexism and bias of one tribal member from Pine Ridge is typical: "'The

Tribal Council is ridiculous,' said a man I shall call Edgar Running Bear because he asked me not to use his real name. 'Two of them are stupid women who have not even had a sixth grade education, one of them is a hopeless alcoholic, and they're all prejudiced'" (LaFarge, cited by Kentfield in Wax and Buchanan 1975:127). It would appear that we have a body of data for comparison of tribal councils through time. The structural compositions, vested interests, formation of corporations, roles of "white consultants," position of full-bloods, and percentage of mixed bloods could form part of a research focus. The "moccasin telegraph" (a very real communication network on reservations) indicates that the present incumbent president of the Ogalala Sioux Tribe sponsored a study that clearly indicates that the mixed-blood ("breed") element is in decision-making positions and occupies most jobs on Pine Ridge, leaving the more traditional full-bloods in powerless positions. One can posit the notion that this picture may be true of most tribal councils.

The influx of returned enrollees (also in the mixed-blood category) to form corporations based upon EDA, minority business, foster age, and other funding for minorities programs needs to be examined for comprehension of the dynamics of modern reservation life. Research of this type must consider residual traditional (equated frequently with full-blood) Natives. These persons form subsystems and are often referred to as "hard-core" or "drop-outs" (or, more realistically from their viewpoints, "push-outs") from educational systems. Powerless people maintain in their "hard-core-ness" the qualities of life that allow for the continuity of tribal traditions. They, in my estimation, are the vestigial and valued components of reservation personnel and the vanguard that allows our culture and traditions to be maintained. However, they are often seen as "deviants" and "target populations" to be changed by the proposal-writers for tribes and Indian organizations. They supply raw material for the funding of programs.

In urban areas, the rise and fall of Indian organizations, the function of tribally-based associations, the nature of conflict and factions, the effects of funded programs, and aspects of Native identity all need research from an insider's point of view. It is possible, however, that researchers—if they are Indian students—might be viewed as "young kids not dry behind the ears." If they are white, they may be co-opted into jobs—such as proposal writing—within Native elite groups or coerced into giving glowing accounts about the falsified functioning of tribal councils or urban Indian groups.

In the strident emphasis on self-determination one could investigate the dissonances between the federal watchdog (BIA) mandated to protect the trust responsibility of the tribes and this new dictum. Equally significant is the examination of reservations as emerging energy resources and the impact of resource development on the human components. This focus is especially pertinent to "white backlash" in the context of whites' and Indians' symbiotic relationships in border towns near the reservation. Building upon models presented by Jorgenson (1972) and Braroe (1975), Native-initiated modes of research are badly needed. The need for new methods and theories is implicit in Thornton (1977). Moreover, the impact of Native American studies departments upon reservations and urban conglomerates presents new avenues for research and evaluation. This points to new and exciting combinations of laypersons in the communities and of Native students and professionals to develop new research strategies.

In the realm of Native-controlled education, an update of the effects of proliferating community colleges upon Indian education is of high priority (Medicine 1975). Have community colleges been adaptive in reorienting high school education to meet the research needs of their constituencies? Have they effectively dealt with the high drop-out rates in high schools? Where have graduates of these colleges gone in terms of completing their educations? These questions and others are being addressed by the American Indian Higher Education Consortium in Denver. A cursory examination of the data returned in the uneven collection by various community colleges points to the need for research design methodologies in this area.

Echoing the standard mea culpa heard at each annual "tribal tite" (the association's annual meeting) of "anthros" who are constantly accused of studying the "powerless peoples," one could make a plea for studying "around" and not only "up," as Laura Nader (1969) suggests. Such groups as the Interstate Congress for Equal Rights and Responsibilities, which has views on Indian rights and governmental responsibilities, offer a choice research potential. Racism and reservations are other topics that can effectively be combined in current research on the Indian scene. More important, the results of such findings should be widely disseminated, not only to Tribal Councils but also at community meetings.

Native American studies programs have served as repositories for American Indians in higher education. That is, virtually every Native individual in a college or university is thought to be in this ethnic department. The programs, however, are not to be thought of as the only places in which Indians in higher education are housed. Native American studies departments' value is considerable:

> These programs tend to attract the educationally disadvantaged and culturally different people into the state college or university arena. It provides them an area of study in which they can gain a sound foothold of confidence and, hopefully, the skills to complete a college education. In essence Native American Studies . . . serve[s] as a stepping stone to advance the education of the Indian student, regardless of Tribe or nation, while also exposing the rest of society to the attributes of the culturally different. (Otis 1976:18)

References

Braroe, Niels Winther. 1975. *Indian and White: Self-Image and Interaction in a Canadian Plains Community*. Stanford: Stanford University Press.

Jorgenson, Joseph. 1972. *The Sun Dance Religion: Power for the Powerless.* Chicago: University of Chicago Press.

Kemnitzer, Luis. n.d. "Reservation and City as Parts of a Single System: The Pine Ridge Sioux." Department of Anthropology, San Francisco State University (ms.).

Kentfield, Calvin. 1975. "Dispatch from Wounded Knee." In *Solving "The Indian Problem":* *The White Man's Burdensome Business,* ed. Murray L. Wax and Robert W. Buchanan, 127. New York: New York Times Co.

Medicine, Bea. 1971. "The Anthropologist and Ethnic Studies Programs." *Indian Historian* 4(1): 15–18, 63.

———. 1975. "Self-Direction in Sioux Education." *Integrateducation* 78(Nov.–Dec.): 15–17.

———. 1977. "More of Sioux Women Educators." [University of South Dakota] *Institute of Indian Studies News Report,* no. 71 (May): 8.

Nader, Laura. 1969. "Up the Anthropologist—Perspectives Gained from Studying Up." In *Reinventing Anthropology,* ed. Dell Hymes, 284–311. New York: Pantheon Books.

Otis, Morgan G. 1976. "A Native American Studies Program: An Institutional Approach." *Indian Historian* 9(1): 14–18.

Thornton, Russell. 1977. "American Indian Studies as an Academic Discipline." *Journal of Ethnic Studies* 5(3): 1–15.

U.S. Department of Health, Education and Welfare. 1977. *A Study of Selected Socio-Economic Characteristics Based on the 1970 Census,* vol. 3: *American Indians.* Publication 75–122: 3848.

Washburn, Wilcomb E. 1975. "American Indian Studies: A Status Report." *American Quarterly* 27(3): 263–74.

CHAPTER 9

The Interaction of Culture
and Sex Roles in the Schools

In the perusal of the literature pertinent to this essay, there is little data directly focused upon the interaction of culture and sex roles as it relates to Indian females. This is, of course, not surprising. Although Native American cultures have been the emphasis of anthropological and ethnological research for countless generations, specific studies pinpointing the influence of culture and sex roles, especially as it pertains to females in schools, are strikingly lacking. It is mainly in the life histories extant in the anthropological literature and those few about Native females that we are able to obtain a view of the roles of women in the diverse cultures of Native North America. It was an attempt on my part to fill this vacuum by publishing a bibliography of the roles of women in Native North American societies (Medicine 1978).

Many ethnographies of various tribal groups present sketches of socialization processes that involve the internalization and actualization of sex roles. Excellent sources for these studies specific to certain tribes may be found in *The Ethnographic Bibliography of North America* (Murdock and O'Leary 1975) and the Human Relations Area Files, which are usually found in any state university library. Because much of the material obtained from tribes before they became "vanishing Americans" was couched in terms such as "primitive education" or "learning to become a Kwakiutl," the rubric of "schooling" in Western terms was not seen as pertinent. Traditionally, sad to relate, anthropological studies have been collected with a view of life in an "ethnographic present" or the pristine past. Many of these ethnographies portray tribal life-ways as they existed before the advent of the European colonizers. There are, however, some studies on child training that are superb models for outlining the socialization of children and allowing the comprehension of cross-cultural child training

(Hilger 1951, 1952). These have been explicit in outlining the role of learning in "primitive societies" that had no reading, writing, and arithmetic as we know it in the Western European sense. Yet if we look at children's games, for example, the Micmac stick game, we find a high level of abstraction involved. More important, socialization studies have allowed for a comprehension of what it means to children who have grown up in a tribal tradition and have internalized tribal values.

This traditional research stance has confounded the importance of ethnographic reporting. For non-Indians reading these reports, it projects an image of past behaviors and attitudes to which contemporary children are expected to conform. These reports mask the adaptations and adjustments in child-training habits that indigenous societies have had to make as survival strategies. More detrimental in my opinion is the observed fact that many tribal ethnographies are currently being used as bases of what I have referred to as "contrived cultures" of modern "traditionalist" and emerging "medicine men" and "medicine women."

Recently, research about Native Americans has tended to deal with "problems." We find an abundance of studies concerned with Indian alcoholism, family disorganization, juvenile delinquency, homicide and suicide rates, child adoption, and fosterage. Acculturation studies have also been dominant and persistent in the present era. The emphasis on studies and research in Indian education is monumental—and in many cases meaningless. Despite the hue and cry about "being studied" issuing from tribal throats, many situations that are presented to Native groups indicate the need for more studies, or that we "should look into that," or that we "need more research." This essentially is an ambiguity of which many Indian persons are not aware.

It is against this backdrop that the roles of women in Native American cultures must be comprehended. Anthropological researchers among America's indigenous people have initially and predominantly been European males. This has given a significant male bias to the reporting of cultural data. Most informants who supplied information about Native life tended to be males. Many tribes viewed it as improper for Native women to act as informants to white male data collectors. Surprisingly, when Franz Boas sent his students—many of them women—"out into the field," the data collecting followed the same rubrics of research: kinship, material culture, linguistic texts, art forms—those categories that were important to the beginnings of American anthropology.

A little-known fact among Native populations is that Boas first utilized Natives as informants. Later, these persons became involved in collecting data and writing about their own tribal groups. Among these persons were Arthur Parker and J. N. B. Hewitt for the Iroquoian groups, George Hunt among the Kwakiutl, Francis LaFlesche for the Omaha, William Warren on the Ojibwa or Anishinabe, and Ella Deloria on the Siouan groups, specifically the Lakota. This era of the "vanishing American Indian" syndrome has yielded significant studies of some of the tribes and laid the pathway for other Native researchers to follow. Even though American anthropology has been faulted by contemporary Native Americans, the early ethnological studies have captured a quality of life that has been called "memory cultures" by some researchers. These early studies remain as the only baselines of information about some tribes.

But to decry the inadequacies of research pertaining to our cultures and ourselves as Native women deflects from the major issue that should be our main concern. Most saliently, a research caveat should indicate Native perspectives in research design. By that I mean that the time is past for advisory boards. This puts the burden of training our students upon us. We need to have knowledge of the existing literature; the posing of "hunches" (often called "hypotheses" in Western European research); and the formulation of research designs that truly reflect the quality and reality of life as it exists on our reservations and in our rural communities and urban enclaves.

In order to deal with the roles of women effectively, one must clear away demeaning and remaining debris. By isolating the imagery inherent in previous literature, the roles of Indian women surface in a dichotomous fashion and should clarify future research endeavors. As with most Native people around the world, women of darker hue and in politically and economically precarious situations with respect to the colonial powers of the world, Indian women were historically seen as "princess or prostitute." To recall the "Pocahantas as princess" syndrome (Green 1975) as opposed to the picture of the proffered and highly sexed feminine object of explorer, trapper, and trader chronicles places Native American women in the historic framework indicative of the assigned sex role and position that befitted these women of forest, plain, and tundra.

The picture of Native woman as gatherer, drudge, and human pack animal abounds in novels and in historical and anthropological writings and is reinforced and validated in the current media. This image, unfortunately, is also paramount in the minds of many Native men. Exploitation of feminine wiles, wills, and intelligence is apparent in the behaviors and attitudes of many Native men. Paradoxically, Indian women have seemingly adjusted to this double bind and have adroitly managed to coexist in tribal and urban contexts. More tellingly, many Native women have contributed to this continuous cycle by conforming to the same socialization patterns that they witnessed their brothers and male cousins undergoing. Significantly, Indian women have apparently not risen to the call of their white, middle-class counterparts by aligning themselves with the women's liberation movement, although some have participated in the International Women's Year (1975). Others have attended the first International Conference of the Indigenous Women in the New World. Still others are active in the Indian movement. There have been no rigorous studies of involvement. Much of this assessment has been superficial and sentimental.

In teaching courses on Native women, I deliberately use the words *roles* and *cultures* in an endeavor to demolish the image of *the* Indian woman and to place

Elizabeth Cook-Lynn and Medicine, Eagle Butte Powwow, 1990. (Courtesy
of Elizabeth Cook-Lynn)

any research perspective within the estimated two hundred indigenous cultures
viable and vital in contemporary American society. Within these ongoing Native groups lies the strength and adaptive mechanisms that have allowed for
survival through centuries of coerced change and conditioning for acceptance
of a new life-style. Melding to a new way of life has placed tremendous pressures on the traditional sex roles of both males and females. That melding suggests that a careful look at the distinctions between the private and public sec-
tors of the female domain, and the articulation of both in the power structure
of Indian communities is in order.

Cultural change—to become assimilated or, at best, acculturated to the dominant society—has been the basis for an educational system that is similar for
all Native groups. Whether Native societies were matrilineal, patrilineal, or bilateral in social organization was seldom considered in the preordained prescrip-
tion for change to a European model. This was the educational model. Through
education, the move from "primitiveness" to "civilization" was to be accomplished. Education was the key to acceptance. Schools became the primary
agents of resocializing "childlike savages" into responsible citizens in a foreign
power structure. In most instances, coherently functioning Native social systems
were demolished and carefully construed dyadic interpersonal relationships
between the sexes were carefully eliminated. Superimposition of new sex norms,
behaviors, and expectations was part of a global educational policy that was

applied indiscriminately across tribal boundaries in the westward expansion of a new nation oriented and guided by a doctrine of "manifest destiny."

The time of contact was a salient factor in the collisions of cultures and the impact on tribal life-ways. The meeting of Europeans with the Six Nations' matrilineal groups in the East was of a different order than the contact with the warrior societies of the Plains, which had a generally male-dominant cultural orientation. Therefore, in speaking of culture and sex roles it is imperative to specify the tribal culture one is addressing. The cultural components—social organization aspects, value systems, belief systems, and ecological adaptations—should be outlined to assess properly the sex roles of participants in that particular cultural milieu. One must be cognizant of the aspects of culture as a code and see that code as a normative system that underlies cognition and behavior. Essentially, roles are a part of this cultural coding system. Further, the exigencies of cultural contact and change must be delineated.

The agents of change—the educational agent, be it missionary, government agent, or trained Native—and their philosophies are crucial to understanding the changing role of women in the educational process. In all cases of tribal women, we are dealing with a convergence of cultural alternatives and the obliteration of some aspect of Native sex roles and the heightening of other categories in a learning situation that ensures survival of self and cultural continuity. This cannot be negated, for in most human societies the mother is the primary socializer of children. This complexity of role internalization is further complicated by a superordinate decision-making process whose policies have been, and still are, applied indiscriminately to Indian people. The policy often reflects the male bias of the decision-makers and the sexism inherent in the dominant society. Generally and historically, the major thrust of all educational programs directed toward Native populations in North America has been to revamp and readjust Native role categories toward acceptable conformity to a foreign society, on which side rested power and right.

To make these generalizations concrete, one must look at research that deals with the delineation of the parameters of the learning process as it relates to female sex roles in a given culture. This will be attempted on four levels. First, an examination of male and female sex roles will be juxtaposed from the ethnographic literature. Second, the initial impact of cultural change with the learning of new sex roles and expectation will be examined. In the third phase, the types of school-and-society studies that concentrate on sex roles will be delineated. Finally, the direction and emphasis for future studies will be postulated from the previous three settings to a generalized examination of cultural transmission and sex-role learning as it applies to Native populations of females.

In order to provide a tentative model of research into tribal groups, I shall focus upon the Native group known in the anthropological literature as the Teton Sioux, who call themselves Lakota and who speak a dialect of the Siouan language stock, also called Lakota. We look to Murdock and O'Leary (1975: vol. 1, 151) and find the placement of this group in an ecological niche:

> The Teton (Western Dakota, Lakota), including the Brulé (Sicangu), Hunk-papa (Uncpapa), Minnecongou (Miniconjou), Oglala, Sans Arc, Sihasapa (Blackfoot Sioux), and Two Kettle, lived in Western South Dakota and West-ern Nebraska. They now live on a number of reservations in the same area, including the Cheyenne River Indian Reservation, the Lower Brulé Indian Reservation, the Pine Ridge Indian Reservation, and the Standing Rock Indi-an Reservation, all in South Dakota, and on several reserves in Manitoba and Saskatchewan, Canada. They speak Siouan languages and probably number around thirty thousand.[1]

Culturally, the Teton fit into the generalized Plains area, with a dependence on buffalo as a food and clothing supply. It was a mobile, hunting and warring society with a flexible, band-type social organization that had strong emphasis on the *tiospaye* (translated to mean an "extended family"). Kinship is reckoned bilaterally, with a tendency to patrilocal residence. Generally, this culture has been characterized as male-dominant. The Teton Sioux reflect the cultural efflorescence that characterized many of the other Plains tribes, such as the Cheyenne and Comanche, whose cultures changed drastically after the coming of the horse. Other Plains features—the Sun Dance as the major tribal ritual (with the use of a portable tipi made from skin) and the war complex (with coup-counting)—were important features of this life-style.

Looking at ethnographic data, one must always be cognizant of the ideational realm, that is, the value system that serves as underlying sanctions to behavior-al expectations. This is important to the phenomenal orders that are the observ-able events. The value system underlies behavioral norms appropriate to a so-cial identity. It is in this context that sex roles are illuminated in the actualization. Rights, duties, and reciprocal acts are significant features in any social system.

Among the Western Sioux, the four cardinal virtues for men are bravery, for-titude, generosity, and wisdom. Interestingly, the cultural sanctions for women recognized role transitions. The highest virtues are industry, hospitality, kind-ness, and chastity among unmarried females and fidelity and fecundity among married women. The internalization and externalization of these ideals and ap-proved conduct are sanctioned by rituals, supernatural dictates, and ceremonies for women. Incipient women's associations uphold these ideals and provide honor, prestige, and recognition for adhering to the ideals of Lakota womanhood. The Lakota, as with most Plains Indian cultures, are definitely oriented to male pursuits. Women's economic roles are supplementary to male activities. Ethno-graphic studies indicate this. However, there are no studies specifically examin-ing women's roles in economics, as among the Iroquois (Brown 1970).

How was proper role behavior learned, utilized, discarded, and transmitted in the lives of Lakota females? Lakota females learned their expected role behavior through precept and example, as do most children in any nonliterate society. Mirsky (1937) bases much of her data on Ella Deloria's field notes and presents good data on the learning processes of Lakota children. In an outstanding book on the categories of socialization of Native American children, Pettitt (1946:42) states for the Plains tribes generally that the "first plaything is a miniature bow given child as early as four years old by proud father. Mother makes and dresses dolls for girls." It is in the life histories, however, that one obtains the nuances of Native learning systems. Luther Standing Bear (1931:9) indicates that kindness was salient in parents' treatment of children, for they wanted to develop a reciprocal love in the hearts of their sons and daughters. Miniature items of material culture (i.e., cradleboards, dolls, bows and arrows, and games of the hunt and war, the tipi and camp move) are means of learning appropriate role behavior and expectations. The fact is that through the presentation of unsullied models the proper and expected sex role behaviors are transmitted to females and males. As in all Native societies that depended upon informal learning processes, supernatural sanctions and recourse to the value system (combined with the aspects of shame for coercion and honor for prestige) were profound patterns for conformance in Lakota society.

Lakota society presented a symmetry and equilibrium that were learned through observation, imitation, mythology, and folktales. Play was an important aspect in learning one's place in the group. The Lakota allowed siblings of the opposite sex to participate in these peer play groups until about the age of seven years. Then the male and female siblings were separated. The aspect of extreme respect prevailed. Direct eye-to-eye contact during conversation was disapproved.

Social control was through the process common in small face-to-face societies where gossip exerts tremendous pressure for conformity to group norms. To shame the tiospaye was a heinous event. Hassrick (1964) and Deloria (1944) present the most cogent accounts of the role of child training and the enactment of kinship expectations in reciprocal interpersonal relationships. This was the time when a girl learned that her relationship to her brother was one of extreme respect and responsibility. Her future behavior was one where she would do nothing but honor him. That is, she was expected to receive the scalps when he returned from encountering the enemy. She was expected to make his first-born a completely quilled (later, beaded) cradleboard. Her behavior could not detract in any way from his prestige. In turn, he protected her honor and cared for her material needs until she obtained a male to do that. He was instrumental in her choice of husband. Very often, it was a *kola* (friend) or a member of his warriors' society who became his brother-in-law.

Contrary to the often-supposed belief that all Indian cultures are alike, I present some pertinent data on early socialization patterns from two Plains groups. The first is almost identical to the Lakota female expectations. Gladwin (1957:116), in reference to the Cheyenne, an Algonkian speaking-group, writes:

> Though information on childhood sexuality is lacking . . . we do know that the grandparents began early [training of] the child . . . and particularly the daughter did marry in the formal and respectable manner through family gift exchange. Such a marriage was made impossible not only if the girl chose to elope, but even if she were unchaste. To be unchaste a girl did not have to have intercourse with a boy: she was defiled if he touched her genitals, or even her breasts. For this reason, a Cheyenne girl, after her first menses, donned a rope and rawhide cover which acted effectively as a chastity belt.

Contrasting this to the Comanche, a Shoshonean-speaking group, Linton (1945:75) states: "Sexual play between children began at an early age, and was carried on freely as long as the two children were not brother and sister. The Comanche paid no attention to virginity; they took these childhood relations more or less for granted." Thus, besides language stock differentiation, we find that female sex roles are not homogeneous in a culture area in which ecological adaptation and female economic roles are similar. Interestingly, in looking at life-history materials, we see that the internalization of feminine roles is evident and reflective of culture, even though the life histories were collected over a great time variable (Jones 1968; Michelson 1932).

As far as research goes, it could be hypothesized that it is in the areas of child socialization and value constructs that Native American societies seem to have remained more reflective of cultural continuity. That dovetails with theories of cultural contact and change. At the risk of sounding didactic, I reiterate that in order to deal significantly with women's roles, one must isolate them and the cultural values underpinning a tribal group.[2]

As in many tribal societies, among the Lakota the onset of the menses was seen as a liminal period and stressed by isolation and continuous occupation. Besides obtaining advice on her future role from an older woman of good character or her grandmother, quill embroidery and moccasin making occupied the girl's time. This was to ensure industriousness throughout life. Because the division of labor was cooperatively arranged between Lakota males and females, role designation was important at this time. Hassrick (1964:196) indicates: "The division of labor was a cooperatively designed arrangement wherein each sex did that work which they believed they were best suited. That women's work involved the labors of tanning, carrying wood, and on occasion bearing burdens in no way inferred a low status. Evidence to the contrary is offered by the high position of women among the Sioux, the values placed upon virtue, upon childbearing and upon industry and craftsmanship." That the Sioux woman's role was well defined and apparently not distinguished by conflict is commonplace in the literature. There is also evidence that girls were chosen in the "child beloved" syndrome—chosen to cut the sacred tree in the Sun Dance, to be in the retinue of the three attendants, chosen in marriage by an appropriate exchange of horses, or chosen to show evidence of being a faithful wife by sponsoring a virtue feast ("biting the knife") ceremony at the Sun Dance. These were normative aspects of living for Lakota women in the ethnographic present. The fact that sororal polygamy and the mother-in-law taboo were operative indicates an understanding of the dynamics of human relationships.

This is not to say that pre-contact societies were without stresses and human frailties. To give a male viewpoint based upon several reputable woman informants, Hassrick (1964:45) indicates:

> In a society which accepts polygamy as a man's prerogative, in which by the mere beat of a drum a man might announce the dissolution of his marriage, in a group where men's advances were so insistent that unmarried girls were protected by constant chaperonage even to the extent of wearing chastity belts, the ideal of monogamous virtue at first appears out of context. And yet, monogamy was not inconsistent with the Sioux way, possibly if for no other reason than it was really less bothersome. While the double standard undoubtedly had its male advocates, it certainly must have created difficult and embarrassing situations for the girl and her family. Divorce, too, meant a certain upheaval, even outside the family circle. It frequently involved emotional tensions through jealousy, retribution, and unrequited love, and not a few divorces ended in murder.

Wife-stealing presented a dilemma to the Lakota. It was a man's prerogative to cut off his wife's nose. Then she was forever branded as an immoral woman, and her chances for remarriage were slim. My data indicate that frequently her role was that of a *witkowin* ("crazy woman," harlot). Analogous to the male who could not function as a warrior, a culturally sanctioned and institutionalized role, the "berdache" (commonly assumed to be a homosexual) was mirrored for women. By dreaming, a Lakota female could reject her role as wife and mother and become a witkowin. How frequently women had recourse to this option is obscured by the lack of data in the literature. An examination of Siouan folktales and myths and current fieldwork is presenting insight into this question.

The foregoing is an attempt to flesh out the roles of women in a culture before the onslaught of confinement of reservations and the determined destruction of male warriors' roles, with the attendant disruption of the dyadic relationship between the sexes among the Western Sioux or Lakota.

It is the early period of confinement to reservations that poses lacunae in our understanding of the changing roles of male and female in Lakota society in the late 1880s. The destruction of the warrior-hunter-provider role for males can often be found in the reports of military men who stress the vanquishment aspects. The demoralizing aspects of this military feat upon the male psyche are often ignored. The government agents who controlled Native life during the early reservation period can be glimpsed in the reports of Indian agents foisted upon militarily defeated and confined Native populations. It is only through the oral history, and again life histories, mostly male (Standing Bear 1924, 1931), that one glimpses early reservation life. Standing Bear (1931) points out a poignant example of his mother dumping out ration flour (possibly thought to be laced with arsenic) and making a shirt for him from the muslin sack. If a generalization may be made, it is that the female role of mother, sister, and wife was ongoing for the continued care of the family.

But what of the role of women in relationships to the agents and soldiers who guarded the "hostiles" and the general physical deprivation of societies whose livelihood had depended upon a destroyed bison and thus a way of life? We are very nearly bereft of data and statements that could clarify the transitional status of Indian women during this period. The strategies adopted for cultural survival and the means of transmitting it to daughters and nieces are valuable adaptive mechanisms that can only partially be reconstructed. It is only by carefully eliciting data from the seventy- and eighty-year-old women on Northern Plains reservations that we are able to obtain tantalizing bits of information about womanhood during this period.[3]

In addition to Indian agents' reports to the Department of War (later, the Interior), one report about an agent is a gem. Julia McGillycuddy (1941:205–6) writes:

McGillycuddy [her father] was more elated over the institution of the boarding school at Pine Ridge than over any other single accomplishment since the beginning of his services as agent, barring only his organization of the Indian police. The school was a model of its kind, with large halls, airy bathrooms, and sleeping apartments, with small clean beds. The bathrooms were provided with metal bathtubs and with hot and cold water. The living room was comfortably furnished. And the kitchen had a huge range with a capacity of one hundred loaves of bread. Everything was in perfect order when the children, a certain number from each camp, were brought to the school.

On the opening day, hundreds of curious Indians—bucks, squaws, and children—hung about the building wondering just what was going to happen to the two hundred youngsters sequestered with it. McGillycuddy advised pulling down the shades at the windows in the large bathroom on the ground floor to exclude the gaze of the inquisitive.

The first step toward civilizing these primitive children was to purge them of various uncleanlinesses. The several bathrooms as well as the laundry were the scenes of activity, the hair-cutting to be accomplished first, followed by a bath, which would include washing the heads. It was a labor-saving device.

In each bathroom a teacher armed with shears was prepared to begin operations. Curious peepers stood close to the windows on the ground floor, deeply regretful of the drawn shades which barred their observation of the activities carried on behind them. There the matron seated a small boy and taking a lousy braid in one hand, raised the shears hanging by a chain from her waist. A single clip and the filthy braid would be severed. But unfortunately, at that moment a breeze blew back the shade from the window. The previously baffled effort of a youngster plastered against the casing on the outside of the window was now rewarded by a fleeting glimpse of his playmate seated in the chair and a tall lean woman with a pair of shears in her hand prepared to divest the boy of his hair—a Delilah bring calamity upon an embryo Samson.

Like a war whoop rang out the cry: *"Pahin Kaksa, Pahin Kaksa!"* The enclosure rang with alarm, it invaded every room in the building and floated out on the prairie. No warning of fire or flood or tornado or hurricane, not even the approach of an enemy could have more effectively emptied the building as well as the grounds of the new school as did the ominous cry. "They are cutting the hair!" Through doors and windows the children flew, down the steps, through the gates and over fences in a mad flight toward the Indian villages, followed by the mob of bucks and squaws as though all were pursued by a bad spirit. They had been suspicious of the school from the beginning; now they knew it was intended to bring disgrace upon them.

McGillycuddy's raised hands, his placating shouts, and his stern commands were less effective than they had been on occasions of threatened outbreak. He was impotent to stem the flight. He calmed the excited teachers, assuring them that the schoolhouse would soon again be filled with children. But their faces expressed disappointment as well as chagrin over the apparent failure of his attempt to civilize the Sioux.

This small vignette graphically presents the impact of new social institutions on the Lakota. It does not, however, present a view of women's roles. We do know from this account, and from Lakota oral history, that Native women often returned from eastern boarding schools such as Carlisle to become matrons in such reservation boarding schools. One can only conjecture about the individual psychic toll of a Native woman caught in this dilemma.

Interesting to posit is the conflict resolution and adaptive means that Native women utilized during this period. Much of role internalization in a situation of cultural conflict can be seen in the life-history material, as, for example, Hopi. Although one can look in vain for data reflecting women's changing roles, articles as "Sioux Women at Home" (Anonymous 1891) are within the journalistic reporting that points to Lakota women in the stereotyped beast-of-burden tradition.

Among the Western Lakota, the Episcopal Church and the Jesuits provided most of the early educational models. The standards established by Captain Pratt in the Carlisle mode were prevalent throughout "Indian country." Half of the time was devoted to industrial training—blacksmithing and agriculture for boys and housekeeping for girls. As part of the policy "to civilize" and "to humanize," Indian students were placed in boarding schools and stripped of their cultural backgrounds. Native languages were forbidden, military discipline was the norm, and corporal punishment was utilized. This pattern of education continued into the 1920s. With the instigation of the Indian Reorganization Act in 1934, the Collier administration heralded a new era. It is from the research generated in this period that we have significant studies of schools and Indian personality.

During the Collier administration at the Bureau of Indian Affairs, large-scale investigation of the current status of Indian children resulted in many studies (Joseph, Spicer, and Chesky 1949; Kluckhohn and Leighton 1962; Leighton and Leighton 1944; MacGregor 1946; Thompson and Joseph 1945). These milestone studies are seldom consulted by researchers—both Indian and non-Indian. By utilizing interviews, school records, and psychological tests, including the Grace Arthur Point Performance Scale (short form), Goodenough Draw-a-Man Test, Kuhlmann-Anderson Test, Stewarts' Emotional Response Test (revised), Bavelas Test of Moral Ideology, Murray's Thematic Apperception Test (revised), and the Rorschach Psychodiagnostic Test, some interesting statements may be made about Lakota females. For our purposes, the data found in MacGregor (1946:195–98) are revealing:

The girls follow much the same development as the boys until they reach adolescence but they appear to reach the various stages a year or two earlier than the boys, as white girls do.

The youngest group of girls, aged eight to ten, feel that the family serves as a great protection to them, as do the boys of the same age group. But the departure of a member from the family circle, or the sickness or death of a relative, upsets the girls' feelings of security in the family even more than it does the young boys'. The girls appear to acquire the pattern of thoughtful and kind behavior and to enjoy the social relationships outside the family at an earlier age than the boys. Their greater enjoyment of going to school and being among the crowd on holiday occasions reflects both a little more maturity and the confinement imposed upon them at home. The little girls do not give as many responses as the boys about being afraid of being left alone, probably because they are kept closer to their mothers. The youngest girls show better social integration because they indicate less concern about themselves and more interest in the welfare of others.

Girls of this age group become involved in fights and quarrels, but they are disturbed about this behavior and the troubles made for them by others. They express also some fear of the opposite sex and show that they are already aware of their sexual role and the conduct expected of them. Fear of the physical environment is also clearly evident from their responses. Even to a greater extent than the eight-to-ten-year-old boys, the girls of this age group are afraid of animals and especially snakes. This fear is excessive and may reinforce their general apprehension which develops later.

Girls of eleven to thirteen continue to expand their relationships with social groups outside the family. School creates an excellent opportunity for this, and the pleasure of attending school increases. The family does not decrease in importance but now imposes stronger restrictions on the girls' behavior, obviously because they are approaching or entering adolescence. The consciousness of their sexual role dominates the behavior of the girls themselves. They appear more afraid of the advances of men and boys and the criticism of the community. They are also interested in clothes and personal ornaments.

Because modesty and restrained behavior are expected of girls, fighting makes them feel deeply ashamed. Evidently they try to control such behavior but express some of their aggression in stealing. They show both embarrassment and anger about such behavior, which indicates that they become participants as well as objects of it.

By the time the girls become adolescent or post-adolescent, their behavior changes and in some directions their anxieties increase. They are kept in the home and given a strong position there. Interest in the solidarity and security of the family is maintained. School assumes a more serious aspect as the girls become more interested in getting an education. They continue to have a good time there, and they are now also interested in getting a job, although to a lesser degree than boys of their age. It is in their relationships and attitudes outside the family and formal school life that the girls show the greater change. Life about them appears to cause more apprehension and creates more social difficulties than at any earlier age. They are more afraid to be alone, more afraid of the dark, of ghosts, and of what may befall them or their relatives. They are also more anxious now about being sick or dying. The type of responses about sickness and also "getting well" suggests that some of their concern about sickness is associated with menstruation.

The older girls appear to have lost some of their anxiety about direct aggression from others, especially boys. They are now having boyfriends without feelings of shame or excessive fear. The rough behavior of boys may arouse their anger rather than fear, and they often strike back. But they feel that this contact is very bad, worse than stealing. In fact, "stealing" drops out of their replies to the Emotional Response Test, although it appears as bad conduct in the Moral Ideology Test responses.

In addition, MacGregor indicates that "the position of women in the family and community has risen, and their function in the family is often more important today than that of the men" (118). He notes that changes in role and status have led to hostility on the part of both men and women, with resultant family break-up. In delineating the type of training girls received in this period, we see:

Girls are taught the essentials of home management, including nutrition. They may also learn at school a number of crafts which will bring additional income into the home, and many become skilled weavers and potters. Allied with the vocational training in some respects is the performance of school maintenance work by the students. Helping in the school kitchen and dining room may also be helpful to girls. But operating the school laundry machines, cleaning the campus and classrooms, and similar chores fall into the category of institutional labor, whatever training value may be connected with them. (MacGregor 1946:142)

Thus, even though the philosophical basis of education is oriented to Lakota culture (except weaving and pottery), the boarding-school pattern was and is still operative.

This is an enduring pattern in boarding-school education. It is extremely difficult when looking at the more recent studies (i.e., Fuchs and Havighurst 1972; Havighurst 1970) to see the precise picture or role differentiation in schools. The delicate matter of learning sex roles in schools and the effect of changed curricula and school settings are not important factors in these studies. What is important is the statement made by MacGregor concerning familial relationship: "Mother-daughter relationship is commonly a very lasting one, and, after marriage, the daughter is constantly returning home to have her babies, or help her mother in emergencies" (58). However, the mother-son bond is just as strong, if not stronger. He notes the great dependence of a boy on the mother.

There is vast significance, at least for this tribal group, in the conclusion reached by MacGregor: "Women have increased their importance in family life and have already emancipated themselves from their former supplementary role. Through organized clubs and guilds, parent-teacher associations, and the community and tribal council, they have accepted active community leadership" (214).

By looking carefully at the published sources, I have attempted to summarize the changing roles of a Lakota woman through time. In this case, the data were concentrated on Pine Ridge. This endeavor could be replicated, and indeed should be, for each tribal society to give a cross-cultural perspective. As Goldfrank indicates, "The very fact that the Sioux of today can afford to avoid a testing of his communal strength on the realities of today, allows him to preserve an anachronistic system of child-training which remains the continued source of inner peace under desperate communal conditions" (1943:151). Statements such as these in the anthropological literature should challenge Native researchers to question—anachronistic or adaptive.

The task at hand is to present research proposals to build upon cultural differences and isolate general coping mechanisms that are characteristic of tribal societies undergoing change. The imperatives are to see Native American women in this context. At the outset, it must be stated that each Native woman has undergone a secondary socialization process of translating and transforming experiences from one cultural base to another. Encountering differing norms, motivations, and expectations of bicultural experiences has been our lot. An examination of these social forces, which have formed a personal experience for each of us, should be realistically appraised. Many of us do not often reflect on these experimental situations, which have allowed us to cope in several different cultural and subcultural arenas.

Of greater concern are the effective and affective influences we have upon others—spouse, families, and children. "Family" in this sense is a broader-based phenomenon than the usually evoked nuclear family. The aspects of fictive kin, female supportive systems, female bonding, and the other means of coping in reservation and urban life should be part of this awareness. We should be aware of the literature on contemporary Indian life-styles.[4]

The concept of male dominance should be seen in cross-cultural settings. An example of this would be to look at dyadic relationships between males and females in cultures that have been reported as matrilineal and patrilineal. The nature of conditioning experience by girls and boys should be examined. This would deal with aspects of tribal sexism. What are female strategies for control of the domains? Insofar as is possible, cultural institutions and residence patterns should be seen as facilitators of sex roles and sex differences. What are the characteristics of contemporary tribal life-styles? In light of this, attitudes and values of the people should be seen as affective activators for behavior. In each case, the contemporary situation should be explicated in light of the past to show the dynamics of present-day culture.

The type of family structure and its fragmentations and strengths, the types of role dysfunctions (male/female homosexuality) and aspects of controls exerted by women, the nature of social control, the reward and punishment systems of child training, aspects of role modeling and significant others (i.e., grandmothers), and the viewing of schools as transitional institutions are only some of the areas that need investigation to shed light on the role of American Indian women in North American society. In contemporary tribal societies, how are the parameters of power, authority, and influence along sex lines perceived and activated? It is only when we can state empirically and analytically the cultural configurations of Indian female sex roles, as learned in family kinship systems and school situations, that our understanding is enhanced and our options are clarified.

Notes

1. Assessing this, one notes that the Standing Rock Reservation is in North and South Dakota, with the agency at Ft. Yates. The demographic statement "probably number around thirty thousand" is common where Native Americans are concerned. Because Indians were first enumerated in the 1970 census in a distinct self-ascribing category, this first demographic deficiency must be acknowledged for research purposes. A statement that there appears to be no one source for reliable data concerning Indians is mandated.

2. I am appalled by the statements made by contemporary Indian "leaders" that clans were the basis of social organization of Indian tribes. This, in essence, is viewing *all* Native societies from a perspective of tribal ethnocentrism rather than from the frequently accused white

ethnocentrism. This fallacy is more dangerous, in my view, because a Native statement carries double jeopardy. I have articulated this view at the National Education Association's Conference on Values at Tahlequah, Oklahoma, in April 1976, in response to this same point made by Lloyd Elm and Eddy Benton. My suggestion is that all Native writers be cognizant of the cultural backgrounds of the groups they are discussing and explicate this information.

3. Intriguing and provocative bits of conversation abound in my field notes. Ella C. Deloria, for example, stated in reference to early reservation days, "Times were hard in those days. Some of the head men even sold their daughters to the soldiers. Of course, our families didn't" (Vermillion, S.D., 1969). In recounting genealogies of the early reservation period, I am amazed at the intermarriage and the infusion of genes from whites, the Chinese, and blacks into Native populations. My research with the Piegan shed some interesting aspects of culture change and women's roles, for example, "Warrior Women of the Plains" (Medicine 1972).

4. See, for example, Guillemin (1975). Although this study is of Micmac (Canadian) Indians in an American city, it presents a realistic view of Indian women and their relationship to other females and males. Studies of the role of conflict and its resolution, female bonding, and sharing information about men, jobs, and coping strategies should impart new insights into research on urban Indian families. Models for research into contemporary reservation life are not too plentiful; see, however, Medicine (1969).

References

Anonymous. 1891. "Sioux Women at Home." *Illustrated American.* New York: Bible House.
Brown, Judith K. 1970. "Economic Organization and the Position of Women among the Iroquois." *Ethnohistory* 17(3–4): 151–67.
Deloria, Ella C. 1944. *Speaking of Indians.* New York: Friendship Press.
Fuchs, Estelle, and Robert J. Havighurst. 1972. *To Live on This Earth: American Indian Education.* Garden City: Doubleday.
Gladwin, Thomas. 1957. "Personality Structure in the Plains." *Anthropological Quarterly* 30(4): 111–24.
Goldfrank, Esther S. 1943. "Historic Change and Social Character: A Study of the Teton Dakota." *American Anthropologist* 45(1): 67–83.
Green, Rayna. 1975. "The Pocahantas Perplex: The Image of Indian Women in American Culture." *Massachusetts Review* 16(4): 698–714.
Guillemin, Jeanne. 1975. *Urban Renegades: The Cultural Strategy of American Indians.* New York: Columbia University Press.
Hassrick, Royal B. 1964. *The Sioux: Life and Customs of a Warrior Society.* Norman: University of Oklahoma Press.
Havighurst, Robert J. 1970. *The Education of Indian Children and Youth: Summary Report and Recommendations, National Study of American Indian Education, Summary Report and Recommendations.* Minneapolis: Training Center for Community Programs, University of Minnesota.
Hilger, Inez. 1951. *Chippewa Child Life and Its Cultural Backgrounds.* Bulletin 146. Washington: U.S. Bureau of American Ethnology.
———. 1952. *Arapaho Child Life and Its Cultural Backgrounds.* St. Clair Shores: Scholarly Press.
Jones, D. G. 1968. *Sanapia: Comanche Indian Woman.* New York: Holt, Rinehart and Winston.
Joseph, Alice, Rosamund B. Spicer, and Jane Chesky. 1949. *The Desert People.* Chicago: University of Chicago Press.

Kluckhohn, Clyde, and Dorothea Leighton. 1962. *The Navaho.* Rev. ed. Garden City: Doubleday.

Leighton, Alexander H., and Dorothea Leighton. 1944. *The Navaho Door.* Cambridge: Harvard University Press.

MacGregor, Gordon. 1946. *Warriors without Weapons.* Chicago: University of Chicago Press.

McGillycuddy, J. C. 1941. *McGillycuddy, Agent: A Biography of Dr. Valentine T. McGillycuddy.* Stanford: Stanford University Press.

Medicine, Beatrice. 1969. "The Dakota Family and the Stresses Therein." *Pine Ridge Research Bulletin* 9:13–23.

———. 1972. "Warrior Women of the Plains." Presented to the International Congress of Americanists. Rome.

Michelson, Truman. 1932. *The Narrative of a Southern Cheyenne Woman.* Washington: Smithsonian Institution.

Mirsky, Jeanette. 1937. "The Dakota." In *Cooperation and Competition among Primitive Peoples,* ed. Margaret Mead, 382–427. New York: McGraw-Hill.

Murdock, George Peter, and Timothy J. O'Leary. 1975. *The Ethnographic Bibliography of North America.* 4th ed., vols. 1–5. New Haven: Human Relations Area Files Press.

Pettitt, George A. 1946. *Primitive Education in North America.* Berkeley: University of California Press.

Standing Bear, Luther. 1924. *My People, the Sioux.* Edited by E. A. Brininstool. Boston: Houghton Mifflin.

———. 1931. *My Indian Boyhood.* Boston: Houghton Mifflin.

Thompson, Laura, and Alice Joseph. 1945. *The Hopi Way.* Chicago: University of Chicago Press.

CHAPTER 10

Native American
(Indian) Women:
A Call for Research

It is counterproductive to dwell on the paucity of published works on Native American (American Indian) women.[1] There is virtually no research in this area and no research agenda for the future.[2]

One reason for the underdevelopment of research on Native women is that, traditionally and contemporarily, research on "Indian problems" has categorized Native Americans as a single group and constructs differentiating, tribal-specific structures. Socioeconomic status, residence patterns, and educational achievements as well as gender remain fuzzy. Indian tribes, urban conglomerates, and females and males have often been lumped together and glossed into pathological parameters. The pervading view of *the* Indian problem has focused research agendas upon such dissonances as poverty on reservations and general economic development strategies, which very often are context-insensitive and not ameliorating. General trends in Native drop-out rates from educational systems, suicide and homicide statistics, and the poor self-images of Indian students have predominated in educational research. Dominating all research about Natives is an interest in alcohol consumption and "drinking styles" of aboriginal people. These foci, in my assessment, have caricatured Native people in a very unflattering way and have made an understanding of them impossible.

A second reason, related to the first, is that published material on North American Native females is bound inextricably within male-produced ethnographic accounts. Such accounts usually portray Native women in one of two stereotypical ways: as the dismal drudge exemplified in the male-dominant warrior societies of the Plains, such as Cheyenne, Comanche, Lakota (Sioux), or Kiowa, or the matriarchal matron of the horticultural groups, such as the

Iroquois. Gender and role variation reflecting the differentiated social structures and cultures of Native American tribal groups is thus obliterated.

Distorted images of Indian women have been perpetuated by the continuing male bias of mainstream writers. The "princess or prostitute" syndrome of much anthropological, historical, and missionary writers is presently reinforced by the portrayal of Native women in the media. The tribal, viable, residual, and syncretic roles of indigenous women in contemporary racist and sexist American society has neither been delineated nor rarely even acknowledged. These unifocused, pathological, and stereotypical approaches have successfully covered the rich variation of gender differences in socialization patterns. Studies dealing with the adaptive strengths of male and female indigenous people are sparse. Only recently have feminist theories been applied to ethnographic data (Albers and Medicine, eds. 1983), and life histories of Native women in Canada and the United States have begun to appear (Blackman 1982; Powers 1986).

Although these life histories are valuable in understanding the diversity of individuals in Native cultural systems, they have generally not been used to improve theoretical constructs pertaining to Natives. Controversies arising from the application of constructs such as matrilocality, for example, have not been the concern of Indian-oriented research. Indeed, many researchers do not seem to be aware of different family structures in matrilineal and patrilineal Native societies that do, of course, play an important part in gender difference and role expectations (Medicine 1983). Nor are distinct family structures that characterize Indian families seen as significant variables in comprehending primary socialization patterns of and by females and males (Medicine 1981). Studies of female-headed households in cross-tribal perspective, for example, might greatly enhance our understanding of patterns of child training and the competencies of schoolchildren.

What research exists suggests that many general "truths" about Indian people could be challenged. For example, recent work with the Menominee indicated that eye contact between an elder teacher and a child was necessary for informal teaching to proceed, and any disruption on the part of the child was challenged (Medicine, unpublished field notes 1987). Similarly, I have heard Lakota (Sioux) parents state, "Look me in the eyes!" when addressing children and grandchildren. Yet the idea that all Indians avoid eye contact is pervasive in educational and psychological reports.

The paucity of existing research and the challenges to conventional thinking that seem to be emerging in the work of Native researchers point to the urgent need for research agendas created and conducted by Natives. It is imperative that Native women begin formulating constructs and tentative hypotheses based upon our own unique experiences and observations. This is one way in which our disciplines, our institutions, and our constituencies can be effective. In what follows, I describe my attempt to conduct research on the process of professionalization, which characterizes the experiences of the few Native women who have pursued higher education. The limited existing information led me to generate many more questions than a single study could answer.

Native American Undergraduate Females

A search of ERIC files yields little pertinent information directly related to the professionalization of Indian females. The unpublished paper by Clara Sue Kidwell (1976) is typical. Her findings, constructed from fragmentary, diffuse sources, are summarized in this portrait: "The Native American woman college student: She is more likely to have attended a non-BIA high school, will probably come from a home in which English is her first language (or if a Native language is her first language, it will be the language always spoken in the home). She will be majoring in some field of education or social service and will be somewhat more likely than her Indian male classmates to persist and complete her degree" (1976:14). This summary of the general demographic trends is barely a start. So many other facets of Native women college students' experiences in contemporary North American society need investigation. What are these students' experiences in school? How do they differ from the experiences of Native women who do not go to college? What are their experiences at home, in kin groups, and with mainstream society? What are their educational goals? What future work opportunities do they aspire to or expect to find? In what ways have they internalized their Nativeness? In what ways do they expect to contribute to their Native group? In what ways are their experiences similar to or different from those of other minority college women?

Native American undergraduate women appear to share one strong concern with other minority women—the area of dating. The wish and behavior expected by peers and family is to date and marry Native men. Many of these males are dating, or are already married to, non-Native females. This is a dilemma, for very often these same men will castigate Indian women who are involved with Caucasians or other minorities. Native undergraduate women have expressed the fear that uneducated Native men may not marry a university graduate. In what ways do these concerns affect the school—and work—related experiences of Native women in particular? What are the implications if a majority of female Native Americans pursue higher education? What is, or will be, the impact for kin and family structures? These are but a few of the questions to be formulated into research designs, published, and disseminated to appropriate interest groups.

Research to answer such questions is clearly within the province of those colleges and universities (i.e., Arizona State, Harvard, the University of Arizona, Pennsylvania State) having specialized Native American programs. Implicit in this proposal is the possibility that Native undergraduate students, by the very nature of their experiential participation in a secondary enculturation process, might construct new theoretical models and research tools that would elicit more significant and meaningful results.

This research necessitates working in Native groups surrounding the universities, involvement in activist causes, and attendance at yearly conventions of intertribal Indian associations. Surprisingly, the effects of this "culture-contriving" and bridge-building across tribal cultures have also not been explored as part of the Native higher education experience. This involvement centers on powwows and "Indian awareness weeks," with lectures by Native intellectuals and activists and "medicine men." In these activities, Native women must deal with the chauvinism and gender bias of the Native American leadership: men. And yet these activities are deemed essential by that leadership for undergraduate life, as a way of achieving esprit de corps and traditionality or at least some semblance of "Nativeness."

Despite the need, I note a great reluctance by Native undergraduates for research and writing. Although it has been determined that this is true for the larger society, the need here is acute. In particular, an increase of ethnographic research at the undergraduate level would raise the consciousness of Indian females in the entire realm of research and subtly present options for graduate school.

Native American Women in Graduate School

There is also little known about Native women graduate students. It is not clear how many Native females enter graduate school, nor are we certain about their motivations. It is clear, however, that since the 1960s and the conscious effort on the part of institutions to recruit minorities more Indian women are in graduate school.

One constant of the Native American female graduate student is endemic: poverty and a lack of resources to alleviate it. This is characteristic of both sexes, regardless of places of origin, and permeates all levels of training. There is evidence of lack of information about graduate fellowships, especially research and teaching fellowships in the departments of choice. Since the 1960s, programs such as the Ford Foundation Fellowships for minorities have been beneficial for some. The availability of fellowships has, however, intensified competition between the sexes and has presented problems of Indian identity. Self-identification (as in the 1980 census) has (and is) causing much discontent in the reaping of such benefits. Persons claiming to be of $\frac{1}{32}$ or $\frac{1}{64}$ Indian blood are often found among the rosters of Native Americans in graduate school. This has caused some factions in Native communities to become more intense. Native consensus, true or not, is that disproportionate numbers of these self-ascribed Natives appear to obtain fellowships in graduate schools. This raises difficult questions among graduate students regarding "Indians of convenience" versus "Indians who have been Indians all their lives," although whether Native women are disproportionately disadvantaged over Native men is not yet clear. At any rate, lack of resources characterizes all American Indian students.

Kidwell provides a somewhat more extensive profile of American Indian graduate females:

> Poor in economic terms; somewhat older than most graduate students, married or divorced, and in many cases, a mother (since 1960, single females have appeared): an individual who, more often than not, is entering a discipline which is new to her, for her undergraduate work may have resulted from inappropriate counseling; a person who is clearly conscious of role and gender expectations reflective of her tribal background; a person who is the recipient of many pressures to "work for the benefit of Indians" and quite unsophisticated as to the mentorship and cohort system in graduate school, thus, her role tends to be somewhat lonely. Her dating behavior, if she is single or divorced, is devoid of interaction with native males, for they tend to be married. Unrealistically, she is under peer pressure to date native males, but often dates Chicano males, or none at all. She tends not to be involved in the Feminist Movement, but may allot some time to Indian organizations on the state or national scene. (1976:17)

From an American Association for the Advancement of Science report we find that the need to assume some attributes such as aggressiveness was a burden for some women of minority cultures, such as some Native American ones in which behavioral modes or patterns are more sharply defined by gender and age than they are in the majority culture (Malcolm, Hall, and Brown 1976:18).

Other salient factors that can be extracted from this report are the need for role models in graduate schools, more counseling as to research methodology and factors involved in job-seeking, involvement in professional organizations, and information regarding postdoctoral fellowships (Malcolm, Hall, and Brown 1976:19–21). Nevertheless, most facets of Native women graduate students' lives are undocumented and need investigation. What is the size of the roster of Indian women in Ph.D. or Ed.D. degree programs? What are their areas of specialty? What are their tribal identities, work experiences, ages, marital statuses, number of children, and places of origin (reservation, off-reservation community, or urban center)?

Native American Women: Early Professional Years

This section is founded upon the least solid data: the four scientists and one student in the AAAS report (Malcolm, Hall, and Brown 1976). This report concentrated upon only five Native females with graduate degrees in, or about to enter, the "hard sciences." Based on the AAAS report, some information is available about the early career paths of these American Indian women. One Native American, holder of a Ph.D. in psychology, began immediately after graduation in a tenure-track position in teaching and research at the university where she obtained her degree. She is now a full professor in another western university. Another person with a degree in social work (and psychology) is presently in an Indian studies program, with a joint appointment in psychology. It would appear that the employment picture reflects their job preferences and personal capabilities. Little data on the process of their professionalism are available, and it has not been possible to get detailed information regarding the other three American Indian women's professionalism and work experiences.

My own informal conversations with female holders of newer Ph.D. degrees indicate certain expectations about their future careers. The women expect that other Native Americans, especially males, will exert pressures for commitment to Indian organizations. One of them indicated that she was made to feel guilty when she decided to return to an academic position. In order to return, she had to modulate her commitment to Indian associations, Native-related concerns, and Indian studies programs. Yet the two areas are confounded. Younger scholars whose identity seems tied to obtaining a Ph.D. degree report a more positive self-image following heightened awareness of Indian heritage.

One can say something about the "publish or perish" aspect of academe. One psychologist and an anthropologist have published adequately and fulfilled the presentation of self and papers at professional meetings. These individuals are also highly visible and greatly involved in tribal and urban Indian research needs and educational innovation. This activism plays havoc with their professorship roles, however, and tenure committees very often do not take community involvement into consideration. Instead, female academicians are often accused of "not being able to say no" (to requests from Indian groups, that is) or of being absent from campus when they go to reservations or urban areas to work with Indian tribes, schools, and groups.

Therefore, the position of Native American professors in an ordinary academic situation is an enigma. If Native American females are not involved in "work for their people," Native criticism abounds. If they are committed to their people's needs, they are looked upon by their academic cohorts as "doing social work" and not theoretical or scholarly work in the European tradition. It is inconceivable to white academicians that both may be possible.

Summary

Research on the Native American female experience in professionalization, as well as other research on Natives, needs to be placed in a framework that takes into account the varied contexts, roles, and commitments that compose the experience of their lives. Tribalism, tribal sovereignty, viable cultural and linguistic traditions, land bases (reservation and communities), and treaty obligations place each tribe in a distinctive category. This is often reflected on the self-images and achievement motives of both genders, and it forms the background of gender-related behaviors and worldview. It is essential that delineation of differential sex roles and status categories for Native American women be achieved. Placing this within the subordinate society's parameters and influences will focus upon the reaction of females of all tribes to the common experience of oppression in U.S. society.

Notes

1. This essay discusses the unasked and unanswered research questions on the educational status and experiences of Native women. It summarizes what little is known about three categories of Native women (undergraduate students, graduate students, and professionals) and suggests necessary starting points for embarking on a research agenda. In addition, this essay advances tentative explanations for the current status of research on the education of Native women in the United States.

2. The situation is currently changing; however this statement was true at the time of original publication, 1988.

References

Albers, Patricia, and Beatrice Medicine, eds. 1983. *The Hidden Half: Studies on Plains Indian Women.* Washington: University Press of America.

Blackman, Margaret B. 1982. *During My Time: Florence Edenshaw Davidson, a Haida Woman.* Vancouver: Douglas and McIntyre.

Kidwell, Clara Sue. 1976. "The Status of Native American Women in Higher Education." Presented to the Conference on Native American Women, sponsored by the National Institute of Education, Albuquerque, Oct. 12–13.

Malcolm, Shirley Mahaley, Paula Quick Hall, and Janet Welsh Brown. 1976. *The Double Bind: The Price of Being a Minority Woman in Science.* Washington: American Association for the Advancement of Science.

Medicine, Beatrice. 1981. "American Indian Family Cultural Change and Adaptive Strategies." *Journal of Ethnic Studies* 8(4): 13–23.

———. 1983. "Indian Women: Tribal Identity as Status Quo." In *Woman's Nature: Rationalizations of Inequality,* ed. Marian Lowe and Ruth Hubbard, 63–73. New York: Pergamon Press.

Powers, Marla N. 1986. *Oglala Women.* Chicago: University of Chicago Press.

Gender and Cultural Identities

Changing Native American Roles in an Urban Context *and* Changing Native American Sex Roles in an Urban Context

Mitakuyepi oyasin chante waste ya nape chiyusa pe. I am greeting you in my Lakota language. When I am home, living on the reservation, this is the way I would normally speak to a gathering. I will translate this greeting because it very neatly, in my mind, encapsulates what has happened here. *Mitakuyepi oyasin* means "all my kinpersons," *chante waste ya* means "with a good heart," and *nape chiyusa pe* is "I shake hands with you." This is very symbolic because it speaks to the whole issue of kinship: *Mitakuyepi oyasin* includes not only other humans but also, as Black Elk states (and his words have been repeated often), the rest of the creatures—in the air, in the waters, and all around us. *Chante waste ya* means that we approach our respective work with good hearts. I am proud of my many tribespersons because they have done a wonderful job in opening their hearts on an issue of great sensitivity. *Oyasin* means that all variations of persons are seen as kin in the Lakota worldview. The greeting symbolizes the circle—the kinship circle. Metaphorically, all persons shake hands, and this, I think, is beautiful. The greeting indicates an inclusivity and acceptance of all persons.

Now perhaps I should begin with some designation: "Not a 'berdache' [*sic*], not a plastic medicine person, but an anthropologist and a Lakota woman." As an anthropologist, I have had to put up with a lot of nonsense from within the discipline and outside of it, and even from some Native communities other than my own. The chapters that follow that are written by Native people (and some of the others) contain the basis for some of the disenchantments that have made Native people doubt the value and veracity of anthropology. But in spite of these matters I am still an anthropologist, and I still maintain ties with Native communities throughout North America.

I became involved in gender studies after speaking with a handsome young Kiowa man many years ago. Later, another Native woman from his "culture area" approached me and said, "Isn't it terrible that this good-looking man is gay? And that is what happened when the Europeans came to us." "No, you certainly don't know anything about your culture, if you can say this," I replied. This then motivated my work.

The fact is, in many communities in Native North America a growing homophobia is evident. That concerns me. I feel that we have to deal with this frightening situation in some way. I responded to the woman's remark by writing a paper in 1979, "Changing Native American Sex Roles in an Urban Context," which I never published elsewhere but is provided as part of this chapter. I published on "Warrior Women of the Plains" (1983) and began to examine the contours of gender terms in my own Lakota language. By examining Native terms for gender classifications, the nuances of naming and behavior will become clearer.

Persons of Lakota or Dakota heritage, as well as others, might quote *"koshkalaka* [means] dyke" from Paula Gunn Allen's writing (1986:258). I did not correct her at the outset because at that time it was a sensitive issue. I knew that a lot of Native women who were just beginning to assert themselves as lesbians might say, "Oh, you're just lesbian-bashing." Being an anthropologist, being bashed by so many other Native people, I did not want to put anyone in that situation. "Koshkalaka" means simply "young man," "youth," or "post-pubescent male." We Lakota have another term, *wikoshkalaka,* which means "young woman," "a post-menarche female," or a "young woman who is *isnati* [lives alone or apart]," often referred to as living in a "menstrual hut" in the anthropological literature. Moreover, in talking with many of my elders (both male and female) and considering the analysis of words, I asked, "Is there a word for women who are like the *winkte?*" There was none. In 1993, when I discussed this, I heard the term *winkte winyan,* for some of the elder females had seen one. Here, again, the term *winkte* was used but with the term for woman, *winyan,* added.

Winkte, the Lakota/Dakota term for "gay or homosexual male," has assumed pan-Indian or intertribal connotations and been translated as "wants [wishes] to be a woman." In a deeper, structural linguistic sense, it means to "kill women." This latter interpretation caused some ire among gender researchers when I first mentioned the translation (Medicine 1987). At the first Wenner-Gren Foundation conference and the subsequent American Anthropological Association session on "Revisiting the 'North American Berdache,'" we heard the term *koshkalaka winyan;* the word *winyan* had been added to Allen's use of *koshkalaka.* If we stick with Allen's meaning and usage, adding *winyan* might be considered redundant or, more often, emphatic: "dyke-woman" or, in other contexts, "lesbian-woman." Although Paula Gunn Allen has written me that the information given her was wrong, and the interpretation of "koshkalaka" was incorrect, the term is used unabashedly in women's studies courses as a result of the continued romanticization of Native American gender and sexuality.

Several other terms in the Lakota language are used to indicate gender characteristics. One, *bloka,* may be translated as the penultimate characterization of masculinity. It was a metaphor for the buffalo bull: ferocious, fearless, and fecund. The term was used to connote the best qualities of a provider and caretaker. *Winyan tanka* posed the desired characteristics of womanhood: virginity in maidenhood, industry and generosity in marriage, and priestliness in old age in order to receive the honored Bite the Knife Ceremony without approbation. By contrast, *bloka* indicated men who exuded power on the vision quest, on the warpath, in horse raids, on buffalo hunts to provide for the *tiospaye* (extended family), and in protecting and cherishing women and children. These characteristics are mythic to the many contemporary men for whom the term means only sexual prowess. The term *bloka egla wa ke* has been translated as "thinks she can act like a man" in striving and excelling in such masculine achievements as riding horses and owning and providing for cattle and ultimately family and tiospaye. The term has been used to refer to women who indicate tendencies that may be construed as lesbian characteristics, or it might be considered to fit that constellation of behavior (Medicine 1993).

We must be very careful in using, or contriving, English translations for Native terms. We also must be aware of the ways language is changed and the meaning of Native terms altered and then used to meet the needs of disenfranchised groups and individuals as a possible response of self-interest. While I was in Canada, I investigated the Algonkian (Algonquian) term for "two-spirited." The use of "two-spirit" as a pan-Indian term is not intended to be translated from English to Native languages, however. To do so changes the common meaning it has acquired by self-identified two-spirit Native Americans. Translating the word *two-spirit* into some languages could lead to misunderstandings that could have adverse effects on the person using the term. One should be cautious and careful to contextualize gender terms and how they are used in Native communities. *Spirit* is an extremely variable term, and in some Native languages connotes sacredness.

What follows was written in 1979, and, like Jacobs's essay (1968), it has had a life of its own, being copied and distributed among Native American women and men who, at that time and even now, call themselves "lesbian" and "gay." I have agreed to its publication here because what I said then still applies to many situations and because it provides historical roots to contemporary efforts.

I am pleased to have been part of the sessions that led to this book and am pleased to be part of this book. The issues we are dealing with are very delicate in Native communities and in anthropology. What happened with the interaction of aboriginal people of all nations and anthropologists of all stripes during the course of the Wenner-Gren conferences was precedent-setting. We have set a model. I think that there should be more of this interaction in the anthropological profession. You should take very seriously what you read in these pages so that we may proceed with purpose and clarity, and an unknowing public can be informed.

Changing Native American Sex Roles in an Urban Context

Many Native American societies—especially the Plains tribes—have provided an outlet for male sexual deviancy in the institutionalized "berdache" (called *winkte* in Siouan and *hemaneh* among the Algonkian-speaking Cheyenne), which has been equated with homosexual in most introductory anthropology text books.[1] Seemingly, there was no analogous role for Indian women. Reexamination and explication of sex roles in contemporary Indian societies indicate a shift in the feminine role to accommodate an emerging (or latent) lesbian orientation. Urban organizations such as GAI (Gay American Indians) will be analyzed as to their function in meeting actualized roles of Native Americans. Here I examine male and female roles in an urban, intertribal context and suggest further research needs.

Contrary to popular belief, movements of Native Americans to urban centers have had a long history (Medicine 1973; Officer 1971). The relocation program sponsored by the Bureau of Indian Affairs in the 1950s greatly increased the trend toward urbanism as a way of life for Indians in contemporary society. This division of B.I.A., renamed the Employment Assistance Program, is still fostering the migration of reservation Indians to cities. The current population figures for urbanized Indians reads variously between 50 and 60 percent of an approximately one million Native inhabitants. This urban variation in census enumeration is typical of statistical data regarding Indians in all areas.

The literature on Native American urbanization has characteristically dwelt upon such problems as alcoholism, poverty, unemployment variables, family break-down, and the return rate to reservations, which form an integral part of the total picture in the life-styles of present-day Indians of all tribes.

Little has been done to deal with the coping strategies of individual Indians. This paper seeks to concretize some of the ideas advanced by Southall (1973) and utilizes data relating to changing sex roles of Indians in an urban context. Southall's neat, "vitamin-like"—(KEPLV)—representation of variables is an extremely challenging method for examining role relationships when applied to the urban experiences of certain self-ascribed Native Americans. Studies (Hirabayashi and Kemnitzer, eds. 1976; Price 1968) have stressed an unequal emphasis on the value of kinship and ethnic (K); economic and occupational (E); political (P); ritual and religious (L); and recreational, leisure-time, and voluntary (V) upon some of the discrete categories for analysis proposed by Southall in urban research. This is to suggest that a partitive analysis of role enactments by Native Americans in cities typifies much urbanization research.

LEFT: Beatrice Medicine, Toronto, 1992. (Courtesy of Terence Durant)

BELOW: Beatrice Medicine, 1992. (Courtesy of Don Doll)

In general, therefore, the examination of role relationships has been uneven for the urban experiences of Native Americans.

Within the urban Indian experience, I shall attempt to examine the voluntary coming-out-of-the-closet process for individuals of Indian ancestry. The term is used to indicate the one that homosexuals use to vindicate a change in sex role orientation and actualization. This English equivalent is also preferable to such Native terms as the Siouan *winkte* (womanlike, or wishes-to-be-a-woman) which, like the Siouan term *washicu* (white person), assumes greater prevalence in intertribal vernacular in urban settings.

Many Native American societies—especially the Plains tribes—had traditionally provided an outlet for sexual "deviancy" in the institutionalized role of "berdache" (Jacobs 1968). Unfortunately, this social role—winkte among the Siouan Lakota-speakers (Hassrick 1964:133–35) and hemaneh among the Algonkian-speaking Cheyenne (Hoebel 1960:77)—has often been equated with male homosexuals in most introductory anthropology texts and classes. Among the Lakota (Teton Sioux), there is evidence that other facets of action were bounded within the winkte gloss—ritualist, artist, specialist in women's craft production, herbalist, seer, namer of children, rejecter of the rigorous warrior role, "mama's boy" (Hassrick 1964:134), and the designation commonly stated in anthropology books. Therefore, the multiplex categorizations in the following statement are extremely appropriate in the elucidation of such a role in an urban setting: "It is the conceptual idea of the particular, defined structural position which I call role and every instance in which it is played, whether by different persons, or by the same person to a number of others, I call role-relationship" (Southall 1973:75).

In addition, Southall's reference to Banton's contention that "high moral density is associated with small population groups where everyone knows everyone else so that deviance in role performance by one person affects all the rest" (1973:80) has relevance to new role enactment on the part of some tribal individuals. The tightly constricted ethnic enclaves of reservations certainly present restrictiveness to role change. There are some instances of ritual role change in some tribes that are temporary and specialized. A certain surreptitiousness and secrecy has been evident in many reservation communities as far as these sexual "deviants" are concerned. Southall indicates, however, that he does not consider sex or age as roles for (his) present purposes, because neither is a universal generator of role relationships. "There is no question of the importance of sex and age in qualifying performance and attitude, but they do not in themselves give rise to basic role-relationships" he states (1973:76–77). It may be suggested that new role relationships in an urban context be examined. The fact that Native American homosexuals are coalescing and amplifying bonding mechanisms that fit into the (V) category may have implications for the urbanizing process and sex roles.

As indicated previously, the ethnological record concentrates primarily upon the examination of the male homosexual role. Apparently, if we rely upon the male-biased reporting of early anthropological accounts dealing with sex roles among Native Americans, there was no corollary expression for Indian females. Gender-based studies in socialization and role differentiation are greatly lacking in anthropological research upon contemporary Native American groups. Schaeffer (1965) presents most of the ethnohistorical data on a Kutenai berdache living in the nineteenth century.[2] In most of the literature dealing with this perceived "deviancy" in Native societies, there are few data on female sexual expression. Seemingly, there is sparse information that can give us dimensions of feminine enactment of an analogous sex role. There are, however, narratives in the myth structure of some tribes which center upon lesbian behavior (i.e., Lowie [1909:50] for the Assiniboine and Jones [1907:151] for the Fox). There are other references to "female transvestitism" scattered throughout the ethnological literature on American Indians (Hill 1935). Hassrick (1964:135) writes: "Lesbianism seems to have played a much less obvious part in the life of the Sioux. Certain dream instructions given to young women in particular, the Double Woman's Appearance—hint at a kind of sanction for female perversion. . . . And yet there exists no record of old maids among the Sioux. Furthermore, there seem to be no examples of female inversion, and the role of women within the society appears to obviate the development of any meaningful causes."

Recent reexamination and explication of sex roles in contemporary Native American societies indicate an increase in overt actualization of homosexual roles. There is, in some instances, a shift in the feminine role to accommodate an emerging (or latent) lesbian orientation. The latency is seemingly more general in reservation communities than in urban areas. Acknowledgements of "gayness" have been indicated to me by Indian males and females, with males more predominant numerically. (I do not think that I am divulging secrets or breaches of trust but feel that such a statement is in order. I do not wish to give the impression of participant-observer.)

The dormant, or suppressed, sexual orientation in women is now (1977–79) being verbalized in reservation communities and may be due to the impact of mental health programs among some Lakota and on other reservations. It may also be a function of the heightened awareness of the plight of women in general. Such new manifestations of sexual inequality as shelters for battered women and the formation of the White Buffalo Calf Women's Society are factors for consideration in a changing society. Enactment of the new sex role is still not salient upon most reservations, however. There is evidence that the governmental agencies, as the mental health programs of the Indian Health Service, are beginning to deal with the emotional trauma of Native people, and there is the possibility that more cases involving lesbian tendencies may be forthcoming as the data are collected.

Again, the congealed interaction of small groups and the onus placed upon such individuals (males, historically, and now females) as the result of generations of an imposed ethical and moral system have apparently taken their toll on the participants in Native societies. Emphatically, the ritual roles of such tendencies, especially for the male actor, have been a part of the total religious repression, as with the Sun Dance among the Sioux. The wholesale denigration of Native belief systems in which individuals with this sexual inclination could manifest actualization has affected the attitudes of Indian persons in the present day. The learning of new cultural and sexual mores in the Christianization process also has relevance for attitudes regarding so-called perversion.

Psychologists in the Indian Health Service have mentioned lesbians among other Indian groups (Apache and Navajo, for example). These scattered inferences of Native lesbianism are reflected in the treatment modalities in the reservation health system. That is, the implication of "deviancy" is indicated, and mental health facilities are then utilized by the "deviant." This raises some interesting implications for the study of powerless people and administered human relations, and it also has significance for urban anonymity.

It is possible that overtness on the part of Native women homosexuals is more reflective of a change in the social climate in the larger, heterosexual white society. It is also significant that expression of lesbian sexual preference is more conspicuous in urban areas.

The lot of the Indian male homosexual in contemporary American Indian life has not been easy, just as it has been difficult for his white counterpart. Many Native American women in leadership positions have maintained that male homosexuality is a result of contact with Europeans and, mostly, have held such sexual "perverts" with disdain. In general, ridicule by fellow tribespersons has been the rule.

Moreover, male-male preference has been recognized and tolerated to various degrees in reservation communities. In some areas, particularly the Lakota-speaking areas, the aspect of *wakan* (power) has prevailed in some traditional communities. However, the orientation of most males to these persons has been one of intolerance. In addition, the male dominance and "macho-like" expressions of males in Indian militant and reform movements have placed these individuals—especially the males—in a triple bind. That is, there is not a sanctioned outlet in a changed and changing social milieu. The constraints of superimposed religious systems of the larger society have prevailed upon the ethical code of the reservation communities, and the marginal character of these individuals has fostered urban migration. To quote Randy: "I was like a lot of Indian people who came to the city. During the forties and fifties, the Bureau of Indian Affairs relocated many Indians to the cities. A lot of them were gay Indians who had 'lost' the respect of their tribes. They came to the cities and turned suicidal, alcoholic, and stereotypically cross-dressed" (Katz 1976:500–501).

This is not to say that the majority of migrants to urban areas fit this sexual designation. Nor is it possible at this time to say with certainty whether the urban atmosphere did allow the seeking of new sex roles. It is possible, however, to state with certainty that the urban milieu did offer greater avenues of accessibility to the homosexually oriented. This availability is highly valued by the participants. It is not possible to trace the transformation of individuals into this sexual role. The type of childhood experience (reservation, urban, or foster home), educational experience (parochial or federal boarding school or living at home), and early sexual experimentation (male and female prostitution) are all factors that are presently under investigation.

Of importance in the urbanization process is the formation of the San Francisco voluntary organization. GAI was formed in July 1975 to meet the needs of this displaced group, foster group interaction and solidarity, and provide a support system to meet the specialized needs of an ethnic group.

Equally interesting in the formation of this special interest group is that two persons—a Paiute male and a Lakota (Sioux) female—were instrumental in organizing the association. The male organizer is explicit in stating that he first became conscious of the institutionalized role of homosexuals in pre-contact societies by reading the gay press. Basic to organizing is a search for Indian pride and a mediation between tradition and change. They were also concerned with dispelling the "image of Indian as macho militant" (Katz 1976:502), which has been so prevalent in the Indian protest movements. Sexism is rampant in such movements as the American Indian Movement (AIM), where militant men often say they are fostering Indian unity by having girl friends in each tribe and by fathering as many children as possible. The intolerance toward homosexuals has been equally enormous. Starting with a nucleus of ten members, GAI now numbers about thirty members representing some twenty tribes in an organization that is predominantly male. The association certainly shows variety in role relationships that transcend tribe and race, for the interaction extends to occupiers of other roles in an urban context.

Observations of the members of the group at Bay Area powwows and political meetings indicated that they were often ridiculed and taunted when they appeared at such functions. Certainly, the group has been involved in protests in the Bay Area, has attempted to educate Indians and others about their status and needs, and has presented radio shows in the greater metropolitan area.

At the present time (1979), the GAI group needs reassessment. Of significance in the arena of role relationships is the fact that individuals of Native ancestry who have homosexual proclivities appear to be gravitating to urban centers, especially San Francisco, for actualization and appreciation of their sexual orientations. Individuals, mostly male, from South Dakota (Sioux), Michigan (Ojibway), Washington State (Flathead), and Idaho (Nez Percé) have sought an urban life-style in contrast to the sexual repression they often find on the reservations. Significantly, face-to-face relationships in small communities are forfeited to urban masses and role-relationship differentiation.

Again, the "macho-like" attitudes of most Native Americans in the home communities are articulated toward these urban migrants when some males state, "Yes, you can 'come out of the closet' when you are in San Francisco, but you have to 'go back in' when you come home."

The entire ramifications of homosexuality among Native American males and females in contemporary life on reservations and in urban settings have not been researched thoroughly. This essay has attempted to call attention to its dimensions as the problem is perceived by role participants and chart the social parameters.

Notes

1. *Editor's note [from the original publication]*: What follows is Medicine's now-classic 1979 essay. As noted in the Introduction and in her remarks, the essay has been circulated in the Gay American Indian underground since it was first given, in much the same way that Jacobs's 1968 "berdache" paper was circulated in gay underground channels.

2. *Editor's note [from the original publication]*: The tribal name is also spelled Kootenai, Kotanae, and Kootenay. See Nisbet (1994:134–38) for a brief account of Qánqon, a Kootenai female "berdache."

References

Allen, Paula Gunn. 1986. *The Sacred Hoop: Recovering the Feminine in American Indian Traditions.* Boston: Beacon Press.

Hassrick, Royal B. 1964. *The Sioux: Life and Customs of a Warrior Society.* Norman: University of Oklahoma Press.

Hill, W. W. 1935. "The Status of the Hermaphrodite and Transvestite in Navaho Culture." *American Anthropologist* 37(2) pt.1: 273–79.

Hirabayashi, James, and Luis Kemnitzer, eds. 1976. "Urban Indian Research Project." Unpublished ms. San Francisco State University.

Hoebel, E. Adamson. 1960. *The Cheyennes: Indians of the Great Plains.* New York: Holt, Rinehart and Winston.

Jacobs, Sue-Ellen. 1968. "Berdache: A Brief Review of the Literature." *Colorado Anthropologist* 1(2): 25–40. In Wayne R. Dynes and Stephen Donaldson, eds. 1992. *Studies in Homosexuality,* vol. 2: *Ethnographic Studies of Homosexuality.* New York: Garland.

Jones, William. 1907. *Fox Tests.* Publications of the American Ethnological Society, vol. 1. Leiden: E. J. Brill.

Katz, Jonathan. 1976. *Gay American History.* New York: Thomas Y. Crowell.

Lowie, Robert H. 1909. "The Assiniboine." *Anthropological Papers of the Museum of Natural History* 4: 42. New York: American Museum of Natural History.

Medicine, Beatrice. 1973. "The Native Americans." In *Outsiders, USA,* ed. Don Spiegel and Patricia Keith-Spiegel, 392–407. San Francisco: Rinehart Press.

———. 1983. "'Warrior Women': Sex Role Alternatives for Plains Indian Women." In *The Hidden Half: Studies of Plains Indian Women,* ed. Patricia Albers and Beatrice Medicine, 267–80. Washington: University Press of America.

———. 1987. "New Perspectives on the Siouan Term *Winkte.*" Paper presented at the New Gender Scholarship Conference, University of Southern California.

———. 1993. Field notes in possession of the author.

Nisbet, Jack. 1994. *Sources of the River: Tracking David Thompson across Western North America.* Seattle: Sasquatch Books.

Officer, James E. 1971. "The American Indian and Federal Policy." In *The American Indian in Urban Society,* ed. Jack O. Waddell and O. Michael Watson, 9–65. Boston: Little, Brown.

Price, John A. 1968. "The Migration and Adaptation of American Indians to Los Angeles." *Human Organization* 27(2): 168–75.

Schaeffer, Claude E. 1965. "The Kutenai Female Berdache: Courier, Guide, Prophetess and Warrior." *Ethnohistory* 12(3): 195–216.

Southall, Aidan. 1973. "The Density of Role Relationships as a Universal Index of Urbanization." In *Urban Anthropology,* Aidan Southall, 71–106. New York: Oxford University Press.

CHAPTER 12

"Warrior Women": Sex Role Alternatives for Plains Indian Women

In much of the ethnohistorical and ethnographic literature on Plains Indians, females are characterized as docile human beings and drudges. Such characterizations serve as a counterpoint to the commonly described male attributes of aggressiveness and bravery. But when one moves beyond the idealized generalizations and examines actual descriptions of individuals and their activities, it becomes apparent that there was considerable variation in the roles of women and men.

One role, which apparently was widespread in North America, is the "warrior woman." Besides references (Denig 1961; Landes 1968; Lewis 1941; McAllester 1941; Seward 1946) to the appearance of this role among Plains Indians, it has been reported in such widely separated societies as the Kutenai (Schaeffer 1964), the Navajo (Topper 1971), Tlingit (Knapp and Childe 1896), and the Ottawa (Thomas Duggan's Journal 1793).[1] The existence of the warrior woman role not only challenges pervasive ideas about the passivity of Native women but also offers an excellent case of example for examining female role variations in American Indian communities.

The purpose of this essay is to describe and analyze the behavior of Plains Indian warrior women not as deviant and idiosyncratic but as healthy and self-actualized. More specifically, it argues that the warrior role for women was institutionalized in Plains Indian communities and that it was one of several culturally accepted positions that accorded women power and prestige in areas typically identified as "masculine."

Background

The subject of sex role reversal has been popular in the literature on Plains Indians. Most discussions of this subject, however, center around the role of the male "berdache" (Jacobs 1968). While female role reversals have been described in several sources (Lewis 1941; McAllester 1941; Seward 1946; Denig 1961; Schaeffer 1964), there has been a disproportionate emphasis on the berdache.

The usual explanation for the institutionalization of the berdache, and the one originally enumerated by Ruth Benedict (1934), is that certain men were unable to meet the demands of masculinity and aggressiveness in the warrior role. From this, it is also assumed that the berdache—donning the attire of women, imitating their voices, acquiring their mannerisms, and following their domestic occupations—provided a necessary outlet for men who did not fit into the typical male role (Hassrick 1964). And finally, it is commonly asserted that rejecters of the masculine warrior role were individuals with unproductive vision quests.

Although it is true that berdache took on behaviors and activities associated with women in Plains Indian societies, their role did not exactly correspond with that of women. Among the Lakota, for example, *winkte* ("wishes to be woman," i.e. womanlike) continued to engage in masculine activities. They often accompanied war parties, and they could support themselves through hunting. In addition, they carried on certain activities that were viewed as normative in their role, including the naming of children in a ritual way, dispensing herbal medicines, and prognosticating the success of war parties. In these and other activities, berdache received a measure of respect and prestige in their community. And even though their social position was not enviable, it was better than that of a man who was a repeated failure as a warrior.

Sue-Ellen Jacobs (1968) has suggested that the warrior woman may have been the female counterpart to the pervasive and widely reported berdache. Insofar as many warrior women combined achievements in masculine occupations with traditional female roles, there was a parallel. There was also a similarity in the sanctioning of sex role reversals through supernatural means. Among the Lakota, women changed gender identities through recurrent dreams, whereas men sanctioned their sex role reversals through vision quests. Yet in both cases, supernatural visitations were interpreted by religious practitioners and accepted by kin and community. Thus, through institutionalized dreams or visions both sexes could assume other roles without seriously damaging their social acceptance and self-esteem. The parallels, however, stop at the level of description. When it comes to customary explanations of sex role reversals, the one commonly applied to the berdache does not appear applicable to the case of warrior women. It seems unlikely that women could not meet the demands required of females in most Plains Indian societies. But then the whole idea that sex role reversals, for either women or men, constituted deviant forms of escapism from "normal" behavior is open to question.

Instead of looking at sex role reversals as a form of "deviance" derived from "incompetence" in the roles associated with a person's gender, it might be more productive to examine them as normative statuses that permitted individuals to strive for self-actualization, excellence, and social recognition in areas outside their customary sex role assignments. In this light, changing sex role identity becomes an achieved act that individuals pursue as a means for the healthy expression of alternative behaviors.

Female Role Variability

In the nineteenth century, major changes were taking place in the social status of Plains Indian women. As Oscar Lewis (1942) so carefully demonstrated with the Blackfoot, the involvement of Plains Indians in the Euro-American hide market brought about major changes in the situations of women. Among these changes was the growing economic dependence of women. Increasingly, female labor was engaged in the processing of hides, a commodity whose acquisition and trade were largely in the hands of men. The economic dependency of women had important consequences on their social rankings within their families and in their communities at large. Generally, their status declined, and they became more vulnerable to the interests and machinations of men.

Although Plains Indian women had become more dependent and vulnerable, there were many different avenues through which they could act in independent and decisive ways. These included socially sanctioned role alternatives and participation in certain female sodalities as well as many different options of a situational nature.

The most detailed and complete discussions of female role alternatives appear in the literature on the Piegan of Alberta and Montana. Among the Piegan, there was a small group of women, called "manly-hearted women," whose ambition, boldness, and eroticism contrasted with the prevailing ideal of female submission and reserve (Lewis 1941). Although the Piegan, along with other Plains groups, put a premium on male dominance, they accorded these women exceptional privileges and prestige in areas typically associated with men. Manly-hearted women excelled in every important aspect of tribal life: property ownership, ceremonialism, and domestic affairs.

As children, manly-hearted women were often favored with more food, toys, care, and attention than other siblings. Such favoritism, which, incidentally, was widely distributed among northern Plains groups, must have had a profound impact on a child's sense of self-assurance and independence. Indeed, favorite female children among the top Piegan often led in childhood games, played boys' sports, and took for themselves the names of great warriors. Moreover, some indulged in sex play early in life.

As adults, the self-esteem and drive of favored females led to superiority in men's as well as women's work. These women attained wealth by taking on the economic roles typically played by men, and as a consequence they attained a level of self-sufficiency that permitted them independence in other realms as well. They selected dance partners; they also cursed when the occasion demanded it. Some dominated their husbands and exposed them to ridicule (Lewis 1941:181). Yet in spite of that, their position in their households was secure. According to Lewis (181), this security was related to their passionate and unconventional sexuality. They allowed their husbands sex play that other women refused, and they expressed their dominance in assuming the male position in intercourse. Such privilege is especially remarkable in view of the prevailing ideology of male dominance, which included wife beating and disfigurement for infidelity. The predominant picture of the manly-hearted women certainly presents an anomaly in the customary view of Plains Indian women as submissive and oppressed.

When the manly-hearted female role is examined in the light of other socially sanctioned status positions for women, it becomes apparent that it is not a "deviation" but one of several alternative female roles. These optional positions can be studied by examining four different Native role categories among the Canadian Blackfoot. These are: (1) *ninawaki* (manly woman); (2) *matsaps* (crazy woman); (3) Sun Dance woman; and (4) *ninaki* (chief woman or favorite wife).[2] (For an interesting diagrammatic representation of these categories, see Seward 1946:120.)

The ninawaki corresponds to the manly-hearted woman of the Piegan. This category identifies a woman in whom aggression was developed to the point where she behaved like a man. (For another interesting discussion of masculine striving among Kaska women, see Honigmann 1944:4–163.) Some of these women, although not all of them, engaged in warrior pursuits.

"Ninaki" refers to an able and respected female who is capable of doing a job as a chief. This term, however, has a second meaning: "the favorite wife of a man." John Ewers (1948:100) refers to this favorite wife as a "sits-beside-me-wife." According to Ewers, this woman had the responsibility of carrying the ceremonial equipment of the man (93). She also shared responsibilities with the man in caring for the sacred bundles and in conducting certain ceremonies. She may have been a sexually favored wife. Usually, this woman was exempt from household work, and only a wealthy man could have afforded such as person in his household. It must also be noted that these women appear to have been trained for this role as children, and like the manly-hearted women they received the kinds of special privileges accorded to a favorite child.

"Matsaps" designates a "crazy woman" but with special references to sexual promiscuity. Among the Lakota, a correlate female figure is *witkowin*. Sexual promiscuity exhibited by a witkowin was sanctioned through certain types of dreams. Dreaming of the *Anog-Ite* (Double Face Woman) or dreaming incessantly of the *Wakinya* (Thunder Beings) released a Lakota woman from her commitments to the cultural ideals of virginity or marital fidelity (Wissler

1912:93). Oral history material suggests that there were incidences where women who had witkowin-like dreams were given away by their husbands. That occurred not in the manner of "throwing away the wife," which typified divorce. Instead, the husband, recognizing the affection of his wife for another, dressed her in her finery, painted her face and the part of her hair, and led her on a fine horse to the man she esteemed.

The Sun Dance woman represented in Piegan society, and among the Lakota society as well, the extreme of womanly virtue. Before marriage she was a virgin. She was never unfaithful to her husband, nor did she remarry after his death. These women were rewarded by assuming an honorary position in the Sun Dance. Among the Lakota, there was also the prestigious Bite the Knife Ceremony in which postmenopausal women were honored for their virtuousness.

The female role categories of the Canadian Blackfoot, which also have correlates among other Plains groups, indicate that there was a range of special statuses for women. Although two positions, that of the favorite wife and Sun Dance woman, epitomize the idealized features of femininity, they were no less important and accepted than those that linked women to manly pursuits. These varied role categories also suggest that the idealized behavior of women was not as rigidly defined and followed as has been supposed.

Besides the evidence of female role variability provided by the categorical statuses just mentioned, there is also the well-known diversity of behavior associated with a woman's birth order. Among the Dakota, for instance, birth order positions had a powerful impact upon how children were raised and what behaviors were expected of them. Such differential treatment must have had a major influence on later adult behavior. There was also variations in treatment and expected roles of wives from the first- to the last-married, and there were differences in how women behaved in their various kinship statuses (i.e., older sister, younger sister, daughter, mother). Unfortunately, the varied social positions of women in Plains Indian societies have not been well documented, and as a consequence it is difficult, if not impossible, to make conclusive statements about the dynamics of psychological and behavioral variations among women that correspond with recognized role diversity.

Women and Warfare

The fact that there were a range of socially accepted roles for women in Plains Indian societies permits us to understand the role of warrior women as one aspect of this variation.

The most detailed account of a warrior woman comes from the writings of a well-known trader on the Upper Missouri, Edwin Denig (1961:194–200). The woman was a Gros Ventres who was captured by the Crow when she was twelve years old. She already exhibited manly interests, and her adoptive father encouraged these inclinations and trained her in a wide variety of male occupational skills. Although she dressed as a woman throughout her life, she pursued the role of a male in her adult years. She was a proficient hunter and chased big game on horseback and on foot (Denig 1961:196). She was a skilled warrior, leading many successful war parties. In time, she sat on the council and ranked as the third-leading warrior in a band of 160 lodges (198). After achieving success in manly pursuits, she took four wives, whose hide-processing work brought considerable wealth to her lodge (198–99). Although this woman's manly-oriented life may have been exceptional, it was socially recognized and esteemed among the people with whom she lived.

Other reports of female warriors are not as complete, and most do not distinguish between women who pursued warfare as a life occupation and those who joined war parties on a situational basis. Among the Blackfeet, there appear to have been women who pursued warfare as an extension of their manly inclinations (Lewis 1941; McAllester 1941). There were also women, usually childless, who accompanied their spouses on raiding expeditions and who may (or may not) have been actively involved in fighting (Ewers 1967:329). And finally, there were women who took on the role of warrior only for a short time and for a specific reason (e.g., to avenge the death of a relative [Lewis 1941]).

Cheyenne women, according to George Grinnell (1946:147), also engaged in warfare. Although many appear to have accompanied war parties as "helpers," some fought in battle, raided for horses, and counted coup on the enemy. The participation of women in warfare, however, appears to have been less common in the late nineteenth century than it was in earlier times.

There were also women warriors among the Dakota. Ruth Landes (1968:39) indicates that although women were tacitly barred from joining war parties, many did participate in war for glory as well as revenge, and some even led war expeditions (49). Women who had achieved war honors played an important role in the *winoxtca*, the female equivalent of male *akicita* (soldiers). These women were called upon to police other women in the campsite and to punish female offenders (69). It is noteworthy that although the female warrior role was apparently common among the Eastern Dakota (i.e., Mdewakanton, Sisseton, and Wahpeton), it has not been reported for the Western Dakota (Teton).

These are a few examples of women's reported participation in Plains warfare and raiding. The motivation for women to engage in war can only be conjectured. First, there was the prestige and glory that accrued to counting coups, obtaining guns, killing and scalping, and cutting tethered horses from within a tipi circle. Women who were capable in these activities could achieve prestige and wealth independently, as the case of the Crow female warrior indicates. Second, there was the need for women to be assertive and able to fight for reasons of self-defense. In a period of history when Plains Indian populations were engaged in bitter and unceasing rivalries with neighboring people, it was imperative that women be prepared to fight and assert themselves, not only at times when they were alone but also when men were present in camp. And, finally, women were also motivated by revenge and engaged in warfare to avenge a relative's death. It is important to recognize that reasons for female engagement in warfare—defense, glory, and revenge—were not different from those that inspired men to fight.

Even when women did not participate in warfare directly, they played a very important role in supporting the military activity of men. Robert Lowie (1934:106) mentions the importance of women's auxiliaries in the military societies of the Crow, and George Grinnell (1946:10–12, 20–22) discusses the importance of women in the scalp ceremonies and social dances that followed the warriors' return. Besides their participation in formal institutions, women supported military ventures in other ways. Among the Dakota, for instance, women expected their husbands to avenge a brother's death. They also pressured husbands to acquire horses to increase the wealth of their lodges, and they encouraged husbands to obtain co-wives (including women captured in war) to assist in the processing of hides and other domestic duties.

Whether Plains Indian women participated in military activity directly or supported it in an indirect way, it is clear that they saw their own well-being, and that of their kin and community, in terms of a social system that revolved around warfare. In this system, prestige and wealth centered around success in the warrior role. The typical status configurations of women mirrored this orientation. As a female grew, her status was typically reflected in the warrior position of her father, then of her brother, husband, and sons. But it could also be reflected in her own warrior status, which, if successful, was achieved and pursued along masculine lines.

The idea that some Plains Indian women followed masculine roles and behaviors, either on a permanent or situational basis, does not deny the idealized and normative patterns of female passivity and dependence in Plains Indian societies. But even though the general ethnographic picture paints Plains Indian women in a dependent role, it is clear that they had other options that included assertiveness and independence. In social settings where maleness and femaleness were separate and contrasting spheres, as they certainly were in Plains Indian societies, the roles of manly-hearted women and berdache were sources of mediation. They offered men and women opportunities for displaying cross-sex talents in socially approved ways, and in doing so they were probably essential to the psychological well-being of people who lived in societies that had highly dichotomized gender expectations.

What is clear from the information presented here is that Plains women and men were able to assume a range of roles that were either consistent with or contrary to their customary gender ascriptions. Unfortunately, such notions as "warrior society," "male dominant," and other male supremacist expressions have set the tone for the analysis of male and female behavior in Plains Indian societies. Consequently, the rich complexity of female gender roles and the variety of relations between women and men have been largely obscured.

In this regard, the shared beliefs and strategies for obtaining status is well-documented for Plains Indian men. Comparatively little information, however, is available on how women pursued alternative roles, how they achieved self-actualization in a male-oriented social system, and how they managed conflicts between personal strivings and societal norms. But it is precisely because many ethnographers of Plains Indian communities assumed, a priori, the existence of a modal and rigid personality profile for females that such questions were not asked. While a new generation of scholars has begun to pursue questions such as these, their answers may never be complete or conclusive. Regrettably, the kinds of data that might illuminate and clarify the nature of female role reversals in Plains Indian societies have not been recorded. At least for the pre-reservation period, it is now too late to uncover such material with any degree of depth. In the end, all that remains on this fascinating subject are cursory references, which, although suggestive, are not sufficient to fully reconstruct the nature and dynamics of role variability among Plains Indian women.

Notes

A different version of this essay was originally presented at the International Congress of Americanists (Rome, Italy, 1972). It was a preliminary statement to call attention to the problem of women's status in the male-dominant societies of the Northern Plains. It emphasized the need to reexamine ethnographic data to provide new insights into this issue and to chart courses for future research involving Native American women. I wish to thank Patricia Albers and William James for their considerable assistance in drafting this essay.

1. Martin Topper records a historical case of a Navajo woman avenging her son's death and leading a Navajo war party on a successful raid against the Hopi. Topper's informants were Percy John and Donald Dejolie (field notes, 1971). The reference for the Tlingit is as follows: "It was usual for an old woman of rank to sit in the stern of the canoe and steer, for even in some battles, women were leaders in battles" (Knapp and Child 1896:64). Christian Feest, Museum fur Volkerkund, Vienna, sent the following reference in 1972: "November 14. An Ottawa sent by Egushewa de Bout Call'd on me in his way to inform me he was sent to acquaint the Ottawas that one of the prisoners a Frenchman taken by the little Otter's part had shot the Indian who owned him, whilst asleep and Tomahawked the Indian wife, Tis a considerable loss to this nation as both the man and woman were leaders of Parties in war, and I greatly fear that all the other prisoners will be sacrificed to avenge this murder" (Thomas Duggan's Journal 108).

2. L. M. Hanks, Jr. (personal communication) confirms that the Blackfoot term for manly woman, *ninawaki*, differs from Lewis's term for manly-heart: *ninauposkitzipzpe*. These terms need further clarification in use and transcription.

References

Benedict, Ruth. 1934. "Anthropology and the Abnormal." *Journal of General Psychology* 10(1): 49–82.
Denig, Edwin Thompson. 1961. *Five Indian Tribes of the Upper Missouri*, ed. John Ewers. Norman: University of Oklahoma Press.

Ewers, John C. 1948. *The Blackfeet, Raiders of the Northern Plains.* Norman: University of Oklahoma Press.

————. 1967. "Blackfoot Raiding for Horses and Scalps." In *Law and Warfare,* ed. Paul Bohannan, 324–44. Garden City: Natural History Press.

Grinnell, G. B. 1946. *The Fighting Cheyennes.* Norman: University of Oklahoma Press.

Hassrick, Royal B. 1964. *The Sioux: Life and Customs of a Warrior Society.* Norman: University of Oklahoma Press.

Honigmann, J. J. 1944. "The Kaska Indians: An Ethnographic Reconstruction." *Yale University Publications in Anthropology* 51: 4–163.

Jacobs, Sue-Ellen. 1968. "Berdache: A Brief Review of the Literature." *Colorado Anthropologist* 1(2): 24–40.

Knapp, Frances, and Rheta Louise Child. 1896. *The Thlinkets of Southeastern Alaska.* Chicago: Stone and Kimball.

Landes, Ruth. 1968. *The Mystic Lake Sioux: Sociology of the Mdewakantonwan Santee.* Madison: University of Wisconsin Press.

Lewis, Oscar. 1941. "Manly-Hearted Women among the South Piegan." *American Anthropologist* 43(2) pt.1: 173–87.

————. 1942. "The Effects of White Contact upon Blackfoot Culture." *Monographs of the American Ethnological Society* no. 6, n.p.

Lowie, R. H. 1934. *The Crow Indians.* New York: Holt, Rinehart and Winston.

McAllester, D. 1941. "Water as a Disciplinary Agent among the Crow and Blackfoot." *American Anthropologist* 43(4) pt.1: 493–604.

Schaeffer, Claude E. 1964. "The Kutenai Female Berdache: Courier, Guide, Prophetess, and Warrior." *Ethnohistory* 12(3): 193–236.

Seward, G. H. 1946. *Sex and the Social Order.* New York: Macmillan.

Thomas Duggan's Journal. 1793. In "Copies of Papers on File in the Dominion Archives at Ottawa." 1887. *Michigan Pioneer and Historical Collections.* 12: 104–9.

Topper, Martin. 1971. Field notes.

Wissler, Clark. 1912. "Societies and Ceremonial Associations in the Oglala Division of the Teton Dakota." [American Museum of Natural History] *Anthropological Papers* 11: n.p.

CHAPTER 13

Indian Women: Tribal Identity as Status Quo

[Editor's note from the original publication]: Individuals are often perceived as having a special nature by virtue of membership in a particular group, defined biologically through sex, race, or tribe. This has been used as a source of strength by members of oppressed groups and also as an excuse for oppression by outsiders. Slogans such as "black is beautiful," ideas of women's special gifts, and ideas of "nativeness" have all been used as sources of pride and ways of achieving group cohesion in the face of external threats. Such ideas are difficult for group members to accept, however, involving as they do significant deviations from the values promoted by the dominant culture.

* * *

> No one had any doubt that the Indians were completely human—
> the Indian girls soon proved that; and if they were human, then to
> the theological mind, there was no real problem with their origin.
> Said Roger Williams: "From Adam and Noah that they spring, it is
> granted on all hands."
> —Blakeless 1961:22

No matter from what vantage point, the Native perception of American Indian women is biologically based. Traditionally, most Native societies assigned social roles that valued women for their biological as well as their economic production. Both guaranteed the survival of the group. That the social roles of Indian women were extremely varied and differentially enacted in indigenous tribal groups need not be amplified here. But it seems essential to reiterate that many traditional views of Indian women are still strongly ingrained in the socialization of both sexes in all tribes. The essence of "Nativeness" as such permeates much of the dyadic interchange between the sexes. It is important, therefore, to understand indigenous images of women. The interplay of images, perceptions, beliefs, and resultant actions on the part of both genders is a significant feature for the comprehension of Indian women's roles in contemporary society.

This chapter examines the interaction of sex roles, indigenous viewpoints, and superimposed directives that impinge upon an American Indian or an Alaskan Native female in present-day society.

The identity of a person of Indian descent is tied to tribalness—that is, to a social grouping based upon biological relationships. Thus, the very nature of a Native female is biologically defined by virtue of enrollment in her tribe, her blood quantum, and recognition by her natal community. Increasingly, tribal enrollment is not only prerequisite but also the recognition that her tribe is labeled as federally recognized. Other persons of Indian ancestry are members of non-federally recognized entities. There are some cases where tribal enrollment has been closed, but recognition is given by issuing cards. Thus, membership in the tribe, based upon Indian heritage, is validated by "card-carrying" individuals.

Rather than enter into the anthropological debate about the term *tribe*, I prefer to use the definition that is generally elicited when Indian people are themselves concerned with the term. To most, "tribe" defines a cohesive social group based upon language, culture, and a geographic place of origin. In general, a specific "life-way" is indicated by such terms as *the Indian way* or the specific tribe's life-style—for example, "Navajo way" or "Lakota [Sioux] way." Many Native individuals use "the Indian way" to cover multicultural congeries of Indian groups, thus posing a dilemma of definition.

For most American Indians and Alaska Natives, belonging to a Native group is important. Implicit in belonging is the aspect of acceptance and acknowledgment of some sort that one is a member of a corporate group. To most Indians, the tribe represents an identity symbol—a reservoir of a distinct way of life and a source of power, wisdom, and vision. As a construct, however, "tribe" can be either a source of constraints or of strengths in offering various alternative ways of living. Essentially, the tribe presents a biological imperative that is a subtle but forceful mechanism of control, for basic to the role of women is the production of children, which allows the tribe to continue. This mandate must be understood in the ethno-genocidal context to which Indians of all tribes have been subjected. Many tribes (for example, the Lakota Sioux) still do not acknowledge womanhood until a child is produced in an acknowledged union. Among certain Pueblo groups (Santa Domingo, for example), a child born to a woman indicates her fertility and so enhances her value as a potential mate.

Cultural dimensions, therefore, are important in these definitions and expectations. This raises issues such as the effect of biculturalism, which is often posed as the rationale for American Indian leadership modes. All these concepts of leadership need reexamination with a view to the ideological underpinnings of the group in question. The fact that "leadership" as a domain has different philosophical bases in Native as opposed to dominant society is important to an understanding of Indian women's roles in contemporary societies.

External forces and imposed policies have, and will continue to have, far-reaching consequences upon Indian women. The congressional hearings held throughout the nation to decide "who is an Indian" speak to the question of identity, which often has been decided outside the indigenous power structures. At this time, decisions are mainly biologically based but have some social determinants. These are both external and indigenous. Tribal council decisions in determining enrollment in tribes are important components in the structure of the ideology of urban and reservation Indian populations. Essentially, enrollment committees decide who is eligible for inclusion. Much of the decision-making rests upon who is in power at the time, and kinship networks are often deciding factors. Some external decisions may be a part of super-structural definitions that state, for example, that only Natives with a quarter degree of Indian blood will be allowed to attend Bureau of Indian Affairs schools. Standards for amounts of "Indian blood" that allow persons of Indian ancestry access to special educational benefits, such as Title IV programs, are other considerations. Increasingly, ethnicity is a salient concern for both reservation and urban Indian populations. By any standards—indigenous or imposed—the image of Native women presents options and constraints, and this is built into self-image and self-actualization patterns for these females.

One must examine the tangle of sex roles, Native views, interracial and intertribal marriages, and superimposed directives that impinge upon Native people in contemporary society, whether the tribal or the dominant one. Indian females are found in all segments of society—white and Native, reservation and urban. Place of residence is a limiting factor in choosing alternatives. Many urban Indian women feel that they must return to their reservations to birth their children. Indeed, some tribal councils often will not enroll babies who are born off the reservation. Many women feel that their children must be sent back to Native communities for part of their socialization. According to some, these actions posit tribal identity.

Therefore, it is difficult and dangerous to generalize about a single ideology for indigenous women due to tribal distinctions and differences. One must specify tribal group and tribal values in order to understand accurately the belief systems and values that give directives. Such factors as social change and degrees of adaptation to the dominant society are important variables and must be taken into account to understand Native women. Perhaps the prevailing ideological base that pertains to all tribal women is the adaptation mode to another, more dominant, society. Some ideological frames are clearly articulated in the present groups. Others are unclear and murky.

The remainder of this chapter will concentrate upon one body of doctrine—

Laura Takes the
Gun and Medicine,
Little Eagle, 1993.
(Courtesy of Todd
Epp for the Sioux
Falls *Argus Leader*)

that of the Teton Lakota (commonly referred to as "Sioux"). This society has also been referred to as a "warrior society," as "male dominant," and as *bloka* in the Sioux language, which can be equated to the Spanish "macho" or to "male dominance" in English.

According to oral tradition, the White Buffalo Calf Woman brought seven sacred rites to the Teton Lakota (see also Black Elk 1967). The significant feature of the visit of the culture heroine is the Sacred Pipe. Essentially, this mythic occurrence is constantly invoked by most Lakota people—male and female—as indicating the high esteem in which women are held in the culture. There have been many interpretations of this mythological character. Hassrick succinctly gives the following analysis as validating the subjugation of women and as justification for a double standard:

> The Oedipean nature of the White Buffalo Maiden legend may owe part of its origin to the masculine character of the society. The role of the two scouts, one representing greed and lust and the other respect and temperance, typifies the dual nature of the Sioux character. The White Buffalo Maiden symbolized not only the mother but more significantly, the sister, and she characterized herself as such. In her was embodied the female kin toward whom males must sublimate the sex drive under penalty of death. Conversely, she became the protector of women against the lust of men. That the sex act carried such strong taboo dramatizes the conflict under which the Sioux male existed and suggests the origin for the double standard. The need for symbolizing such restrictive association for a related female seems to have found compensation in the attitude that unrelated females were the natural target for male seduction. Such women were fair game. The lustful hunter was destroyed not so much for his uncontrollable lust as for his breach of a taboo and his commission of a sacrilege.

That the Sioux chose for their tutelary deity a woman, rather than a man, indicates their concern to revere feminine qualities. That the Buffalo Maiden was, in fact, the Goddess Whope, wife of Okaga, the South Wind, enforced the proposition that the Sioux savior was completely and wholesomely feminine. She firmly established a rigid yet healthy realistic sexual pattern to which both its men and women could subscribe, and which they could respect. (Hassrick 1964:222–23)

I quote this in full, for seldom in the ethnographic record is such an explicitly masculine interpretation of a mythological narrative found. This interpretation seems to give ideological justification for strong control over women. I note, however, another variation of the myth of the White Buffalo Maiden from a Native Lakota male religious practitioner (from the *yuwipi* cult). Lame Deer indicates: "The White Buffalo Woman then addressed the women, telling them that it was the work of their hands and the fruit of their wombs which kept the tribe alive. 'You are from mother earth,' she told them. 'The task which has been given you is as great as the one given to the warrior and hunter.' And therefore, the sacred pipe is also something which binds men and women in a circle of love" (Fire and Erdoes 1972:253–54).

In a more recent statement, a practicing religious leader, Stanley Looking Horse, further notes: "It is told that the red bowl of the pipe shall represent the feminine aspect while the tube handle of the pipe shall represent the male aspect. Thus, inclusion of everyone is intended, and if we honor this commitment, then our people will be able to see a great generation" (Medicine 1979b).

Through the use of Siouan symbolic structure, the sexual, social, and economic expectations of female behavior are clearly articulated. The cultural mandates from symbolic and mythic structures did actually reflect duality and complementarity in economic and social roles. The survival and continuity of the group depended upon this functional relationship. This was enacted and validated in such ceremonies as the Sun Dance.

Native evaluations of Lakota womanhood are significant, however. The creative ability of the woman to produce children was seen by the Lakota as a powerful act. The Native term for pregnancy, *eglushaka,* translates into English as "growing strong." The *wakan* (sacredness, or power) of a female's menstrual period could weaken the wakan components of such male things as medicine bundles, war bundles, shields, and other paraphernalia, which belonged to the men in the *tipi* (dwelling). Thus, at the menarche, an emergent woman was placed in a small shelter outside the tipi. This act of isolation was called *ishna ti* (to live alone). It is still used metaphorically to refer to that "time of the moon." In her menstrual dwelling, she was visited by women who were postmenopausal. The isolation was an opportunity for learning excellence in crafts such as quilling and tanning hides. Other womanly knowledge involving sexuality and child care was also dispensed. At this time, according to the Lakota view, a woman embodied power and sacredness exactly as she did in a pregnant state. Some interpretations for the Yurok, however, surround such special times with an aura of pollution (Douglas 1966).

Further, virgin women embodying the sacred White Buffalo Calf Woman were selected to symbolically chop down the sacred Sun Dance pole in the annual Summer Ceremony. Older women, mostly postmenopausal, assumed the honorific role of the Sacred Pipe Woman.

At present, when difficulties arise in the Sun Dance they are often attributed to women who attend the event at the "time of the moon" without knowing the aspects of their power. Indeed, male religious practitioners often blame any untoward event that occurs at such a ritual upon the presence of menstruating women. These new attitudes are a sign of women's repression, no longer an acknowledgement of feminine power.

Such sacred symbols as the White Buffalo Calf Women often serve as a convenient sign that sexual equality is the normative aspect in contemporary Lakota life. The image of this cultural heroine is used as the epitome of Lakota womanhood. That can furthermore be manipulated into the general cultural values of generosity, fortitude, integrity, and wisdom. Ella Deloria, a Native anthropologist and linguist, writes of the Lakota:

> Outsiders seeing women keep to themselves have frequently expressed a snap judgment that they were regarded as inferior to the noble male. The simple fact is that woman had her place and man his; they were not the same and neither inferior nor superior.
>
> The sharing of work also was according to sex. Both had to work hard, for their life made severe demands. But neither expected the other to come and help outside the customary division of duties; each sex thought the other had enough to do. That did not mean, however, that a man disdained to do woman's work when necessary; or a woman, man's. The attitude on division of work was quite normal, however it looked to outsiders. A woman caring for children and doing all the work around the house thought herself no worse off than her husband who was compelled to risk his life continuously, hunting and remaining ever on guard against enemy attacks on his family. (Deloria 1944:39–40)

Native viewpoints and oral history accounts seem to corroborate Ella Deloria's contentions. With the destruction of the Native way of life and the restriction to reservations, disequilibrium was initiated and increased as new belief systems were instigated and forced upon this group of Indians as they were upon others. Leacock (1955) mentions the effects of Christianity upon an Algonkian group in Canada, indicating that a male superiority complex may have been part of an acculturation process. Certainly, the imposition of partilineality upon many American Indian groups resulted in the use of the father's surname. Hamamsy (1957) notes a change in the matrilineal Navajo social structure as a result of superimposed policies. Mary Shepardson's presentation of Irene Stewart's story adds much to a Native perspective of social change in one Navajo woman's life (Stewart 1980).

There is a drastic need to reexamine the cultural contours of ongoing belief systems in Native North American societies to juxtapose traditional and super-imposed ideology and sex role behaviors.

Although attitudes of male superiority are evident in the social organization structures of modern societies, bilaterality was characteristic of the Siouan society in the past. How the change toward patrilineal descent was impressed upon the Lakota and other Plains societies must be examined to assess its contribution to the observable increased masculine bias.

With the prohibition of the Sun Dance as a "heathen ritual" in the 1800s, a patriarchal male god who condoned punishment for sin did much to disrupt social and economic equity between the sexes. In the early reservation period, the pressure to assimilate all Indians persisted. The treatment of all Lakota males as enemies who were to be conquered demolished the male roles of warrior and hunter. Women's roles as household provisioner and caretaker and rearer of children continued. However, under pressure from change agents ("boss farmers" and "matrons" who taught new skills—farming for men and cooking new foods and sewing new fabrics for women) there was disorientation of economic roles, and attitudes toward each sex changed. A subtle subordination was imposed on Lakota women. Most did not wish to devalue the demoralized males in their extended families. As a survival mechanism, women became workers in the formal acculturating institutions, such as schools and churches. Some were recruited to go away to school to become teachers or at least matrons in boarding schools. The pressures to accommodate to another, new society were strong. In many cases, an occupational adaptation meant survival for self and kinship units. Much of this adaptation was self-selected with disdain for the Native culture. Some alternatives were chosen as means of rejecting the Native society and escaping to a new worldview and language. Some women simply rejected all aspects of the new society. In any case, coerced cultural change was standard.

There are several possible interpretations of this acculturation process. One is that females who were not "properly trained" in a Native cultural system aspired to leave. Another explanation might be that those supporting and committed to the traditional gender ideology remained secure in their kinship networks, economic niche, and natal community. Another segment of females may have compromised and developed a nexus of occupational involvements away from the Native group while maintaining a tribal affiliation in kinship bonds, rituals, and aesthetic arenas. Therefore, the ideology and identity tied to tribal-ness were enacted differently in personal realms.

Development of these patterns was possible within a changing social order. Clearly, the superimposed ideology of a dominant "American white" culture enforced changes from tribal traditions to a foreign culture. It may be accurately stated that contemporary Lakota Sioux sexism is embedded not only in the biological arena but also in some Native ideological structures that have been firmly buttressed by Christian ideology and legal patrilineal codes.

The newly reactivated ritualistic systems, such as the Sun Dance, *Wopila* (giving thanks and offerings), and *Yuwipi* ("tying up" the shaman) ceremonies, have acknowledged that the foundations for the Native belief systems were presented by the White Buffalo Calf Woman. But male orientation in the revitalized Native belief structure is strong (witness the Lakota Medicine *Men's* Association, which is headquartered at Rosebud Reservation, South Dakota). Lakota maidens are still selected to be the four virgins who chose and cut the sacred tree; a revered older woman is chosen as the Sacred Pipe Woman. Some women dance in the Sun Dance voluntarily. This is the extent of feminine involvement in this revitalized religious rite. Of course, food preparation and auxiliary features of the ceremony such as the give-away rely upon women's work. (A give-away is a ceremony for the distribution of food, clothing, and other goods in order to make ownership more equitable.) In more traditional areas, however, men still cook the beef. Women, moreover, often carry on the other rites, which are and have been a part of the Sun Dance ritual, such as the Wiping the Tears Ceremony, which is still performed at only one Sun Dance among the bands on Standing Rock Reservation. These secondary rituals, such as naming ceremonies, focus upon the underlying values of the culture: generosity, fortitude, and, ultimately, compassion. However, most male ritualists assume greater importance in these rituals, as do the males who are "pierced" in the Sun Dance. Women have offered bits of skin from their arms, but that is a recent innovation.

It is also important to examine the views and attitudes of Native men. Some Sioux males, for example, readily admit that they are chauvinistic and that they like this state of affairs. Others give lip service to the old traditions and the complementarity of the sexes. Some are decidedly pro-female and orient their daughters toward leadership roles, both in the indigenous and the dominant societal contexts. This may account for the fact that Standing Rock Reservation had two tribal chairwomen in the 1940s and 1950s. Only recently has there been another chairwoman in another reservation (Lower Brulé). The few Lakota males who consciously train their daughters for leadership roles are not in the ascendancy, however. This encouraging attitude was more characteristic of a previous generation. There is, nonetheless, a strong core of Lakota women who are in positions of influence, both on and off the reservations.

Why, then, do some women adhere to the ideology of male superiority as embodied in the concept of bloka? To some, it is a tradition that is needed to validate their "Indianness." To others, the commitment is essential inside the tribal community, while a more aggressive and assertive style is more in keeping with the interactions outside the Native community. To others, the ideology emphasizes sacrifice or the more commonly used phrase "helping my people." Whatever the perception, the process most often involves female subordination. Traditional socialization along gender lines also is an important consideration.

When one examines Native ideologies, one often finds that they are built upon divinely sanctioned controls. These Native charters are often utilized to revamp symbols and maintain the status quo.

Many recent statements from Indian males almost mirror the statements of males in the Black Power movement of the 1960s. Many of the adherents of the American Indian Movement (AIM) have indicated that their goal to promote "Indian unity" is "to have a girl in every tribe." Still other males adroitly manipulate the notion of "commitment" to Indian causes to involvements that ensure the birth of children. The production of children is also seen by males and some females as a means of combating the genocidal actions of the federal government, thus the tremendous outcry at the sterilization of American Indian women and at the difficulty of obtaining accurate information about its extent. Both Native American males and females are concerned about the ethnocidal and genocidal practices that have been the lot of American Indians.

There are other areas where contemporary Indian women are pressured to conform to the Native ideology. One concerns intermarriage with non-Indians. Indian men often resort to the powerful implication of lesbianism or frigidity in soliciting sexual favors from women. Besides decrying professional women as "women's libbers," many Native men attempt to control female activism by indicating that "we know what she needs" (sexual encounters of a Native sort, of course). Many Native women allow themselves to be manipulated in this way. Contemporary Indian sexuality has not been researched in an adequate fashion. Aspects of homosexuality—traditional patterns and also manifestations in the present—have only begun to be examined (Medicine 1979a).

That pressures to conform to "tribal norms," that is, to marry Native men, are strong is noticeable in the disproportionate numbers of professional women, now divorced, who were previously married to white men. Another observation indicates that some professional Native women have married Native men whom they met while teaching classes in prisons. The impact of intermarriage and miscegenation is also blurred at present but is an important consideration relating to "Indian identity."

Affirmative action also has a biological basis as far as Native women are concerned. This is especially true in the academic arena, where many tenure positions are occupied by individuals (males and females) who claim Indian ancestry. Thus, it might be best to end this chapter by stressing that the ideological bases for tribal women are varied and need to be delineated. Perhaps the most common themes running through tribal histories are cultural suppression and racism. To analyze how tribal women have coped with this in association with study of the male and female ethos and worldviews reflective of Native gender ideologies would add much to the comprehension of American Indian women of today. Analysis by insiders and outsiders with this caveat in mind would greatly strengthen knowledge about the dynamic character of women's roles.

References

Black Elk. 1967. *The Sacred Pipe: Black Elk's Account of the Seven Rites of the Oglala Sioux,* ed. Joseph Epes Brown. Norman: University of Oklahoma Press.

Blakeless, John. 1961. *The Eyes of Discovery: The Pagent of North America as Seen by the First Explorers.* New York: Dover Publications.

Deloria, Ella. 1944. *Speaking of Indians.* New York: Friendship Press, 1944.

Douglas, Mary. 1966. *Purity and Danger: An Analysis of Concepts of Pollution.* Baltimore: Penguin Books.

Fire, John/Lame Deer, and Richard Erdoes. 1972. *Lame Deer: Seeker of Visions.* New York: Simon and Schuster.

Hassrick, Royal B. 1964. *The Sioux: Life and Customs of a Warrior Society.* Norman: University of Oklahoma Press.

Hamamsy, Laila Shukry. 1957. "The Role of Women in a Changing Navajo Society." *American Anthropologist* 59: 101–11.

Leacock, Eleanor. 1955. "Matrifocality in a Simple Hunting Society (Montagnais-Naskapi)." *Southwestern Journal of Anthropology* 11: 31–47.

Medicine, Beatrice. 1979a. "Changing Sex Roles in an Urban Context: Native Americans." Presented to the Central States Anthropological Society, Milwaukee.

———. 1979b. Unpublished field notes.

Stewart, Irene. 1980. *A Voice in Her Tribe: A Navajo Woman's Own Story,* ed. Doris Ostrander Dawdy; foreword by Mary Shepardson. Socorro, N.M.: Ballena Press.

CHAPTER 14

The Role of American Indian Women in Cultural Continuity and Transition

American Indian and Alaskan Native women are perhaps the most neglected and grossly treated in the literature of minority women. This is true especially in research on speech forms and patterns of language usage in American Indian and Alaskan Native communities. Research on the language patterns of women in these communities suffers from the mistaken notion that such an entity as "the monolithic American Indian" exists. To speak of speech patterns typical of "the American Indian" and to make generalizations across tremendously complex and varied linguistic differences is obviously dangerous. There are an estimated 206 distinct languages being spoken by the Natives of North America that reflect totally distinct language stocks, many of them being as dissimilar as English and Chinese (Chafe 1962). Such multiplicity of languages makes it extremely difficult to speak of the linguistic aspects of "the American Indian woman."

It is important to point out, however, that although there is great variation in American Indian languages, traditions, and customs, there is a common experience that these communities share historically as a result of language policies and practices imposed by the various political institutions and education systems governing them. For example, many of the unique language systems of American Indians have been obliterated through the education policies of a federal government that has often sought to eliminate the cultural and linguistic differences of indigenous tribes in order to pressure them into becoming part of the dominant culture. In some cases, this suppression of language has resulted in the tribes' decline or death. Today, language retrieval and revitalization are seeking to undo the results of this linguistic oppression. In other cases, this oppression has had less devastating effects on American Indian communities and instead resulted in varying degrees of Native language use among contemporary Native people. As a result, one finds that there are extreme variations in the communicative skills in Native languages from one tribal community to another, both on reservations or in urban areas.

The power of linguistic domination by the superimposition of an alien tongue—English—and an education system, both of which serve as instruments of social control, have markedly affected the structures, uses, and attitudes of the languages of subordination. Indian women are particularly affected by these sociohistorical circumstances for a variety of reasons to be discussed below. American Indian women perform at least three distinctive social roles through their patterns of language use in their communities. They maintain cultural values through the socialization of children; they serve as evaluators of language use by setting the normative standards of the Native or ancestral tongue and English; and they are effective as agents of change through mediation strategies with white society.

Enforcers of Tradition

The historical pattern of English language domination has been especially significant for Indian women—the primary socializers of children.

The introduction of the majority language—English—placed and continues to place a heavy burden on Indian women because adopting the English language often has meant losing linguistic symbols of culture and gaining male bias carried by the semantic system of English. One example is found in the very different way gender is handled in some American Indian languages and English.

Standard English, with its male bias, has often obviated the rich, gender-based distinctions that exist in the ancestral language. To cite one example, Lakota Sioux, in any of its three dialects—Lakota, Dakota, or Nakota—has significant obligatory structural markers to indicate first-person woman's speech as opposed to man's speech. For the most part, these markers consist of suffixes. For example, *"Hanta yo"* would be a command muttered by males to indicate "Get out!" *"Hanta ye"* would be the equivalent referential meaning for female speakers.

Aside from the more obvious linguistic obligatory markers that exist in American Indian ancestral languages and not in English, there are also an entire set of kinship terms serving to depict social and familial relationships in American Indian culture. These do not exist in their English translation. Women are indirectly affected here again. For example, in Lakota, gender-specific terms exist to indicate birth order and vocative designations, so for females the simple term *brother* would be distinguished in one of two ways, depending on age: *tiblo* (older brother) versus *mi-sunka-la* (younger brother).[1] Conversely, similar terms are used by males to indicate feminine gender and age (or birth order). Moreover, in the bilateral kinship system, the terms are extended to parallel cousins or cross-cousins, depending on the sex of the speaker. As a result, one can understand the confusion that a superimposed kinship system such as the English model brought to social structures and reciprocal relationships, in this particular American Indian culture, and to others. In those cases where an ancestral language has literally died or barely continues to exist, often even linguistic marking of female-female relationships, feminine bonds, and responsive relationships has been obliterated.

Building on these ancestral kinship designations, mothers usually indicate proper behavior to daughters and other "daughters" in kinship equivalencies such as female parallel cousins. One may commonly hear such affective assessment given to daughters: "White persons don't have the proper kinship names for brothers. But you know you respect your older brother and take care of your younger one."

It may be that some Lakota persons as well as other American Indian groups have accepted, or have been forced to accept, the new kinship models imposed by the white culture and language. Although specific linguistic designations may no longer exist, other culturally revealing patterns of language usage remain. One such vestige is the "joking relationship." Such verbal interaction, with a sexual connotation, as an older sister's husband often extends toward his wife's younger sister or her younger female cousin reflects a language usage pattern that denotes the continuity of an ancient cultural form. Perhaps English or the ways of white people have not been effective in destroying core cultural values. In Lakota communities, women continue to participate in joking relationships, usually at public events. The jokes are always stated in Lakota, for it is felt that this type of humor is best expressed in the Native tongue. Nuance and repartee reflect skillful manipulation of language and add to the enjoyment of the group. Some women are known for their remarkable wit and subtlety in "joking" and their verbal skill in "putting men down."

There are other instances where women of the older generation that stayed at home and attended local schools rather than going away to governmental or parochial boarding schools are known to have greater knowledge in oral history or knowledge of traditional techniques and material items. These women are often envied for this unique and valued information, not only by other women but also by Lakota males. It is in the rich folklore and legendary domain that much knowledge is being lost in cultural transmission to children, especially grandchildren. These youngsters tend to be monolingual in English, and thus stories detailing "how it was in the old days" are usually told in English. Folktales and proverbs, which have traditionally served as prescriptive devices, are not totally significant in contemporary communities in the Native idiom. Cultural retrieval programs have succeeded in collecting folktales and legends in English, however. Folktales have also been recorded in the Native language. Whether in English or the Native language, these have relied heavily on women's contributions, both as storytellers and translators of Native oratory.

Cultural Brokers

One particular role that women have played, and continue to play, in many American Indian cultures is that of mediator between their own community and white society. They are often vested with this role because of their facility with the English language. In many communities, women acquire English more readily than men, and their resulting competence often places them in the role of mediator. One can hear statements such as the following made by a Brulé Sioux male from the Rosebud Reservation: *"They* [BIA administrators, county welfare workers, judges, and police officers] listen to women when they talk to them."

Although there is realization of the need for such mediators on the part of Indian men, there is at the same time a great deal of dislike, criticism, and frustration. Males often criticize women for learning the English tongue "too well," because getting too close to white society is taken as a sign of assimilation and consequent rejection of one's own cultural values. But the fact that women are put in the role of mediators becomes a point of frustration for males. They envy them for their bilingual skill, especially for the power associated with it in the dominant society. In a sense, such language usage patterns make males feel helpless in the face of oppression and racism in a dominant white society. This emasculation often leads to conflict between males and females, exhibited too often toward wives in verbal or physical battering. Such conflict is especially onerous for men in the Northern Plains Indian societies that have been labeled "warrior societies." Because male self-valuation has produced a sense of superiority, the "macho" image is eroded by such speech usage patterns, and the locus of control in male-female relationships is seen by males as being usurped.

Lakota Sioux adults can be seen in dual roles as cultural conservators and cultural innovators in the area of language use. The traditional role of cultural guardian is seen vividly in an example from Ella Deloria (1944:43), who uses it to include all adults:

> Nor was it any wonder that small children rapidly learned their social duties, since the training constantly given them was calculated to condition them and direct them in that way. All grown-ups by tacit consent seemed to "gang up" for that purpose. Even before a child was aware of his kinship obligations they make sentences and put the correct words and formal speeches into his mouth for him to repeat to this or that relative. It was their informal but constant system of education in human relations and social responsibility.

It has been acknowledged that the major socializers of children were the Lakota females, even though both men and women taught the proper kin terms that guaranteed smoothly working *tiospaye* (extended family) relationships in a traditional setting. It was this sharing of child training that was quickly submerged in a new superimposed system of patriarchal orientations, a system foisted on the Lakota as part of the acculturational process, which held to the ideal that the training of children was entirely in the women's domain. Along with the demolition of the warrior role among the Sioux and the fact that women were often sent to get the rations that were doled out in the early reservation period, women also began the subtle but functional assumption of the role of cultural broker or mediator. In addition, women were often recruited to work in the houses of missionaries and other agents of change. In order to interact on this level, women learned the English language as means of survival in a rapidly changing situation. They also taught children that interaction in two different worlds required entirely different languages and a new behavioral pattern.

Interestingly, women were recruited along with the men to attend off-reservation schools in such far-removed places as Hampton, Virginia, and Carlisle, Pennsylvania. It was in these schools that the Native language was suppressed and both sexes learned to excel in reading and writing English. It was usually Indian men who said they had completely lost their ability to speak the Native tongue after returning to the reservation. Oral history accounts, such as those of the Standing Rock Reservation, substantiate that women were often called upon to deliver speeches at community events such as Christmas and New Year's celebrations, weddings, and other public events.

In the public sphere as well as the private ones, Lakota women are groomed to be expressive. Even today when I return home, I am expected to address the crowds at powwow celebrations and other community events. The skill of public speaking was and is now equally accessible and available to both Lakota males and females.

At the time when tribal councils first functioned on reservations, some Lakota members often took their daughters to observe the meetings, and they thus became aware of the *pogo* (political climate of a new institution). Because meetings were conducted in English and Lakota, fluency in both languages was enhanced. It was not surprising that Standing Rock had a female tribal chair in the 1940s and another in the 1950s. This may have been unusual, but the thrust to biculturalism and bilingualism was seen as a means to understanding the superimposed culture with a strong background in the Native one. Females fulfilled both.

As mothers, women have played an important role in educating their children in the proper use of the English language through games devised for that purpose. Such training has added a great deal to the success of their children in school. Often contextual situations are pointed out to indicate the proper vernacular mode to the child. Students who lived at home had parental surrogates within the kinship network as well as parents who supported their efforts. Speech-making was still part of the expected behavior pattern. More important, before the days of relevant Indian curricula, many mothers encouraged the use of oral history, legends, and Native materials to write histories of the various villages or towns on the reservation as a means of interesting students in improving writing competency in English.

Evaluators of Language

Women in American Indian communities hold a wide variety of different attitudes toward language usage. They range from very traditional ones that tenaciously adhere to ancestral language and values even though English is also used to a more assimilationist one in which children are not addressed in their ancestral language. Some families try to maintain a truly bilingual home. As mothers, women play a decisive role in the whole matter of language choice, because it is often their decision that determines which language the child will acquire naturally. Some continue speaking the ancestral language to the child but send the child to a school in which English is the only language of instruction. Others speak English only. Still others follow a bilingual model through the use of more modern bilingual schooling. For example, some southeastern groups such as Lumbee or Pamunkey, although claiming to be Native, do not have a cultural or linguistic base that reflects a tribal character. On the other hand, such groups in the Northeast as the Passamaquody or the Penobscot have retained a Native language base. In the Southwest, the Navajo evidence a high degree of monolingualism in their Native language. It could be argued that women have contributed greatly to these variations in bilingualism. A long-distinguished "Indian" trait seems to center on Native autonomy; the choice is usually made by the mother or maternal surrogate as to which language or languages will be used and consequently learned by the child. It is often the case, however, that one hears such statements regarding the loss of language as, "I'm sorry that my mother did not teach me my Native language."

This essay has discussed various aspects of women's roles in American Indian communities as manifested by the use of the ancestral language and English. As males and females within these communities have acknowledged, the impact and importance of Native women in cultural and linguistic continuity are noteworthy.

Note

1. There are, of course, many language communities throughout the world that have been in contact with English and yet have retained such distinctions as age and familial relationship in their use of English. Nigerian English "senior brother" and "junior brother" is one such example. The fact that Lakota and other American Indian communities may not retain such distinction marks the extent of the cultural oppression that the adoption of the English language in the United States has imposed.

References

Chafe, Wallace L. 1962. "Estimates Regarding the Present Speakers of North American Indian Languages." *International Journal of American Linguistics* 28(3): 161–71.
Deloria, Ella. 1944. *Speaking of Indians.* New York: Friendship Press.

CHAPTER 15

North American Indigenous Women and Cultural Domination

$\mathbf{M}$any immigrant groups in the United States celebrated a quin-centennial of the "discovery" of a New World in 1992. However, most of the 1.5 million Native people in the United States who live in isolated reservation areas, or the 50 percent of the Native population who live in urban areas, are rejoicing in their survival. Their cultural survival against centuries of genocide, legal restrictions on religion and language, and superimposed systems of law that were meant to completely obliterate Native law-ways and customary systems of marriage and kinship, and, more devastatingly, demolish belief systems that were considered "pagan" is indeed remarkable. This pattern of conquest and domination exists in many areas of colonization by European powers.

At present, it is agreed that there are approximately 325 distinct tribal groups in the United States (American Indian Policy Review Commission 1977–78). Their viability in cultural life-styles and linguistic persistence lends credence to adaptiveness and tenacity. This contradicts the common view of policymakers and religious practitioners that American Indians would inevitably join a mythical melting pot. American Indians of all tribes have been the focus of administered human relations since the beginning of contact with a dominant and domineering governmental system that prevails to the present day. American Indians and Alaska Natives (not Native Americans) have a comprehensive system of laws, federal statutes, and rules stipulated by Congress, which distinguishes them from other so-called minority people. Thus they have a constant need for lobbyists and self-help associations to monitor every session of Congress carefully and apprise them of—and in some cases circumvent—legal actions that would erode the special status of tribes as "domestic nations" and abrogate treaties on which tribal sovereignty is based. The need for eternal vigilance as each session of Congress convenes has led to the establishment of watchdog groups such as the National Congress of American Indians (founded in 1944) and the politically astute Native American Rights Fund, which is composed of indigenous lawyers of both genders. Besides these pan-tribal organizations, many tribal governments maintain offices in Washington, D.C., to monitor legislation and inform their tribal constituencies.

It is well documented in the ethnographic literature on North American Natives that the imposition of the patriarchal nuclear model of European kinship has extinguished many systems of matrilocal residence as part of the thrust toward civilization, according to standards of custom and law of the conquering nations (Hamamsy 1957; Kehoe 1983; Leacock 1981). Eleanor Leacock documents changes in Naskapi culture due to the fur trade, the effects of missionization, the patrilineal models regarded as basic for legitimacy of the union's issue, and the impact of a money economy on a hunting and gathering society in Canada. More important, she delineates the changes in male-female relationships that indicate a marked difference in decision-making in Native societies where egalitarian principles had prevailed. This pattern of colonialization is mirrored among the Iroquois, Navajo, and other indigenous groups.

Because the Naskapi reside in Canada, one must mention the Indian Act of 1876, which gave status to Natives who were direct descendants in the male line. Women who married outside the band (to Europeans, métis, or non-status males) lost their Indian status, as did their children. Conversely, non-Indian women, mainly European, who married Native men became fully endowed with rights to live on the reserve and register their children in the band. They were also entitled to health, education, and welfare benefits. Now [in 1993], *Native* and/or *Aboriginal* are the preferential terms used in Canada, although *Treaty* and *Non-Treaty* are also used. Only in 1985 was this law changed to end racism and discrimination against Canadian Native women. The issue of Native women wishing to return to reserve lands and to Native rights, especially for education, is a source of discord in many Canadian Native communities today (Bourgeault 1983).

This essay, however, deals only with specific cases that involve unequal treatment of Indian women in the United States. In most pre-contact societies, Native women shared equally with men in social, economic, and ritual roles. Most ethnographic accounts (for the Plains culture area) emphasize the dynamic, dyadic interplay of both genders in the ongoing enterprise that allows indigenous societies to exist (Albers and Medicine, eds. 1983). Perduring images of Indian women as drudges and beasts of burden and the "princess or prostitute" syndrome of first encounters are still part of the interethnic interchange and center in legal transactions. Recent feminist writings have contextualized the high status of Indian women in many societies, especially those of the "warrior" societies of the Northern Plains (Albers and Medicine, eds. 1983; Allen 1986; Van Kirk 1980). The emphasis on feminine skills did not disturb the egalitarian nature of Native societies. The feminine "culture hero" of given cultural man-

Jean Schensul, Medicine, and Faye Harrison at the Society for Applied Anthropology's Malinowski Award Ceremony, Baltimore, 1993. (Courtesy of Michael Chapman)

dates—such as the sacred White Buffalo Calf Woman of the Lakota (Sioux) or Changing Woman among the Navajo—was and still is an ongoing focus of these belief systems. These feminine icons are constantly evoked by participants in these cultures as an ongoing means of social control, especially in wife abuse.

The placement of Indians on reservations, the destruction of male roles, and the diminished valuation of Indian women had great demoralizing and long-lasting effects on Native populations. In the destruction of aboriginal lives, the legal repression of Native languages and belief systems, such as the Sun Dance among the Lakota, cut at the very heart of Native life-ways. The Christian ethic of patriarchy—a male god and a patrilineal kinship model with the imposition of patrilineal family names—virtually eclipsed the autonomy of Native women.

The introduction of alcohol as a control mechanism in the early fur trade era also had perduring repercussions in early reservation placements. In general, apathy and despair seemed to reign in early reservation life. More devastating, a pattern of administered human relationships ensued. With the demolition of traditional leadership patterns and the establishment of new "chiefs" with more acquiescent orientations, patterns of paternalism were firmly established. In addition, new patterns of legalized law-ways undercut established and functional Native legal codes. For example, punishment for murder among the Lakota was the adoption of the transgressor into the kinship unit to make up for the loss of the murdered one. Only entities such as the Pueblo in the American Southwest—where continual residence in aboriginal habitation sites was common—were somewhat immune from these tremendous dislocations. Gender disequilibrium and social anomie are often referred to as the "culture of poverty" or "reservation culture" in present-day parlance. These factors, along with racism, discrimination, and unemployment, are part of the everyday life of indigenous people in North America.

In the history of Indian-white relations in the United States, the forcible removal of children from families and the belief that education and Christianization were important forms of civilizing "wild Indians" were disastrous government policies. In addition, the dominant society felt that "women were the cradle of civilization." Thus, the role of Indian women as change agents was fostered. Early in the educational process, Indian women were utilized as matrons, cooks, maids, and laundry workers. The benefits of a new life were instilled in them, and intermarriage was encouraged; thus it was hoped that they would direct their children away from "heathen ways." It is important to recognize that federal and parochial schools constituted the main destroyers of Indian families and kin networks. The Protestant ethic was the super-ordinate force in this indoctrination.

The use of Native languages was expressly forbidden, and the cultural basis of ritual, value configurations, and kinship terminology was undercut and replaced with a meaningless cultural infrastructure. More far-reaching, the boarding school experience demolished parenting skills, and the consequences of that intrusion are still evident today. In this context, it is evident that socialization according to tribal traditions was negligible.

At the present time, there are many instances of legal inequities in the lives of Indians, both male and female. In "Indian Country," as the tribal land bases (reservations) are often called, jurisdictional issues abound. Reservations are situated within counties that are within states. On reservations, federal Bureau of Indian Affairs (BIA) legal forces prevail. The tribal police are mainly concerned with the seven major crimes of federal policy. The tribal court on most reservations operates with its own legal mandate. As disequilibrium regarding proper behavior becomes more evident in homes, larger systems of new laws prevail. Because reservations are within states, BIA police are often in direct conflict with state police in legal jurisdiction. For example, on Standing Rock Reservation, which straddles mid-North Dakota and South Dakota, three control mechanisms are evident. South Dakota does not have jurisdiction on state roads within the reservation. This has been a battle with the state since the 1950s. When the state referred it to the Supreme Court, tribal sovereignty ruled.

In cases involving Indian women, such as spouse or child abuse or welfare issues, jurisdictional mandates blur the enactment of justice. In off-reservation or "border towns," where many Indian women live in legal or consensual ("Indian marriage") unions, there is often little recourse for them in abuse cases. Municipal and county police may ignore these abuses—both physical and sexual—on the pretext of jurisdictional uncertainties.

In cases of child abuse—especially in cases where grandmothers (the mainstay in many Indian families) wish to obtain custody of minor children—mothers tend to utilize state courts, where European kinship systems are often evoked, in order to circumvent grandparental rights. Removal from family contexts prevented boys and girls from connecting with parental surrogates. The European modus operandi was physical punishment to "save the child." In other cases, state laws might be negated. In South Dakota, for example, some counties recognize tribal court orders and others do not. In some cases in which a spouse is of another race—generally European—the implications of legal codes are horrendous. A case that has publicized this problem vividly is that of a Dakota woman who removed her child from Washington state to her natal reservation. The young male child then was abducted by his white father and taken out of South Dakota. Tests for paternity determination were initiated. A final resolution to this and other cases plays upon state versus tribal jurisdiction.

Wife abuse—when reported—is often dismissed as a "domestic issue," especially in border towns. The recent establishment of shelters for abused women and children is a sign that some tribes are confronting the need.

In the 1960s and 1970s, many Indian activists, including females, claimed that Indian women had been sterilized without their knowledge or consent. Outright claims of genocide were leveled against the Bureau of Indian Affairs and the Indian Health Service, which maintains hospitals on reservations. This was a time of ethnic ferment in the United States, and it is not possible to obtain accurate data on these claims.

In that same era, white social workers removed many Native children from Indian homes and placed them in foster homes and/or made them available for adoption. Many of the dissonances of Native life—for both men and women—were alcohol-related. However, in many instances, the standards used to judge the quality of a home were middle-class norms. The functions of extended families and Native kinship obligations were seldom considered. This led to hardship among women and grandparents who wished to maintain care of their children.

To avoid these problems, several historical factors must be contextualized and particularized for each individual in a tribal matrix. One factor, of course, is the loss of parenting skills. Another is poverty—the dismal statistics constantly evoked when one speaks of Indians, including high unemployment, alcoholism, and lack of job and educational skills. A major factor is the interface of powerless people with superimposed legal systems.

Alcohol constitutes yet another problem. Legal prohibition against Indian consumption of alcohol was operative from the 1800s into the mid-twentieth century. In 1953 that prohibition ended, and there was a great rise in alcohol-related crimes and social problems among Indians, particularly the battering of women and neglect of children. Currently, excessive consumption of alcohol by pregnant women is resulting in an accelerating rate of fetal alcohol syndrome in many tribes. These disorganizational factors, plus concern for children, led to the passage by Congress of the Indian Child Welfare Act in 1978. The act mandates that social workers must find foster homes within tribal communities and encourage adoption by tribal people. Unfortunately, the money needed for casework and alleviation of this problem is not forthcoming from the federal government. Tribes are hampered by lack of economic resources and the destruction of cultural norms that formerly allowed for the absorption of orphans and neglected children into extended kin networks. The need is still evident in many Indian enclaves—both reservation and urban.

One possible amelioration of these dissonances is the passage of the Indian Religious Freedom Act of 1978, which allows for a return to Native rituals and belief systems. This has had a positive effect in many communities, for previously heavy alcohol-users have utilized old beliefs as support systems in sobriety. The truism that alcohol is an imported evil is also helpful. Many alcoholism treatment programs use Native beliefs as a coping mechanism. The efficacy of these indigenous strategies has not been evaluated. However, attendance at meetings to maintain sobriety appears to be increasing.

From this very partitive presentation of complex issues that impinge on Indian women, one should note that there are many externally construed laws and statutes formulated and promulgated by a myriad of federal agencies. These include the Bureau of Indian Affairs, which acts in a trust position, as well as the U.S. Public Health Service, Housing and Urban Development, Environmental Protection Agency, and others. Both the BIA and the HIS still essentially direct and/or limit the types of occupational selections that Indian women make. In addition, tribal councils make decisions regarding loans for higher education. HIS policy regarding sex education programs, medical care, prenatal and other "female" concerns, and care for urban residence sets priorities for the quality of life of Indians. Housing and Urban Development has instituted such notions as clustered housing in reservation communities, which has exacerbated in-group tensions, peer pressure to drink, the sexual abuse of children, and, in general, has aided in the erosion of family effectiveness within a kinship frame. More recently, the EPA has pressured some tribes to accept nuclear waste on reservations, which has potential for serious damage to future generations. In sum, external policies continue to have horrendous effects on Indian people. All of these impinge upon tribal and individual decision-making in contemporary life. What is important is that when discussing the roles and statuses of Indian women, their tribal group must be specified.

Regarding the legal and social rights of indigenous women, the Wanrow case (1971) serves as a good example of the conflict between tribal tradition and non-Indian law. In Washington state, the mother of a sexually abused boy shot the perpetrator. The defense attempted to show that she was acting within her tribal cultural mores. The attempt failed in federal court. Thus women are often caught in a triple bind of customary law and beliefs and state and federal jurisdictions. The mother currently is working for an advocacy group that defends treaty rights. Although this may be a cause célèbre, it highlights legal discrepancies for all Indians.

It is also notable that in Nebraska, Montana, and North and South Dakota the incarceration rate for Indian men is exceedingly high, and much is alcohol-related. Moreover, the structure of tribal societies is being affected. Growing numbers of Native households are headed by a single parent, usually a female. The strength of women in legal matters is evident. Men often say to Indian women in their kin networks, "You go talk to the judge, he'll listen to you." Again, this leads to perceptions among whites that Native women tend to be "more dependable" and "more aware of time" than Indian men. However, both male and female status in the face of interethnic encounters reflects racism and second-class citizenship. This situation is further confounded by the low economic status of Indian families, which minimizes their effectiveness in negotiating in the legal system.

A further example of imposed legal policies that have had deleterious effects on traditional tribal government was the passage of the Wheeler-Howard Act of 1934 (often referred to as the "Indian Reorganization Act") under John Collier's administration at the BIA. In tribes that accepted this legislation, the act set up tribal councils based on the premise that men should be the leaders. The model often circumvented the role of women in tribal government and allowed male control. For example, among the matrilineal and matrilocal Navajo, councils consist mainly of men at the present time. Thus the act has eroded the position of women in decision-making. Although there are instances of female chairpersons, such as at Standing Rock in 1950 and 1960, this has not been the norm. Recent figures, however, indicate that many women are assuming these elected positions in tribal groups. Witness the recent reelection of Wilma Mankiller to head the Cherokee tribe in Oklahoma.

Although there are many examples of legal actions detrimental to Indian customary law, the Martinez case demonstrates how these tribal decisions may evolve from female actualization in legal contests. The 1978 case of *Santa Clara Pueblo v. Martinez* arose out of the wish of a Santa Clara woman married to a "full-blood Navajo" to leave her home in Santa Clara village to her daughter. The tribal council (not the indigenous one) disagreed on the grounds that she was married to an outsider. As indicated by Pueblo anthropologist Edward Dozier (1970), a strong dual governance of aboriginal secular and religious functions existed (and still exists) in many pueblos. Martinez appealed to the Supreme Court, claiming sex discrimination. The Court ruled that a female tribal member "could not bring a case against the tribe in a federal court. The Indian Civil Rights Act of 1968 did not expressly abrogate sovereign immunity by subjecting the tribe to civil suits in federal courts" (Wilkinson 1987:49). The decision was made in spite "of any act of Congress providing for the protection of civil rights" (Wilkinson 1987:49). Unfortunately, it seemed a signal for some tribes to allow their tribal councils to permit enrollment only for individuals whose father was an enrolled member of that tribe. In cases of consensual unions, a child cannot be enrolled unless a man signs an acknowledgment of paternity (as on Standing Rock Reservation). Other unfortunate consequences are certain to arise from this decision.

In summary, I would state that the status and role of Indian women declined after the formation of reservations. During this time, state and church policies imposed a patriarchal and patrilocal model, the privatization of communal property, and a system of increased administration of human relationships, which did much to diminish tribal women's status and aspirations.

Fortunately, the political and economic influence of women has grown since the 1960s. Women of the Northern Plains in particular have maintained a power base and prestige structure that is tied to artistic efforts, the manipulation of educational avenues, welfare and economic enterprises, and ritual participation. It is also encouraging to note that since the 1970s there has been an upsurge in the number of Native lawyers—at last count, seven hundred. More than one-third of these are women. A Lumbee was the first woman to argue a case successfully before the U.S. Supreme Court. If women serve as judges in tribal courts on Indian reservations or penetrate the legal systems in off-reservations border towns, these developments will greatly improve the legal status of all Indians in the United States.

Notes

Albers, Patricia, and Beatrice Medicine, eds. 1983. *The Hidden Half: Studies of Plains Indian Women.* Washington: University Press of America.

Allen, Paula Gunn. 1986. *The Sacred Hoop: Recovering the Feminine in American Indian Traditions.* Boston: Beacon Press.

American Indian Policy Review Commission. 1977–78. *Meetings of the American Indian Policy Review Commission.* Washington: Government Printing Office. [Summarized as General Accounting Office. 1978. *Review of the American Indian Policy Review Commission.* Washington: Government Printing Office.]

Bourgeault, Ron. 1983. "The Development of Capitalism and Subjugation of Native Women in Northern Canada." *Alternative Routes* 6: 109–40.

Dozier, Edward P. 1970. *The Pueblo Indians.* New York: Holt, Rinehart and Winston.

Hamamsy, Lila Shukrey. 1957. "The Role of Women in a Changing Navajo Society." *American Anthropologist* 59: 101–11.

Kehoe, Alice B. 1983. *North American Indians: A Comprehensive Account.* Englewood Cliffs: Prentice-Hall.

Leacock, Eleanor Burke. 1981. *Myths of Male Dominance: Collected Articles on Women Cross-Culturally.* New York: Monthly Review Press.

Van Kirk, Sylvia. 1980. *Many Tender Ties: Women in Fur Trade Society in Western Canada, 1670–1870.* Norman: University of Oklahoma Press.

Wilkinson, Charles. 1987. *American Indians, Time, and the Law: Native Societies in a Modern Constitutional Democracy.* New Haven: Yale University Press.

CHAPTER 16

Carrying the Culture: American Indian and Alaska Native Women Workers

One of the most striking characteristics of American Indian and Alaska Native women as a group is their cultural diversity. There are more than five hundred "federally recognized" tribes in the United States (including 197 Alaska Native village groups), all of whom view themselves as sovereign nations based on treaty agreements with the federal government (U.S. Department of the Interior 1988). Each tribal heritage includes a linguistic background and life-style particular to that tribe. The diversity of Native American tribes is further intensified by the contrasting rural and urban environments in which they live. Approximately one-third of the 1.4 million Native American people live on rural reservations. Thus, in order to fully understand the occupational issues of Native American women, one has to understand the cultural context of tribal and individual variation.

Unfortunately, government officials, policy analysts, and authors often fail to make these cultural distinctions, characterizing all groups under the rubric "American Indian" or "Native American" and thus negating the diversity of tribal cultures and characteristics. This tribal distinctiveness—as Navajo or Kiowa—is further blurred when indigenous women are categorized as "women of color" and are generalized in the data dealing with minority women. In many cases, they are excluded as an entity. Moreover, there is an absence of demographic and socioeconomic studies specific to Native women.

Overview of the Native American and Alaska Native Population

In general, data indicate that the Native American population is young, with a median age of twenty-three years, contrasted to the U.S. median age of thirty years (U.S. Bureau of the Census 1981). Two-thirds of Native families have children under eighteen years of age, as opposed to one-half of all families. Accordingly, the 1983 birthrate for Indian and Alaska Natives was significantly higher than the birthrate of the general U.S. population (twenty-nine births per one thousand Indian and Alaska Native people compared to 15.5 births per one thousand people for all races in the United States). The Native American infant death rate during the years 1982–84 was 10.2 per one thousand live births, 1 percent lower than all other races in the United States (U.S. Department of the Interior 1988). Suicide rates, however, are particularly high among young males of Native groups (Bechtold 1988). Life expectancy from 1979 to 1981 was sixty-seven years for Native males compared to seventy-five years for Native females.

Overall, the educational achievement rate of Native people is well below the national average. The 1980 census states that about 8 percent of Indians complete four years of college or more compared to 16 percent of the total population. Most of the degrees are earned by Native women.

The socioeconomic status of American Indian and Alaska Natives is considerably below the national level. Female-headed households account for 23 percent of all Indian households, 5 percent higher than the general population. These households have a median income of $7,000, which is below the median income for all female-headed households and approximately $5,000 below the poverty threshold for a family of four (U.S. Bureau of the Census 1981). Because Indian families tend to be larger than the norm, their poverty may be aggravated. Compounding the problem of poverty, housing units on many reservations lack basic facilities. More than one-fifth of the houses lack an indoor toilet, and 16 percent of households on reservations do not have telephones.

Unfortunately, although there were many studies of urban Indians in the 1960s, current data on non-reservation residents is lacking. However, a 1978 governmental report indicated that most Indian women heading families were urban residents: "Female-headed households showed even less likelihood of being located outside of the central city" (U.S. Commission on Civil Rights 1978). Thus, although there is little specific data on Native American female-headed households, it can be surmised that their situations are comparable to those of other minorities in the inner cities.

There are numerous factors that have significant impact on the socioeconomic status and quality of life in contemporary Native communities. The list includes low income, a high educational drop-out rate, a low educational level, teenage pregnancy, single female–headed households, child and spouse abuse, alcoholism, and an increase in fetal alcohol syndrome (Dorris 1989). These issues are part of daily life for most indigenous women and have an impact upon their roles in their families and communities and in the labor force.

Concerns of Native Women

If there is a commonality among Native women, it is in their adjustment to superimposed policies of administered human relationships, a fact that has dominated the life-styles of indigenous people since the time of colonial contact. Much of the dire socioeconomic reality can be attributed to generations of external decision-making and colonialist procedures from a myriad federal agencies (Bureau of Indian Affairs, Housing and Urban Development, Health and Human Services, and others) that direct Native life at all levels. Repression of Native belief systems and Native languages has been countered by concerted efforts of many women to preserve cultural ways, languages, and a worldview that reflects unique tribal life. The adage "women are the carriers of Indian culture" sums up this important fact of Indian life.

Cultural survival is the primary concern among many Native American women and strongly influences their efforts to address the economic and socioeconomic problems facing their people. For instance, Native American women play a vital role in the well-being of the extended kinship group, which, by pooling the resources of its members, is able to survive the conditions of poverty and a hostile culture (Medicine 1981). The economic survival of these extended families often depends upon the effective coping mechanisms of female members. For example, women often act as unpaid workers in the traditional ways of collecting and harvesting (Medicine 1981). Grandmothers in particular are highly valued in contemporary life, not only for these unpaid services but also for the perpetuation of the culture. In addition, women act as mediators in the legal systems of the dominant society, sometimes entering local and national political spheres. These activities are uncompensated, but they are expected behavior necessary to maintain a family structure.

Work-force Issues of Native American and Alaska Native Women

Gaining access to the work force of the dominant culture has been difficult for many Native groups because aspirations for occupational fulfillment have often been directed by outside decision-makers. Partly to blame are the government agencies (deemed the "civilizers" by some Native people) that implement social service programs designed to serve the educational, family, and child welfare needs of Native populations. These programs, reflecting the values of the dominant culture, emphasize the acculturation of Native people to the larger society's norms through education. Women have been steered in the direction of such occupations as nursing, teaching, and social work. It would appear that many occupational opportunities for women will continue to be in the "helping" professions because government agencies, the primary employer on reservations, exhibit a hiring practice that favors women. As a result, women's incomes tend to be higher than men's in some reservation economies (Albers and Breen n.d.).

Employment opportunities for Native Americans in the educational field vary according to the hiring practices of educational institutions. Issues of identity often cloud employment in institutions of higher education because applicants claiming Native ancestry are hired in order to meet the organization's affirmative action goals. (Most Indian people have a tribal enrollment document to validate their ancestry.) In a recent survey of teachers in the agency town of Standing Rock Reservation, North Dakota, almost 50 percent of a total of fifty teachers are Native women (Medicine 1989). In contrast, an earlier study of the employment practices in Montana indicated that in one school district with a total of four hundred classroom teachers, only one was Indian (Montana Advisory Committee 1974). Tokenism is also evident at the University of Montana, where only thirteen of 1,040 faculty and non-faculty employees are Indians (Montana Advisory Committee 1974).

Although American Indian women have been part of a growing labor pool of women, increasing from 35 percent in 1970 to 48 percent in 1980, Native women have had limited access to higher-wage managerial and professional occupations. Only 16 percent of Native people were in managerial and professional occupations, compared to 23 percent for society at large. Employment has generally been concentrated in the lower range of employment—the laborer and service categories. Because this is the area in which more discriminatory factors are operative, it is apparent that indigenous females are caught in a triple bind of gender, prejudice, and isolation in reservations or in urban areas, where they must compete with other minority persons for jobs.

Exclusion of a Native American category in analyzing employment trends, or the general use of the blanket term *minority,* is evident in reports dealing with women workers. Therefore, what follows is a compilation of available data indicating trends in the employment patterns of Native women (which appeared in the 1970s). In a speech on Native women in the work force, Shirley Hill Witt has stated, "You should know that only 11 percent of Indian women employed outside the home are in professional and technical work. And only 2 percent are employed as managers and administrators. . . . More than 36 percent of all Indian women have no income at all" (Witt 1979).

Table 16.1, reprinted from the U.S. Department of Labor's *Handbook of Women Workers* (1975), identifies the percent of Indian, Aleut, and Eskimo women in ten general occupational categories (U.S. Department of Labor 1975:57). Such data is seldom contextualized and does not consider cultural variation, which is so important in the occupational levels achieved by Native women (Whiteman 1980).

In a rare glimpse of occupational distributions (1976), American Indian/Alaska Native women came "13.3 percentage points closer to the majority female pattern" (U.S. Commission on Human Rights 1976). That sudden advance could be the result of more Indian women seeking higher education in an attempt to achieve economic equity (Medicine 1988). However, another report indicated that the improved picture was still dismal: "The relative economic improvement of American Indian/Alaska Native and Black female-headed households resulted in median household per capita incomes that were only one-third of the majority population's median per capita income in 1975" (U.S. Commission on

Table 16.1

Occupation	American Indian	Aleut and Eskimo
Professional, technical workers	11.1	8.8
Managers/administrators	2.4	5.2
Sales workers	4.0	3.1
Clerical workers	25.1	26.0
Craft and kindred workers	2.1	1.0
Operatives (including transport)	18.7	10.7
Laborers (except farm)	1.3	1.4
Farm workers	2.3	1.7
Service workers	26.3	34.3
Private household workers	6.7	8.0

Civil Rights 1978). In addition, "the disparity for American Indian/Alaska Native and Puerto Rican female-headed families is even greater because they were five times more likely, as a group, to be in poverty in 1975 than the average majority family" (U.S. Commission on Human Rights 1976).

The current position of Indian women in the world of work is difficult to assess. A 1982 resource guide entitled *Ohoyo One Thousand* lists one thousand professional American Indian and Alaska Native women "who identify with 231 tribes and bands." It notes that "sixty-nine women [in 1983] were heading their tribal governments—chiefs!" The guide also includes Native women with academic doctorates and another seventy-two in doctoral study, sixteen of the estimated forty-nine women medical doctors within the population, and twenty-nine of an estimated sixty women lawyers (Anderson 1982).

Conclusion

Due to the impact of affirmative action programs in universities and professional organizations such as the American Indian Psychological Association, the entrance of Native women into the professions of law, medicine, and the social sciences is likely to continue. As a result, there is evidence of a growing division of women into the lower strata of service-oriented occupations in reservation and urban enclaves and an upper-middle-class group whose affiliation to tribal groups is minimal. The life-styles of this emergent group is more oriented toward the middle class and tends to mirror the middle-class achievements of white females. The women in this category tend to be more visible in white-oriented associations (i.e., the women's movement) and thus, like their European counterparts, are embedded in the society of the dominant group. The entrance into professional fields by the offspring of Indian employees of government bureaucracies such as the Bureau of Indian Affairs or the Indian Health Service accelerates the growth of this upper-middle-class group.

In contrast, many women in Native communities are primarily concerned with the preservation of the language and culture from which Indian and Alaska Native culture and identity stems. When tribal women gather together in conventions, as the North American Indian Women's Association, the concern is for the preservation of Native family, culture, and survival. The means of survival is contextually defined in the tribal background of each individual woman; they survive despite their disadvantaged position in the national work force.

References

Albers, Patricia C., and Nancy Breen. n.d. "Deciphering the Census for Trends in the Status of American Indian Women." Unpublished paper.

Anderson, Owanah. 1982. *Ohoyo One Thousand: A Resource Guide of American Indian and Alaska Native Women.* Wichita Falls: Ohoyo Resource Center.

Bechtold, Donald W. 1988. "Cluster Suicides in American Indian Adolescents." [American Indian and Alaska Native Mental Health Research Center] *Journal of the National Center* 1 (March): 26–35.

Dorris, Michael. 1989. *The Broken Cord.* New York: Harper and Row.

Medicine, Beatrice. 1981. "American Indian Family Cultural Change and Adaptive Strategies." *Journal of Ethnic Studies* 8 (Winter): 13–23.

———. 1988. "Native American (Indian) Women: A Call for Research." *Anthropology and Education Quarterly* 19(2): 86–92.

———. 1989. Field notes.

Montana Advisory Committee to the United States Commission on Civil Rights. 1974. *Employment Practices in Montana: The Effects on American Indians and Women.* Washington: N.p.

U.S. Bureau of the Census. 1981. *We, the First Americans.* Washington: Government Printing Office.

U.S. Commission on Human Rights. 1978. *Social Indicators of Equality for Minorities and Women.* Washington: Government Printing Office.

U.S. Department of the Interior, Bureau of Indian Affairs. 1988. *American Indians Today.* Washington: Government Printing Office.

U.S. Department of Labor. 1975. *1975 Handbook of Women Workers.* Washington: Government Printing Office.

Whiteman, Henrietta V. 1980. "Insignificance of Humanity, 'Man Is Tampering with the Moon and Stars': The Employment Status of American Indian Women." In *Conference on the Educational and Occupational Needs of American Indian Women.* Washington: U.S. Department of Education, Office of Educational Research and Improvement, National Institute of Education.

Witt, Shirley Hill. 1979. "Native Women in the World of Work." In Bulletin 0404, *Women of Color Forum: A Collection of Readings,* ed. Toni Constantino, 41–61. Madison: Wisconsin Department of Public Instruction.

CHAPTER 17

Lakota Star Quilts: Commodity, Ceremony, and Economic Development

During the nineteenth and early twentieth centuries, most Native people living in North America were subjected to great cultural disruption, displacement, and relocation by the U.S. government. As Native people resettled, they found new ways of maintaining traditional practices, as commented upon by Ella Deloria in *Speaking of Indians*:

> The people began to make ingenious adaptations of some elements of their old life to the new. For instance, at one period they transferred the art decorations of the tipi to the log house. Out of G.I. muslin they made very large wall coverings, a carryover from the dew-curtain of the tipi and called by the same term, *ozan*. On these they painted beautiful designs and made lively black-and-white drawings of historical scenes or hunting or battle or peace-making between tribes, and courtship scenes, games, and suchlike activities of the past. People went visiting just to see one another's pictographs and to hear the stories they preserved. (Deloria 1944:93)

Quilts made to provide warmth have been part of Lakota Sioux households in North Dakota, South Dakota, and Montana since the beginning of the reservation period. Lakota Sioux women of the Northern Plains reservations began making patchwork quilts as utilitarian replacements for buffalo robes and other skin bed coverings. According to ethnohistorian Christian Feest, "Nowhere did patchwork quilting become of importance as on the Northern Plains, where quilts were used increasingly as substitutes for painted skins after large scale hunting had been abandoned" (1992: 151–52). The introduction of quilts into western Sioux reservations was undoubtedly linked to the presence of missions on the early reservations.[1]

Everyday quilts made of tops of simple square or geometric patterns, using scraps of wool, cotton, and other materials and filled with batting, were commonly called *owanke* (to spread) or *owinza* (to cover). Called *sina ek cheka* (translated as "ordinary shawls" or "blankets"), they have long been a favored textile in Lakota Sioux households. Feest notes that "the predominant use of the *star* quilt or *sunburst* design may be best understood as a direct continuation of one of the earlier symbolic hide painting traditions" (1992:151–52, emphasis in the original). Originally labeled *wichapi shina* (star robes), these quilts assumed distinctive values in Lakota life.

Female quilting groups formed and continued in the pattern of the older traditional porcupine quillwork societies, and involvement in these societies fostered recognition of women's contributions to the community. Women's groups also were fostered by missionaries to promote industriousness. To excel at quilting became a matter of status for many Lakota women as well as important economically, and quilts began to function as both commodity and ceremonial object (Albers and Medicine 1983). But the dispersal of these quilts seems less important than their economic and ritual roles in contemporary Lakota Sioux reservation life.

Seldom is a star quilt used as an ordinary bed covering in reservation homes; rather, star quilts are used in ways that distinguish their meaning and role with Lakota Sioux life. They are employed as door coverings for dwellings or shelters at ceremonial events and are worn by healers in *Yuwipi* (curing) ceremonies. More important, star quilts have long been a critical element in give-aways and the life-cycle events, from birth to death, of the Sioux.

Miniature star quilts often are made or obtained by members of a *tiospaye* (extended family, usually a sister of the father) for a newborn child. Because cradleboards and cradleboard coverings are not functional in contemporary times, a gift of a star quilt to a child is purely honorific, serving to recognize the child's entrance into the extended family. This practice, most often observed by "traditional" and/or full-blooded families, gives the item—called *alesza* (to urinate upon)—added symbolic value. The gesture also validates the Lakota term for child: *wakan yesa* (a sacred being).

Interestingly, many paternal aunts (the father's sisters) give this gift whether the child is a result of a legal marriage or a consensual one—recognition of the child is the significant issue. Some children receive the gift of a star quilt later in childhood or at a naming ceremony, which may be in adolescence. At whatever age, the star quilt is a symbol of prestige, sentiment, and "belonging." Some youths take their star quilts with them when they venture out of the community to search for work, recreation, or attend college. Doing so may represent an emotional tie to kin and community.

From the establishment of the reservations until very recently, every "proper" Lakota maiden was expected to have a hand-quilted star quilt in the household goods she took to her new home upon marriage. This custom may have declined, however, due to the prevalence of consensual or "Indian" marriages and the waning of the "exchange" feature in contemporary marriages.

Today, star quilts are the most valued and prestigious items in the death customs of the Lakota. In prior times, the buffalo robe, painted with a star motif, was used to wrap the body of the deceased for scaffold burials. Now, a star quilt often is used to cover the coffin. Most families bury the quilt with the departed; some remove the quilt and give it as recompense to the religious practitioner who conducts the ceremony. Until recently, it would only be given to a Christian minister; now it may also be given to the individual conducting a traditional ceremony. Traditionally, the Lakota threw beaded moccasins into the grave to assist the departed on the Lakota steps to the Milky Way—*Wanagi Omani* (Spirit Road)—and the entrance into the Land of Deceased Relatives. For those who do not have beaded moccasins, the star quilt now serves this purpose. Some acculturated Lakota have begun to substitute commercially made Pendelton blankets for star quilts, although quilts are preferred.

No matter how poor a Lakota family may be, there is a concerted effort to obtain a star quilt for funerary rites. Upon hearing of a death in their family, many women of all ages quickly gather to make the requisite quilts. Working efficiently, they are able to produce one in approximately four hours. These may be hand-quilted or simply "tied" with yarn or thread. If the quilters are not paid immediately in cash, they are compensated by gifts a year later during the memorial feast.

At the memorial feast, star quilts reach their apex in ceremony and prestige in many of the Lakota Sioux and Dakota Sioux reservations. In this *Wanagi Yuhapi* ("keeping the spirit" of the deceased), the *wasiglapi* (affronted) keep a lock of hair of the deceased for a year. During that time, the entire tiospaye begins to make and collect items for the release of the dead person's *nagi* (spirit) at the memorial feast. This time of mourning is also a time of industry for all. It is a time of humility and a time to make by hand, if possible, the necessary items. The number of star quilts made often is a mark of respect and love for the deceased. They also add to the prestige of the family. At the memorial feast, the quilts, sometimes numbering fifty to a hundred, are displayed in ceremonial structures called boweries. During the course of the memorial feast, the quilts are given to the guests of the family as thanks for their participation in the ceremony.

Star quilts also have entered the political area, with gifting to politicians and elected tribal, state, and federal offices. An unforeseen act of possible reciprocity is enacted when a tribal group or tribal officials gives a star quilt to a political figure. The October 15, 1986, *Lakota Times* featured Sen. Lawrence Pressler thanking a political tiospaye for receiving a star quilt: "Your beautiful quilt is one of our most cherished possessions" (6). Also pictured was Senator Tom Daschle, who held a "victory feed" at the Pine Ridge, Rosebud, and Cheyenne River reservations. At Rosebud, he was given a star quilt by the Vietnam Veterans' Association. This is the Sioux way of enmeshing politicians. Daschle is expected to reciprocate the gift in his subsequent legislative actions. When a bill is introduced in Congress to abrogate Indian treaties, tribal advocates should, perhaps, refer to this ultimate gift and expect proper decisions. But perhaps the Lakota metaphor of "giving to honor" is too subtle for the political arena.

In the important contemporary powwow circuit and in the recently proliferating Sun Dances, the giving of star quilts has become an established component of ritual exchange, particularly in Sioux communities. Quilts are often given to the singers or drum groups as a means of thanking the musicians for excellent performances or for singing an honor song. Often, however, the singers may, in turn, offer the quilts for sale in order to obtain gas money to return home.[2]

The proliferation of star quilts as ceremonial items and their use in the honorific aspects of reservation and larger society events have led to an increased demand for quilters. The last twenty years also have seen an explosion of interest in quilts and quilting within non-Native communities and a corresponding interest by non-Natives in acquiring Sioux quilts. This has enabled some Sioux quilters to augment their household incomes substantially through sales of quilts, both to other Sioux and to outside audiences.

The burgeoning demand also has fostered the establishment of economic organizations on reservations to help supply the quilts needed for ceremonial uses and also provide a means of income. As early as 1983, a cottage quiltmaking industry was founded on the Cheyenne Reservation. The *Lakota Times* reported, "This organization was a dream of two women, Marcia O'Leary and Deleen Kougl, a dream come true. The business provides opportunities for many women from the reservation to use not only their talents but also to incorporate years of tradition and heritage into present-day use through designing and creating hand-quilted star quilts and other hand-made products."

Another quilt business, founded in 1985 on the Sisseton-Wahpeton Reservation by a church-based economic grant program, specialized in decorator pillows (University of South Dakota 1987). Meanwhile, at one of the border towns adjacent to the reservations, a factory has been recently established to manufacture "Dakota quilts." Unfortunately, the factory does not employ any Indians and is simply trying to capitalize on the growing popularity of star quilts in the marketplace.[3]

Although quiltmaking activities have been initiated for economic development on many Lakota Sioux and Dakota Sioux reservations, many of these endeavors have relied primarily upon outside funding, and they have not had a great economic impact on the lives of women. It remains to be seen if the market will sustain the new cottage-craft industries. The majority of tourists in the Black Hills near Sioux reservations is interested only in buying Indian trinkets—tomahawks, beaded belts, and headbands made in Hong Kong—and not willing to purchase the higher-priced yet authentic, locally handmade quilts and other crafts. However, the adaptations of the star motif to lower-priced items such as sofa pillows, baby buntings, purses, and carrying bags seem more marketable. Within the context of the community, though, making and giving quilts has had a great impact on traditional systems of economy and prestige.

As star quilts have become increasingly more important to the ceremonial and ritual activities in contemporary Lakota Sioux and Dakota Sioux life, so has the influence of women in the maintenance of these traditions. As Patricia Albers observes, at Fort Totten, a Dakota reservation, "An area where women's influence had grown was in the social networks that organized and supported ceremonial activity on the reservation. Women were primarily responsible for building what the Dakota called 'collections,' that is, an accumulation of gifts to be distributed at these give-ways. . . . Most of these items were . . . reproduced directly by female labor, as in star quilts—one of the most prestigious goods in ceremonial exchanges" (Albers and Medicine 1983:130). Albers (1974) has also noted, "[Other quilts were] purchased through female incomes. Since women made most of the contributions to give-ways, it was their prerogative to decide to whom gifts would be given in the social networks that linked the Dakota at Devil's Lake to Indian people from neighboring communities in Canada and the United States. Through this activity a number of women gained considerable prestige and renown not only at Devil's Lake but on other reservations as well." This status has resulted in a saying often heard at social gatherings: "Women are the carriers of culture."

Notes

1. Jeanne Eder, an Assiniboine Sioux scholar, researched the appearance of quilting at the Fort Peck Reservation in Montana and presented the data in a slide show: "My Grandmother's Star Quilt Honors Me."

2. The recycling of quilts through exchange, sale, and gift-giving would be an excellent study of the movement of ceremonial goods throughout the Great Plains in the United States and Canada; a quilter's distinctiveness is also a mark of significance in this transfer.

3. I, as an anthropologist, have been trying to obtain information on this enterprise and have been unable to do so. This situation speaks to larger issues on the part of indigenous anthropologists and on the study of powerbases in the dominant society.

References

Albers, Patricia. 1974. "The Regional System of the Devil's Lake Sioux," Ph.D. diss., University of Wisconsin-Madison.

Albers, Patricia, and Beatrice Medicine. 1983. "The Role of Sioux Women in the Production of Ceremonial Objects: The Case of the Star Quilt." In *The Hidden Half: Studies of Plains Indian Women,* ed. Patricia Albers and Beatrice Medicine, 123–40. Washington: University Press of America.

Deloria, Ella. 1944. *Speaking of Indians.* New York: Friendship Press.

Feest, Christian F. 1982. *Native Arts of North America.* London: Thames and Hudson.

[University of South Dakota]. 1987. *Institute of Indian Studies New Report* 110(Feb.): 7.

The Lakota star quilt parade, Bullhead Powwow, 1998. (Courtesy of C. E. Burke)

PART 4

Beliefs and Well-Being

Native American Resistance to Integration: Contemporary Confrontations and Religious Revitalization

The fact that Native Americans survive with unique cultural distinctiveness reflective of tribal differences never ceases to amaze integrationists.[1] Historically, Indians have used both confrontation (wars, uprisings, and protests) and conciliatory acts (education, forced and selective conversions to Christianity, and self-help associations like the National Congress of American Indians, among other devices) as adaptive strategies to resist total assimilation into a dominant social system and a loss of cultural integrity.

It is certain that in the worldviews of most American Native people, the bounded and culturally defined universe of belief systems and indigenous value orientations are critical for the maintenance of basic philosophical systems that are reflected in personal life-styles. These often form the bases for resistance to integration. Worldviews allow for alternatives for changing adaptations that threaten tribal and individual maze-ways.

This essay attempts to explore in a tentative fashion an increasingly significant religious ritual—the Sun Dance of the Lakota Sioux. Examining the ritual in a contemporary framework, it appears as a mechanism for mediation of individual identity and absorption into the larger society. It also heralds a means of intensifying and guaranteeing cultural continuity in the face of perceived repression and reaction to social problems engendered by living within dual societies and acts as an access to enhanced ethnic identity. More salient, it may be seen as a rejection of coercion to religious systems that have long been dissonant with Native beliefs.

In the heightened return to Native religious beliefs, the Christian faiths that are ministering to the Sioux have altered their rituals to include Native elements. Thus, we see the Catholics utilizing a pipe as a sacred symbol in the mass (Steinmetz 1970). The Episcopal Church has also used Lakota symbols in the design of altar cloths and priestly vestments. This may be an overt attempt to retain Native adherents; it also indicates an awareness of increased Native religious concerns on the part of the proselytized people. I have not assessed the role of Native clergy in this attempt to mediate between Native ritual and Christianity. Finally, the revitalization of a Native belief system appears to be emerging as an essential to the establishment of a required ethical system and as a means of strengthening Indian identity in the contemporary United States.

Messianic movements and nativistic aspirations by American Natives in response to the superimposition of new life-ways have been well documented in the anthropological literature. Wallace (1969) has described the syncretic Code of Handsome Lake, which has supplied a viable religious code for the Seneca and other Six Nation groups. Specific for the group under scrutiny, Mooney (1896, 1965), Walker (1917), Deloria (1929), Miller (1959), Melody (1976), and countless others have written about the Sun Dance and the Ghost Dance. The analyses have centered upon events in the nineteenth century and have presented the view that by participating in such classic millenarian movements as the Ghost Dance a pristine, aboriginal culture would be restored among the Sioux, and the white intruders would disappear from the Natives' land. A return of departed kin and decimated animals that contributed to the well-being and sustenance of the tribes would ensure the continuity of an uninterrupted Native life. This reaction to domination is certainly comprehensible when one apprises the situation of that time. As Underhill (1977:259–60) writes:

> Those who needed the new gospel most tragically were the Sioux. Up to now, they had felt themselves conquerors, the only Indians who had not lost a battle with the whites. They had kept the Bozeman Trail open for ten years. They had demolished Custer's command. But some of their chiefs had seen the change coming. On the promise of tools, food, and clothing they had accepted a huge reservation where they could still hunt deer, even if the buffalo were gone. There, they had expected to camp as they pleased, meeting the whites on equal terms, while they considered the "new road" at their leisure. Then, somehow, nine million acres of their best land were gone. The bands found themselves confined on small, separate reservations and treated like a conquered people. They went through the hardships of drought, locusts, and failure of supplies as did the other Plains tribes. They soon began to divide into factions: the "friendlies" who were tired and ready to succumb and the "hostiles" who hoped for war. To the Indian agent, they were all rebellious savages. He was a political appointee whose orders were to "keep the Indians quiet," and his usual idea of doing this was to summon the military camped at various forts located around the country. The Indians resented the forts located in their old hunting grounds. And they resented the tough little pioneer towns crowding close to the reservations. Men in saloons of those towns spoke of killing a Sioux as "making him into a good Indian."

The forgoing selection is presented not to evoke sympathy but to provide a contextualization that often provokes nativistic movements that are oriented to social change. These conditions are also historical facts that are utilized by many participants in contemporary, radical movements and serve as a rationale for concerted action and articulation to change socioeconomic conditions among Native Americans today.

Present-day conditions in most areas where Native Americans reside have not changed drastically. Decreased infant mortality, improved health conditions, and a possible greater longevity have been quoted as measures of a changed quality of life. Rather than dwell upon the many dismal images depicting present-day Indian life, the following succinct statement from the American Indian Policy Review Commission's final report will suffice: "Today, available statistics on Indians in the United States continue to paint a picture of widespread deprivation unequalled by any other United States sub-group. Whether men or women, living in the city or country, Indians in the United States suffer from inadequate education, and relatively poor health, low incomes, poor housing, and sanitary conditions generally regarded as unacceptable" (1977–78:90).

Understandable then is the formation of the American Indian Movement (AIM) in Minneapolis in 1969. It was an apparent reaction against poverty, inequity in employment, racism, and police harassment. Comprehensible also is a response to exclusive and elitist university education and a hope for a more relevant education for minority students, which was basic to the establishment

Medicine with Jean O'Brien at the Weisman Museum of Art, Minneapolis, 1995. (Courtesy of Warren Bruland)

of ethnic studies departments (Medicine 1971). Further radicalism by university students led to the seizure of Alcatraz Island in 1969 (Talbot 1978). Deloria (1973:15) writes: "Shortly after the island was closed as a prison in 1964, a number of Sioux Indians then living in the San Francisco Bay Area landed on the island and claimed it under the 1868 Fort Laramie Treaty with their tribe. In 1964 there were few people around in the Indian community who were willing to risk a prison sentence to demonstrate a legal technicality, so the invasion sputtered and died. For the record, the first invasion of Alcatraz Island was led by Allen Cottier, Dick MacKenzie, and Adam Nordwall." The significance of this assessment is that social movements are reflective of the most propitious sociocultural climate in which they can be generated for effectiveness.

It is important to recognize that the confrontative act that captured the imagination of the world precipitated other "land grabs" of excess federal property like the military installation near Davis, California, which resulted in the establishment of Deganaweda-Quetezcoatl (D-Q) University for Native American and Chicano (Mexican-American) students who previously, through inferior educational preparation, had been barred from academe.[2] Another take-over of federal property was the seizure of Ft. Lawton near Seattle, where an urban Indian coalition—the United Indians of All Tribes Foundation—was eventually founded. It has operated as an innovative and ameliorative service model for urban Indians who had migrated to this area during World War II and the subsequent relocation period of the 1950s.

Increasing radical action culminated in the caravan of Indians of all tribes and ages in the "Trail of Broken Treaties" entourage to Washington, D.C., in 1973 (Burnette and Koster 1974). There, the Bureau of Indian Affairs building was seized and held for some time. This basically was an action against the bureaucratic ineptitude of a governmental agency. However, the most vehement and grim confrontation was that of Wounded Knee II, which was directed against a so-called puppet government. This reaction to dominance—not only by the Bureau of Indian Affairs but also through the elected tribal council established by the Indian Reorganization Act of 1934—has had the most disruptive effect on not only the Wounded Knee hamlet but also on the entire reservation of Pine Ridge in South Dakota. The repercussions of kin against kith, intra-group hostility, mutual distrust of such indigenous entities as the "traditional chiefs" and the newly formed Lakota Civil Rights Association, and the ubiquitous tribal council are great. One must caution, however, that although Wounded Knee II called national attention to the asserted illegalities of the tribal chairman, the situation described there can easily be duplicated on many other reservations in the United States. Frequently, elected tribal councils form a Native elite group supervising a "traditional" and/or "full-blood" and powerless constituency. Nepotism and self-aggrandizement are more frequent than expected in this indigenous bureaucracy.

Native Americans do not live in a social vacuum even though many live on reservations and some live in urban ghettos. The ripple effect of these confrontations and the demands for retribution—both monetary and in land returns—have affected perceptions and behaviors of members in the larger society. Retaliatory acts such as the formation of the Interstate Congress for Equal Rights and Responsibilities, organized in 1976 with headquarters in Martin, South Dakota, plus the Cunningham bill to abrogate all treaties with Indian tribes, which was unsuccessfully introduced in the 1978 Congress, are but two salient features of the so-called white backlash movement recently generated in the United States. It was primarily the Cunningham bill and the reaction to repression that formed the basis for the "Longest Walk," which culminated in Washington, D.C., in the summer of 1978. It was that peaceful protest that stressed the spirituality of Indian people. Religious practitioners and elders figured prominently in the walk.

The previous account has spelled out the social parameters of contemporary American Indian life. Continued confrontations have seemingly resulted in intensified restrictions by the dominant society. In South Dakota, for example, there is a renewed attempt by the state to achieve legal jurisdiction over Sioux reservations. Rosebud Reservation lost the fight against state jurisdiction in 1976. Attempts for previous state control were successfully thwarted by the combined efforts of the seven reservations in 1955. A Lakota viewpoint is expressed by Frank Ducheneaux, Sr., then chair of the Cheyenne River Sioux Tribal Council: "Somehow or other the idea has grown that Indian reservations are no-man's lands of lawlessness and that the tribal councils are fostering that lawlessness by opposing State jurisdiction on the reservations" (1956:20). Of significance in that quotation is the implication that important elements of autonomy and cultural identity are basic to Native American identity and uniqueness. Moreover, the fight to maintain an aspect of "Indian-ness" has been a continual one. Concerted efforts to maintain legal and cultural integrity have been and continue to be valued and defended.

There are, however, subtle pressures that tend to reinforce the desire for cultural maintenance and ethnic identity among most tribes in the United States. The federal government's tenacious trust in its treaty obligations to the various tribes is basic to tribal sovereignty.

Although South Dakota has been viewed as a vanguard of racism and discrimination toward Indian people (Stevens 1978), these situations exist in most areas where Native Americans live. At present, the Boldt decision, which ruled in favor of tribes in a fishing rights struggle in Washington state, is being challenged. Repression seems rampant in many areas.

What has not been largely discernible in the realm of confrontation and voluminous verbalization of Indian rights is an increasing involvement in Native belief systems. It is clear that aspects of spirituality and a revitalization of indigenous beliefs to meet the needs of a wide variety of pan-tribal participants in a social movement of protest became inevitable and imperative. An ethical and philosophical base was not strongly evident in the early actions, although there was the odd reference to "spiritual needs" (Deloria 1973; Harvey 1970). The one compelling ritual of rebellion that has, and is increasingly achieving, inter-tribal commitment is the Sun Dance of the Teton (Lakota) Sioux. It appears conceptually apt and adaptive and meets the functional prerequisites of modern individuals of Indian ancestry searching for a Native identity, an ideology, and a religious experience.

This religious ritual, historically seen as the ultimate expression of paganism, possibly because of the elements of self-torture as a means of supplication to the Wakan Tanka (Great Sacredness), was banned by governmental decree among the Sioux in the 1880s. As Burnette (a Rosebud Sioux) and Koster (1974:30) indicate, "The Sun Dance was a symbol of solidarity—all the various bands of the Sioux nation would assemble for the ritual. Because of this, the Sun Dance came in for a heavy dose of suppression by White authorities."

Because the ceremony rallied Sioux bands who were seen as enemies by the U.S. government, the ban not only undercut the philosophical basis of a Native society but also was a powerful means of social control. Valentine McGillycuddy, the agent at Pine Ridge, outlawed the Sun Dance in 1881 in direct contradiction of the 1868 Sioux Treaty, which allowed for the practice of indigenous religion. He threatened any full-blooded Lakota Indian who participated or attended the Sun Dance by withholding rations. He also threatened to imprison half-breeds who attended (McGillycuddy 1941:167–68).

Since the 1950s, when the Sun Dance was reactivated as a public event on Pine Ridge Reservation, this ritual and others of a minor quality—Yuwipi (To Tie One) and Wopila (To Give Thanks)—have proliferated in the contemporary life of the Lakota Sioux on most major reservations in South Dakota. Until recently, the Sun Dance of the Lakota has been mainly a restatement of ethnographic data (Melody 1976; Powers 1977) that was previously published. Mails (1978) has provided extensive ethnographic descriptive data on contemporary Sun Dances—the leaders, the intercessors, and the observed ritual and ceremonial actions. The transformation of the Sun Dance is implied in Burnette and Koster (1974:30):

> The Sun Dance was forbidden for many years, although traditionals risked jail or beatings to hold small ceremonies in secret. More recently the Sun Dance has been practiced openly, but some non-traditional Indians have tried to capitalize on it by allowing concessionaires to set up hot-dog stands and carnival rides just outside the consecrated dance circle. At Pine Ridge, a tribal politician named Dick Wilson, later to win fame or notoriety at Wounded Knee II, organized a rodeo as part of the Sun Dance celebration. Many older Indians found this, and the charging of admission to old Indians who wanted to watch the dance, more insulting than the government's previous suppression. The traditionals and some of the young activists took to holding their own Sun Dances away from the fairgrounds and carnival atmosphere.

The description is important, for it was the general ambiance of the ceremony when it became a ritual event in the realm of activism.

As the minor rituals of Yuwipi and Wopila tend to meet the more individualistic and functional needs of family and kin on Lakota reservations, they have been transmitted to urban centers. These, and related ceremonies called "sweats" (using a sweat lodge, or *inipi*) and "prayer meetings" (peyote meetings of adherents of the Native American Church), have achieved new dimensions in such metropolitan centers as Denver, San Francisco, Los Angeles, and Seattle. Participation in Sun Dances is producing ritualists who have been called "instant medicine men" or "self-styled medicine men." Whatever the dynamics of a proliferating Native religious ethic, this transformation clearly shows the ceremonial networks of Native Lakota Sioux beliefs. They are also reflective of the complementarity of urban and reservation in the life-styles of modern Indians.

The Wounded Knee II confrontation in 1973, with the resultant disruptions in life on Pine Ridge and encounters with tribal, state, and federal authorities, precipitated the movement of the Sun Dance encampment. Presently, the intertribal and international character of participants has centered upon Green Grass on Cheyenne River Reservation in South Dakota, where the Sacred Calf Pipe of the Ocete Sacowin (Seven Council Fires of the Lakota nation) has traditionally been lodged and revered.

It seems obvious that a major symbolic act of being a "traditional" Native American is "to Sun Dance" and, eventually, "to pierce." Participation in this ritual is rapidly becoming a symbol of traditionality and an ethnic marker for many Native people of all tribes—those who are affiliated with the American Indian Movement, those who live in urban areas, and those whose quest for identity and individual or social change necessitates the search for a symbolic and ritual system. The Sun Dance, with its history of repression and expression of torture for self and society, appears to meet manifest needs of many present-day Natives. Significantly, the participation in this symbolic and ritual system transcends tribal affiliation and previous belief orientation. Urban Indians of Lakota heritage return to dance, to observe, and to obtain the benefits that accrue from attendance. Chippewa Indians are encouraged to participate in this ritual that belonged culturally to their traditional enemies. One Chippewa (or, as they prefer to be called by their own linguistic designation, Anishinabe) indicated that he knew it was a Lakota rite. As an Anishinabe, he felt he had no right to participate, although he was criticized because he declined to become involved. Micmac Indians from New Brunswick, Canada, felt obligated to regain an Indian identity by making a pilgrimage to Pine Ridge—even if they did not partake of the ritual experience. Members of the American Indian Movement have used participation and, more important, piercing as a new badge of commitment.

The intertribal character of participants over a period of time has not been tabulated. One can gauge the increase of dancers when one notes the increase—

from fifty-seven dancers in the 1976 Sun Dance at Green Grass to ninety in 1978. Since 1975, the Minneconjou Indian Culture Society from the tribal museum at Eagle Butte, headquarters of the Cheyenne River Indian Agency, apparently has given substantial monetary aid. Advertising with printed posters and supplying food and gas money for the dancers and stipends for the principal medicine men are some ways in which the ritual is subsidized. Thus, the larger tribal polity is involved in an indirect way. The director of the museum is a returned urbanite whose husband has acted, and continues to do so, in the Hollywood movie industry.

Data relating to economic reimbursement is not available at this time for the Green Grass Sun Dance. However, a tradition of paying Sun Dance leaders has been well established on Pine Ridge. For example, Frank Fool's Crow, who was eighty-seven years old in 1978 and is noted for his religious zeal and commitment to the Lakota religion, was paid $500 in both 1976 and 1977 for conducting the Sun Dance there. Money is forthcoming from the coffers of the tribal council and is distributed through the Sun Dance committee, which supervises the logistics of the ritual (Lewis 1972:45–58).

Since the move of the Sun Dance ritual to Green Grass, the area has assumed more sacredness, for the symbol of the sacred calf pipe is a cherished tradition among the Lakota. Sacredness of land is also exemplified via the lodging of the Sacred Pipe there. The Sacred Pipe still remains in the family who has had it for generations. At this time, the proscription that the symbol of Lakota religion not be opened still mandates activities surrounding the ritual object. The pipekeeper's father is becoming increasingly active in ceremonies that predominate in reservation life. He is present at naming ceremonies, powwows, funerary rites, and rites of reintegration immediately following the deaths of individuals in more traditional Lakota families.

Speaking of the increase of other ceremonial events in the Plains, Deloria (1973:253) notes, "Other tribes have seen an increasing interest in recent years as specific ceremonies became the objects of people's affection. Naming ceremonies in some tribes appear to have become much more numerous, as urban Indians seeking a means of preserving an Indian identity within the confusion of the city have asked reservation people to sponsor naming ceremonies for them. They have traveled sometimes thousands of miles and spent thousands of dollars to be able to participate in such events." Native ritual, then, is assuming more importance in the lives of Indians today.

In a recent book entitled *Oglala Religion*, Powers makes a very important statement in a short summation: "At the white man's end of the scale they [Oglala] observe technology and change. But at the Oglala end, they see ideology and continuity. There they find a connection with the past expressed in the concept of *wakan*, that which is sacred, but also, that which is old" (1977:205). The essence of Lakota belief and identity is expressed and actualized in the concept of wakan. It is this substructure of a moral and ethical system that forms a philosophical base, which is cogently analyzed by DeMallie and Lavenda (1977). The essence of the power that is actualized by Native Lakota-speakers and ritual participants is captured by their statement: "The concept of power is a key to understanding the cultural systems of the Siouan peoples of the Plains. It symbolizes a natural philosophy and serves as an integrating concept of the Siouan universe" (1977:153).

The underlying basis of a ritual for establishing and sustaining an ethnic identity on an intertribal plane, then, poses some questions as to the deep-seated commitment and emotional tone of such a philosophical base. Later, they state: "It becomes clear that the Dakota concept of power, conceived of as an attribute of things and persons, is by no means an impersonal force shared by all to a greater or lesser extent. Impersonally, *wakan* remains an unknowable, unrelatable concept; only through the actions of *wakan* in the specific life forms of the world does this power become knowable and meaningful. It is always intensely personal in its manifestations" (159).

To bilingual and bicultural Lakota Sioux people, this concept has been an organizing principle in the Native belief system and has been transmuted to encompass the "holy" and the "sacred" aspects of the Christian sects to which many Siouan-speakers belong. Therefore, the question looms enormously in the examination of the Sun Dance as an emergent religion that can deal effectively with a multitribal group of participants.

An examination of the motives of recent Sun Dance dancers is needed for theoretical development of nativistic movements in the present day. Theoretical contributions of Wallace, deriving from his revitalization and maze-way resynthesis models plus Aberle's (1966) "cultural deprivation" formations, have important implications for analyzing the modern revivalistic ritual of the Lakota Sun Dance.

For some present-day Sioux Indians, participation in Sun Dances hinges upon a "reformative" desire. Often, individual motivation and participation in such religious ritual is noticeably absent from anthropological literature. In reporting on current religious revivals (Amoss 1978), aspects of psychological processes, social organizational features, and the idiosyncratic motivations for individual involvement are left unclarified. In attempting to develop a typology of social movements, Kopytoff (1964:86) refers to "reformative" movements as a cluster of "ideological referents" and a "desire to change existing culture or parts of it." It appears, therefore, that a problem to be "solved" by Sun Dancing is a potent motivation for some Lakota people. In this case, the problem to be solved—or at least diminished—is the excessive use of alcohol on some reservations. The data that point in this direction are not in the great intertribal Sun Dance (Pine Ridge and Green Grass) but in the smaller, community-based ceremonies (Mails 1978:47–60). Other problems stemming from social and economic deprivation, extreme poverty, and a disadvantaged position in a dominant and racist society can also be seen as latent functions (Jorgensen 1972).

In addition, participation in the intertribal Sun Dance is an important political statement for many. It is also, as previously noted, a means of ethnic identity and clearly a manifestation of nativism. In a description of Pine Ridge Sun
Dances for the 1969–70 period, Lewis writes:

> Today the Sun Dance retains important functions, but the emphasis has shifted
> from religious to social functions—and an economic factor has been added.
> Much of the spiritual significance is lost in the commercial aspects of the cel-
> ebration. The ritual as performed today is awesome and colorful, but is a mere
> fragment of the traditional ceremony. The motives of the dancers are more
> superficial and even trivial and their sacrifice is certainly less. Still, more and
> more people, including young adults, consider the Sun Dance to be *the* "Indi-
> an religion," *the* Dakota religion, or at least the most conspicuous public dis-
> play of old religion or revived aspects of it. (1972:47, italics in original)

If one extends Aberle's term *redemptive* to the analysis of participation in contemporary Sun Dances, one can readily see the primary objective of seeking
change for individuals.

Another feature that has been discussed in Jorgensen (1972), with data for the
Great Basin cultures, particularly the Ute, has been the Sun Dance as an instrument of power to a powerless people in dealing with social inequities. This is a
ritual means of coping with social and economic deprivation. As far as emergent Lakota Sun Dances are concerned, the sparse data on individual reasons
for involvement do not allow for cross-cultural comparisons. The data presented
above, given by "M.D.," certainly does not indicate how the motives attributed
to the dancers were derived. Jorgensen presents a useful mode of analysis that
he labels an "agentive" approach to social action, which offers possibilities for
further and future analyses.

In the dynamics of motivations for individual participation in ritual structures there is little that gives clues to an emic approach. The fact that a total of
eight Sun Dances was held in South Dakota in 1978 speaks to the increased
emphasis upon the functions—both latent and manifest—of the ritual.

Although examining the rationale for individual participation is not the aim
of Mails's (1978) book, his rich, descriptive accounts of ritual and symbolic forms
are important. The difficulty in obtaining articulations for involvement for each
dancer is acknowledged. Motives for participation were transmitted by William
Schweigman (Eagle Feather) via tape recordings. Native interpretations and
rationales in the genesis of indigenous revitalization movements are generally
absent in the ethnographic literature. This is especially true for Native people
involved in the recent confrontative milieu. Since the 1960s, most tribal people
have categorically rejected anthropologists, although dyadic pairs of Natives and
non-Natives have appeared as coauthors, for example, Burnette and Koster
(1974), Lame Deer and Erdoes (1972), and Pelletier and Poole (1973).

Bharati raises a relevant point: "The question of whether an anthropologist's being born and raised in an informant or subject society affects his work is certainly an interesting one" (1959:258). This poses many questions for research into revitalization movements or indeed any research done by indigenous persons. Many of us have been subjected to cries of "subjectivity" or "where is the data?" In the area of belief systems, this holds equally for Native investigators and those Native innovators who are, in a sense, attempting to reconstruct a philosophical system to meet changing times and needs.

Further, Bharati continues, "The ultimate reduction in the study of religion seems to lie in symbology. I suggested earlier that we might be better off if we jettisoned symbol talk altogether in the investigations of religions that do not use 'symbol' emically" (262). He further states a need for a "definitional genre, built on a linguistic matrix or a set of ethnosemantic data. A linguistic theory might generate the logical deduction of a belief pattern that might then be called a symbol. In an ethnosemantic theory, the actors themselves would create a body of stipulated meanings capable of being conventionalized, from which 'ex-post-facto' symbols could then be deduced" (262).

If we view emic analyses as a factual portrayal of a people's involvement with the sacred symbols in an emotional and cultural context, then various levels of interpretation may emerge from the examination of the Sun Dance. Deloria (1973:269–70) observes that "the primary thesis of tribal religions, the relationship of a particular people with a particular land, and the belief of many tribal religions that certain places have special sacred significance must itself be tested in the years ahead. Young Indians must once again take up the vision quests, the search for revelations and dreams, and the responsibility to make the tribal community come alive even with the tremendous hurdles that exist in the modern world." This caveat is being executed, for within the past year several young Lakota men have sought vision quests. The sacred and symbolic Bear Butte north of the sacred Black Hills in South Dakota has been ascended. Some seekers have a sacred approach. Some, mainly urban folk, have punctuated their vision-questing with descents and respites for watermelon and/or carbonated soft drinks!

What is tantamount in the building of a belief system and symbolic structure is that the basic, underlying value configurations that traditionally formed the basis for a functional and meaningful belief system be comprehended and actualized. In the spirit of self-determination, which is the next dictum to the Native people of the United States, execution of the codification of a Native belief system may be achieved if Lakota medicine men and other ritualists as intercessors, along with female participants like the Sacred Pipe Woman and others, examine the moral and ethical code and place it in a meaningful framework for operating in a modern world.

The reaction to oppression needs to be mediated. Many militants of the 1960s had completely decried the conversions to Christianity and the adaptations to a "white" life-style. Cries of "Apples!" or "Sell-outs!" or "Uncle Tomahawks!" and other pejorative descriptions were commonly utilized. A search for a "new traditionality" can be seen as a gloss for the new searchers for a Native belief. Many statements in the rich oral history of our tribes have reinforced the written facts that Native Americans made adaptations to a new life-style as a means of survival. The fact that Native languages were suppressed poses some problems in the transmission of esoteric songs, prayers, and ritual behavior in Native languages, which are being retrieved in many tribes. The need for intercessors and adepts who are bilingual, or who are willing to learn a Native language, is an important factor in concretizing a ritual structure. The need for apprentices who are articulate in the Native language and can deal with ethnosemantic and philosophical rubrics is an aspect of cultural transmission that may ensure cultural continuity and integrity.

At the present time, there are few individuals involved in religious revivals who are examining their own motivations and actions as ritualists and participants. At the present time, the complete individuality of the various Sun Dance leaders has concentrated upon ritual performance and ego gratification. The underpinnings of the theological and philosophical bases still remain largely unexamined and unanalyzed.

In assessing the impact of the Lakota Sun Dance, one is aware of the manifestation of one of the four cardinal virtues of the Lakota—generosity (the other three being fortitude, bravery, and integrity). Thus, by invoking the virtue of generosity, a generosity of inclusiveness could account for the acceptance of half-breeds, members from other tribal groups, and, in some cases, Canadian Indians. This value of individual autonomy could also explain the wide variety of "medicine men" now proliferating in the United States.

The Sun Dance of the Lakota, then, complies with an expressed need for a ritual that surpasses idiosyncratic tribal identities and derives from a "culture of subordination" that has been common to all tribal people in North America. Based upon a ritual of suppression, it is now seen as a mode of resistance to integration. An outstanding feature of involvement is to manifest the positive aspects of being a Native American. As a reenactment of positive ethnic identity, it serves as an important cultural marker transmitting pride in Native life.

Notes

1. The term *Native Americans,* the most recent gloss for North American aborigines, is now in disfavor with many tribal groups and individuals. The National Congress of American Indians, a powerful self-interest group, has passed a resolution (1978) opposing its use at their last convention. Throughout the historic Indian-white interface, such names as "North American Indians," "American Indians," "Amerindian," "Indian-American," and "First-Americans" have been in vogue at various times. In this essay, I use Native American and American Indian interchangeably. As for the focus on the essay, the Lakota, who are often labeled "Sioux," "Teton Sioux," "Western Lakota," and "Dakota" in the anthropological literature, I use the term *Lakota,* for I am referring primarily to the Western Sioux who speak

the Lakota dialect of the Siouan language. I also use such designations as "Rosebud Sioux" to indicate the reservation as a social system to which one assigns oneself. This is accepted procedure by most Lakota Sioux.

2. Interestingly, D-Q University conducted an intertribal Sun Dance in the summer of 1976.

References

Aberle, David F. 1966. "The Peyote Religion among the Navajo." *Viking Fund Publication in Anthropology*, no. 42. New York.

American Indian Policy Review Commission. 1977–78. *Meetings of the American Indian Policy Review Commission.* Washington: Government Printing Office.

Amoss, Pamela. 1978. *Coast Salish Spirit Dancing: The Survival of an Ancestral Religion.* Seattle: University of Washington Press.

Bharati, Agehananda. 1959. "Anthropological Approaches to the Study of Religion: Ritual and Belief Systems." In *Biennial Review of Anthropology,* ed. Bernard J. Siegel, 230–82. Stanford: Stanford University Press.

Burnette, Robert, and John Koster. 1974. *The Road to Wounded Knee.* New York: Bantam Books.

Deloria, Ella. 1929. "The Sun Dance of the Oglala Sioux." *Journal of American Folklore* 42: 354–413.

Deloria, Vine, Jr. 1973. *God Is Red.* New York: Grosset and Dunlap.

DeMallie, Raymond J., Jr., and Robert H. Lavenda. 1977. "Wakan: Plains Siouan Concepts of Power." In *The Anthropology of Power: Ethnographic Studies from Asia, Oceania, and the New World,* ed. Raymond D. Fogelson and Richard N. Adams, 153–65. New York: Academic Press.

Ducheneaux, Frank, Sr. 1956. "The Cheyenne River Sioux." [Association of American Indian Affairs] *The American Indian* 8(3): 20–30.

Harvey, Byron. 1970. *Thoughts from Alcatraz.* Phoenix: Arequipa Press.

Jorgensen, Joseph G. 1972. *The Sun Dance Religion: Power for the Powerless.* Chicago: University of Chicago Press.

Kopytoff, Igor. 1964. "Classification of Religious Movements: Analytical and Synthetic." In *Symposium on New Approaches to the Study of Religion,* ed. June Helm, 77–90. Seattle: University of Washington Press.

Lame Deer/John Fire, and Richard Erdoes. 1972. *Lame Deer, Seeker of Visions.* New York: Simon and Shuster.

Lewis, Thomas H. 1972. "The Oglala (Teton Dakota) Sun Dance: Vicissitudes of Its Structure And Function." *Plains Anthropologist* 17(55): 44–49.

Mails, Thomas E. 1978. *Sundancing at Rosebud and Pine Ridge.* Sioux Falls: Center for Western Studies.

McGillycuddy, Julia. 1941. *McGillycuddy, Agent: A Biography of Dr. Valentine T. McGillycuddy.* Stanford: Stanford University Press.

Medicine, Beatrice. 1971. "The Anthropologist and American Indian Studies Programs." *Indian Historian* 4(1): 15–18, 63.

Melody, Michael E. 1976. "The Lakota Sun Dance: A Composite View and Analysis." *South Dakota History* 6(4): 433–55.

Miller, David H. 1959. *Ghost Dance.* New York: Duell, Sloan and Pearce.

Mooney, James. 1896. "The Ghost Dance Religion and the Sioux Outbreak of 1890." In *Fourteenth Annual Report of the Bureau of American Ethnology,* pt. 2. Washington: Government Printing Office.

————. 1965. *The Ghost-Dance Religion and the Sioux Outbreak of 1890.* Chicago: University of Chicago Press.

Pelletier, Wilfred, and Ted Poole. 1973. *No Foreign Land.* Toronto: McClelland and Steward.

Powers, William K. 1977. *Oglala Religion.* Lincoln: University of Nebraska Press.

Steinmetz, Paul B. 1970. "The Relationship between Plains Indian Religion and Christianity: A Priest's View." *Plains Anthropologist* 15(48): 83–86.

Stevens, Don, and Jane Stevens. 1978. "South Dakota: The Mississippi of the North." [American Indian Historical Society] *WASSAJA: An Indian Newspaper* (June–Oct.): 6–7.

Talbot, Steve. 1978. "Free Alcatraz: The Culture of Native American Liberation." *Journal of Ethnic Studies* 6(3): 83–96.

Underhill, Ruth. 1977. *Red Man's Religion: Beliefs and Practices of the Indians North of Mexico.* Chicago: University of Chicago Press.

Walker, J. R. 1917. "The Sun Dance and Other Ceremonies of the Oglala Division of the Teton Lakota." *Anthropological Papers of the American Museum of Natural History* 16(2): 51–221.

Wallace, Anthony F. C. 1969. *The Death and Rebirth of Seneca.* New York: Vintage Books.

American Indian Women: Spirituality and Status

Native American women in traditional societies were deeply embedded in the spiritual universe that permeated every phase and aspect of their life-ways and life-cycles.[1] As a generalization, this seems to be valid across tribal cultures in the pre-contact situation. This truism is also reflective of the delicately but well-integrated gender roles of males and females in Native societies before the onslaught of imperialistic European contact.

Beyond these all-encompassing statements, one must elect to examine each tribal entity in light of the ethnographic and oral history records and to explicate the varied roles and statuses in each distinct culture. Thus, it is almost a travesty to discuss "American Indian women's spirituality," writ large. Not only are tribal differences important, but the selective adaptations that Indian people of all tribes have made in cultural contact and change are also real factors that must be constantly in the forefront of any discussions dealing with American Indian women who have been socialized in a tribal milieu. This caveat is often ignored in feminist writings about American Indian women. The common stereotype of a monolithic Indian woman seems prevalent.

Spirituality in presently extant tribal groups is also extremely varied. There are degrees of traditionality apparent in the continuation of Native belief systems. There are commitments to Christianity that have many adherents. There is, at present, revitalization of Native religions such as the Sun Dance among the Siouan groups, which is attracting males and females of all tribes and all ages. This is significant, for the Sun Dance has been repressed and outlawed as a "pagan" rite and "heathen" practice since the 1880s. Other religious ceremonies among many tribes, as the Native American Church or peyote religion, have been equally harassed. Scarcely comprehended is the fact that all Native religions were seen as savage myths. The road to civilization was the destruction of the Native beliefs and languages that form the basis for the philosophical and ethical systems of Native Americans. It speaks to the spiritual resilience of Native people of the New World that their belief systems have persisted at all.

To give a view of feminine spirituality that was the operative in traditional cultures, one tribal experience will be presented. This is necessary because many tribal groups do not wish to have their belief systems publicized. In many areas of Native North America, spiritual realms and their manifestations are well-guarded. Niethammer (1977) presents a potpourri of "religion and spirituality" experiences for women in societies ranging from Coast Salish in the northwestern part of the United States to Menominee and other Algonkian-speakers in the Woodlands culture area of the Midwest. An example of these spiritual events was vision-questing among the Nez Percé of Idaho in which "every ten-year-old child was sent to the mountains to seek a guardian spirit" (Niethammer 1977:360). From this statement, one must surmise that both boys and girls were submitted to this initial rite.

The different enactments and experiences along sex lines are not clear, however, in many ethnographies. That statement is not a derogation of ethnographic interpretation but a dilemma that confronts those who write about the Native societies of North America. The tribal variation is so great, and the reporting has been so androcentric, that feminine roles and behaviors in traditional societies are often blurred or nonexistent in ethnographies.

Whatever the tribal group, feminine aspects were fully integrated into its lifestyles. However varied the interpretations or enactment of belief systems and manifestations of spiritual experiences, most Native groups provided complementary spiritual roles for men and women. Thus, there were ceremonies for males and others for females that were tied to the developmental aspects of the life-cycle. Closely correlated to these ceremonial events was the all-endowing and perduring cultural mandate of "power," which was equated with supernatural force that permeated all objects—animate and inanimate. This omnipotent and pervasive spiritual force was known as *wakan* among Siouan-speakers, *orenda* among the Iroquoian groups, and had still other categorizations. This spiritual force served as a powerful enforcing element and basic organizing principle in directing one's life—for both males and females. It was the matrix and nexus of spirituality for both sexes.

In keeping with the caveat of secrecy and respect for other Indian women's belief systems, discussion will center upon the Teton Lakota (often called Sioux). This presentation will not violate a sacred trust, for much of this brief focus upon Siouan spirituality is more fully explicated in major ethnographies such as Hassrick (1964) and Black Elk (1953). The following is a description of the salient features of a Lakota Sioux female's maturational phases, which evoke *wakan* (spiritual power) and direct her life.

A Lakota mother, upon birth of a female child, would follow certain prescriptions to ensure the child's indoctrination into the proper role of a "good" Lakota female and the guarantee of wakan powers and protection. As with the son's, in this "male dominant" warrior society the afterbirth was placed in a tree as an offering to the Wakan Tanka (Great Sacredness). This act was indicative of the sacredness of the tree as a symbol of the Sun Dance, in which the tree is seen as a mediator between earth and sky—persons and *wakan* (powerful sacredness).

Furthermore, in the Sun Dance Ceremony, the highest honor for a virgin maiden was to be chosen to symbolically "cut" the sacred tree. Placing the afterbirth in the tree put the individual in proper relationship with the *wakan* (power that permeated the entire universe). After the umbilical cord fell off, it was placed in an amulet that was shaped like a turtle or a sand lizard. Because these two beings are strong and difficult to kill, they are fitting figures for protective amulets. Interestingly, two were made by the mother (or her mother) during her pregnancy. One was merely a decoy to protect the child from malevolent forces. Good and evil powers were recognized as actual arenas of interaction.

A naming ceremony for children occurred four days after birth. At this time, well-wishers thanked the family for the feast and asked that the child be healthy until "the ears were pierced." The father asked a brave warrior to pierce the boy's or girl's ears at the next Sun Dance. This act, which happened when the child walked, indicated that the religious and ethical system of the Lakota would be accepted fully. Thereafter, the Lakota way of life was his or her modus operandi.

For Lakota girls, the next major rite of passage was the female menarche. Essentially, this complemented the boy's vision quest. For the girl, this event was especially meaningful and significant. The Ball-Throwing Ceremony or the Buffalo Ceremony marked the event. Either recognized the wakan nature of femininity. Creativity in producing life was seen as a powerful aspect of Lakota womanhood. There were many symbolic aspects involved that focused upon the wakan attributed to the female. Sexuality of symbols—the drinking of red chokecherry juice, the actions of the male religious practitioner who initiated the fecundity of buffalo, and the special painting of red designs on the face and head of an emergent woman—all recognized creativity. All were spiritual acts that had great import on changed female status and role.

The power of creation inherent in women was recognized by isolation in the menstrual hut outside the *tipi* (dwelling) of the household group. Subsequent isolation has often been described in the ethnographic literature as pollution. However, it was felt by the Lakota that the power of women was so great at this time that it could destroy the potency of the medicine bundles and war paraphernalia of the males in the extended family (*tiospaye*). During the initial isolation, the young female concentrated upon the arts of quilling and making moccasins to ensure her future industry and diligence. Creativity—the potential of fertility, fecundity, and power—was highlighted by these rites, which marked a change in status and heralded the continuity of the group and the life-way. Songs, chants, dance, and expressive verbal admonitions—sacred and es-oteric—were part of this ritual of honor for women.

Possibly the most widely recognized and aspired-to rite of recognition and respect for Lakota post-pubescent girls was to be chosen as one of the four vir-gin maidens to symbolically cut the sacred Sun Dance tree each summer. This was a vivid manifestation of regard for females who lived the ideals of the soci-ety. It was also an effective means of social control for young women. Nonethe-less, it almost always elicited the attentions of a young warrior well-endowed with war coups and hunting and horse-stealing skills. Horses were offered to the family of the girl as a respectful way of asking for her hand in marriage. This has often been seen by observers as an indicator of the low status of Plains In-dian women. Because there was a general recognition of status and a reciprocal gift-giving from her family, however, it indicated a sacred and respectful qual-ity to the union. Women who were not wed with this exchange or who eloped with their prospective mates were seen as uncaring persons because they had no emotional affection for wakan postulates in the Lakota way of life.

Marriage was also seen as a significant phase of a woman's life for the conti-nuity of the group and the perpetuation of a distinctive and honored life-way. Therefore, creative force was expected. Pregnancy was and is called *eglushaka* among Lakota-speakers. It translates as "to make oneself strong." Care and con-sideration were the lot of women during this period. After the child was born, a lengthy period of lactation (up to four years) was enacted for the benefit and love of, and concern for, the child on the part of both parents. There was a strong su-pernatural proscription against sexual intercourse during this period—again for the health, esteem, and love of the child. This mandate also explains the func-tional aspects of the ideal marriage pattern of sororal polygamy, which had di-rectives other than sexual ones. Sisters (and "sisters," i.e., female cousins in the tiospaye) shared not only a husband but also economic and household chores in a "warrior society" in which there may have been a scarcity of males. What is significant from the indigenous viewpoint is that harmony and respect were re-ciprocal and reflected one's commitment to the wakan character of Lakota life.

As the woman passed her reproductive years, which were not onerous with repeated pregnancies, she assumed a hallowed place after her menopause. Her status increased. Her age correlated with the wisdom of her years. Respect for her grew, as did her knowledge of esoteric rites and rituals. Her wakan charac-ter was evinced. The power of a menstruating, creative woman was mediated. The ultimate melding of wakan and feminine status was the honor of being the Sacred Pipe Woman in the Sun Dance. This was recognized by the populace as an assumption of the role of the legendary White Buffalo Calf Woman who brought the Sacred Pipe and the Sun Dance ritual to the Teton Lakota in the mythic past.

Throughout the adulthood of a Lakota woman, spirituality was evidenced and reaffirmed in daily rituals that upheld the ideals of Lakota society. For females, the four cardinal virtues were fortitude, generosity, industriousness, and wisdom. The Quilling Society, a group for women who evidenced industriousness; participation in the Scalp Dance to honor one's male kin; initiating a Bite the Knife Ceremony to commemorate one's faithfulness to a husband; and interacting in the numerous naming ceremonies all evoked sanctions that focussed upon the organizing principle of spiritual life—the wakan. Events of high emotional affect and common daily occurrences displayed the inextricable bond between belief and behavior and enriched the feminine perspective on life.

Throughout the life-cycle of a female Lakota, the characteristics that personified a "good woman" were enacted and validated by the spiritual underlying principles that directed accepted modes of behavior. Although virtue and chastity were the basic assumptions for qualities of womanhood, as with the male "berdache," women had the culturally sanctioned option of expressing excessive sexuality (and other deviations from the norm) through dreaming of the Double-faced Woman. But the majority, it appears, followed the normative pattern. Hassrick (1964:122) notes, "They also set such a high standard for women that those who achieved it were accorded significant status and respect; in a sense they attained a goddess-like quality." Feminine spirituality among the Lakota was integral and integrated in every act of life.

As with most Native cultures of North America, conquering Christians wreaked havoc with traditional belief systems. The adaptive strategies utilized by females during this critical change period are not well documented. Hints of changes in beliefs and attitudes are given in such works as Ella Deloria (1944) and Standing Bear (1928, 1933).

Indian women of today are also the least comprehended of minority women. Essentially, one can state that those females who are socialized in Lakota tradition still are bound to cultural principles that focus upon the expectations of being female in Lakota society. Others have not chosen these dictates and have chosen to become relatively acculturated to the dominant society's values and norms. Still others are searching for an identity via return to traditional religion—mainly participation in the Sun Dance, which has now achieved an intertribal character.

Contemporary spirituality has not grasped the interest of researchers among Indians. Secrecy aspects and a greater determination on the part of Native Americans to control the types of research projects are a few of the reasons why that is so. Some Siouan writers, however, have attempted analyses (Deloria 1973, 1979; Medicine 1979, 1980). Certainly, the participation of Indian women in the larger women's movement in the dominant society has not been the focus of research and publication. Until this is attempted in a rigorous fashion, our knowledge of American Indian women and contemporary spirituality will remain dim.

Note

1. Terminology for natives of North America has been variable. Though most groups prefer to be glossed with their native name, as Lakota for Sioux and Dine for Navajo, names as Amerindian, Indian-American, and so on have been somewhat capricious. Native American is the latest categorization. Most groups do not object to American Indian. I use the last two interchangeably in this paper.

References

Black Elk. 1953. *The Sacred Pipe: Black Elk's Account of the Seven Rites of the Oglala Sioux*. Edited by Joseph Epes Brown. Norman: University of Oklahoma Press.

Deloria, Ella. 1944. *Speaking of Indians*. New York: The Friendship Press.

Deloria, Vine, Jr. 1973. *God Is Red*. New York: Grosset and Dunlop.

———. 1979. *The Metaphysics of Modern Existence*. New York: Harper and Row.

Hassrick, Royal B. 1964. *The Sioux: Life and Customs of a Warrior Society*. Norman: University of Oklahoma Press.

Neithammer, Carolyn. 1977. *Daughters of the Earth: The Lives and Legends of American Indian Women*. New York: Collier Books.

Medicine, Beatrice. 1979. "Native American Resistance to Integration: Contemporary Confrontation and Religious Revitalization." Unpublished paper.

———. 1980. "Indian Women: Tribal Identity as Status Quo." Presented to the National Association for Women's Studies, Bloomington, Indiana.

Standing Bear, Luther. 1928. *My People, the Sioux*. Edited by E. A. Brininstool. Boston: Houghton Mifflin.

———. 1933. *Land of the Spotted Eagle*. Boston: Houghton Mifflin.

CHAPTER 20

American Indian Women: Mental Health Issues Which Relate to Drug Abuse

The Problem

Despite the fact that equity is an important issue in matters dealing with minorities, there has been scant attention given to the plight of American Indian and Alaskan Native women in the arena of mental health services.[1] That persons from this gender category have historically been involved in the "caring" professions as practical and registered nurses, in counseling and guidance, and in Native systems of curing has not been a factor in the consideration of this segment of the Native populations. Indeed, the stress upon "medicine men" has grossly overshadowed feminine healing and support systems in many indigenous enclaves.

Moreover, the glossing of demographic data of tribal groups also hinders total comprehension of sexual differences in health matters. In attempting to present the health needs in the present, one must scrutinize reports dealing with disparate matters to obtain scattered facts. To cite one example that would have implications for one particular tribe and its female members, Kunitz (1977:399) notes that among the Navajo, the sex ratio changes to favor women over men. The population tends to be very young, which indicates a high dependency ratio and the likelihood of an increase in the size of the nuclear family. These demographic factors would certainly have implications for the roles of women in that society. But there are other factors inherent in male and female relationships that are not readily disclosed by mere demographic data. The fact that role reversal in leadership and economic patterns was already occurring in some regions of Navajo-land had been documented by Hamamsy (1957). The fact that men had obtained jobs as wage-earners in a matrilineal society had impact on the mental health of Navajo women. Of interest at present are the reactions of women in this society to the emergent male leadership and composition of the tribal council. That role incompatibility is increasingly difficult for Indian women of all tribes in present-day society is a situation that seems to permeate all tribal structures. This fact may be highly conducive to drug abuse.

The anthropological literature dealing with areas that might be remotely connected to the mental health needs of Native females is sparse. For purposes of meeting research needs, any attempt at coalescing the scattered studies that pertain to Indian women is of paramount priority. Studies (Alvarado 1970; Haynes 1977; Slemenda 1978), although touching on the delicate issue of population control, are attempts to flesh out the parameters of an important area of contemporary life for females. It is, however, significant to note that these studies are oriented primarily to efficacy in contraceptive use. Each represents different interpretations of birth control that are reflective of the sociocultural backgrounds of the groups involved. Necessarily, any research dealing with Native American groups will reflect this bias. This is a primary research caveat that is uniquely distinctive to tribal groups—generalizability is often unrealizable although often expected in research designs as set out by federal agencies.

My experience with Native groups—in urban areas and on reservations—indicates that there is a need for information about pregnancy, birthing procedures, and birth control. In an unpublished study on Teton Dakota beliefs about the health problems of their children (Gaalswyk 1979), the stated request of mothers in a small hamlet on Standing Rock Reservation in South Dakota was for birth control information for their teenage daughters. That information was elicited by the researcher, who was concerned with the notion of "giving something back to the Indian community after obtaining data there" for her M.A. thesis. This is also a new approach to research in Native communities.

Although these studies on health aspects of Indian females center upon pertinent areas that are only beginning to be investigated, the research does not enter into the psychological and motivational areas of Indian women's lives. It is within these psychological domains that tendencies toward drug abuse are embedded.

A research priority that needs clarification is the interface of urbanization and other demographic features. Uhlmann's tentative study (1972) indicates such needs. She notes a lucanae of models in researching fertility among American Indian women, which accounts for voluntary birth control and other variables such as delayed marriage, education, occupation, and migration. She derives her data from the Papago in Tucson and appears to generalize it to "American Indian Women." This fallacy often obscures the tribally and geographically specific behavioral norms that make reporting on American Indian women so precarious.

What and how do generalizations regarding this diverse gender population emerge? In one of the few studies that delineates differing orientations to such tests as the TAT, Bigart (1971) presents data that support Louis Spindler's (1962) study of Menominee women, which indicated that Indian and white psycho-

Medicine at the Native American Education Systems College, Twentieth Anniversary Pow-wow, Chicago, 1995. (Courtesy of Faith Smith)

logical differences were less important for Indian women than for Indian males. Indian women in a Salish Flathead community that Bigart examined showed a significantly greater concern than on-reservation whites in the "relative importance of dominant and equal (or advice) relationships to older people." This research indicated that "technological acculturation has little connection with a projected shift towards White psychological patterns among the Indians" (1972:232) of this Salish Flathead community composed of the Salish Flathead, Pen d'Oreille, and Kootenai tribes.

Laurence French (1976) discusses social problems of Cherokee women that resulted from ambivalence over the loss of traditional heritage and blocked access to white culture. This led to normlessness and confusion in role identity and is often seen as an impetus to alcohol consumption (Medicine 1976–84). The usual descriptors for Indian communities, such as family disorganization, alcoholism, illness, and mental health problems, resulted in increased consumption. He states that women suffer more than men because they lack avenues for aggression. Women were disproportionately represented in Cherokee society, were victims of male violence, and were the primary socializers of children due to family fragmentation.

In a recent article, Eileen Maynard (1979:15) characterizes Oglala women as having "retained much of their traditional role and even, in many cases, have expanded their role to include employment and social action. These changes in sex roles have produced great family instability with matrifocality and matri-centered families becoming more common." This may be a factor in the reports of high alcohol abuse among Sioux women, as cited by Joan Weibel-Orlando (1984). *This characterization of male and female relationships, coupled with the descriptions given by French, are important benchmarks upon which to build future research.* The trend is also noted in Metcalfe's (1979) writing, where she describes Navajo women in an urban setting as "both 'making it' in the city and at the same time remaining Indians or, what is more to the point from their perspective, 'Navajo.'" Later, she states, "For a few women this dual participation involved feelings of personal ambivalence, as if they were trying to cover both bases without being solidly grounded in either. However, about one-third of the women showed a positive self-image and healthy personal adjustment along with their bicultural behaviors. In other words, they were moving securely within both worlds. There were indications that retention of their Navajo cultural traits, instead of being a problem, was part of the positive adaptive strategy" (28). Her sample consisted of twenty-three Navajo women.

Interestingly, Louise Spindler is now introducing data that suggest the Menominee feminine behavior is not explainable with "the conducive base [that] provided models of role flexibility that made the role behaviors of the leading women credible for a large audience of Menominee. The cosmopolitan adaptation of a few Menominee women made their role behaviors in the new political situation possible for them" (1962:39). She does, however, caution that "all female-linked roles do not change at the same rate." Further, she cautions that "one feels that we have, on the whole, not been precise enough in our analyses of specific attributes or dimensions to provide the necessary data base for such generalizations" (39).

The foregoing, which is a highlight of some of the most recent studies dealing with American Indian women, remains in the configurational framework of such earlier works as Lurie's *Mountain Wolf Woman* (1966, Winnebago), Landes (1938, Chippewa), and even Spindler (1962). It is in more recent works such as Shipek (1970) and Jones (1972) that gender-specific training for females is given meaning and can be utilized for the development of research proposals. Such collations as Katz (1977) and Niethammer (1977) are too partitive to be effective. I have tried (Medicine 1978) to deal with issues confronting Indian women at present.

How are the more realistic concerns of women in reservation and urban communities articulated? It is extremely difficult to define these needs. Needs assessments, which are constants in these communities, very often do not focus upon feminine concerns—except perhaps in the educational realm for meeting their children's needs.

It is not easy to obtain a comprehensive and cogent statement of mental health needs from American Indian and Alaskan Native women. The most comprehensive is possibly the "Report of Special Populations Subpanel on Mental Health of American Indians and Alaska Natives" (1978). This report is in a "not for distribution" category, however, and thus its impact is limited. There is no distinct treatment of women's needs. These unique needs are covered in areas under alcoholism or destruction of Indian families and recognition of "the traditional medicine man and woman as healers of emotional, mental, and physical disorders" (1978:43). Shockingly from my point of view, the very explicit and realistic recommendations from the training symposium (Trimble and Ryan 1978), which met simultaneously with the White House conference, do not dwell upon mental health needs based upon gender difference.

How then does one obtain this type of concern? It is possible to obtain some information from attendance at national Indian women's organizational meetings. There are several national organizations and a few regional ones. Unfortunately, besides the resolutions that are passed at these conferences, documented statements of these needs are seldom forthcoming. Thus, at this time, one is only able to gather these statements and see if any implementation might be forthcoming. Unfortunately, many resolutions instigated at Native American conventions are tinged with political overtones. In general, however, they tend to express valid concerns.

The most predominant and enduring Native American Indian Women's Association (NAIWA), which was formed in 1970, has annual meetings every June. Concerns that have been constant during the past decade have been the changing roles of women in many tribal societies and dissonances in male-female relationships: increased divorce rates, consensual marriages, one-parent families, family disorganization, battered spouses and children, and ongoing concern with child fosterage and adoption. Underlying these, but never mentioned, are the economic underpinnings of urban and reservation communities, which are basic to many of the problems that are reinstated yearly. Alcoholism is a problem viewed in gender-specific realities.

The regional Indian organizations have had interesting and specific activities that are tied to community needs. One example is the White Buffalo Calf Woman's Society on Rosebud Reservation in South Dakota, which has established a home for battered women and children and has engaged in other alcohol-related activities. One is an honoring ceremony for those Lakota females from that reservation who have achieved advanced degrees from institutions of higher education. Interestingly, men from the group wanted the same kind of honoring ceremony. Most important, this act was a modern version of the Quilling Society, in which excellence among Lakota females is recognized and publicly acknowledged. This example is only one in which bonding mechanisms among women may be activated for substance abuse control.

There are infrequent statements by American Indian women on issues that affect them. Tillie Blackbear, a Rosebud Sioux and vice-chairperson of the South Dakota Coalition against Domestic Violence, indicated at a workshop on "Domestic Violence—a Native American Perspective" held at the Colville Indian

Reservation, "Acceptance means that people feel that domestic violence—in fact violence in general—is the only way to deal with a problem. That is a tragedy." Her statement was reported by Ray Gonzales, editor of the Colville *Tribal Tribute,* and printed in the National Indian Health Board's *Reporter* on July 19, 1980. Further, Blackbear stated, "Family life is an idealized social myth. It is a myth characterized by love, kindness, and harmony. In reality, family life is often characterized by violence in a probate setting." According to Blackbear, persons who use violence as a problem-solving method have often been raised in a home where violence was common and are "simply using the methods they learned as a child." She felt it important to break that cycle, although the solutions she proposed were not explicit in the reporting.

Various publications dealing with Indian women often list concerns. French (1976) discusses social problems of Cherokee women. He sees their dilemma in terms of cultural ambivalence, a loss of traditional heritage, and lack of access to white culture. Family disorganization, violence, alcoholism and illness, and mental disorders are seen as consequences of normlessness and confusion in role identity. He feels that women suffer more than men because they are denied access to aggression release and status enhancement, which seems to be accessible to Cherokee men. He notes that women are disproportionately representative in Cherokee society, are often victims of male violence, are the primary socializers of children, and often serve as household heads following family disintegration.

Issues of battered spouses, abused children, alcohol and drug abuse, sterilization, parent abuse, and other features of social disorganization often overshadow adaptive strategies that have allowed for cultural continuity. Underlying these manifestations of disequilibrium in Native societies are the ever-present realities of racism, sexism, and classism. The contours of these social facts are basic to understanding the mental health needs and priorities of the feminine contingent in present-day tribal groups.

Underlying these are self-perceptions of being a Native female in a dual social system—tribal and non-Native. Group membership—which must be seen as choosing alternatives that are situationally defined and tied to a natal group that predestines expectations—often poses dilemmas that require constant assessment of one's role and expectations of being a Native Alaskan or American Indian woman. The alternatives must always be evaluated, as are role requirements that might be sources of difficulties or temporary or ongoing maladjustment. Perception and efficient enactments of these parameters are of crucial importance in the mental health of Native women.

At a recent meeting in Augsburg College in Minnesota, the American Indian Women of Minnesota, Inc., addressed central concerns that included career development, battered women, health care, and employment rights. These issues were discussed in forums such as the Women's Educational Equity Communications Network and have not been reported. One obvious danger is the difficulty in obtaining cogent summaries of such feminine gatherings from persons who have attended (or from the officers or organizers, for that matter). That is also true for NAIWA. Most of its officers are employed and are raising families, and they seem to be activated only during the days of the annual meetings.

In addition to the actual discussions of issues at national meetings, various publications dealing with women's issues often list concerns. For example, the issues of battered spouses, abused children, alcohol and drug abuse, steriliza-tion, parent abuse, and other deviancies speak to the social disorganizational variables of contemporary Indian life on reservations and in off-reservation areas. These variables are all tied to the mental health of Indians—both males and females. Thus, it is necessary to construct research strategies that focus upon sex differences tied to age and socioeconomic categories. Class and status (tra-ditional versus progressive) categories are still viable and ongoing in contem-porary Indian life. Neo-traditionality (i.e., a return to Native religions) is a newer perspective for consideration. There are aspects of positive coping mechanisms that have allowed Native people to persist. These, however, have seldom been critically examined.

Research formulations in the mental health field are multitudinous. One may look at the litany of deviances, or one may examine the underlying framework of how Native people have managed to persist in seemingly untenable positions of poverty and frustration. In that vein, female bonding behavior—within the kinship bond or in fictive kinship situations—would be a novel approach. This would fit within the demands of networking, which is almost a requirement for the equitable funding of women's programs. The achievement of satisfactory roles—as professional and the maintaining of "traditional" (i.e., curing and religious roles)—needs amplification.

One area that is seldom mentioned in research priorities is that of sexual politics. This may take different forms. Sexual and intellectual exploitation of women in terms of the status quo of traditional sex role assignment is a very real dilemma for Indian females. Indian women have established some bond-ing behavior—kin or non-kin. Doing so has not been an easy task for some younger women who are recent in the professional ranks. These younger women feel isolated and devastated by relationships with Indian males—whether lov-ers, husbands, or brothers. A more enduring and meaningful relationship seems to have been the father-daughter dyad. Women have often been the forerunners in professional occupations in their tribes. Very often they have been ridiculed for striving to achieve. Moreover, the double-bind aspect has been more acute for them. They have had the dual roles of keeping families together and trying to make a living. There are many strands to positive mental health practices evidenced in the coping strategies of such women.

In this arena, women find a need for counseling sessions. Many persons who have sought professional counselors have indicated a lack of awareness of cul-tural differences and thus have been frustrated with this experience. Some, however, have utilized counselors. There is surfacing, as part of the bonding mechanism, evidence of peer counseling—or at least the narrating of similar experiences. It seems that Native females who have sought psychiatric counseling do not feel they are qualified to counsel peers. Some even think that it is dangerous to do so—and rightly so in many instances. This is the area that I feel must yield the most data for comparability and for training students of Native descent to do research. A continuum of traditional, para-professional, and professional counselors' styles and techniques needs to be researched at this time.

There are other general types of research projects that must be initiated. Some stem from aspects of sexism and racism in the larger society. Racism is one feature that could be postulated to apply with equal valence across all tribes. Sexism as activated within the larger society should be further defined for Native societies. Classism is a newer phenomenon with many tribes. This is especially true with Indian women when academic degrees, activism, and community involvement are involved. Beyond economic considerations, aspects of traditionality and acceptance by members of tribes are also features, as is self-ascribed identification. These variables can be recombined into bonding mechanisms that fit various issues and orientations.

Of prime importance in presenting data about Indian and Alaskan Native women is the typicality notion. This has not been properly or effectively addressed in much research upon women. The percentage of women who fit categories is seldom explicated. This seemingly reflects the gloss of the Native woman; any analysis of feminine behavior should confront the generalizability of the results of research. This, then, would lead to comparability and thus highlight similar or divergent traditions in the changed and changing societies of Native North America.

There are voiced statements regarding a lack of support systems for Indian women who have recently completed the baccalaureate degree. Analyses of marriage patterns indicated that Indian males continue to exhibit a tendency to marry females in the larger society. Pressures—by Indian males and their cohorts—upon Indian women to marry tribal members is great. There seems to be no effective informal or formal pressure exerted upon Indian males to do likewise. Indeed, many Indian males indicate that Caucasian females are more adaptive to their idiosyncratic behavior and more readily learn cultural requirements if the male is oriented to traditional activities such as Native religious and powwow activities. If one examines the marriage pattern of "medicine men" or incipient "medicine men" this tends to be confirmed.

Besides sentimental reasons and matrimonial ties, Indian women are increasingly verbalizing a lack of professional support systems in the occupational realm. There are several informal support networks that have functioned for some time. Besides peer group and kin affiliations, an enlarging support system of teacher and student relationships is evident. There is little evidence of mentorship in the Anglo sense, although some Indian women speak of "proteges." In general, truly friendly, egalitarian relationships seem to emerge in some areas that cut across generational ties.

This brief statement, then, outlines the dilemmas of, and portends an area of anxiety for, the professionally emergent Native American female.

Note

1. This is no more significant than in the study of drug abuse among American Indian women.

References

Alvarado, Anita. 1970. "Cultural Determinants of Population Stability in the Havasupai Indians." *American Journal of Physical Anthropology* 33(1): 9–14.

Bigart, Robert James. 1971. "Patterns of Cultural Change in a Salish Flathead Community." *Human Organization* 30(3): 229–37.

French, Laurence. 1976. "Social Problems among Cherokee Females: A Study of Cultural Ambivalence and Role Identity." *American Journal of Psychoanalysis* 36(2): 163–69.

Gaalswyk, Judith R. 1979. "Teton Dakota Beliefs about Health and Illness Problems of Their Children." Unpublished M.A. thesis, University of Washington.

Hamamsy, Laila Shukrey. 1957. "The Role of Women in a Changing Navaho Society." *American Anthropologist* 59(1): 101–11.

Haynes, Terry L. 1977. "Some Factors Related to Contraceptive Behavior among Wind River Shoshone and Arapahoe Females." *Human Organization* 36(1): 72–76.

Jones, David E. 1972. *Sanapia: Comanche Medicine Woman.* New York: Holt, Rinehart and Winston.

Katz, Jane B., ed. 1977. *I Am the Fire of Time: The Voices of Native American Women.* New York: E. P. Dutton.

Kunitz, Stephen J. 1977. "Underdevelopment and Social Services on the Navajo Reservation." *Human Organization* 36(4): 398–405.

Landes, Ruth. 1938. *The Ojibwa Woman.* New York: Columbia University Press.

Lurie, Nancy O. 1966. *Mountain Wolf Woman, Sister of Crashing Thunder: The Autobiography of a Winnebago Indian.* Ann Arbor: University of Michigan Press.

Maynard, Eileen. 1979. "Changing Sex-roles and Family Structure among the Oglala Sioux." In *Occasional Papers in Anthropology No. 1: Sex Roles in Changing Cultures,* ed. Ann McElroy and Carolyn Matthiasson, 11–15. Buffalo: Department of Anthropology, State University of New York.

Medicine, Beatrice. 1976–84. Field notes

———. 1978. *Native American Women: A Perspective.* Las Cruces: ERIC/CRESS.

Metcalfe, Anne. 1979. "Reservation-Born-City-Bred: Native American Women and Children in the City." In *Occasional Papers in Anthropology No. 1: Sex Roles in Changing Cultures,* ed. Ann McElroy and Carolyn Matthiasson, 21–34. Buffalo: Department of Anthropology, State University of New York.

Niethammer, Carolyn. 1977. *Daughters of the Earth: The Lives and Legends of American Indian Women.* New York: Collier Books.

"Report of Special Populations Subpanel on Mental Health of American Indians and Alaska Natives." 1978. Unpublished report submitted to the President's Commission on Mental Health.

Shipek, Florence Connolly. 1970. *The Autobiography of Delfina Cuero: A Dieguiño Indian.* Riverside: Malki Museum Press.

Slemenda, Charles W. 1978. "Socio-cultural Factors Affecting Acceptance of Family Planning Services by Navajo Women." *Human Organization* 37(2): 190–94.

Spindler, Louise S. 1962. "Menominee Women and Culture Change." *Memoir of the American Anthropological Association,* No. 91.

Trimble, Joseph E., and Robert A. Ryan. 1978. *An American Indian and Alaska Native Mental Health Training Symposium: A Summary Report of the Proceedings.* N.p.: n.p.

Uhlmann, Julie M. 1972. "The Impact of Modernization on Papago Indian Fertility." *Human Organization* 31(2): 149–61.

Weibel-Orlando, Joan. 1984. "Alcoholism Treatment Centers as Flawed Rites of Passage." *Medical Anthropology Quarterly* 15(3): 62–67.

CHAPTER 21

New Roads to Coping:
Siouan Sobriety

Alcohol use and abuse among American Indians and Alaskan Natives have been, since the 1960s, the most widely studied aspects of contemporary tribal life-styles. However, systematic interpretation of the results of these studies is both taxing and frustrating, due in part to the many different assumptions that underpin the investigation of such phenomena. Those features, which seem amenable to preventive intervention, often prove to be illusory targets that are irregularly glimpsed from behind a cloud of interpersonal and psychological problems. Only the recently emerging longitudinal studies of specific tribes—several of which pay particular attention to the social contexts of drinking—allow for the kind of information that will ultimately lead to the design of effective alcoholism prevention programs (Kunitz 1977; Levy and Kunitz 1974; Waddel and Everett 1980). Coterminously, studies that concentrate on the cognitive dimensions of alcohol use and abuse within this special population present new data that can be of considerable value to providers in the actual delivery of services. Unfortunately, few if any of our current training programs, whether preventatively oriented or not, have incorporated these fresh insights into their curricula.

The purpose of this essay is to illustrate that ethnographic observation of drinking patterns and the awareness of the various ways in which the underlying cognitive dynamics may be expressed are critical to understanding the experiences of Indian alcoholics, their achievement as well as maintenance of sobriety, and to the formulation of successful strategies for coping with the diverse pressures that initially contribute to alcoholism in Indian people. With this end in mind, then, I delineate the tendencies toward, and the maintenance of, sobriety among individuals on the Standing Rock Reservation who have learned to cope without the use of alcohol. My major concern is to describe maintenance mechanisms. What are the forces that propel an individual into attempting sobriety? In what activities does a sober individual engage after attempting sobriety? What are the support systems that are most conducive to maintaining sobriety?

"Everyone Drinks!": A Lakota Rationale for Drinking

Most observers of drinking styles among the Lakota have noted that the aim of drinking is to get drunk as quickly as possible (Kemnitzer 1972; Maynard 1969; Mohatt 1972). Some have described the social setting in which drinking behavior is learned. Kemnitzer, basing his perceptions on Pine Ridge, provided the following synopsis, which is relevant to all Sioux reservations:

> Although the main environments for social drinking are homes, cars, parks and bars, in all of these the whole family is included. Small children are present at drinking parties, and infants are taken to bars and there suckled, or beer and wine is mixed in their bottles. Children under twelve play around the drinkers in bars, and by the age of fifteen are in drinking groups of their own, but do not participate in public bar drinking until they are older. Adolescents are also sniffing gasoline and glue as well as drinking alcoholic beverages. The drinking culture is also expressed in the play of younger children:
>
> Two young boys are playing with toy cars. They pretend to load the cars with people, drive the car to White Clay for wine, get drunk, and wreck the cars on the way home. Little girls playing with dolls make up a situation where the "parents" get drunk and fight.
>
> Young children are also coerced by older children and adolescents to sniff gasoline and to drink. Thus, values and behavior reinforcing traditional drinking patterns are transmitted by example and instruction to children of all ages, and drunken behavior becomes "normal" behavior for a significant segment of the population. (1972:139)

Although the "significant segment of the population" is not specified, patterns of participation in drinking behavior clearly are well established by the time a child becomes a member of his or her adolescent peer group.

This conditioned propensity for alcohol is carried into the nexus of reservation and border town. In describing the "culture of excitement" for the Sioux, White (1970) depicted the following folk-way: "For the Sioux Indian one of the most important is chronic drinking to excess. This is the easiest way to quick elation and excitement, a way to relax and forget the fears and insecurities of one's life. It is also a means for the Sioux, who by tradition is dignified and reserved, to be loud, raucous, and cocky in his repartee. In his elation, he forgets any sense of inferiority and gains a feeling of power and assurance—ready to accept any dare" (1970:189). In his categorization of the folk-ways said to be characteristic of the "culture of excitement" (which could be well correlated with the "culture of poverty"), White included such norms as the "readiness for physical violence," "violation of the law or vandalism," and "sex play." He stated that this culture is "shared by men and women of all age groups" (190) and is found in the "Sioux lower-class subgroup which, with its focal point on the lives of bars on Rapid City's Main Street, tends to be a world apart even from the rest of the Indian community" (189). His description fits a type of urban nomadism (Spradley 1970) and the drinking behavior in urban areas as described by Ablon (1964). A similar picture of drunken behavior and subsequent maladjustment is evident in the behavior of other American Indians (Dosman 1972; Graves 1970, 1971; Hackenburg and Gallagher 1972; Price 1975).

Hurt and Brown (1965) noted that the patterns of alcohol consumption have become concretized since the Eastern Dakota began using alcohol. Their study of the urban Dakota, an Eastern group in South Dakota, indicated that excessive drinking was not typical of drinkers in earlier periods. However, as this group became urbanized, a noticeable increase in consumption was discernible. It appears that intensified contact with white communities has fostered alcohol use among the Eastern and Western Siouan groups. Besides drinking to satiation and stupor as a final stage, most writers agree with Kuttner and Lorincz (1967) that drunkenness allows Sioux individuals, particularly males, to display aggressive comportment that is under control in a state of sobriety.

Women and Drinking

There is little on the drinking styles of Indian women in the literature on alcohol. Maynard (1969:40) provided these observations of the Pine Ridge Reservation: "In the case of the women, the attitude is quite different. In some situations and among some groups women are also under pressure to drink. In general, however, the woman who does not drink is respected and the woman who drinks is criticized. Especially open to censure are women who neglect their children because of drinking or who hang around bars unescorted."

White (1970:189) indicated that in his Rapid City group both men and women were "equally ready to fight physically." Moreover, women apparently figured importantly in the subgroup's sexual code, which was not explicated except to point out that "at the bottom of the group (in status as well as the meaning of life) are the women who have become prostitutes and the complete derelicts known on Main Street as the 'winos'" (192). He observed that men stationed at the air base, cowboys coming into the city, and traveling construction workers often become "friends" who as long as they are in the area support some Indian women. An important consideration in relationships between Lakota males and females is the pressure of the peer group for males to continue in their drinking patterns. This usually leads to a dissolution of the marriage and the woman's dependence on Aid to Dependent Children. It also leads to isolation from married friends. Very often, single Lakota women, after a marriage failure, gravitate to a life on the Main Streets of the Northern Plains communities.

Whittaker (1962) notes that in contrast to their male counterparts, women on the Standing Rock Reservation show less tendency to drink large amounts of liquor at a single sitting. However, he observes that a larger amount is consumed than by the white sample population in Iowa. Speaking of a time in the 1950s, he delineates a pattern of generational differences among Indian women in which the number of women who drank increased twice as fast as that of males; it has nearly quadrupled over recent generations. He also notes that woman tend to stop drinking when children are born. These trends continue into the present and characterize contemporary (1970–80) drinking patterns on most Lakota Sioux reservations (Hurt and Brown 1965; Kemnitzer 1972; Maynard 1969; Medicine 1969; Mohatt 1972).

As mentioned, from 1960 onward, drinking by females of child-bearing age became more frequent. Women's response to their husband's eternal "boozing" has been to join them. This attitude is more usual than one might imagine. As many Lakota women say, "If you can't lick them, join them." After pleading for years for abstinence or at least sporadic drinking on the part of their husbands, they begin to accompany the men to bars and begin to drink. For some, this is only a transitory act. They stop when they have convinced their husbands to lessen their alcohol consumption. For other Sioux women, drinking becomes a way of life. There are some Sioux women, as with Indian women of other tribes, who are able to go into a bar or restaurant and "drink like whites." In border towns off the reservation, this means that they might have a cocktail or beer before a meal or go to a local bar where live music is featured. Others do not go to bars or drink at all. These are often older women or those who have achieved sobriety.

Lakota women have been aware of the use of alcohol since the days when it became legal to purchase it—and even before then. Some who came from families who were o ki se' (literally, "halves," or "half-breeds" as they are called in reservation English) often saw their fathers drink liquor. Some of these individuals, lacking the physical features stereotypically associated with Indians, could purchase liquor. Others were bootleggers. If one's father was white, very often that person purchased liquor for Indian friends and relatives. Some women made wine from the wild grapes and wild chokecherries that grew on the Northern Plains.

Many young women who grew to adulthood during the early years of the repeal of the ban on alcohol consumption (after 1953) learned to drink as part of their adolescence. As for males, learning to drink became almost a rite of puberty for a significant number of young women. Introduction of alcohol thus was (and remains) a part of growing up for both sexes.

A gradual introduction to alcohol consumption is accomplished by several means. Generally, and at the present time, a female learns drinking behavior in the family setting. This means that in most cases her father and mother are both drinkers and her introduction to drinking is not a problem for them. Indeed, there are many families who actively encourage young daughters to accompany them on drinking bouts. Some families carefully guard their daughters from peer group interaction, but the numbers in this category have steadily declined since the 1950s.

In families that actually encourage daughters to drink (or may not discourage their participation), there is a sense of fatalism. The girls will drink no matter what they, as parents, do. This attitude has several latent aspects. By allowing the daughter to drink, she may become a form of insurance as a source of alcoholic beverages, especially if she falls into the pattern of border-town existence previously described as the Main Street syndrome. A young Indian female is often able to recruit white ranchers, farmers, and even police officials to support the drinking habit she acquires. Moreover, her extended kin, if composed of heavy-drinkers, also shares in this symbiotic relationship. Indian women who fit this description very often form liaisons with bar owners, bartenders, and businessmen to guarantee a source of liquor. In many cases, this goes beyond merely supplying liquor and may become a form of livelihood. The survival strategies of Indian women "winos" and transient single men in contemporary tribal life have not been examined. Most Lakota people do not look down upon this type of behavior. Derision is not part of the attitude that such persons engender. Rather, "Poor thing! He/she can't help it" is often heard when Lakota people refer to persons ensnared in alcohol addiction.

That these actions are not peculiar to the Standing Rock or Cheyenne River reservations is readily evident from other entries in the literature. Describing a town in eastern South Dakota, Hurt wrote:

> A further characteristic of the Indian in Yankton is the numerical superiority of women (141 women and 121 men). Since the sexes are almost equal in number under the age of 18, women are more numerous in the adult group. Men are apparently more transient, leaving Yankton for larger industrial areas, moving back to the reservation, or simply wandering along the open highways. The women are less mobile because their responsible sex role involves care of large numbers of children usually found in the urban Indian family. (1961–62:227)

Referring to the social milieu, Hurt further stated, "Unless an Indian is a mixed-blood, he has little social contact with the white man except for members of the lowest socio-economic class. In particular, contacts between young Indian girls and older white men are fairly frequent in bars and in automobiles" (227).

Traditional mechanisms of social control have not adapted to the new lifeway and are not functional. One remnant of traditional male and female "sibling" behavior is illustrative. The institutionalized *hakatakus* (to follow after them) refers to expected behavior for a Lakota female's "brothers"—biological and sociological. They were expected to serve as her guardians, "watching and protecting her from other men" (Hassrick 1964: 123). This seemingly anachronistic custom is still apparent in some, more traditional families. It certainly is not as prominent as it was in the early reservation period, lasting until the late 1950s among the majority of full-blood *tiospaye* (extended families). This is only one example of the breakdown of social institutions and the resulting demoralization of a people. It also represents an acculturational process in which new norms and values were not realistically represented by the agents of socialization and religious forms that followed the suppression of Native belief systems.

In summary, Lakota women fulfill a variety of roles at the intersection of alcohol and everyday living. Some women are willing participants in the drinking game. Others have been compelled to join, hoping to salvage a marriage or to hold a man's attention. Others serve as caretakers, driving drunks home, feeding them, cleaning them, and helping them through their escapades in many ways. Still other women act as intercessors or mediators in interethnic encounters in the "off-reservation" towns bordering Indian enclaves. Women, wives, mothers, sisters, aunts, and cousins appear with bail money, plead with non-Indian judges, contact lawyers, and maneuver to keep Lakota males out of jail. There have been instances in which women have granted sexual favors to law officers. A subtle racism in the judicial system is recognized by all, Indians and whites. This is reflected in the common request expressed by Lakota males when they plead with the women of their tiospaye to intercede in their behalf with the legal system: "They listen to you."

Men and Drinking

The most common response of Lakota males to "why do you drink?" is, "Everyone does it." There is a strong impetus to drink, especially among males. Peer pressure is great and is markedly clear during the adolescent period. However, it carries into the adult years in the form of the traditional friendship group (*kola*-hood), which has become a "drinking buddy" sodality. Previously, I referred to the tensions inherent in a marriage or liaison that involve conflicting loyalties to the peer group and to a stable marriage. Acceptance by one's comrades very often is the more potent force. For Lakota males, this frequently is a result of frustration and perceived failure to obtain jobs and to provide a livelihood for their families. Self-actualization and meeting the expectations of the larger kin group (the tiospaye) are difficult to fulfill in many contemporary Lakota communities. The inability to "pull one's weight," as Lakota say, in a social structure in which the survival of the unit depends upon equitable contributions of time and effort is a heavy burden. It is especially onerous for male members of the extended family. The inability to provide strikes at the very core of *bloka*-ness (Lakota masculinity).

The drinking proclivities of Sioux males have been described graphically in the literature. Blakeslee (1955:34) referred to "several Dakota males of different ages and degrees of acculturation" who engaged in "riotous eating and drinking which took place the first two weeks after the arrival of the subsistence check. The end of the month was sober and lean." He noted that although the "older men frowned on drunkenness, all opposition to drinking behavior was passive."

Among Lakota males, drinking alcoholic beverages, and participating in the daring exploits that mandates, is thought of as a validation of manhood. This is evoked as bloka, which is used as a modus operandi for all Lakota males—whether or not they are fully bilingual. Its translation into English is noted as "male superiority," but it is more accurately equated with the Spanish macho, or male chauvinism. The behaviors and attitudes of Lakota males are tied to this notion of masculine potency. Male supremacist attitudes are fully ingrained in the socialization process. The "warrior syndrome" has been explicated in several ethnographic monographs (Hassrick 1964; MacGregor 1946; Province 1937). The stress on the value of males continues and yet has not been completely assessed in the continuity of cultural ideals, despite powerful sanctions that are brought into play. As one example, a Lakota female is not fully recognized as a mature woman until she has produced a son. Similarly, males feel inadequate until they have fathered a son. A very decided male bias is part of the socialization processes for both male and female children.

In discussing the "culture of excitement," White offered further insight into this androcentric bias when he stated, "Within the strictly matriarchal Sioux family the relationship of the mother to the boys is observed to be unusually salient, while in the boys there is frequently a dislike, even contempt, for the absent father or the present but worthless father" (1970:193). The internalization of the androcentric ideal is a powerful force in motivating boys entering adolescence to drink. The dare "prove you're a man!" is a great incentive to action and is commonly invoked in peer relationships during a male's maturational process. It appears to intensify during puberty but seems to continue throughout a male's lifetime if he is to be accepted as a member of the Lakota male peer group—a kola group. The interrogation "Ni bloka he?" (Are you a male?) is sufficient to thrust a young or old Lakota male into any feat of daring. It is also part of the expected behavior that might be provoked as a reaction to a dare, ranging from reckless driving to self-mutilation such as withstanding cigarette burns on arms or hands while remaining stoic and bloka. The Native utterance "Ai! A-tash bloka sni!" (Not like a man!) is sufficient to demolish a male Lakota who aspires to membership in the group.

Interestingly, a male who resists taunts and dares or who exhibits feminine characteristics is often dismissed as *winkte* (womanlike) or a homosexual. There is an awareness among some Sioux people that the enactment of the latter role was institutionalized in pre-reservation days. Others are as merciless as members of the dominant society. Generally, however, a recognized and accepted winkte (true homosexual) is not harassed and tempted to drink. The English equivalents for "winkte" are "sissy" or "mama's boy," terms of derision for repeated resistors of alcoholic beverages. But because most Lakota males wish to be accepted, this cultural ideal of Lakota masculinity is exceedingly effective in inducing men of all ages to consume alcohol.

For Sioux men, involvement in sharing, especially of alcoholic beverages, and continued participation in peer groups can be counterproductive and can undermine marital bonds. An inability to care for their families is not unique to Lakota men, however. Lang (1979) and Westermeyer (1972), writing about the lives of Indian men in general, have indicated that apathy and continual drinking are major factors in marital discord and, when combined with discrimination and racism, contribute to the negation of self.

It is possible that these feelings of inadequacy and emasculinity covertly motivate the dependence upon alcohol so evident in the studies of drinking styles among Lakota males. Early exhortations to drink in order "to be a man" remain constant throughout the masculine experience, and drinking conformity is demanded by "drinking buddies" or peers. To refuse is to be "too good to drink with us."

Mohatt (1972) attributed the rationale for drinking among Lakota males to the concept of power; the *wakan* (power domain) is familiar to most of them. Traditionally, the search for power was a means of self-actualization and self-direction. The *hanbleceya* ("crying for vision," or "vision quest") was an institutionalized means of achieving an altered state of consciousness in order to receive a vision that would become a mandate for action in one's adult life. By fasting, drinking water, and concentrating upon the *wakan* (omnipotent power base), the senses were altered. A visionary "guardian spirit" would appear and become a guide to the future life of each individual male. However, this explanation does not seem plausible, given that Lakota males have not actively pursued vision quests since belief systems were suppressed in 1882. (There have been attempts at hanbleceya since 1960, but the new experiences are cloaked in secrecy by most participants.)

The Stages of Drunkenness

There is a definite pattern to the drunken behavior of Lakotas, especially Lakota men. It begins by drinking a great deal of any available alcoholic beverage. This is the "feeling good" stage, when talking, joking, and "bragging"—telling tales of daring and success—occur, often referred to as a "laughing spell" by some males (Mohatt 1972:274). It is followed by a period of maudlin reminiscences that can lead to tears, one of the few times when Sioux males resort to tears in public. This phase can be traumatic for young children who may be present. After this comes a stage of bellicosity and belligerence. Kuttner and Lorincz (1967) suggested that drunkenness allows Sioux individuals to display aggression that is under control when they are sober. This aggressive behavior often results in fights and acts of violence. The final state is to become comatose, called "passing out" by Lakota in reservation vernacular. That stage—passing to an ultimate state of stupor—does not exactly correspond to Kemnitzer's states of drunkenness. His documentation sequences drunken states at Pine Ridge as follows: "initiating a party," "first animation," "slightly high," "tipsy," "happy," "depression," "indignation," and "fights" (1972:139–40).

The Lakota themselves do not have such elaborate distinctions, but certain stages of inebriation can be identified and show the differences in indigenous perceptions of the drunken states. Jules-Rosette (1978:570) posited that descriptive vocabularies "both alter the experience through indexing it and are transformed by the experience." This description is especially apt when the vocabularies of both Lakota and English are juxtaposed to depict stages of inebriation. The emic elements of drunken behavior are outlined in table 21.1.

It is readily apparent that the Lakota utterances evoke the experiences described. Native referential terminology is different from the white mode when the Lakota discuss drinking among themselves. The gloss *alcoholic* is a term borrowed from health practitioners on reservations and is used to describe someone who is habitually drunk. Of any other person who drinks occasionally, it is usually stated that "he or she drinks" (yat ka'un). If a person drinks alcohol frequently, one says in Lakota, "Ito mani s'a" (that person gets drunk).

Table 21.1. Comparison of Standard English/Lakota Vernacular Terms for Various Stages of Intoxication

Standard English	Vernacular English[a]	Lakota Dialect Siouan
Non-intoxicated	"sober"	*ito mani sni* (drunk not)
		t'an ables ya na un (composure having)
Slightly intoxicated	"getting tight"	*ag'a* (wavering, uncertain)
	"feeling good"	*ki tan la o waste' sni*
	"getting high"	(slightly not well, not in good shape)
	"gone"/"polluted"	*ito kes kes omani* (in an unusual way, walking). Presently, these translations are given: to stagger,
Intoxicated	"drunk"	*ito mani*[b] (a contracted form of reeling, spinning, and getting dizzy)
		tuktel iya ye (where gone is unclear)
		ti yes ni (not at home)
Comatose	"passed out"	*o t'e* (dead)
	"dead drunk"	*o t'e xpi ya* (deadly sleep)
		o t'e ito mani (dead drunk)
Delirium tremens	"the shakes"	*chan chan un* (shaking, in state of)
	"D.T.s"	
Hallucinations	"seeing snakes"	*skan skan wa yanke* (moving things are seen)
		zu ze cha wa yanke (snakes are seen)
		taku t'ok t'okcha wa yanke (strange things are seen)

a. In the literature on bilingual education, vernacular English is often referred to as "reservation English," "Indian-English," or "red English." Native languages are often called "Indian" by Native people themselves; thus, one hears the phrase "speaking Indian."

b. Riggs (1851:96) translates *I-to'-ho-mni-* as an adjective: "dizzy, light-headed, drunk."

The English term *alcoholic* refers to one who purchases alcohol when money is available and then becomes drunk. That this pattern is usual and predictable is given. The annual income for males on Standing Rock Reservation for 1970 was $1,861 and $1,447 for females (U.S. Department of Commerce 1973:163). The general lack of money makes continual drinking impossible and is pertinent to the binge drinking syndrome. It is also an adaptive feature. Sporadic drinking at least allows Lakota persons to maintain regular nutrition programs and thus does not foster alcohol-related malnutrition. Cause of death among the Lakota is often diagnosed as cirrhosis of the liver. The vernacular is simply "cirrhosis" or, in Lakota, *pxe-shica* (bad liver).

Social Controls

Among the Lakota, although one's being is bound up in kinship (Deloria 1944; MacGregor 1946; Mirsky 1937; Schusky 1975), coercion or control by kin is seen as a transgression against the individual. Moreover, alternative forms of social control are weakly developed. These mechanisms, which once took the form of *akicita* (soldier) societies, were formulated to meet certain specific needs, for example, regulation of the hunt. Some aspects of the ritual cycle were eradicated in the early reservation period that together with the disappearance of the hunter and warrior roles render traditional patterns of male self-actualization almost impotent. Akicita societies were replaced by agent-appointed police, who were called *maku maza* (metal breasts) and seen as enemies rather than peacekeepers. The name and attitude still apply to the tribal police of today.

Field's (1962) arguments regarding relationships among social structural features of traditional societies and drinking behavior are relevant. In his critique of Horton's research on anxiety, Field concluded that "drunkenness in primitive societies is determined less by the level of fear in a society than by the absence of corporate kin groups with stability, permanence, formal structure, and well-defined functions" (58). He based his initial hypotheses upon assumptions about the role of "solidarity and respect." He speculated that individuals in close-knit societies that operate on respect for authority tend to drink moderately and act passively when drunk. The Pueblo societies of Native North America are a ready example to contrast with the loosely structured societies of the Northern Plains.

Yet it seems that Lakota do not currently think of drinking as a problem, whereas recent reports on the Hopi (Levy and Kunitz 1974) indicate that, at the present time, they evidence a high incidence of cirrhosis of the liver. That appears to be due to solitary and sustained drinking as opposed to Lakota patterns of imbibing, which tend to be sporadic, enthusiastic, and without sanctions from the kin group or community at large. It still is not clear, but one can surmise that the binge or spree drinking episodes of the Lakota do not result in a flagrantly high rate of cirrhosis of the liver.

The fact that drinking periods are tied to availability of funds mitigates a persistent pattern of imbibing. Indeed, economic limitations have also been noted by other researchers (Leland 1976). Field's speculations are based on coded materials drawn from an analysis of early cross-cultural studies (Field 1962; McClelland et al., eds. 1972; Whiting and Child 1953), which were, in turn, derived from the Human Relations Area Files and therefore are subject to the biases of these source documents. However, there is no denying that a loosely structured, less well-defined social organization, coupled with diffused authority, is more likely to allow drunkenness among its members. Control predicated on kinship relationships is noticeably lacking in such groups as the Lakota (Goldfrank 1943; MacGregor 1946; Mirsky 1937).

Despite the common and unquestioned bit of folk-wisdom that "all Indians are drunks," there have been many persons—males and females—of Lakota ancestry who have not been drinkers. Although the number of teetotalers is declining, they generally range from thirty-five to eighty years in age. Lakota women are the largest group in this segment. Some women in their seventies have never tasted liquor other than sacramental wines. These persons fit into the category of total abstainers. There are other women who drank in their youth but who, upon reaching thirty-five or forty, stopped entirely and voluntarily. There is only one women, fifty-five, who was a "heavy drinker" and stopped when she became a Mormon. Of the ten persons in one community of ninety adults who were converted to Mormonism and became abstainers, following the nonalcoholic code of their new faith, four persons (one married couple) began drinking after two years of achieved sobriety. They explain their lapses as becoming "Jack Mormons."

By what means do the persons who, in reservation parlance, are "confirmed drunks," "habitual drunkards," "alcoholic," or *ito mani k'tca* (supreme or ultimate drunks) achieve a continuous sober state?

Factors Bearing on Sobriety

When Lakota regard individuals who have previously been drinkers, they state, "Wana yat k'e sni" (now that person does not drink). Sobriety is envisioned as a state that a person elects to reach by self-determined action and a very conscious plan. This state is known as *puza* (dry), which metaphorically means "does not take in any liquid" ("liquid" refers to alcoholic beverages). The path through which this sober state is achieved is the exercise of *chin ka cha*, which best translates as "personal autonomy" (often "will power" in reservation English). This sober state is appreciated but is not widely acclaimed—as is, for example, being a good "traditionalist," being generous in giving feasts, or being a good war dancer. It appears that being "reformed"—as some Lakota say—has been a part of the maturation process that men follow. It is not a predictable event. White (1970) mentions a "reformed" friend of the male clique in Rapid City but does not define this status. Among the Standing Rock Sioux, "reformed" usually means that one has given up the habit of drinking. The prevalent folk-view is that being sober means "not drunk"; being reformed is the complete disuse of intoxicants; and "cured" is seen as a permanent state reached by persons who heretofore had been heavy drinkers. They are described as "staying sober" (*yat k'e sni*).

Abstinence and Controlled Drinking

Drinking alcohol, simply called "drinking" or *yat k'an*, and abstinence are distinct from the state of sobriety described above. The former means to drink in a social manner initially but with the possibility of turning into a prolonged bout or binge. This involvement depends upon the chin ka cha configuration of individuals who might be involved. Abstinence means not drinking at all. Seldom are these Lakota persons participants in group drinking events. In some drinking groups, the pressure to imbibe may become intolerable. Statements such as "you think you're too good to drink with us," or "I didn't know you're a *wasicun* (white person)," or "so you're not a Lakota anymore" are examples of pressures to drink and can be unnerving to nondrinkers. In other drinking groups, those who state they do not drink are seldom pressured to imbibe. This is not a usual pattern, however.

The major orientation of individuals toward sharing and immediate gratification may override considering the control of drinking. Periodic "falling off the wagon," as the Sioux label a "slip," occurs. It is usually coincident with the first of the month or the payment of leases within a kinship group, usually in December. For most persons, the resumption of drinking indicates that periods of nondrinking are of a temporary nature. These periods are also difficult to distinguish from times when money is lacking.

Abstinence is seen as "never drinking," as in the Siouan *yat k'an sni*. Thus, the Lakota notion of abstinence indicates that a person has never indulged in alcoholic beverages and maintains that stance. Abstinence can cost dearly. Consider the following for another Native group: "However, except for a number of women, there are few abstainers among the Naskapi. In fact I knew of only one adult male (sixty-five years old) who claims never to drink and whose claim is substantiated by others. Furthermore, he is a virtual recluse whose most frequent interactions are with some older Montagnais who, as far as I could gather, do not drink either" (Robbins 1973:109).

Quitting Drinking and Pressures

Women tend to stop drinking by the time they are thirty-five or forty. This is explained simply by saying that they are *winyan tanka* (women, big), which has connotations of "maturity" in Lakota. When pressed, they indicate that they are "too old to drink" or that "their children are grown now." Some mothers say that when they attempted to reprimand their children about drinking, their past drinking days were used to negate their admonitions. Therefore, they feel that if they are to control their children, they should set an example. Maintenance of sobriety is not a difficult task for the majority of them.

As for the Lakota males, some of them also begin to "level off" in their drinking by age forty onward. Some become complete nonimbibers. The most common response from men who have achieved complete sobriety to the question, Why did you quit drinking? is, "I was tired of drinking and carousing." Many of them indicate that sobriety is not an easy road to follow. They specifically mention the taunts by drinkers who urge them to drink with them, the lack of support groups, the loneliness initially encountered, and the "lack of friends." Many report that the ridicule and disbelief in their new status is equally onerous from white people in the towns. One informed me that when he went into the trading center, he was most often greeted with, "Well, chief! I remember when you used to drink!" He responded, "Yes, and I was a better drunk than you were!"

Folk Beliefs and Sobriety

Few folk beliefs exist about the onset of uncontrolled drinking among the Lakota today. A major deterrent used by the full-bloods invokes the concept of *wacunza* (to cause harm). Grobsmith (1974) interpreted this concept as "immanent justice." A Native interpretation is that an implicit and always unspoken consequence of an untoward act is to bring misfortune upon someone by that action. Thus, if children cry needlessly or for no obvious reason, they are told that they are going to wacunza someone in their family. When one who has not been drinking (has been in a sober state for some time) begins to imbibe alcohol, or if one who has never drunk liquor begins to drink excessively, the person is told that wacunza will result. This uncontrolled behavior is also thought to result in the injury or death of a closely related member of the tiospaye. A segment of the population also believes that excessive drinking after the death of a loved one can result in the habit of constant drinking. This is called *ah' yah* (to make habit-forming). Most traditional Lakota will not drink for a year, or at least six months, after the death of closely related kin.

Some women believe that excessive drinking can cause miscarriages or stillbirths, however, a majority of women do not drink during a pregnancy. For some, this may be a time when they give up drinking entirely. A few young women in their twenties who were carrying illegitimate children often drank excessively but did not state a reason for this.

Dimension of Sobriety

Dimensions of sobriety and abstinence from intoxicants are seldom mentioned in studies on Siouan drinking. Therefore, Whittaker's work is extremely pertinent. Religious beliefs or ethical considerations have often been stated as reasons for nondrinking by many people. Among the Standing Rock Sioux in 1961, only 9 percent of the abstainers indicated these reasons (Whittaker 1963:81). Some respondents offered health or efficiency as a reason for sobriety. However, 47 percent of the Sioux sample could not offer an explanation for not drinking. In his report to the tribe, Whittaker notes: "Forty-seven per cent of the Indian group either could not or would not give a reason for abstaining. Discussions with Indian leaders concerning this and the large numbers of drinkers who did not give a reason for drinking revealed the general consensus that these people had very likely never given the matter much thought" (1963:29). His study group consisted of formerly heavy-drinkers; 26 percent of the Indian abstainers had previously indulged in drinking four or more times a week. Forty-three percent of those who later abstained reported having stopped drinking between the ages of twenty and forty.

In answer to the question of how an alcoholic can stop drinking, 73 percent of Whittaker's respondents answered that it simply took will power, 21 percent thought the drinker would require help, and 6 percent thought religion would be the answer (Whittaker 1963:83). The emphasis on "will power" is striking. It is the closest English vernacular term for the Lakota concept of chin ka cha.

Whittaker was struck by the lack of social controls to mitigate excessive drinking. He states that drinkers were not punished. Any deviant or unusual behavior that happened while drinking was excused, and the drunk was incorporated immediately into the group. In reference to an earlier description of male superiority in Siouan society, he noted that women were expected to remain with a drinking spouse. Moreover, "beating a wife when drunk was not disapproved by over a third of the respondents" (85).

The following observation by Whittaker is also important to this discussion: "Questioned about attitudes toward abstainers, 58 per cent said they thought a person who refrains or refuses to take a drink is 'commendable,' 14 per cent did not care one way or the other, 17 per cent either did not know or expressed no opinion, 3 per cent were hostile to such a person, 5 per cent thought this must be a person of great will power, and 3 per cent said they had never seen anyone refuse a drink and hence could not answer the question" (86). Not caring or not knowing, which suggests noninterference, hostility, and reference to will power, are reflective of Sioux attitudes toward alcohol consumption.

"I Got Tired of Drinking": Interpretations of Intents and Continuities of Siouan Sober States

"I got tired of drinking" is a recurrent theme throughout many of the explanations given by Lakota persons as to why they stopped drinking alcohol. This phrase in English is a direct translation from the Lakota term *ta watl yesni*, which was elicited by two psychologists on Standing Rock Reservation (Johnson and

Johnson 1965). They interpreted it as signifying to be "totally discouraged." The Native term is more appropriately transcribed as "tiredness" of an obnoxious situation or as "approaching with dread." Placed in the context of alcohol use, it can be interpreted either in Lakota or reservation English as simply deploring a life of drinking alcohol. Rejecting a life of dissonance and dissipation due to drinking and attempting to assume one that is more productive without alcohol is at the heart of this process.

A major question concerns how the Sioux restructure a defensible self-image after a long period of alcohol use and abuse. Braroe (1975), writing about the Cree of Canada, observed:

> Feeling guilty for transgressing a moral rule is not the same as being guilty. One feels guilty when one's action is felt as a blemish on the inner self, when one has violated standards that are accepted as part of one's identity and are used to evaluate one's own moral worth. Obviously, Indians do not experience the guilt that Whites associate with their own drinking and readily use to evaluate Indians' drinking. There is one very revealing exception to this pattern. During the Sun Dance liquor is forbidden, and no one present in the circle of tents around the sacred lodge may possess or consume it. This rule is observed and enforced by the majority of the band, and the few who break it are scolded, a sanction apparently strong enough to dissuade infractions by most of the community. This is the sole occasion on which drinking appears to be a source of guilt on the reserve. When I asked why alcohol was forbidden at this time and at no other, an Indian man replied positively: "Because the Sun Dance is an Indian thing and drinking is a White thing." (1975:141)

This passage illustrates the compartmentalization that allows Indians to coexist with non-Indians in separate socioeconomic and ritual spheres.

It is apparent that guilt or shame are not effective means of discouraging Lakota drinkers; a period of self-assessment and a reevaluation of directions in one's life is necessary. Although Levy and Kunitz (1974) attributed male Navajo drinkers with a lack of introspection, they nevertheless indicated that many Navajo men do stop drinking at middle age and without apparent external coercion or difficulties on their part. Levy and Kunitz wrote: "Aging itself causes a cutting down of drinking" among the Navajo. Further, "In any event, the high proportion of Navajo males who have quit after years of heavy drinking leads us to question the chronic addictive nature of 'Indian alcoholism'" (1974:137).

Aging does not seem to be as important a variable in Siouan sobriety, although it has some relevance. In fact, there are a few women (three) who began to drink for the first time in their lives in their late fifties and early sixties. This was unusual, however, and was tied with the loss of close kinpersons. As for Lakota males, many continue drinking to the very end of their lives. No great censure is directed at these aged drinkers. Some community members say, "Well, they have nothing to look forward to."

Therefore, the assumption of a sober state as a new way of life is a highly idiosyncratic act for Lakota individuals. Withdrawing from the world of drink on all Lakota reservations and social groups is a very painful process. Peer pressure is extremely intense. Social isolation is a price one must pay by selecting this alternative way in order to ensure the continuance of abstinence. Extreme pressure is applied to force persons to begin drinking again. One reformed drinker mentioned that the "hardest part of being sober is the loss of friends." Courage and a certain self-isolation seem in order for the maintenance of sobriety.

Lakota Self-Analysis

A period of introspection or an increased awareness of self occurs in the move to sobriety. One Native term that is used to describe this phase—*ah wa bleza ki* (to examine one's self)—means to cogitate or become introspective. The term involves a type of "self-analysis" within the indigenous frame. It has great implications for a change in behavior and is based upon the psychotherapeutic beliefs of the Lakota people. When they seek advice from a Native practitioner *wa pi ya* (curer), *wi cha sa wakan* (holy man), or *winyan wakan* (holy or sacred woman) and ask for aid—for either physical or mental disturbance—supplicants are asked to *ah bleza* (examine) their actions. The underlying premise here is that unless one is able to cogitate upon one's actions, and place some perspective upon these acts, one is unable to deal with problems believed to be based in interpersonal relationships. As a practitioner frequently states, "Tok'sha he ah bleza ki" (Eventually, the person who is causing distress may examine his/her acts and will rectify the situation). This, admittedly, is a very diffuse modality.

The process places the burden of remedial behavior upon self-actualization and the character of the person who causes the dissonance. This is the ultimate focus upon individual autonomy (chin ka cha), which is characteristic of the Lakota Sioux. There is no force outside the individual, such as wakan or slight feelings of guilt via the Christian ethic, that places the responsibility upon the individual to change. The attempt to effect change resides entirely within the individual. This, then, may offer an explanation as to why many Sioux relate achieving sobriety to will power.

The great emphasis on individualism, or at least individual decision-making, as to one's life and behavior is tied to these concepts of personhood. This may also explain the lack of controls that exist beyond the individual and why kinfolk elect to remain apart from the control apparatus when it comes to drinking and nondrinking behavior. The entire decision is placed upon the individual. The person is also allowed an unstructured freedom of choice by the equally significant term: *chin ka cha*, which in this useage has connotations of "he/she prefers to be that way." When these terms are used, they signify that no outside force is able to intervene and effect significant change in a person's behavior. This is a delicate issue, for the Lakota person might at any time *wa chin ko* (most commonly translated as "to pout") and withdraw. This concept has been developed more explicitly elsewhere (Lewis 1975, note 1).

It appears, then, that intervention and behavior modification, which is the crux of sobriety, are self-induced and constructed in such a manner as to withstand the pervasive, calculated and continuous pressure of a peer group, beginning with adolescents and continuing with age-sets that are like the kola-ships that continue in contemporary Lakota life.

Ceremonies and Abstinence

There are specific times when Lakota people do not imbibe. Religious events, whether Native or Christian, are times when sobriety prevails; others are during certain rites such as naming ceremonies, birthing times, or funerals. Any untoward drinking is certain to bring censure upon the offenders by tiospaye members and gossip from the community. Men never drink when hunting. Many who are more traditional utilize charms and certain roots during this event, and liquor is forbidden. The prevailing pattern of white behavior is assumed by the more acculturated when fishing: Men, and sometimes women, drink beer at this time. Utilization of alcohol is exceedingly prevalent at rodeos, where whites and Indians interact. This appears to be a pattern across the Northern Plains (Braroe 1975). Drinking, although often officially banned, is common at powwows. These are largely social events on reservations and in urban areas. As is common in the larger society, alcoholic beverages are also assuming importance at birthdays for adults, weddings, and divorces.

The Sun Dance ritual and other older ceremonies such as the Yuwipi (a curing ceremony) forbid the presence of anyone who has used alcohol. Smoking anything, specifically *pezi* (grass, i.e., marijuana) except the sacred tobacco is also proscribed. These rules are strictly enforced, and anyone with a suspicious odor—even that of perfume—is usually turned away from the ceremony. Participants in these ceremonies are not supposed to drink alcohol. But this is not rigidly enforced—nor can it be—in their daily lives away from the ritual cycle. There are instances (outside the ritual cycle) of newly emerging "medicine men" becoming intoxicated on speaking tours to universities or in their lives on reservations.

It is obvious, however, that some persons participate in the Sun Dance for therapeutic reasons, as those persons of Lakota heritage do, to seek a transformation of the individual. The search for supernatural aid to eliminate dependence upon an intrusive and abusive item—alcohol—is a new departure in the ritual. This is a variant from the previous function, which was the preservation of the social order and participation primarily for the welfare of the group. This buttresses Jorgensen's (1972) analysis of the Sun Dance of the Ute and Shoshone, an event seen by participants among many tribes as an alternative to drinking and a means of possibly achieving rigorous temperance.

Besides serving other functions—prestige and honor in participating, status in scarification marks, compassion for people by offering prayers, and enhanced Indian identity—"sun-dancing" for the contemporary Indian male is a means of controlling the excessive use of alcohol. A revitalized ritual, the Sun Dance has not been completely integrated into the symbolic belief structure of the Sioux. As a repressed religion, with the underlying structure of Native language and value systems also suppressed, complete integration and manifestation of belief are still being formulated—especially on an individual level. Increasingly, the Sun Dance is becoming a pan-Indian or intertribal phenomenon, and other tribes—Shoshone, Cree, Micmac, and others—also seek enlightenment in a Native faith. Moreover, the Sun Dance is a regularized event performed on an annual basis. It may, however, occur in various places on Sioux reservations during the summer months. Although an intense rite and evocative of deep religious feelings, it is not of sufficient duration to have lasting effects as a mechanism of alcohol control. Participants come from different Sioux reservations, and there is little esprit de corps or continual intensification. There is no sustained support system that might function throughout the year in isolated Lakota communities or in urban areas.

Some Lakota persons—again, most often males—attend the Yuwipi Ceremony as a means of obtaining help for their drinking problems. Although this is primarily a curing and/or clairvoyance ceremony, depending upon the wishes of the initiator or patient, there are reasons for its performance. Participants in the ritual, other than the patient, ask for help by supplicating and imploring the Wakan Tanka (Great Sacredness) and supernatural spirits. Kemnitzer, in reference to the Oglala Sioux, indicated: "Others also ask for help; people who had lost things, people giving thanks for previous help, men worried about a wife's illness, and women worried about their husband's drinking" (1978:3). A Yuwipi Ceremony may be held specifically for a person who has a drinking problem and is usually initiated by his parents or members of his kin group. All persons present meditate on his problem and pray for him. However, whether or not the ceremony is held to control a drinking problem, anyone who is present may ask the spirits for aid. There is no evidence, however, that anyone has been cured through this rite. It is, nonetheless, the only indigenous support system besides the Sun Dance. Many persons attend the Yuwipi to call attention to the fact that they are cognizant of their drinking problems. The religious practitioner does not assume an active role in the treatment of the person who publicly acknowledges his affinity for alcohol. He merely requests supernatural aid.

When individuals of either sex seek aid from a religious practitioner or Native counselor, the person does not receive stringent directions for change. He or she is merely asked to *ah bleza* one's actions and implement change. There is strong emphasis on *chinka cha* (individual autonomy) and reason and will to change. The therapist listens and may give advice in a nonthreatening nonjudgmental manner.

Pursuing the Sobriety Cause

Since the 1970s, governmental agencies, tribal governments, and Indian associations such as the National Congress of American Indians have expressed concern over the problems of alcohol use. Major emphasis has been on intervention strategies.

The states of abstinence and sobriety in contemporary Native societies have not been examined. However, patterns of abstinence have been historically evident. This fact has been outweighed by attributions in the social structure of a superimposed society. Concerned Native people seem to have subscribed to the "problem" orientation and have not looked to nonindulgence. As seen from the Lakota Sioux data, Native beliefs of expected behavior based upon gender considerations (i.e., male superiority and female subservience) are powerful forces at play in contemporary indigenous social systems.

Sobriety as an achievement seems based upon an enhanced awareness of self and society and certain introspective processes. Age, sex, status, and economic state are important considerations. But the social climate is also significant. Social movements and positive nativistic orientations may create a means to control drinking and assert abstinence patterns. After generations of cultural suppression and forced acculturation to the dominant society, it is only since the 1960s that a conscious revitalization movement has assumed ascendancy in most Sioux reservations and urban Indian enclaves. Allied to this resurgence is the belief that alcohol is an introduced evil that was part of the genocide and ethnocide policies of the conquerors. This is a subtle orientation, verbalized in other contexts such as the American Indian Movement and other protest organizations.

The ideologies of these new movements are important in current Indian life. Voluntary organizations such as the National Congress of American Indians and the recently formed North American Indian Women's Association have also delineated the problem of alcoholism among their constituencies. They often manifest their concern by giving workshops on the issue. Of significance is an increasing Native awareness of the effects of alcohol in Indian communities. This heightened consciousness and spirit of self-determination may be positive forces in sobriety maintenance.

References

Ablon, J. 1964. "Relocated American Indians in the San Francisco Bay Area: Social Interactions and Indian Identity." *Human Organization* 23(4): 296–304.

Blakeslee, C. 1955. "Some Observations on the Indians of Crow Creek Reservation, South Dakota." *Plains Anthropologist* 5: 31–35.

Braroe, N. W. 1975. *Indian and White: Self-Image and Interaction in a Canadian Plains Community.* Stanford: Stanford University Press.

Deloria, Ella. 1944. *Speaking of Indians.* New York: Friendship Press.

Dosman, E. J. 1972. *Indians: The Urban Dilemma.* Toronto: McClelland and Stewart.

Field, P. B. 1962. "A New Cross-Cultural Study of Drunkenness." In *Society, Culture and Drinking Patterns,* ed. D. J. Pittman and C. R. Snyder, 48–74. New York: John Wiley.

Goldfrank, E. S. 1943. "Historic Change and Social Character: A Study of the Teton Dakota." *American Anthropologist* 45(3): 306–21.

Graves, T. D. 1970. "The Personal Adjustment of Navajo Indian Migrants to Denver, Colorado." *American Anthropologist* 72 (1): 35–54.

———. 1971. "Drinking and Drunkenness among Urban Indians." In *The American Indian in Urban Society,* ed. J. Waddel and O. M. Watson, 274–311. Boston: Little, Brown.

Grobsmith, E. 1974. "*Wakun Za:* Use of Yuwipi Medicine Power in Contemporary Teton Dakota Culture." *Plains Anthropologist* 19 (64): 129–33.

Hackenburg, R. A., and M. M. Gallagher. 1972. "The Costs of Cultural Change: Accidental Injury and Modernization among the Papago Indians." *Human Organization* 31(2): 211–26.

Hassrick, R. B. 1964. *The Sioux: Life and Customs of a Warrior Society.* Norman: University of Oklahoma Press.

Hurt, W. R. 1961–62. "Urbanization of the Yankton Indians." *Human Organization* 20(4): 226–31.

Hurt, W. R., and R. M. Brown. 1965. "Social Drinking Patterns of the Yankton Sioux." *Human Organization* 24(3): 222–30.

Johnson, D. L., and C. A. Johnson. 1965. "Totally Discouraged: A Depressive Syndrome among the Sioux." *Transcultural Psychiatric Research* 11: 141–43.

Jorgensen, J. G. 1972. *The Sun Dance Religion: Power for the Powerless.* Chicago: University of Chicago Press.

Jules-Rosette, B. 1978. "The Veil of Objectivity: Prophecy, Divination and Social Inquiry." *American Anthropologist* 80(3): 549–70.

Kemnitzer, L. S. 1972. "The Structure of Country Drinking Parties on the Pine Ridge Reservation, South Dakota." *Plains Anthropologist* 17(56): 131–42.

———. 1978. "Yuwipi." *Indian Historian* 11(2): 2–5.

Kunitz, S. J. 1977. "Underdevelopment and Social Services on the Navajo Reservation." *Human Organization* 36(4): 398–404.

Kuttner, R. E., and A. B. Lorincz. 1967. "Alcohol and Addiction in Urbanized Sioux Indians." *Mental Hygiene* 51(4): 530–42.

Lang, G. C. 1979. "Survival Strategies of Chippewa Drinkers in Minneapolis." *Central Issues in Anthropology* 1(2): 19–40.

Leland, J. 1976. *Firewater Myths: North American Indian Drinking and Alcohol Addiction.* Monograph no. 11. New Brunswick: Publication Division, Rutgers Center for Alcohol Studies.

Levy, J. E., and S. J. Kunitz. 1974. *Indian Drinking: Navajo Practices and Anglo-American Theories.* New York: Wiley-Interscience.

Lewis, T. H. 1975. "A Syndrome of Depression and Mutism in Oglala Sioux." *American Journal of Psychology* 132(7): 753–55.

MacGregor, G. 1946. *Warriors without Weapons: A Study of the Society and Personality Development of the Pine Ridge Sioux.* Chicago: University of Chicago Press.

Maynard, E. 1969. "Drinking as Part of an Adjustment Syndrome among the Oglala Sioux." *Pine Ridge Research Bulletin* 9: 33–51.

McClelland, D. C., W. N. Davis, R. Kalin, and E. Wanner, eds. 1972. *The Drinking Man*. New York: Free Press.

Medicine, B. 1969. "The Changing Dakota Family and the Stresses Therein." *Pine Ridge Research Bulletin* 9: 1–20.

Mirsky, J. 1937. "The Dakota." In *Cooperation and Competition among Primitive Peoples*, ed. M. Mead, 382–427. New York: McGraw-Hill.

Mohatt, G. 1972. "The Sacred Water: The Quest for Personal Power through Drinking among the Teton Sioux." In *The Drinking Man*, ed. D. C. McClelland, W. N. Davis, R. Kalin, and E. Wanner, 261–75. New York: Free Press.

Price, J. A. 1975. "Applied Analysis of North American Indian Drinking Patterns." *Human Organization* 34(1): 17–26.

Province, J. H. 1937. "The Underlying Sanction of Plains Indian Culture." In *Social Anthropology of North American Tribes: Essays in Social Organization, Law, and Religion*, ed. F. Eggan, n.p. Chicago: University of Chicago Press.

Riggs, S. R. 1851. *Grammar and Dictionary of the Dakota Language*, rev. ed. Vol. 4 of *Smithsonian Contribution of Knowledge*. Washington: Smithsonian Institution.

Robbins, R. H. 1973. "Alcohol and the Identity Struggle: Some Effects of Economic Change on Interpersonal Relations." *American Anthropologist* 75(1): 99–122.

Schusky, E. L. 1975. *The Forgotten Sioux: An Ethnohistory of the Lower Brulé Reservation*. Chicago: Nelson-Hall.

Spradley, J. P. 1970. *You Owe Yourself a Drunk: An Ethnography of Urban Nomads*. Boston: Little, Brown.

U.S. Department of Commerce, Bureau of the Census. 1973. *1970 Census of Population: Subject Report, American Indians*. Publication PC(2)-1F. Washington: U.S. Department of Commerce.

Waddell, J. O., and M. W. Everett. 1980. *Drinking Behavior among Southwestern Indians: An Anthropological Perspective*. Tucson: University of Arizona Press.

Westermeyer, Joseph J. 1972. "Options Regarding Alcohol Use among the Chippewa." *American Journal of Orthopsychiatry* 42 (April): 398–403.

White, R. A. 1970. "The Lower-class 'Culture of Excitement' among Contemporary Sioux." In *The Modern Sioux: Social Systems and Reservation Culture*, ed. E. Nurge, 175–97. Lincoln: University of Nebraska Press.

Whiting, J. W. M., and I. L. Child. 1953. *Child Training and Personality: A Cross-Cultural Study*. New Haven: Yale University Press.

Whittaker, J. O. 1962. "Alcohol and the Standing Rock Sioux I: The Pattern of Drinking." *Quarterly Journal of Studies on Alcohol* 23(3): 468–79.

———. 1963. "Alcohol and the Standing Rock Sioux II: Psychodynamic and Cultural Factors in Drinking." *Quarterly Journal of Studies on Alcohol* 24(1): 80–90.

CHAPTER 22

Alcohol and Aborigines:
The North American Perspective

Natives of North America present an aboriginal population of diverse cultural and linguistic dimensions. As with other aboriginal people, they inhabit a present filled with stereotypic images. Besides being assigned to the monolithic category of "North American Indian," the most pervasive and enduring is that of the "drunken Indian." But, as some sociologists suggest, there may be a kernel of truth in that perception. The word *alcohol* as it pertains to Native people in the "New World" (another misperception) evokes emotional considerations and dangerous labeling on all levels. Like other disparaging "othering" of aboriginals, labels such as "lazy," "stupid," and "undependable" are often attributed to males and "sexually promiscuous and licentious" to women. Much of this categorization is based upon the North American Indian's "inability to hold alcohol," an attribute believed by many non-Natives to be genetically based.

To emphasize how early these attitudes are ingrained into members of the dominant or larger society, I recall an incident. At a lecture and dance performance by an Indian male in a California museum, the entertainer asked, "Are there any questions?" I was amazed that the sole response was from a young male child, approximately five years of age, who asked, "Do you drink?"

It may be reasonable to assume that many stereotypes about "others" are learned very early in the socialization of children. Perhaps we may assume that such attitudes about "drunken aboriginals" hold. I have witnessed them directed toward aboriginals in Australia, Maoris in New Zealand, and Native people in Siberia. I suggest that we are dealing with an image that is almost generic at present. It is historically and legally based and hinges upon being a universal truth in Native and non-Native interaction.

In view of the many assumptions and subjective statements about the inappropriateness of indigenous inebriation, its use in the aboriginal world needs clarification. To clarify the misinterpretations, it seems imperative to present a perspective in historical and sociocultural terms. A discussion of alcohol's absence or presence in the ethnographic record of each tribal group might facilitate an understanding of this controversial issue.

The production of alcoholic beverages is tied to such obvious variables as the availability of resources to allow for its production. Therefore, the interdependence of suitable raw materials, knowledge of brewing and distilling techniques, and patterns of consumption are unique attributes of the total picture of each tribal group's use of alcohol. Significantly, there appear to be several considerations in the sociocultural level of those groups of American Indians that fostered or limited the manufacture of alcohol. It is commonly assumed that the cereal grains used to distill inebriating beverages were strictly limited to tribes that practiced horticulture. However, some tribes utilized fully developed horticultural systems and yet did not manufacture alcoholic spirits (Driver and Massey 1952). On the other hand, there is evidence that some Native groups brewed intoxicants from the vegetal materials they gathered. Thus, ethnohistorical materials for specific tribes must be presented with prudence and extreme caution.

It is a commonly accepted fact that most American Indians did not use alcohol before the contact period. As MacAndrew and Edgerton (1969:100) indicate, "Except for a few southwestern tribes, the North American Indians had no alcoholic beverages prior to the coming of the white man." However, before European contact, the New World was not entirely without alcohol. In Mexico, for instance, Natives developed alcoholic beverages, primarily from maize. Wild plums, pineapple, and sarsaparilla roots were also used. After the conquest, brandy and tequila were a further refinement of distilled liquors. Items such as sahuaro and pitahaya cacti and mesquite were also used.

Maize beer manufacture consisted of three techniques: chewing grains to facilitate fermentation, sprouting maize grains, and using stalks. Sprouted-corn beer spread northward to the San Carlos, Mescalero, Lipan, and Chiricahua Apaches, where it is known as *tiswin*. As early as 1894, Bourke indicates that tiswin was a sacred intoxicant of the Apache. Interestingly, Bourke refers to a Cherokee sour-mash corn gruel. It is also remotely possible that some tribes of the Southeast (Virginia and the Carolinas) produced a persimmon wine. If it was indigenous, it did not spread among the neighboring tribes, for knowledge of alcohol manufacture was not evident in Indian cultures of the eastern seaboard.

Alcohol Consumption and Ritual

It is in the Southwest, however, that imbibing alcoholic beverages assumed ritual proportions. It has been stated that among the Apache, women made tiswin before the reservation period (Flannery 1932). Curley (1967) indicates that men assumed its preparation after 1873. Levy and Kunitz (1971b:62) note, "The Western Apaches are thought to have made a cactus beer before their initial contacts with the Spanish, although maize beer diffused northward probably a century ago. In any event, the manufacture of a fermented beer and its secular use was noted as an important problem among the Western Apaches immediately after the establishment of the reservations by early administrators." Basso (1970) indicates that among the Cibecue Apache, women make the intoxicant *talpi* (*tulapai*), which is still used in a ceremonial context in a girl's puberty rite (*nai'es*). The salient aspect is that Native-brewed alcohol is imbibed within a ritual framework.

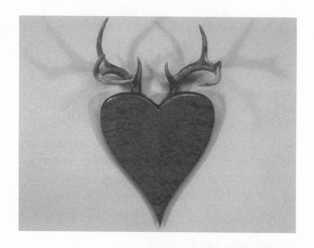

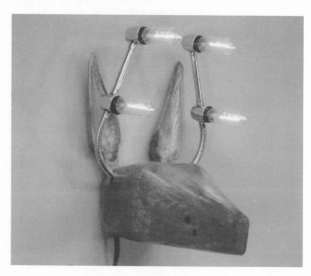

ABOVE: *Deerheart II*
©1997 by Ted Garner
(wood, aluminum, and
lacquer; 19 by 10.24 by
9 inches). (Courtesy of
Ted Garner)

RIGHT: *Ideadeer II*
©1997 by Ted Garner
(wood and glass; 16 by
13 by 18 inches). (Courtesy of Ted Garner)

The above information on this hunting and gathering Athapaskan-speaking society, with clan organization and a previous warrior society, indicates that in the history of alcohol use within such a group, understanding the sociological features or sex roles pertaining to the manufacture of alcohol, confinement on the reserve, and the patterns of aboriginal consumption are necessary antecedents to understanding current conditions. Such studies as L. B. Boyer (1964), R. M. Boyer (1964), and Curley (1967) stress deviance and imply a deficit scene—lack of responsibility in adults, absence of effective role models, ineffective socialization practices, dependence upon government, and other "culture of poverty" syndromes. R. M. Boyer describes horrendous drunken behavior that may be a part of drunken aggression in many areas where American Indians presently reside.

Only when the use of intoxicating beverages and the resultant behavior are placed within a total and dynamic cultural context one will be able to assess alcohol's integral part in viable Native cultures. For the Apache, Basso (1966) notes that the use of tulapai, the Native beer, is a means of cementing reciprocal relations with clan relatives. He describes the impact of wage work on the purchase of beer and wine (Basso 1970), behavioral responses (silence) to drunken verbal abuse, and the reactions to drunken Apaches at ceremonials. Such evidence of Native responses to alcohol use in present-day societies offers interesting interpretations.

Regularized and ritual use of a fermented drink made from the fruit of the sahuaro cactus is a long-standing tradition among the Pima and Papago Indians (now referred to by their linguistic name, Tohono o'Odham) of Arizona. Underhill (1953:196) succinctly states in reference to maize cultivation: "Perhaps their first ceremony should be called 'impregnation' rather than 'birth,' for it was at this time, just before the summer rains, that the juice of the giant cactus was fermented and drunk with solemn ritual. Such ceremonial drinking, as we have mentioned, was widespread in Mexico and South America, but before White arrival, it was not practiced north of the border, except by the Pimans. Their belief was that, as men saturated themselves with liquor, so the earth would be saturated with moisture. In a short time after the drinking festival, the rains came."

Waddell (1975) has indicated that, among contemporary Papago, social bonds between males are important considerations in examining drinking styles. Contextually, the drinking pattern is fourfold: with family in the home, as the wine ceremonial (*nawait*), on other festive occasions, and as part of idiosyncratic conviviality. In an urban environment, Waddell (1975) found that "social credit" (i.e., sharing alcohol) was the basis for an egalitarianism that met the needs of Papago migrants and further fostered personal power.

From Ritual to Deviancy

In the prolific literature on drinking among American Indians, despite the focus on a certain tribe or the use or non-use of alcohol in pre-contact days, contemporary drinking patterns are often seen as deviant. Most studies deal with an unspecified number of persons, usually male and most often in an urban situation. The only exceptions are the long-range studies on the Navajo by Levy and Kunitz (1971a, 1971b).

There has seldom been an ethnohistorical study of one particular tribe to pinpoint the introduction and continuing use of alcohol within that group. Much of the current literature on imbibing styles derives from the notion that drinking alcohol constitutes a "problem" for Indians because they cannot "hold their liquor." In addition, during the period of funded research, citing Indian alcoholism as a major social problem has often guaranteed funds to deal with this major dissonance and maladaption. The converse side of the question— Indians as abstainers or achievers of sobriety—has not been explored.

MacAndrew and Edgerton (1969:110) continue, "Outside the Southwest, the Indians of what is now the United States and Canada had no alcoholic beverages before the coming of the white man." Why alcohol did not spread farther north from Mexico is a puzzling but unanswerable question. It was cherished in Mexico, and it later became sought all over North America. Yet the fact remains that the vast majority of North American Indians, although they possessed many wild and cultivated plants suitable for fermentation, did not produce alcoholic beverages prior to the period of European contact.

I am well aware of the fact that many subaltern or "people of color" researchers are often accused of subjectivity or bias. Therefore, I present in full the conclusion of an article written by Patrick J. Abbott, M.D., and entitled "American Indian and Alaska Native Aboriginal Use of Alcohol in the United States":

> The use of alcohol originated in Middle America but rapidly diffused to Northern Mexico and from there to the Southwestern United States. The majority of aboriginal production and use of alcoholic beverages was in this region. However, there were a surprising number of scattered accounts of intoxicating beverage use throughout the United States prior to White contact. For the most part, the use of alcoholic drinks required an agricultural base, but not in all instances. The reason for this is primarily that alcoholic beverages were made from domesticated plants, although there are examples of liquor being derived from wild plants. (1996:1–13)

Aboriginal use generally did not involve excessive drunkenness but rather controlled and supervised use—often in highly ritualized occasions. Further, accounts of American Indians' initial encounters with alcoholic beverages did not describe reckless or disinhibited behavior. The first recorded account of alcohol being given to American Indians was in 1545 by Jacques Cartier, and it occurred without incident. As MacAndrew and Edgerton (1969:114) aptly describe, "When the North American Indians initial experience with alcohol was untutored by expectations to the contrary, the result was neither the development of an all-consuming craving or an epic of drunken mayhem and debauchery."

It was with ongoing white contact that the use of alcohol assumed more destructive aspects. The reasons for this are beyond the scope of this review and are discussed elsewhere (MacAndrew and Edgerton 1969). Several hypotheses are likely, however: Alcohol became increasingly more available through the active commercial and fur trade; tribes did not have to divert valuable food supplies into producing alcoholic beverages; the alcohol content of beverages increased dramatically with the introduction of distilled spirits (which had been largely unknown to American Indians except the Aztec, who had some familiarity with rudimentary distillation processes) (Bourke 1894); and, perhaps most likely, outside contact brought massive social and cultural change. Social rules governing drinking behavior shifted as a result of these changes. Alcohol became a menace, not necessarily because it was novel in use but as an expression of a dramatic sociocultural shift. Abbott follows the standard "cultural area" approach and gives information on aboriginal alcohol use for the tribes in that category.

It may be concluded that debilitating and chronic alcohol abuse did not reach epidemic proportions among North American Natives until the contact period and resultant cultural change. Historic records and ethnographic accounts are filled with repressive laws, such as the "Potlatch law" in Canada, which repressed religious and artistic expression and confiscated sacred items. Both federal governments of Canada and the United States established legal constraints to suppress aboriginal cultures. Most of the literature dealing with "Indian drinking" points to this destruction as basic to Native anomie and cultural loss and despair.

In an interesting analysis of federal Indian policy in the United States, Robert J. Miller and Maril Hazlett (1996) define five phases based upon the image of the "drunken Indian." The formative years (1789–1871) established "the assumption that the mythical 'drunken Indian' is powerless." This era prohibited Indian consumption of alcohol. In the allotment and assimilation period (1871–1928), "Ineffective federal and racist state legislation cemented the stigma of the 'drunken Indian' as a race helpless to control itself against alcohol." The Indian reorganization and termination era (1945–61) was perhaps the most significant. The repeal of Indian prohibition allowed Indians to drink in public places in the United States in 1953 and in Canada in 1963. The "drunken Indian" became a public hazard on reservations and in off-reservation border towns and urban areas. Many dysfunctional families and communities in contemporary Native life may be traced to this period. In the self-determination era (1961 to the present), legislation "equated Indian health care with alcoholism treatment, [and] the myth of the 'drunken Indian' remained the foundation of federal Indian alcohol policy and its implementation."

Within these periods, Miller and Hazlett examined countless policy decisions made by the federal government—from treaties to current Indian self-determination legislation. These numerous pieces of legislation validated many Indians' beliefs that they are the most regulated ethnic group in the United States. Miller and Hazlett conclude: "The surest road to recovery from the 'drunken Indian' myth in federal policy is for the federal government to support and allow tribes and Native Americans to take the lead in directly formulating and carrying out the solutions" (1996:298).

Buried in Miller and Hazlett's report as a footnote (1996:403) is a statement that addresses the genetic propensity of Native people in the United States toward alcohol. Dr. Everett R. Rhoades (Kiowa), director of the U.S. Indian Health Service, testified before the U.S. Congress in 1991: "There are clearly biochemical and intracellular mechanisms in which the evidence, inconclusive at the present time, is very, very suggestive that there is a difference in the handling of ethanol between the Indian population and the Asian population. . . . The search for genetic markers is well under way. I think it is entirely likely that the answer to alcoholism is going to be in some obscure investigator's laboratory." In response, Sen. John McCain asked: "Are you saying in layman's language that there is some evidence that would indicate that alcohol has a different effect on Native Americans and Asians than it does on non-Native Americans—in other words, that it goes to the brain more quickly, its more addictive in nature? Is that what you are saying?" "I'm suggesting that, yes," Rhoades replied. As for a biological and genetic predisposition to alcohol, my search of the literature has not been conclusive.

Unfortunately, the literature on alcohol and Canadian First Nations people is not as extensive as it is on alcohol and Native Americans. Governmental funding for studies has not been as great. References to alcohol use and abuse is often mentioned, however, in various ethnographic reports for specific native groups. A few books, such as Hornby and Dana (1984) and Shkilnyk (1985) for the Anishinabe (Ojibwa), are the exceptions.

The Persistence of the Image

But a myth persists. The "drunken Indian" image pertains to all Indians—male and female. It is part of the fabric of white and Indian relationship in the past and present. Patterns of alcohol utilization, behavior while drinking, and attitudes toward liquor vary from group to group. Nonetheless, the image of the aborigines who are "unable to hold their liquor" remains.

References

Abbott, P. J. 1996. "American Indian and Alaska Native Aboriginal Use of Alcohol in the United States." *American Indian and Alaska Native Mental Health Research* 7(2): 1–13.

Basso, K. H. 1966. "The Gift of Changing Woman." *Bureau of American Ethnology Bulletin.* Washington: Government Printing Office, 113–73, 196.

———. 1970. *The Cibecue Apache.* New York: Holt, Rinehart and Winston.

Bourke, J. G. 1894. "Distillation by Early American Indians." *American Anthropologist* 7(3): 297–99.

Boyer, L. B. 1964. "Folk Psychiatry of the Apache of the Mescalero Indian Reservation." In *Magic, Faith and Healing: Studies in Primitive Psychiatry Today,* ed. A. Kiev, 384–419. New York: Free Press.

Boyer, R. M. 1964. "The Matrifocal Family among the Mescalero." *American Anthropologist* 66(3): 593–602.

Curley, R. T. 1967. "Drinking Patterns of the Mescalero Apache." *Quarterly Journal of Studies on Alcohol* 28: 116–31.

Driver, H. E., and W. C. Massey. 1952. "Comparative Studies of North American Indians: Narcotics and Stimulants." *Transactions of the American Philosophical Society* 47(2): 260–75.

Flannery, R. 1932. "The Position of Women among the Mescalero Apache." *Primitive Man* 5(1): 26–32.

Hornby, R., and R. H. Dana, eds. 1984. *Mni Wakan and the Sioux: Respite, Relief, and Recreation.* Brandon, Man.: Justin Publishing.

Levy, J. E., and S. J. Kunitz. 1971a. "Indian Drinking: Problems of Data Collection and Interpretation." *Proceedings: First Annual Alcoholism Conference of NIAAA.* DHEW Pub. No. (HSM) 73–9074, ed. M. Chafetz, 217–36. Washington: Government Printing Office.

———. 1971b. "Indian Reservations, Anomie and Social Pathologies." *Southwestern Journal of Anthropology* 27(2): 97–128.

MacAndrew, C., and R. B. Edgerton. 1969. *Drunken Comportment: A Social Explanation.* Chicago: Aldine.

Miller, R. J., and M. Hazlett. 1996. "The 'Drunken Indian' Myth Distilled into Reality through Federal Indian Alcohol Policy." *Arizona State Law Journal* 8(1): 223–98.

Shkilnyk, A. M. 1985. *A Poison Stronger than Love: The Destruction of an Ojibwa Community.* New Haven: Yale University Press.

Underhill, R. M. 1953. *Red Man's America.* Chicago: University of Chicago Press.

Waddell, J. O. 1975. "For Individual Power and Social Credit: The Use of Alcohol among Tucson Papagos." *Human Organization* 34(1): 9–15.

PART 5

Families

CHAPTER 23

The Changing Dakota Family
and the Stresses Therein

Current theories about Dakota family appear to be mainly built upon family structure and interrelationships of the *tiospaye* and the smoothly functioning operational system it was in traditional society. This seems hardly an adequate account for the obvious maladjustment and apathy that seem to typify present-day life on Dakota reservations. I do not wish to contribute further to the pathetic picture of the Dakotas but rather to elucidate the factors and provide a clearer frame of reference for studying the family in contemporary Dakota reservation culture. Perhaps pinpointing future research needs might be a result.

This presentation is tentative and exploratory at best. My essay is an attempt to provoke critical and realistic evaluation of what the present-day family is and what it does and does not do for individuals who participate in a dual, in some cases a triple, social milieu. These exploratory ideas are based upon data from Cheyenne River and Standing Rock reservations, where all areas of the reservations were visited for three months in 1956 and in 1964. Interviews were obtained from several individuals on Rosebud and Pine Ridge reservations, where only two weeks were spent in 1956.

A presentation of the actual functioning of the contemporary Dakota family system, with its inconsistencies and internal stresses, is the object of this essay. It appears necessary to come to grips with this basic unit in understanding the dismal and discouraging Dakota picture, which seems to permeate all recent analyses of this group of American Indians. Many of these analyses have been based upon education, economics, tribal factionalism, administration, and other disturbing factors on the reservations. Malan (1961) has hinted at a few factors that may account for family disorganization.

The term *tiyospaye* still has meaning to most tradition-oriented Dakota, except perhaps the current non-Dakota-speaking generation. To most, the term indicates "family" in the broadest sense. Connotation has changed slightly. *Tiospayaki* ("that extended kin group," or, more popularly, "that family") often indicates a group that might be manifesting "non-Dakota-like" or abnormal behavior. There is an underlying premise here that aggression, hostility, dishonesty, or other less desirable actions are often shown by such extended family groups and may be endemic to that group. In other words, the atypical behavior seems to be part and parcel of the behavioral characteristics of a particular "family." Thus, it is explainable and gives an expected rationale for unusual behavior—drinking, fighting, etc.

The term often used to explain deviant behavior (good as well as bad) is "tiospaye hecun onpi" (that's the way that family lives). These expectations make deviance within the group plausible, such as, "The X family is noted for their fighting and holding wild parties," or "The Y family is noted for its 'smartness' [intelligence]." Acts of aggression and other deviant behavior (rape, extra-marital affairs, and illegitimacy) can be attributed with ease to a particular family. Because such a family consistently performs in an "expected" pattern, there is no reason for public concern. "Family" is, in a sense, an identifying label and a term that has meaning for whites in nearby towns. "Good" and "bad" Indian families are often compared with "responsible" and "no-good" ones.

A Dakota family is grandparent-based. This is undoubtedly a function of the housing situation on the reservation, in that the allotment or land upon which a house is built usually belongs to the grandparent (either maternal or paternal) and operates as a home base for the extended family of sons, daughters, their spouses, and the children and grandchildren of these unions.

There appears to be no clear-cut residence pattern among newly affiliated members of the opposite sex in present-day Dakota life. There is constant movement to and from the homes of either the parents of the woman or the parents of the man. This is usually dictated by the amount of stress and strain that are present at any particular time in any family setting. In addition, a deciding factor may be the economic position of the parents—which family is able to provide food and lodging.

The extended family, with the mobility of the union of procreation, is predominant. The grandparental relationship with grandchildren is dynamic, ongoing, and critical in maintaining a small measure of cohesiveness within Dakota society. An example of this is a situation where twenty-six grandchildren live in and around the grandparents' home. In this case, the male grandparent often gives his grandchildren an aspirin every night at bedtime to ensure a measure of peace and quiet. This appears to be a normative type of family unit, although the number of grandchildren would vary from a minimum of three to into the twenties.

The family of procreation is diffuse and ever-changing. There are many factors operative here. Among these are the complete demoralization of the majority of Dakota women and the equally, if not more, demoralized status of Dakota men. This could be attributed to many causes. Most noticeable, besides the traditional dependency that seems to be a built-in factor, is increased dependence upon Welfare and Aid to Dependent Children (ADC) and greater promiscuity. It was surprising to note that heretofore "stable" or "good" families in the full-blood category are also shattered. The change in family function is noted by most Dakota themselves, but how to remedy it is a further cause of anxiety. Countless cases of moral deterioration and drinking among previously "good" families were pointed out by other Dakota.

There are many temporary liaisons and much illegitimacy. Following the traditional value placed upon children, the child of such circumstances is held to be completely innocent. All transgressions on the part of the members of such temporary liaisons are excused with "you can't blame the child" and other such statements. Indeed, there is still one common characteristic among Dakota grandparents. One often hears such phrases as "it isn't the child's fault." Traditional patterns of permissiveness and excessive indulgence (perhaps typical of grandparents) are amplified, and grandparents are ambivalent about interfering with children's discipline. There is also ambivalence in the statement, "In the good old days, our grandchildren would take care of us, now it is the other way around." The fact that many grandparents are receiving Social Security payments (commonly called "old age") and are compelled to provide for a number of grandchildren must be discouraging. It is often the case that not only must they provide room and board for adolescent grandchildren but also for many of their peer group. The "leveling process" of Dakota society is a real, hard fact.

The parent who neglects a child is not censured directly and apparently feels no sense of over-riding guilt, for he/she knows that the child will be cared for during any unspecified time that the child is "abandoned." The child (or children) is given care and help from any member of the extended family (mainly grandparents and siblings of parents) in such instances when the parents are away on drinking bouts. There seems to be greater articulation and commitment to who should be responsible when parents leave for off-reservation work. There also appears to be an undercurrent of disgust directed against the transient parent but never against the child. That feeling, however, is seldom verbalized when the parent returns from extended drinking bouts in the nearby white communities or throughout the reservations. Usually, a disapproving silence is the only indication of censure. In some instances, other members of the kinship group (those not recently on a spree) will "talk to" transgressing parents. That is not usual, however. The effects of these misdemeanors upon the child have not yet been fully assessed, but certainly they have an effect upon school performance and attendance and future orientation toward life.

It has been noted, however, that in cases where the grandparents might question the behavior of a young Dakota adolescent, the adolescent often retorts: "Well, my father [or my mother] does it, so why can't I?" This can be seen to have a dual implication: "Why do you question my behavior? Obviously, you were not able to control the behavior of your own child," and also, "What is a good behavior for my parents is good behavior for me." As a generalization, the grandparental role as disciplinarian is not strong.

There appears to be an increasing utilization and exploitation of Dakota women by non-Indian males in the whole area of the Dakota reservations. One is able to discern a tremendous amount of miscegenation by a very cursory appraisal of the Indian population. There are many blonde, Caucasian-featured Indians in families formerly known as, and that interacted as, full-bloods. Negroid admixture is also on the increase. There appears to be a growing prestige factor in being able to document one non-Indian ancestor. There is also pride in legal alliances of non-Indians (white, not Mexican or Negro) and Dakota women in most families.

Many instances of "things you shouldn't hear" but "you can see them anytime you go into _____ [a town neighboring two reservations]" were recounted. Some of these things included nude adolescents sitting in tubs in alleys, intoxicated adult women walking down streets, their skirts tucked into their underpants, and countless other examples of the role of present-day Dakota women. In many cases, many non-Indians looked on being Indian and walking down the street as an open invitation.

There are communities reported (by Indians) as having the highest rate of venereal diseases and stillbirths on their reservations (compared to other communities on the reservation). Abortion is practiced, but the means and frequency, and the group of women who do so, could not be determined with any degree of accuracy. It could be postulated that because of the lack of stricture regarding illegitimate births and the Dakota valuation of children, abortions are not resorted to as often as one might think. The ones that have been ascertained were among legally married thirty- to thirty-five-year-olds. One can easily see that such factors as increased Aid to Dependent Children and increased welfare payments might condone the birth of children, even to temporary liaisons. The fact that children are generally cared for by grandparents and other members of the extended family may make the birth of children a less hazardous venture than the uncertainties of abortion.

In any treatment of groups of individuals like the modern Dakota it is easy to overlook the customary life-way, which is that of an underprivileged minority whose major problem is subsistence and whose concern for the present, day-to-day existence is basic to understanding this group's modus operandi. Consistent with this, and as important, is the still vital and often-resorted-to idea of the "generous human being." The area of interpersonal relationships within Dakota families is often insufficiently presented. The idea of generosity (with less emphasis on reciprocity) still characterizes modern Dakota society to a marked degree. It is very real and meaningful (and stressful in many cases). Generosity is a regulating force in family and interpersonal relationships. Reciprocity is another matter, and the fact that it is disfunctional in present life on reservations is very evident.

Training children to be generous begins early in their socialization. This has been noted by many students of the Sioux. As in the traditional culture, the baby of the family is catered to; his every wish is granted, and his needs are cared for by all members of the family. It seems apparent, however, that the first-born of the family is given much more of this care than subsequent siblings. In general, a baby's older siblings are expected to give the baby most things he desires. As the baby grows older, he, in turn, is expected to do the same for younger siblings. We have recorded instances of five- and six-year-olds buying articles (old beads, necklaces, writing tablets, and the usual treats of candy and pop) for their younger siblings.

Coincident with this training in generosity, a great repulsion toward hoarding or saving is instilled in children at an early age. "Don't be so stingy" is a common admonishment to young children. When young children are given money, they invariably go to the nearest store to spend it immediately. True, they often share their purchases with siblings and peers. That is the expected behavior, and such action meets with the approval of adults. Some school-aged children will bring playmates home from school and will furnish them with snacks. Many mothers make a special effort to have goods (bread, jam, coffee, tea) ready for a late-afternoon snack.

It is apparent that training toward giving is still maintained in early childhood. Early socialization is oriented toward the extreme polarity of that in white American society. The phrase "don't be a *wasicu* (white)" still has power over youngsters.

There are other aspects surrounding child socialization that are based on giving. There appears to be no withholding of love on the part of parents (or parent surrogates, especially females) in exchange for good behavior on the part of the child. Extreme permissiveness is still evident.

Another feature that has bearing on child socialization is the "going-ness," or mobility, of contemporary Dakota. Families are willing to travel great distances for shopping and to use facilities such as laundromats. In summer, seasonal variation is supplied by rodeos and "doings" (ceremonials that are religious and social). In fact, cars have displaced horses as prestige items in reservation life. A Dakota individual who owns a car is assured of some sort of income, for he is paid for "hauling passengers." When engaged in this activity, he/she usually takes a child. (Many Dakota males are unable to obtain drivers' licenses due to drunken driving convictions, and most automobiles are registered in a woman's name.) The children who are left at home are given a treat (canned tomatoes or peaches, watermelon, and other fruit, if available) or are given the opportunity to go to the nearest store and "charge something" (cookies, candy, pop) to compensate for their stay at home. If nothing is available, they are specifically asked what they desire to have brought to them.

A form of bribery, then, is a means of social control that has its beginnings in the early childhood of the modern Dakota. This appears to be an ongoing process throughout early and late adolescence. It has not assumed the importance of reward vis-à-vis punishment, but it appears to be mainly a subtle means of a compensatory nature. This can be seen as contributing to the early beginnings of a dependency orientation. This pattern of mobility is especially critical during adolescence. There is a marked increase in situations where young men and women leave their natal homes when things become too tense and move into other homes (within and without) their families.

The sharing of children is another common feature of family life. There is a great fluidity of social mobility among children. This perhaps may have increased with the contemporary non-marriage pattern. Children are often left with members of the kin group (or friends) for undetermined periods of time. That practice is greatly exploited by the younger members of society. If a parent (or parent surrogate) goes on a binge of unknown duration, he is free of worry about the children, for someone in the community will have assumed their care. This often does not follow family lines.

It appears that although contemporary Dakota place high value on children, this is an area of great ambivalence. It seems that the battered child syndrome is an emerging phenomenon. The actual whipping of children by present-day parents, full-blooded or otherwise, is one of the major intergenerational areas of disagreement and discord. Grandparents who observe the whipping of their grandchildren show silent disapproval but are seldom moved to direct action. It was observed that young children who provoke parental ire will often run into the grandparent's cabin or room. There, depending upon degree of parental anger, the child frequently finds refuge.

It was noted that in cases of parental disagreement, a parent often spanked a child (i.e., mother spanking daughter and father spanking son) in order to, as they say, "get back" at the spouse. This form of provocation was also seen in cases when mothers actually threw the child at the father or put it on the ground and walked away—a supreme insult to grandparents.

There is a curious syncretic combination of some aspects of child training. Children are never punished if they admit to a disapproved act. For example, some children may open a can of peaches, eat an entire watermelon, pop a pound of popcorn, or, in a more serious vein, whittle on the family's best chair. If a parent asks who did it and the child responds "I did," then no reprimand ensues. Praise, usually directed more toward toddlers than older siblings, is meted out for trivial acts such as hauling wood into cabins, bringing water, and so forth.

The child is allowed to make many of his own decisions—right or wrong. Although a parent may express a preference for a mode of action, in the final analysis the child makes the decision. A statement by parents and grandparents—"I tried to tell him/her, but you can't tell him/her anything"—usually closes the issue.

The significance of grandparents and their effect on the socialization of young Dakota are further demonstrated by the fact that very often a young child will threaten "I am going to run away to grandmother or grandfather."

As far as grandparents are concerned, the most devastating thing they can say about their children is, "They are stingy. They deprive us of our grandchildren." This is a statement most often heard directed toward young couples who are progressive, have definite views about child training and their children's education, and are "white-oriented" in other values. These individuals often keep their children at home and restrict their mobility.

Dakota hospitality does not appear to be of a compulsive order. Nor does it appear as a need to deny feelings of hostility (although this may be part of the picture). It seems to be a fairly genuine attribute derived from childhood training. Serving food to all visitors is a common and accepted practice. It is only in those houses where "they think they are whites" that this primary point of etiquette is forgotten. It is usual for families to drop into one's home around mealtime and for the visitors to jokingly say, "We are *tiole* (one who looks for a home)." The implication is there, and the hostess feeds the visitors. It is highly insulting to say of anyone, however, that he is tiole in a serious manner.

When one seeks help, as, for example, during haying or branding time, one must provide an initial meal, no matter what time of day. Provision of a place to sleep, if the job is longer than one working day, is also expected. In addition, the host must furnish transportation to and from the helper's home.

It is sometimes possible to get some help from those of the family group who are living at one's house during the summer. Guests are always obligated to help with the chores and housework. In many instances, it is easier to get help from guests than from family. Helping with chores is often left to the discretion of the guest and reflects his early socialization. There is no conscious effort on the part of younger parents to teach their children to help with chores, dishes, and so on when they visit in family members' homes. This type of training is often supplied by the grandparents' generation and is based upon their earlier training and orientation. The traditional way of returning dishes to the hostess was never discussed during my two periods of fieldwork.

Contemporary hospitality also refers to the "setting-up" process that forms the basis of many interactions among the Dakota in non-Indian centers. If one is drinking, one must "set-up" Indian acquaintances in the bar. Non-drinkers (only a small minority) treat each other to meals in restaurants and cafes. One can easily see the diminishment of funds in a short time because of such ventures. Both sexes engage in this practice, which appears to be a carry-over from early child socialization. Usually, drinking bouts continue until all pooled resources are exhausted.

This generosity extends into other areas: gift-giving, the use of clothes and cars, and the care of children. This often leads to a very "un-Dakota-like" (in the traditional sense) attitude. Recounting what one has done for others is a common pattern now ("I did that for them, and here"). This attitude appears to be more common on the intra-familial level and leads to a terrific amount of bickering. It seems to stem from the frustrations of human relationships, the uncertainties of life on reservations, and growing intra-group hostility, all pressed into a dysfunctional traditional behavior that is nonregulatory. This, and sheer belligerence, were given as the most common causes for the noticeably increased intra-familial fights (verbal and physical) that appear to be so much a part of contemporary Dakota existence.

Most Dakota drink for a variety of reasons. Many do so because they "enjoy it" or they "like to have fun." Others try to rationalize their drinking habits in a variety of ways: "I get so tired of staying home with the kids," "I get so mad at the old lady [wife]," and so on.

Usually a Dakota drinking bout starts innocuously enough. There is great conviviality, much "setting-up," and much talk, which becomes rather spirited. The talk is "good talk" and usually centered around the drinkers' childhoods and adolescences. Peer-group affiliations are brought out, as the "good old days" ("when we had such a good basketball team"). Very often, these last remarks lead to verbal fights for the glory of the old high school. It is especially significant that these people are nostalgic about their childhoods and find remembering them so reaffirming and reassuring. It was interesting to note the completeness of their accounts of what had transpired during shared childhood and adolescence.

There appears to be a maudlin sentimentality that prevails and is often a prelude to the onset of hostility and bellicosity. One mixed-blood, twice married, typified the reaction of most people when he stated, "Well, cousin, however it is, this is the way the Dakota live." When last seen, he was engaged in a physical fight with one of his wife's cousins. After this initial period when young Dakota are able to verbalize their hopes and frustrations there is the drinking bout itself, when most are in a stupor of forgetting.

Stresses within the family are a constant threat to its cohesion and stability. The two sexes apparently do not form a tight-knit family unit because they both know that the wife can, and indeed does, leave the husband and rely on a steady income of welfare payments and dole (surplus commodities). It seems that Dakota women are more conscious of the hold—sexual and monetary—they exert over males and are exploiting it greatly. Matrilineality is an increasing factor in present-day Dakota families. The role of a contemporary Dakota male appears to be even more emasculating. There have been instances of a mother proclaiming that a child does not belong to her present spouse. Male frustrations are greatly increased, which contributes directly to other maladjustments in reservation life: drunkenness, felonies (an increasing number of bad checks are being written), and petty crime.

Women are participating in extra-marital relationships more frequently, not only with Sioux men but also with non-Indians. It is known that many women who are becoming "integrated" in surrounding white communities supplement their incomes by prostitution. A corollary is a complete disregard for the traditional upbringing of Dakota daughters. This is seen in the exploitation of contemporary females by whites as well as Indians of all ages.

Giving birth to a child is somehow equated with adulthood among the Dakota, even among the increasing numbers of thirteen- and fourteen-year-old girls who produce illegitimate children. The Dakota phrase "towa cinca tayesni" (literally, "whose child no one knows"), a tremendous mark of shame several generations ago, does not have great significance in present systems of social control. Motherhood (and fatherhood) has always been esteemed among the Dakota. The current emphasis on illegitimacy appears not to be censured by the extreme shame and rejection that might be expected by administrators, social workers, and other change agents working with contemporary Dakota, although older Dakota are quite perturbed by the number of thirteen- to seventeen-year-old females who become mothers.

The idea of prolonged nursing is held up to the current generation as an ideal. The group of fifty-year-old mothers (in 1956) apparently held to the practice of prolonged lactation—the range being from two to five years. This was practiced more with male than female babies. There is a tendency for young mothers, however, to "put the baby on a bottle" because nursing interferes with their activities. There is also increased dependence upon grandparents (or great-grandparents) to provide canned milk for the babies.

For all the apparent looseness of female morality attributed and seen among the modern Dakota, there is a surprising reticence to talk about pregnancy, birth, and related activities. This is a definite change from twenty to twenty-five years ago, when grandmothers seemed to have more to do with sex education and the inculcation of morals. The grandmothers of today do not present such data but try, often belatedly, to instruct their granddaughters in the proper care of children, meanwhile deploring their lack of interest in doing so.

Many young teenagers of today have complained that their knowledge of menstruation and pregnancy was obtained from peers and older sisters rather than their mother or grandmothers. There appears to be a decided hostility, especially by younger daughters toward mothers. The eldest-daughter role is still compatible and not so stressful. Role definition and occupancy apparently follow Dakota expectations. The care of aging parents, young siblings and their progeny, and greater interaction with non-Indians are areas of increasing import.

Sibling stress caused by vying for parental approval and competing for acknowledgment of generosity, gift-giving, and aid of all sorts is a common phenomenon in interactional patterns of present-day Dakota sisters.

The continued value of the male in modern Dakota society as an "ideal" configuration is important. Sons and brothers (especially the eldest) are valued and treated with deference by most contemporary families. Indeed, much of the traditional behavioral pattern regarding this sex preference persists in many families (for example, giving the first game killed by a young adolescent male to someone outside the family or giving boys an Indian name). Traditional androcentric propensities are manifest today. The vast freedom allowed the Dakota male has previously been noted. Present role expectations include ability in athletics, riding in rodeos, sexual exploits, drinking, and breaking broncos if the family is a ranching one (although most Dakota youths follow that means of gaining prestige at one time or another).

Stress among male siblings is not as noticeable as stress among sisters, or perhaps it is more sublimated. It seems to be accepted that an older male child is rightfully entitled to all the attention he receives. Younger male siblings appear to be willing to accept the status quo and operate within its framework. There have been instances of internecine fighting, however, usually between males and usually during drinking bouts. This is an area in which further probing is essential.

Due to the extremely free and easy life of early manhood, the Dakota male seems to find married life quite frustrating, and marriage appears to become more onerous as more children arrive. Subtle pressures are exerted by grandparents who worry about the increasing number of children and the incipient burden that they may eventually create. The older Dakota ideal of few children is evoked and presented as a "way of life" in which concern for the child was great. This ambivalence on the part of grandparents was noted in 1956 and was greatly verbalized during 1964.

It is not infrequent to hear twenty- to thirty-year-old Dakota males remark, "I'm a failure. I've tried everything—even relocation." It is extremely difficult for both Dakota and non-Dakota to comprehend the limited range of employment that is available to this age group. The stereotyped image of Indian unreliability due to alcoholism, time, poor work habits, and all the faults attributed by white society makes the family role a difficult one at best. (There are, of course, as in most stereotypes, some measures of truth in this image.) The Dakota male is in a very precarious position in contemporary reservation society.

It is within this age group that role conflict and incompatibility is most noticeable. Male frustration is shown in not being able to provide a workable model for sons. As a recent superficial study of alcoholism (financed by tribal funds) has shown, there is a marked increase in the use of alcohol for the majority of Dakota of *all* ages. Many grandparents are presently seeking relief from life pressures with the use of *mini-wakan* (liquor). (Many of my peer group pointed this out as the major change in life since we all were growing up in the "good old days.") During the six years between visits to these reservations, the salient feature of change concerned the numbers of Dakota grandparents who had begun to drink.

As far as the Dakota male is concerned, there is a complete dissonance between role expectation and role fulfillment in his adjustment to a changing society. Because of the nurturing, permissive picture the Dakota mother presents to her son, there appears to be greater heed paid to her advice than to the wife's wishes. This indicates that there will be further maladjustments in marriage and may have a great deal to do in accounting for the so-called apathy of Dakota men. Fathers, too, tend to be extremely permissive about the behavior of a male child, although it was fathers (really, grandfathers) who expressed concern about the future role of Dakota men. After a youth's marriage, he is expected to assume the role of breadwinner and caretaker of his children. This is where role unpreparedness and role conflict arise and cause great disruption in the child's socialization process.

There are countless instances of children being born after the death of the man to whom their mother was married. They share in his estate, however, and thus further complicate the heirship problem. Most often, the family's elder brother merely says, "My brother is certainly a good man, he even produces children after his death" (translated from Dakota). In general, there is apathy toward raising a legal issue. Often, it is too difficult to convince agency personnel of one's concern.

The older generation is also bothered by the diffuseness of kin and a lack of identification in pinpointing kinship relations. As an illustration, one Dakota woman whose son had died leaving no children of his own but a widow and her two children by a previous marriage was very concerned about family inheritance. Later, her daughter-in-law formed an alliance with another Dakota man, and when the child from that liaison was enrolled as the son of her deceased son, the older woman became very indignant. She made special trips to the Indian agency, and after several attempts (administrators could not understand her concern) had the child's name removed and proper paternity indicated. It was no easy task. The administrators insisted that the name of the widow was her legal one, and thus the widow's son was entitled to use it and be enrolled under it. This Dakota "grandmother" was concerned about the inheritance rights of the illegitimate child as opposed to the rights of her "real" grandchildren.

As a result of the decided and self-evident favoring of males in contemporary Dakota culture, there appears to be more Dakota women "out among the whites" and interacting with white American society. This may be seen in several ways. Perhaps in one light it is a direct protest against early parental favoritism of males. At the moment, there is insufficient data to support the concept of "aggressiveness of females" based upon this premise. There is great reliance on Dakota women of all ages to interact with administrators, teachers, social workers, and others of the white dominant society. This suggests that Dakota males rely on mothers, wives, and "girl friends" (as the females of their temporary liaisons are designated) to act as buffers in dealing with external society.

There is definite manipulation of police, social workers, and other administrators to receive the maximum concessions. This falls within the realm of the women, which modern Dakota do not see as a loss of prestige. The ability to coerce "them" (administrators) is a mark of prestige. This factor is recognized by some social workers who rely on a white American maxim: "The squeaking wheel gets the grease."

This dependency increasingly extends to women bailing young (and not so young) Dakota males out of jail frequently, which, of course, presents an exceedingly unvalued position for the male, as viewed by white standards. It is seen as accepted behavior by Dakota males, and increasingly mothers are especially questioning the wisdom of such actions. Sisters (in particular the eldest) often perform acts to honor their brother, for example, staging impromptu give-aways when a brother competes in a rodeo. If the brother is a returned veteran, he is greatly honored, and much is given away "in his honor" at the ceremonials that have replaced the old warrior societies (July 4 celebrations, V-J Day, and Veteran's Day, November 11).

At present, it would appear that the "shame culture" is not now a "guilt culture" but perhaps a "get culture." Dakota orientation to contemporary life on the reservations seems to be get what you can to sustain your needs in any way—and by any means available.

Increased violence and strife were especially evident in current (1964) family relationships. There appears to be a complete polarity in the way most families behave, ranging from a saccharine congeniality to a nonverbalized, hostile situation when whole sections of families avoid each other and individuals do not speak to each other for weeks. The only individuals who appear to operate in this time of stress are young children, who are again excused on the grounds that "you can't blame them" or "they are not responsible for the way their parents act."

Among the modern Dakota, it would seem that kinship terminology and usage are shattered and not in evidence. Kinship relationships outside the immediate family are relatively unknown. The retention of traditional kinship terminology is not universally used by the younger generation (in 1964). Young Dakota teenagers are not learning the language. As kinship terms become obliterated, such Dakota terms as *wicakcela* (old man), *winukcala* (old woman), and *kola* (friend) seem to be assuming greater generality.[1] The English terms *uncle* and *aunt* are used more commonly and with no distinction between paternal or maternal affiliations.

One often hears "you can't trust your own relatives" when discussing family and kin with other Dakota. This seems to be very significant in the behavior of the Dakota, where there is much stealing and hocking of items belonging to other members of the family. It is also noted in an increased amount of insufficient-fund checks or checks drawn on bank accounts of those few Dakota who use banks. It would be interesting to know how many Dakotas in the state's penitentiary are there for this felony.

During the summer of 1964, it was seen that material objects such as beaded goods and Indian artifacts were being sold to white individuals in nearby towns. Frequently, adolescent grandchildren will rifle grandparents' trunks and storage places to look for valuables to sell. The practice has now extended to piece-work quilts ("star" quilts), embroidery and crocheted art goods, and shawls, which become barter items for beer in the many local taverns that thrive within the reservations. These are also the prized pieces that form the material items in contemporary Dakota give-aways at ceremonials: feasts and powwows. White purchasers feel that this is their last opportunity to obtain "real valuable Indian artifacts" and hence are eager to provide collateral in a pawn situation or pay cash for them. Some enterprising young Dakota males make the rounds of the reservation, systematically searching old and abandoned houses and home-sites for "Indian things" that can be used to sustain their propensity for alcohol.

There is a noted decrease in respectful relationships between male and female siblings (and first cousins). Indeed, joking between such siblings has now taken on a sexual aspect. This is perhaps a function of the complete breakdown of clear-cut definitions of female and male roles within the kinship group. Weak controls are often brought into play to support an earlier aspect of "shaming," when one person might say of another Dakota, "He/she doesn't know who his/her relatives are." This pattern of unknowing is also evident when one hears young men say, "I was interested in her, but I guess she is some kind of cousin," or "I didn't know she was related to me until my mother told me," or "She's supposed to be some kind of a 'shirttail' relation, but I really wasn't serious about her." There appears to be a complete absence of the kinship terminology among young Dakota adults as a means of regulating their behavior. It is increasingly the case that kinship ties are sublimated to flirtations and relationships of a sexual nature, and there is some reflection of that fact in many temporary liaisons.

There is a transitory attempt to teach kinship during the early periods of the child's life. The significance is among the second ascending generation, in which the roles of grandfather and grandmother are more functional in interpersonal relationships with grandchildren. There is a definiteness about this kinship alliance not found in other relationships today. As far as could be ascertained, this gap can be partially explained by the fact that the "aunt" and "uncle" terminology reflected in the bilateral kinship system are used to indicate siblings, first and second cousins of the parental generation. They are generalizing terms. This may also be a function of the complete use, or nearly so, of the English language, in which there appears to be no great indication of paternal or maternal affiliation. In some instances, a young Dakota may feel the need to indicate how the person is an "aunt" or an "uncle." Usually, the easiest explanation is "he's some kind of an uncle to me" or "she's supposed to be an aunt." It would appear that kinship is important in establishing visiting (and staying) patterns with a minimum regulation of reciprocity, and it exerts some strength in interactions between grandparents and grandchildren. Hospitality based on kinship is invoked more frequently than reciprocity.

It is doubtful that much of this regulation of interpersonal relationships based on clear-cut kinship affiliation is being inculcated into the younger generation. Again, to quote a teenager, "Grandmother bawled me out for seeing him. He's supposed to be some kind of cousin." One hears a good deal of talk about "shirttail" relations in all modern generations. Sometimes the term is used in a joking manner, and sometimes it is said despairingly, as when such kin have lived with one for several weeks.

It might be said that kinship is more a matter of convenience than a control-ling mechanism in present-day Dakota life. Older Dakota recognize that "a good name means nothing to these people now." Fictive kinship appears to be more functional among modern Dakota and is seen as an incorporation of individ-uals into the trans- and/or intra-reservational system. That ensures a recipro-cal pattern of giving at powwows and guarantees a place to stay when one visits other reservations (or districts within a reservation). This has seasonal utility and is operative primarily during the summer "powwow circuit." The older system of honoring a "returnee" to the reservations is ongoing. Honor based upon achievement seems to be the criterion. In these "honorings," cash (for gas) is also a common give-away item. Reciprocity in the fictive kinship system is important. The operation of this system and the system seen in urban Dakota are areas under investigation now.

It would appear that there is considerable interpersonal impoverishment (to use one of Erikson's term) manifest in modern Dakota life, and its incidence seems greatest among the younger generation. A lack of the guiding principles traditionally instilled by parents is critical in this area. The fact that most grand-parents are geared to a life based on "traditional values" and hence present a distorted image of present-day life to their grandchildren is a discrepancy that underlies the discontent and deficiencies of contemporary "mother" and "fa-ther" roles.

The lack of meaningful social controls in the present society, plus the fact that the Dakota themselves recognize a need for "false courage" (mini-wakan) as a prior condition for social amiability and intimacy to ensure introspective ver-balization about their problems, indicates a completely disorganized social sys-tem. The family of procreation and the family of orientation are disjointed, diffuse, and nondirective. Daily personal interactions, especially marked after the onset of puberty in both sexes, tend to be quite barren. As indicated previ-ously, real warmth in conversations centers around "the good old days" of one's childhood or the childhood of an offspring. Early child-training practices ap-pear to act as a focus for continuing Dakota values in the face of exerting and coercing pressures.

The obvious fact that young adults are not trained (either by parents or by parental surrogates such as school and religious personnel) for effective roles in reservation or nonreservation life makes the future of the modern Dakota look quite bleak indeed. In the final analysis, the structuralization of the Dako-ta family is essentially the same except for the increase in temporary liaisons among the younger generation and the brittleness of these arrangements. The tiospaye as a functional unit is not vital to modern Dakota as a regulatory force.

The status of the Dakota male is further undermined by the role of a tempo-rary father, which is filled by many males who assume the relationship but have no great involvement in child care. The role of disciplinarian for a girl friend's children is a transitory thing. Grandparents involved in this kind of a "marital" arrangement generally resent being called by the kinship terminology that they reserve for their own grandchildren. Temporary liaisons of this kind are called "ekceya ktce onpi" (literally, "common togetherness"). Often, such arrangements are instigated and sustained by Dakota females who use their incomes (welfare and/or ADC) as a means of binding males to them. Conversely, and because of the assured independence this income gives women, they can terminate such an arrangement as they desire.

An additional factor for consideration concerns the fact that in any marriage—stable or unstable—there is the knowledge that a woman may control her destiny. Wives in unstable marriages, after a period of time, become eligible for welfare due to the absence of their legal husbands. This creates a decided action toward blocking their return, because that would stop welfare payments. Indeed, if the legal husband returns and by some chance becomes gainfully employed, frequently the wife will manipulate to have him fired or start him on a drinking bout to ensure his removal from a job.

The role of the Dakota woman is becoming increasingly important as she acts in many capacities to manipulate Dakota men—either for their benefit or detriment. It would appear that the functions of the modern Dakota family are in a state of flux and uncertainty. There are greater and increasing role incompatibilities and insufficient and distorted models for young children to emulate. The inability of the Dakota family to meet the stresses and strains of acculturation and adaptation has further crippled, it would seem, the total social adjustment of Dakota individuals. One certain way of extricating oneself from this situation is complete removal, with no return to the reservation except for sporadic and brief visits. Removal, and remaining away, and return are topics for further research, however.

Note

1. It is interesting to speculate about whether this is an absorption of American "white" terminology (Schneider and Homans 1955) or a continuation of the Dakota affectional terms of address I heard during childhood, when these terms were used by strictly non-English-speakers as diminutives and terms of endearment.

References

Malan, Vernon D. 1961. "Theories of Culture Change Relevant to the Study of the Dakota Indians." *Plains Anthropologist* 6:16.

Schneider, David M., and George C. Homens. 1955. "Kinship Terminology and the American Kinship System." *American Anthropology* 57(6):1194–208.

CHAPTER 24

American Indian Family: Cultural Change and Adaptive Strategies

The encompassing phrase "the Indian family" seems a contradiction both in terminology and interpretation. The word *family* leaves one confronted by legal, sociological, and religious reference points of the larger society. Yet American Indians and professionals are constantly confronted by the phrase *the American Indian family*. This gloss covers courses listed in Native American studies departments in certain universities. Again, we are victimized by a dominant-subordinant relationship in which our unique and viable tribal entities are blurred. A monolithic family unit results that many of us categorically accept without question. It is important to develop a general statement that examines American Indian families at the present time and to construct a typology, however tentative, of Indian families that might allow us to assess the structure of this important kinship unit.

Research on American Indians in contemporary society assumes a segmental approach related to "problem" constraints and "problem-solving" assumptions. Multiproblem families—often referred to as "traditional," "full-blood," and/or "hard-core"—have been the focus of studies on what is generalized as "the Indian family." There is seldom an attempt to examine the families of specific American Indians—nurses, social workers, teachers, or BIA employees. I suggest that we should be discussing the underlying orientations, beliefs, and kinship systems of a variety of Indian families. Fortunately, such terms as *the matrifocal family*, which has been applied to blacks, have not yet been transferred to Indian tribes. The term has blurred qualitative differences in the family structure of the black population and provided a clever subterfuge to support a "culture of poverty" concept. For many black families, the cohesion and strengths implied in such an analytic unit seem valid (Stack 1974).

Terms have been applied to Indian families. "Irresponsible," "drunken," "disorganized," and other demeaning descriptions constantly surface in Indian-white (and, I might add, Indian-Indian) relationships. The multiproblem "traditional" or "full-blood" families have been the focus of sociological studies (e.g., Minnis [1963] 1972). One example of such research is reflected in the following statement:

> The important role and influence of grandparents should also be mentioned, since one-third of the families at Fort Hall still have an extended nuclear type of family. Especially during festivals or trips to other reservations parents leave their children with grandparents. This also happens when the primary family is disrupted. From interviews with social welfare workers on the reservation, it was revealed that during Sun Dance festivals, "round-ups," and journeys to neighboring reservations, some parents leave even young children with grandparents for many days or completely alone, neglected, and dependent upon welfare agencies. This is strange ambivalence toward children, with a great deal of affection for them and yet little hesitancy to desert or neglect them. (Minnis [1963] 1972:334–35)

This analysis presents a deficit model and obfuscates a tribal variation that more accurately reflects differential adaptation to the superimposed administrative policies of education, health, and welfare. The common denominator to which this primary institution of procreation and orientation in Indian tribes has been subjected originates in a power structure that has imposed upon (and changed) the basic kinship unit. "Power structure" includes the government, various religious denominations, and educational institutions. These external decision-making bodies have pressured the major socializing units in Indian society. Essentially, a model of a nuclear family, with a single-unit residence pattern, was the requisite of all tribes. This imposed family became the primary instrument in "civilizing" tribal people and obliterating cultural heritages.

By emphasizing problems in Indian families, there has been a loss of the much-needed holistic approach commonly found in early ethnographic studies by anthropologists. In these accounts of a Native group's total life-ways, one examined sex roles, child socialization, mating and marriage patterns, kinship structures, and belief and value orientations. Unfortunately, the data were usually placed in the context of an "ethnographic present" or "the way it was" before white contact. An idealized configuration of tribal life often resulted. However, aside from criticisms of anthropologists as social scientists, this body of data presented a cogent and cohesive picture of the familial actualities of named groups in Native North American societies. The changing emphasis in research produced different conclusions. Acculturation studies from the late 1950s onward have essentially focused on similarities between Native Americans and a supposed monolithic white family structure and culture. Indians are expected to have become "white."

In examining studies of this era, one is still able to effectively discern a pro-totypic "family model," either white or Indian in orientation. Yet acculturation studies provide base-line data that social workers, teachers, nurses, or persons in the "helping professions" can profitably consult, digest, and utilize *if* they wish to understand the rich tribal variations. These studies have been important for one other major reason: They present aspects of social and cultural change that are evident and that continue in tribal communities, no matter where in "Indi-an country."

Indian communities have not significantly profited from other people's re-search, because its focus has been on problems—alcoholism, suicides, family disintegration, and other pathological parameters of contemporary social life. The uncritical proliferation of "helping programs" limits knowledge and com-prehension of Indian families even more. It has been, and is, profitable for uni-versities, service agencies, and tribal groups to obtain funds to intervene and attempt to change the "pathological" character of Indians and their life-styles. We, as Indian people, have fallen into the "funding trap."

Previous natural helping service systems—curing societies (Iroquois) and Women's Craft Guilds (Cheyenne), among others, and the obligations and rec-iprocity of such extended-family structures as the *tiospaye* among the Lakota Sioux—no longer function as mutual aid societies. Indeed, give-aways among the Lakota Sioux are now merely prestige-seeking, wealth-displaying, ethnic markers for many practitioners. It has become a mirror image of the Northwest Coast "potlatch" rather than an accepted and institutionalized way of honor-ing someone by giving to the less fortunate, the mourners, or the ill and infirm in the local community.

The family life of Indians in contemporary society is difficult to summarize in a manner that may be agreeable to all Indians. Indeed, Native Americans are saying what anthropologists were saying in the late 1950s, when any attempt to arrive at postulates or generalizations about Indians was met with "but that is not true about *my* people!" Most generalizations made by an Indian about the Indian situation are greeted with the same anthropological response. In this case, there is not the condescension of "owning" a people but of "belonging" to a tribal entity.

The uncertainty regarding the composition of Indian families can be verified in current studies on Native Americans. Levine states, "Extended family or 'clan' ties are strongly felt; to Indian people, the American 'nuclear family' seems a lonely arrangement" (1965:16). If Levine is equating "extended family" with "clan," the fallacy of the description is evident. There is a qualitative difference between these two units, specifically their instrumentality in the interpersonal relationships of present-day Indian people. Some Indian persons, however, do indeed equate "clan" with "extended family," which is confusing to all. Elsewhere I have written:

In many statements made by Indian "leaders" and some writers . . . , I am appalled at the statement that clans were the basis of social organization of Indian tribes. This, in essence, is viewing ALL native societies from a tribal ethnocentrism rather than the frequently accused White ethnocentrism. More dangerous, in my view, is the fact that because a native person stated this, this fallacy carries double jeopardy. I have articulated this view at the National Education Association's Conference on Indian Values at Tahlequah, Oklahoma, in April, 1976, in response to the same point made by Lloyd Elm and Eddy Benton. My suggestion is that all native writers be cognizant of the cultural backgrounds of the groups they are discussing and explicate this information. (Medicine 1976)

The confusion in terminology is even more important if we consider the structure of contemporary Indian families. I fear that it will have greater relevance when the question of Indian identity and tribal affiliation becomes important. The clan as a social organizational institution is found among such groups as the Pueblos, Iroquois, Navajo, and Apache (e.g., Abrams 1976; Basso 1970; Ortiz 1972; Shepardson and Hammond 1970). In general, a clan is usually defined by anthropologists as "a unilineal kinship group that maintains a fiction of common genetic descent from a remote ancestor, usually legendary or mythological" (Hoebel 1972:691).

To return to the rubric of the "extended family" used so often in referring to contemporary Indian families, we need a Native or indigenous definition, or, as anthropologists call it, an "emic" definition. Hoebel defines an extended family as "a social grouping consisting of near relatives in addition to the mated pair and their offspring" (1972:693). This latter social grouping was quite prevalent in band-type social organization with bilateral kinship systems. We find bands in such groups as the Kiowa, Shoshone, and Lakota Sioux among tribes in the Plains area. Among Teton Sioux or Lakota-speakers, such band designations as Hunkpapa, Oglala, and Sihasapa (Blackfeet) are still recognized. Historically (and still today among Native American tribes), there are matrilineal, patrilineal, and bilateral types of kinship structures. These structures often influenced residence patterns. In matrilineal societies such as in the Pueblo and Iroquois groups, matrilocal residence most frequently followed after marriage.

The marriage pattern also varied in the family structure. Some marriages were arranged, as those among the Winnebago, for example. (See Lurie [1966] for a poignant discussion of the man whom the brother of the book's heroine chose for her.) There are other instances in which fathers selected bridegrooms. In matrilineal societies, a clan's mothers and elder women had much to say in the choice of a mate. How important women's decisions are at present needs to be determined.

Some early reports on marriage customs among the Plains groups were erroneous. Many trappers and traders would notice the family of the groom leading horses to the bride's dwelling and assume that the horses were being exchanged for women. The sanctions of cementing a nuptial tie between two social groups, which often formed the basis of extending family obligations and allegiances, were not understood.

In pre-contact Native societies, clans controlled marriages. For example, among the Navajo, persons from the Salt Clan had to marry outside that group. If that proscription was transgressed, illness could result. Such a marriage carried the onus of incest. We know that this ritual still operates in various degrees among these people. Among the matrilineal Haida, clans functioned in burial ceremonies, and members of one group would officiate at the funerals of members of other groups. The duties of members to each other and to other clans are countless. In some tribes—Ojibway, for example—expected marriage partners were cross-cousins from other clans. In addition, clans are often present in horticultural or sedentary societies.

This rich variation of marriage form and residence pattern presents a body of data that should be considered. More important, the vestigial forms and values deriving from them are aspects to consider in examining the dynamics of family life today. Employing data from Oklahoma, Carol Rachlin writes:

> Indian life does not fall into rigid categories. It is, rather, a complex of interlocking circles, each exerting pressures and control upon others. An individual functions in different capacities in these circles or in groups. The family is the central unit of Indian society now, as it has been in the past. Ostensibly a senior man is the head of each family group, but one must never discount the position of the older women.
>
> The Indian family today retains its old balance, though increase in life span generally has raised age levels. An old person today is someone sixty years or older. These are the sages of Indian life. The active "doers" range in age from thirty to sixty years. Individuals under thirty are either getting an education, starting a new career or making it quite clear "they won't make it."
>
> Tribal politics, while publicly dominated by younger men, is inwardly controlled by the elder members, through the restraints imposed by family ties. The desire of the older members of a tribe to hold to the past, the need of middle-aged and younger persons to hold a continuum and the attractiveness of feeling that one belongs to an in-group has enabled many tribal traditions to survive, though often in altered forms. (1968:172–73)

Rachlin does not mention the type of social organizational structure in which this particular family dynamic operates, although one would postulate that it would be a "band-type" or one of bilateral descent. A generalized Plains pattern, which is implicit in the description, predicates this assumption (e.g., Hoebel 1960; McAllister 1937; Province 1937). However, the metaphor of concentric circles has relevance for the extended family if one sees the two circles as different interest groups.

In searching the literature on Native American definitions of an extended family, Jennie Joe, Cecelia Gallerito, and Josephine Pino remark:

> The extended family is a crucial factor in the lifestyle of Native Americans. Historically, tribes were based on family affiliations. Food, shelter, and survival were supported on a communal approach. Maintaining family stability was so important to Native Americans that tribes evolved safeguards to protect against a family's disintegration as a result of death. Kinships were increased through adoption rituals that existed within tribal ceremonies. Presently, the pervasive factors that have created the nuclear family are affecting American Indians as well. (1976:93)

The authors then retreat into the particularistic tribal variants of Laguna and Mescalero evidence because "they represent the tribes of the authors" (92–93). I am not faulting this attempt to provide unique comparative data, or a range of it, to a select audience—in this case, nurses. My concern is with the ways in which one can profitably generalize the universals of culture contact to enable Native Americans to discuss the totality of "the Indian experience," especially its relationship to contemporary family dynamics. Such a perspective would benefit from Native American experiences and formulations.

John Redhorse, a Cherokee social worker, offers a more realistic appraisal of the extended family:

> First, Native American extended families differ from their European counterparts which define an extended unit as three generations within the same household. Rather, Native American extended families assume a distinct village-type network construct. This, of course, has significant impact upon behavior patterns. During early childhood socialization and for general orientation to a living, individual transactions occur within a community milieu characterized by several incorporated households. Second, extended family structure facilitates transmission of cultural attributes which conserve family patterns and contribute to individual identity. Third, family serves as a major instrument of accountability. It sets standards and expectations which maintain the wholeness of the group through the enforcement of values. (1977:11)

Building upon such a framework, I surmise that extended families aid in survival and serve a number of adaptive functions for members in this quasi-corporate group. In many tribal groups, the extended family is based upon the kinship structure, for example, the tiospaye among the Lakota Sioux.

Extended families are often seen as dysfunctional by middle-class white individuals and Indians aspiring to middle-class standards. In some cases, Indians of both genders have chosen a life-style that approximates the normative values of white America. Jorgensen compares the domestic dependency of Indian tribes to colonial subjugation when he writes:

Some U.S. Indians can move from reservations, gain university education, and become popular authors or high-ranking officials in the Indian service. Individual "successes" such as these are few and far between, even if they are desired and sought by Indians. It is important to stress that *individual* successes are possible, but the probability of such successes are low. On the other hand, tribal or group successes are highly *improbable*. That is to say that success comes to some of those Indians who sever their ties with the wide network of kin and Indian friends and leave the tribal life behind. Success is a narrow individualistic phenomenon consonant with the Protestant ethic. (1978:6, emphasis in the original)

Strategies in maintaining an alternative life-style may include intermarriage (to a white spouse); severing kinship bonds within the Indian community; selective interaction with Indian friends of similar orientation; using Native ritual for an ethnic marker (as in the Lakota Sun Dance or the Kiowa Black Leggings Society); internalizing the values of a nuclear family (with possible serial monogamy); engaging in extramarital affairs; and having a suburban home, two cars, and a savings account. Elsewhere, I categorized these individuals as "Native elites" (Medicine 1978:24–25).

If one were constructing a model continuum, one reference point might be the middle-class American Indian family. The other might be the "hard-core" type that most generally is an operationalized extended family. The basis of this social unit is a matrimonial union of male and female—either legal (licensed), consensual (often referred to as the "Indian way"), or an "Indian marriage." This establishes a relationship in which an alliance between two kinship groups is recognized by the community.

The setting of the cultural background that gives validity to the union may vary, because there are at minimum two viewpoints—that of the individual and that of the community. Qualitatively, the perceptions of a union may vary. There are instances in which "Indian marriages" (consensual) are recognized by the minimal pair but unacknowledged by the kinship group or the larger community. Generally, the "Indian way" marriages that have been arranged by parents or members of either kinship group have recognition in the Native community, and in many cases are of lifetime duration. An "Indian way" marriage establishes a relationship through which the community recognizes an alliance between two kinship groups. The kinship groups of either partner are usually given equal recognition, thus providing a strong, bilateral base to the union. This provides a framework of interaction, forming that which Redhorse and other social workers identify as a network.

The two kinship bases provide a nexus of support and flexibility that allows the united pair to maximize their options within the kinship frame. Most often, the residence pattern of the newly joined sexual pair depends upon such factors as availability of space in a residence of the home of a significant other (parent, step-parent, sibling, cousin, or some more distantly related or fictive kin). The economic state of the pair (or the kin to whom they attach themselves) also determines their residence. Ownership of an automobile (the ubiquitous "Indian car") and the general services available (i.e., hauling water, cutting wood, doing errands, exchange of child care, and caring for the elderly) are all implicitly considered to be helping strategies and contribute to the economic and social well-being of the extended family unit.

Thus, we see that an adjustive form of reciprocity in an "Indian family" is set in place in kinship units in many communities. The ebb and flow of the individual within the kin group produces flexibility and dynamism, which foster survival and adaptation to economic and social exigencies. The enactment of a reciprocity model may be idiosyncratic on an individual level. However, buttressing by a kin group may allow it to operate on a poverty level. Note that American Indian/Alaskan Native families are 2.89 times more likely to live in poverty as majority families. More striking, female-headed families of this group were 5.44 times more likely to be in poverty than an average majority family in 1975 (U.S. Commission on Civil Rights 1978:65).

This reciprocity model may also be dysfunctional. A chronic alcoholic in a family very often "does not pull his own weight," as some Lakota Sioux say. But the Sioux kinship system and network and value structure dictate that one cannot "disown" this person. This situation creates gaps in the network.

In general, a communitywide web of kinship acts as an adaptive mechanism that shelters a newly joined couple. It also allows for movement from one social grouping (extended family) to another when the situation "gets tough." When interpersonal relationships become strained, when stress results, when reciprocity patterns are shattered, and when expectations are not met, a cou-

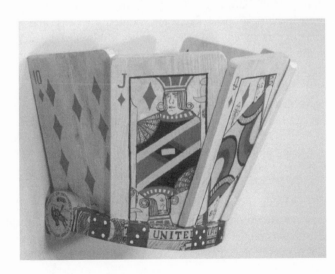

BabyNeedsaBrand-newBonnet ©1997 by Ted Garner (wood, watercolor, and lacquer; 9.5 by 14 by 10.5 inches). (Courtesy of Ted Garner)

262 Learning to Be an Anthropologist and Remaining "Native"

ple's relationship may dissolve or they may move. The structure of the system may realign, but it continues in a new form within the concentric circles of kinship matrices. This expansiveness and retractability can also extend to the urban areas that are part of the total experiential network of most contemporary Indians.

Indian families have a concentric quality that Rachlin likens to "interlocking circles" and that must be seen as part of fluctuations and alliances within the family of sexual union (what social scientists call "family of procreation"). Changes in marriage partners, serial monogamy, or "Indian marriage" arrangements can provide survival strategies for both males and females. Either member of a conjugal pair may separate themselves and ease into the ebb and flow of spheres of interaction, which might be a peer group of males, a peer group of both sexes, or one that is entirely female.

The spheres can also consist of biological kin groups, extended kin groups, or fictive kin groups. If one examines alliances on a monthly basis, one finds that Indian males in some communities most often frequent the homes of their female consorts during the first part of the month, when ADFC checks or other welfare checks are distributed. There appears also to be a direct increase in household inhabitants in grandparental homes whenever a pension or Social Security check is forthcoming. Native females who ally themselves with employed Indian men (and sporadically with white men in off-reservation border towns or white and black men in cities) also practice survival strategies.

The growing tendency for Indian wives to work for wages in Native communities also affects the changing structure of Indian families and the differential economic and social roles of the sexes. Increased placement of children in day-care centers or with economically compensated child-care givers in these communities reflects the trend as well. More data are needed on the frequency of child-care exchange and the utilization of kinship networks for child care in most Indian groups. There is always mention of "grandmother" as a primary socializer in current Native rhetoric but little about the utilization of kin groups in the socialization process of children. The "family of orientation"—that is, the kin groups that have impact on a child and transmit the cultural life-styles of both rural and urban Indians—needs greater attention.

Ironically, the women who are most articulate about the "quality of Indian life" and the Indian family seem to be divorced or unmarried. The entire issue of Indian divorce rates is hazy at this time. Until we have reliable data about the marriage, intermarriage, divorce, and remarriage rates of both genders of the Indian population, it is difficult to obtain an accurate picture of Indian family structure.

The database is further complicated by instances of so-called Indian marriage. One can surmise that this introduced considerable confusion in maintaining kinship structures and, ultimately, tribal corporateness and identity—both individual and tribal. This is further compounded by rates of intertribal marriage, regulations mandated by tribal councils regarding the enrollments of Indian individuals, and aspects of fosterage and adoptions—critical issues in contemporary Indian life. The latter may stem from complex economic and social factors. Generations of imperfect parental role models result from boarding school education—both federal and parochial. Rising alcoholism and drug use among Indians; devalued kinship ties and responsibilities (Medicine 1969); an upsurge of reactions to genocide and lack of birth control knowledge and utilization; and changing sexual mores, tribal values, and socialization beliefs are all factors to consider when speaking of Indian families.

There are obvious maladaptive effects of familial adjustments that must be examined. Seldom considered is the role of the Indian elderly. Building nursing homes on reservations has a dire effect upon both these individuals and their families, although the full impact has not been realized. These actions certainly run counter to an often-verbalized Indian value: respect for elders. A valuable resource for tribal knowledge and wisdom, let alone the continuation of child-rearing practices, is being lost to future generations.

There are an alarming number of requests for funding to counter the abuse and neglect of Indian children. Yet growing evidence of parent abuse (parent-beating) and increased wife/woman-beating on many reservations indicates a dysfunctional family life. The rate of wife/woman-beating is an unknown factor and may be correlated with the concept of macho among Indian men. The fact that shelters for battered women are being established on some reservations and in urban areas indicates that family life is changing in Native communities. There are now instances of women beating men.

The sociological and psychological implications of these dysfunctional aspects of family life must be considered when an emerging ethic or generalization on Indian families is studied. They are significant to any praxis-oriented program. Together, the circularity of individual action welded to the group action of social units such as the extended family allow Indian persons to survive in a racist and economically deprived environment and are considered a basic survival mechanism.

A new methodology (an emic view and a Native perspective) of contemporary Indian family typologies is needed for action-oriented programs. A cross-cultural, intertribal, and intra-tribal approach would increase understanding of the dynamics of family structures. We, as Indian professionals, must assess the commonalities evident in Indian families in various cultural and ecological areas—including urban conglomerates. I suggest a comparative perspective to examine segments of tribal enclaves in specific historical frames and certain geographic (or tribal) areas. Discussions, however tentative, of Indian families should yield comparative data that illustrate variations on the complexity and adaptive strategies that allow Indian persons to survive and Indian tribal customs to continue.

Certain historical facts speak to the viable structure of Indian families. The fact that family structures have not been completely recast in a "white mold" speaks to the survival strength of many domestic units. Due to ecological factors (i.e., separation in reservations of community enclaves), Native American kinship units—which are seen qualitatively as familial units—have remained functional for group survival. Encapsulation from the dominant society has allowed a Native version of a conjugal or domestic unit to persist.

To further understand the dynamics of families, a rigorous study of types and their modus operandi as well as the influence of parents and parental surrogates in child socialization processes will add further refinement. The transmission of those cultural components that fundamentally compose the value structure— and their translation into daily activities—will provide both understanding and improvement. It will also develop better treatment and counseling modalities.

The individual juxtaposed with the kinship group allows dynamic and reciprocal yet selective interaction. Aspects of responsive reciprocity can be differentially enacted in all spheres. There appear to be functional adaptations underlying the tribal diversities. Different responses to power structures and administered human relationships are salient strategies that ensure cultural continuities.

Concentrating on Lakota Sioux kinship units, it may be theorized that the high individualization that is attributed to members of these social groupings (MacGregor 1945; White 1970) may be a form of adaptation to a marginal position with respect to the larger society and to the aspects of socioeconomic impotence and powerlessness that seem characteristic of most Native American groups at present. Individual autonomy is highly stressed among the Lakota and may well function as an adaptive mechanism to the stresses of reservation living and interacting in a racist society. This characteristic may also allow for occupancy of the types of family structures at both ends of the continuum and a flow between each. This idiosyncratic individualism may also allow a person to interact in the concentric circle of conjugal family, extended kin group, and peer group and permit a certain flexibility that is embedded within the group. For the Lakota, the ultimate identity of being and identity may possibly be enacted in certain contextual frames. To be specific, a Lakota male might act exceedingly *bloka* ("macho," or "chauvinist") in his male peer group but present a different self in the domestic group.

To chart the possible direction of compositions of Indian families in the future, one must examine the forces and circumstances of racism and oppression. It behooves us to be cognizant of those forces as they impinge upon Indian domestic units in the present. That Indian people have not been completely assimilated speaks to the strengths and successful adaptive strategies that are operative in a domestic unit that has expansive yet restrictive boundaries. This has been a powerful deterrent to complete amalgamation within white society.

References

Abrams, George. 1976. *The Seneca People.* Phoenix: Indian Tribal Series.

Basso, Keith H. 1970. *The Cibecue Apache.* New York: Holt, Rinehart and Winston.

Hoebel, E. Adamson. 1960. *The Cheyenne, Indians of the Great Plains.* New York: Holt, Rinehart, and Winston.

———. 1972. *Anthropology: The Study of Man.* New York: McGraw-Hill.

Joe, Jennie, Cecelia Gallerito, and Josephine Pino. 1976. "Cultural Health Traditions: American Indian Perspectives." In *Providing Safe Nursing Care for Ethnic People of Color*, ed. Marie Foster Branch and Phyllis Perry Paxton, 81–98. New York: Appleton-Century-Crofts.

Jorgensen, Joseph G. 1978. "A Century of Political Economic Effects on American Indian Society: 1880–1890." *Journal of Ethnic Studies* 6(3): 1–82.

Lurie, Nancy O. 1966. *Mountain Wolf Woman, Sister of Crashing Thunder: The Autobiography of a Winnebago Indian.* Michigan: University of Michigan Press.

MacGregor, Gordon. 1945. *Warriors without Weapons: A Study of the Society and Personality Development of the Pine Ridge Sioux.* University of Chicago Press.

McAllister, J. Gilbert. 1937. "Kiowa-Apache Social Organization." In *Social Anthropology of North American Tribes: Essays on Social Organization, Law, and Religion*, ed. Fred Eggan, 98–169. Chicago: University of Chicago Press.

Medicine, Beatrice. 1969. "The Changing Dakota Family and the Stresses Therein." *Pine Ridge Research Bulletin* 9: 1–20.

———. 1976. "The Interaction of Culture and Sex Roles in the Schools." N.p.: National Institute of Education.

———. 1978. "Higher Education: A New Arena for Native Americans." *Thresholds in Education* 4(2): 22–25.

Minnis, Mhyra S. 1963. "The Relationships of the Social Structure of an Indian Community to Adult and Juvenile Delinquency." *Social Forces* (May): 395–403. Reprint. Howard M. Bahr, Bruce A. Chadwick, and Robert C. Day, eds., 1972. *Native Americans Today: Sociological Perspectives*, 327–38. New York: Harper and Row.

Ortiz, Alfonso, ed. 1972. *New Perspectives on the Pueblos.* Albuquerque: University of New Mexico Press.

Province, John H. 1937. "The Underlying Sanctions of Plains Indian Culture." In *Social Anthropology of North American Tribes: Essays in Social Organization, Law, and Religion*, ed. Fred Eggan, 342–74. Chicago: University of Chicago Press.

Rachlin, Carol K. 1968. "Tight Shoes Night: Oklahoma Indians Today." In *The American Indian Today*, ed. Stuart Levine and Nancy O. Lurie, 160–83. Baltimore: Pelican Books.

Redhorse, John. 1977. "Culture as a Variable in Human Services." *PSRI Report* 2 (7):11–12 .

Shepardson, Mary, and Blodwen Hammond. 1970. *The Navajo Mountain Community: Social Organization and Kinship Terminology.* Berkeley: University of California Press.

U.S. Commission on Civil Rights. 1978. *Social Indicators of Equality for Minorities and Women: A Report.* Washington: United States Commission on Civil Rights.

Stack, Carol B. 1974. *All Our Kin: Strategies for Survival in a Black Community.* New York: Harper and Row.

White, Robert A. 1970. "The Lower-class 'Culture of Excitement' among Contemporary Sioux." In *The Modern Sioux: Social Systems and Reservation Culture*, ed. Ethel Nurge, 175–97. Lincoln: University of Nebraska Press.

PART 6

Anthropology

CHAPTER 25

Ella C. Deloria:
The Emic Voice

Ella Cara Deloria (1889–1971) was a Yankton Dakota woman, who, with some other North American Natives, accepted the invitation of the anthropologist Franz Boas to become a linguistic informant and an ethnological entrepreneur in anthropology classes at Columbia University in 1929.[1] This meant that she served as an emic, or Native, speaker, teaching to anthropologists the various dialects of the Dakota; it also meant that she developed the skills of the anthropologist herself. The emic perspective, plus her scholarly training, made her a unique figure. In addition, because she was a Christian and educated in the "modern" tradition, she was well suited for the role of cultural mediator.

Deloria's association with Boas had begun many years before, when she herself was a student at Teachers' College of Columbia University. Educated at St. Elizabeth's Mission in Wakpala, South Dakota, where her father, the Rev. Phillip Deloria, was the first Indian to become an Episcopal missionary, she then had gone to All Saints School in Sioux Falls, to Oberlin College, and, finally, to Columbia, where she received a B.S. in 1915. Her professional life encompassed teaching in the Bureau of Indian Affairs schools, at Haskell Institute, among others. She also worked as a health education secretary for Indians in the YWCA. This was much the usual occupational pattern for Indian women of her generation. She never married, which, in those terms, also was typical of the professional profile.[2]

Ella Deloria was proficient in both the Dakota and Lakota dialects of Siouan.[3] With Franz Boas, she coauthored *A Dakota Grammar* (Boas and Deloria 1941). They were planning further publications at the time of his death in 1942. Of her work, Boas wrote, "She has a thorough grasp of the grammar and spirit of the language. We have written together a grammar of the Dakota, of the Teton, Yankton, and Assiniboine dialects, and she is thoroughly conversant not only with the forms but also with the very intricate psychological background" (Deloria 1944a [1979]:xiv).

Deloria also worked on her own (Deloria 1929, 1944a). Not only did she single-handedly produce major accounts of Siouan life-ways, but her work as an ethnographic and linguistic informant (as we Native people often are) was also basic to anthropological interpretations of Lakota data by scholars willing to utilize and credit a Native view (Medicine 1978).[4] So voluminous were the notes, papers, translations, and folkloristic and linguistic materials she had gathered that scholars (especially at the Lakhota Project at the University of Colorado) are still at work, planning for future publications of her research.

The project on which she was engaged even until the time of her death at ninety-one years of age was a Lakota dictionary, which she foresaw as entering into psychological and sociological considerations from a Native worldview. She had been given a grant from the National Science Foundation for this work, which she was doing at the University of South Dakota, where an endowed professorship in her name has now been established. Fortunately for contemporary students, the Dakota Press (Vermillion) has recently reprinted two of the publications for which she was best known: *Dakota Grammar* (originally published in 1941) and *Speaking of Indians* (1944b [1979]).[5]

Although the *Grammar* is of great interest to all persons working with Native American material and also to those developing projects in bilingual education, the other two books have greater significance for all teachers of ethnic literature. Ideally, every professor of Native American literature should be required to take a course in anthropology of the North American Indian, but even those who use only a few works, such as those found in anthologies, will attain a greater level of understanding from *Dakota Texts* (Deloria 1932), and any interested layman will enjoy *Speaking of Indians* (Deloria 1944b [1979]). Deloria provides tremendous insight into a culture of Native North America, which is still viable and vibrant. Her writing holds to her ideal that "all life, all the culture of a people, is of one piece. No element of it exists in a vacuum" (1944b [1979]:41).

Speaking of Indians was written when intercultural education was seen as an essential part of the war effort. The book was written for a periodic study by Christian churches, and its last part deals with "Indian Life in Wartime" and the participation of Indians in the military system. The first three sections, however, compose one of the richest and most important studies of culture change on a Sioux reservation and by extension give insight into the culture shock sustained by all Indian people.

She begins with a selection from Stephen Vincent Benét's poem "Western Star" and uses the line "and a scheme of life that worked" as her own starting point. Sections about the actualities of Lakota kinship, child socialization, family life, and coerced culture change are superb presentations and are set in a charmingly written and easily comprehensible style. For example, she comments on "Spiritual Culture Areas":

> We may know a people, but we cannot truly know them until we can get within their minds, to some degree at least, and see life from their peculiar point of view. To do that we must learn what goes on in their "spiritual culture area." By that fancy phrase I simply mean what remains after the tangible and visible part is cleared away. I mean such ethical values and moral principles as a people discovers to live by and that make it a group distinct from its neighbors. I mean all those unseen elements that make up the mass sentiment, disposition, and character—elements that completely blend there, producing in an integrated pattern a powerful inner force that is in habitual operation, dictating behavior and controlling the thought of all who live within its sphere. (Deloria 1944b [1979]:12)

Deloria comments that it "is relatively easy to understand all this interplay of cultural elements in a literate people," but "the unlettered peoples present a problem, for they can only talk, and their words, howsoever lofty, are lost instantly." She considers her own best approach and decides that others can cover the entire Indian scene better than she can, so she will limit herself to "the one people that I know intimately and whose language is also mine" (1944b [1979]:13).

She begins with the kinship system of the Dakotas, with the strict rules that govern all conduct, not only property but also even life itself. Her shared charm and caring interest in any ethnographer or linguist who researched Siouan groups often led her to tell these persons to call her "Aunt Ella" in an act of typical Lakota incorporativeness. This often led to the mistaken belief that these persons had truly been "adopted." This action has often been a source of discomfort and embarrassment for many of the persons in her *tiospaye* (extended kin group). Current "adoption" of non-Siouan individuals involves approval by the tiospaye plus a special name, which may be available, and, more important from the viewpoint of Native society, an expensive give-away to validate the fictive kin alliance.

Adherence to the rules of kinship, hierarchy, and tradition made life in prereservation times tolerable:

> It was this respect for personality that ruled tipi life and made it tolerable for the several, and sometimes many, who dwelt there. Outsiders, accustomed to many rooms, would by justified in asking, "How could anyone have privacy here? How could a man think his own thoughts, packed in with so many?" And those would be good questions for which there are good answers.
>
> The Dakotas managed to achieve privacy in their own adroit fashion. They made their own privacy, and it was mentally effected. Harmonious tipi life was easily possible by each person's knowing and playing his role well. He moved

cautiously at all times, with a nice regard for the rights of others, according to his relationship with each. (Deloria 1944b [1979]:45)

But after the nomadic life was denied to Indians, and when hunting had come to an end, people were expected to become farmers on the arid land assigned them and to live as the white man did:

> Eventually, with pathetic optimism, the Dakotas started putting up their first log houses, patterned after those of the white man. They moved in and set up housekeeping, supposing it would be just that easy. They had not begun to understand all that goes with the new way of living they had adopted.
>
> The houses were small, one room affairs, low and dark—and dank because of the dirt floors. Compared with the well-constructed tipis with their manageable windflaps for ample ventilation, the cabins were hot and stuffy. Germs lurked everywhere, causing general sickness, and the death rate increased. Even if hygiene necessary for controlling the spread of sickness had been explained to them, a conflict would have arisen between its demands and the ancient concern for kinship. "What? Am I to shun my dear ones just because they are ill in order to save my own self?" It was unthinkable. (Deloria 1944b [1979]:60)

Later, things got worse as individual allotments of land were made and each "family unit" was expected to live by itself, often miles from their other relatives. Now every chance to foregather with relatives was precious. "Farmers" left their small gardens to dry up and their stock to fend for themselves while they went away on lengthy visits. Later, they learned to make better, larger houses that had tighter walls and wooden floors:

> The people began to make ingenious adaptation of some elements in their old life to the new. For instance, at one period they transferred the art decorations of the tipi to the log house. Out of G.I. muslin they made very large wall coverings, a carry over from the dew curtain of a tipi and called by the same term, *ozan*. On these they painted beautiful designs and made lively black and white drawings of historical scenes of hunting or battles or peace-making between tribes, and courtship scenes, games, and such-like activities of the past. People went visiting just to see one another's pictographs and to hear the stories they preserved. (Deloria 1944b [1979]:60–61)

As one of the strengths of Deloria's writing lies in her analysis of the learning process in a cultural matrix, the following excerpt seems appropriate:

> Nor was it any wonder that small children rapidly learned their social duties, since the training constantly given to them was calculated to condition them in that way. All grownups by tacit consent seemed to "gang up" for this purpose. Even before a child was aware of his kinship obligations, they made sentences and put the correct words and formal sentences into his mouth for him

to repeat to this or that relative. It was their informal but constant system of education in human relations and social responsibility. (Deloria 1944b [1979]:29)

Myths, legends, and folktales similarly played an important part in the socialization of children and the instillation of values. This fact was important in Ella Deloria's generation, because there was still general proficiency in the Native language. One of the public events of a child's life is a ceremony still held by traditional Sioux in which the child is given a hereditary name that is part of the historic background of a particular family. The present-day English gloss "Naming Ceremony" (for *Hunka*) shows that personality configurations (i.e., Nativeness) still continue.[6] Here is Deloria's description of the ancient ceremony:

> What we might call the formal education of Dakota youth was centered in the tribal ceremonies. The "sermons" recited on these occasions emphasized the ideals that each generation felt it vital to implant in the minds of its boys and girls. Let us look at several of these ceremonies to see what teaching accompanied them.
>
> We may begin with the *Hunka* ceremony performed on the happy occasion of blessing little children. The small candidate was honored by a feast and presents were made to many people in his or her name. The recipients asked singers to laud the child's name in song[,] and all that was very agreeable. But the core of the whole matter was that, by the child's very presence as the center of attention and acclaim, he or she was henceforth a "child-beloved," and was committed as a matter of honor to the practice of generosity, even if at times it might involve great personal sacrifice. (Deloria 1944b [1979]:41–42)

Deloria's scholarly work *Dakota Texts* contains some of the most authentic accounts of traditional Lakota myths and folktales in the Siouan vernacular. But what makes linguistic and literary analysis possible must always be dependent on emic interpreters: Deloria's footnotes are at least as significant as her texts. Because of her work, literary analysis of old Siouan texts are accessible to modern literary scholars—as the texts of many other tribes are not.

Her method, as she describes it, was to write the narrative "down in the original, directly from the story-tellers who related them to me. Each tale is accompanied by a free translation which I tried to keep as simple and close to the Dakota style as possible; and by notes on the grammar and customs. In addition, a literal translation was made" (Deloria 1932:ix).

The legend of the White Buffalo Calf Woman, which is a charter for Lakota belief systems, still survives, as do the Iktomi (Trickster) stories. Deloria defined the Iktomi in this way: "In other words, you simply did not dare have dealings with strangers, because you could not be sure of them. They might so easily turn out to be the incarnation of Iktomi, the legendary spirit of deceit, ready to play a trick on you" (1944b [1979]:20).

One example from the Iktomi cycle will show its strength and vividness and will explicate the translation process in Deloria's work. Deloria defines *Ohu'kaka* as "tales . . . (which) are best known, oftenest repeated, and farthest removed from the events of every day life of the Dakota people."

> They are the real *Ohu'kaka*. To our minds, they are a sort of hang-over, so to speak, from a very, very remote past, from a different age, even from an order of beings different from ourselves. These tales, in which generally some mythological character like Iktomi, Iya, the Crazy Bull, the Witch, or Waziya (the Cold), takes part together with human beings, are part of the common literary stock of the people. Constant allusion is made to them; similes are drawn from them which every intelligent adult is sure to understand. "Like shooting off the sacred arrow," or "They are dancing with eyes shut, to his singing" one hears repeatedly. "He is playing Iktomi" is understood to mean that a person is posing as a very agreeable fellow simply to get what he wants. (Deloria 1932:ix)

For the *Ohu'kaka* "Iktomi Tricks the Pheasants," Deloria gives this synopsis: "While Iktomi sings, the pheasants dance with eyes shut, and he kills the largest of them. Later, while his fowls are cooking, he is caught fast up in a tree and a wolf coming by eats all his food" (Deloria 1932:xi).

That terse precis does not do justice to the richness and vitality of the tale—in Lakota or in the translation. However, Deloria, evidencing her linguistic training and emic perspective, explains such cultural things as the utterance "tok'i hiya ye" (going some where). This movement, which characterizes the opening of every Iktomi story, is explained: "*Tok'i* plus an active verb gives force of independence of interest and motives. Here it means that wolf was going along on his own business, paying not the least attention to Ikto' or his affairs. In other words, if Ikto' had kept still, there would have been no story" (Deloria 1932:22). It also points to the character of the Lakota trickster—that of intruding oneself upon another individual. Thus, the trickster, Iktomi, transgresses cultural norms of Dakota folk, and the tales serve as a tension-reducing mechanism.

In the tale "Iktomi Marries His Daughter" (Deloria 1932:11–19), we see Iktomi as the supreme transgressor, and we also note how Iktomi tales deal with such cultural proscriptions as incest. More important, we see how Deloria includes ethnographic analyses of certain elements that enhance this collection of expressive elements of culture. I extract the utterance *ani'lowa pi*, which Deloria explains as "*lowa*, to sing; *a*, over; *ni*, you." In the *hu,ka* ceremony, they sing (*pi*) over the candidates, waving a particular type of wand decorated with horse-tail hair and in rhythm with the song (15). Later she notes, "The Dakota text says, 'Were your father living, he would no doubt even arrange for them to sing over you.' 'To be sung over' was to undergo the *hu,ka* ceremony, and assume all the privileges and obligations it (*hu,ka*) carried. It was a great honor, indicating the love in which the candidate was held by her parents or other relative who arranged it" (18).

Aunt Ella's intelligence, charming curiosity, and warm dignity allowed her to fit into any social and/or intellectual situation. Her worth as a Native educator has resulted in one dissertation (which I have not consulted) (Murray 1974). She was a many-sided woman. Her work as ethnologist, linguist, and folklorist was marked by vigor and objectivity. A devout Christian throughout her life, she was able, in *Speaking of Indians,* to give graphic accounts of tribal dances, especially the Sun Dance and the Vision Quest, with total respect for their significance to those participants. Had she lived longer, there is no doubt that she would have taken pride in the resurgence of interest in traditional Indian ways, such as she herself helped to preserve.

Ella Cara Deloria and Her Work

Ella Cara Deloria was known for her ethnographic fieldwork with three Siouan-speaking groups: the Dakota, Lakota, and Nakota.

Deloria, whose Native name was Anpetu Waste Win (Beautiful Day Woman), was born during a snowstorm on January 30, 1888, on the Yankton Dakota Reservation at Lake Andes, South Dakota. She was the eldest of four children born to Philip Joseph (Tipi Sapa, or "Black Lodge") and Mary Sully Bordeau Deloria, the granddaughter of Irish artist Thomas Sully. Ella's Native name was seldom used in her interaction with her people, and she later became known as "Aunt Ella" to Native kin and younger anthropologists.[7]

Although she spent most of her formative years among the Hunkpapa and Sihasapa Lakota (Sioux) on Standing Rock Reservation, Ella Deloria, along with other Native North Americans, became a student of her natal Siouan language and cultures. Deloria conducted much of her research on Standing Rock, Pine Ridge, and Rosebud reservations and used the general term *Dakota* to cover all the dialects spoken by these Western Teton groups. Possibly because her father converted to Christianity and was the first Native American to become an Episcopal minister (founding St. Elizabeth's Mission and its school near Wakpala), Ella's involvement with the people at Standing Rock seems to have been largely confined to church-related and educational activities. Participation in indigenous rituals and ceremonies was largely lacking. It was part of the missionizing and educational milieu of the time to negate Native life-styles and strive for education in the context of the dominant society.

Undoubtedly, her father influenced her choice of a teaching career, and she is remembered by reservation residents for her contributions as an educator. Her training included schooling at St. Elizabeth's Mission and All Saints School (also Episcopalian) in Sioux Falls, South Dakota. She won a scholarship and attended Oberlin College in Ohio from 1911 to 1913, when she transferred to Teachers' College of Columbia University and finished with a B.S. in 1915. She returned to teach at All Saints and in 1923 took a job with Haskell Institute, a Bureau of Indian Affairs school in Kansas, where she taught physical education and dance in an experimental program. She was also secretary for American Indian work of the National Board of the YWCA in New York City, illustrating a pattern of professionalism followed by some Native women.

During her career as an anthropological linguist, she not only worked with Boas, with whom she coauthored *Dakota Grammar* (Boas and Deloria 1941), but also with Ruth Benedict. Benedict's influence may be seen in her later work, for she became absorbed in producing a dictionary that probed the psychological implication of the Lakota language. This project, which occupied her from 1962 until her death, was initially supported by a National Science Foundation grant (1962–66) to the University of South Dakota's Institute of Indian Studies.

Her life as an educator was constantly interspersed with fieldwork, which began around 1927. She resigned her teaching position at Haskell to devote time to Dakota research and to publish scholarly works with Boas until his death in 1942. She also sent material on traditional Dakota culture to Ruth Benedict. Deloria traveled to most Sioux reservations to interview elders on Siouan language and cultural topics. She was amused that most Siouan-speakers made remarks about her, believing that she could not understand or speak their language and were surprised and delighted when she responded in their Native tongue. This extended fieldwork resulted in *Dakota Grammar* and in *Dakota Texts,* a rich bilingual collection of folktales, legends, and Iktomi (Trickster tales) told by storytellers from several reservations. *Dakota Texts* is valuable for its commentaries that deal with translation and semantic difficulties, the performance features of stories, and statements regarding the cultural context of the tales.

Deloria also translated, arranged, and annotated the works of other scholars. Particularly important are the George Bushotter manuscripts, a series of texts on Dakota life written in 1887 while Bushotter worked for the Bureau of American Ethnology (BAE) under James Owen Dorsey. Deloria's annotations and comments on these materials remain unpublished. In addition, she translated texts recorded by two missionaries—Gideon and Samuel Pond's collection of Santee Sioux tales and personal histories.

In 1937 Boas asked Deloria to verify and correct myths compiled by James R. Walker, a physician who had lived on the Pine Ridge Reservation from 1896 to 1914 (Jahner 1983). Deloria worked on both the linguistic/phonetic aspects and the content of Walker's materials. She spoke with one of Walker's narrators, Edgar Fire Thunder (age seventy-eight), in investigations of a secret holy men's society reported by George Sword. She also interviewed Ten Fingers, possibly the grandson of the holy man Finger, whom Walker had interviewed, and talked to various people on the reservations. In letters to Boas she frankly discussed which stories people recognized (those of Left Heron and other informants) and which they felt were not really Dakota myths (e.g., George Sword's stories). Because Deloria found no variant tales of those that Sword had related to Walker, she concluded that these stories were examples of creative fiction rather than oral tradition. She recognized that gifted Lakota storytellers such as Sword had elaborated on traditional tales and even incorporated aspects of European folk-lore with Dakota elements into their stories (Jahner 1983).

Ella's letters to Boas reflected the conflict between her professional commitments and deeply felt kinship obligations. She took care of her father during a long illness and lived for much of her life with her sister, Mary Susan, whom she helped support. Mary Susan, an artist known professionally as Mary Sully, did the artwork for *Speaking of Indians* (Deloria 1944b [1979]), Deloria's popular account of traditional Dakota culture.

Deloria often spoke of taking care of her nephews (Vine Deloria, Jr., among them) and obviously derived pleasure in her role as aunt. Her attitude toward Siouan kinship displayed analytical and purposive direction, for she once told her great-nephew, "I am really your grandmother in the Lakota way, but you can call me 'Aunt Ella,' too." Her perspective reflected typical Lakota incorporativeness regarding kinship, which she often conferred upon the younger ethnographer colleagues for whom she acted as an aunt. This speaks to Lakota perceptions of proper behavior for women.

Ella and Mary Susan exemplify two early Siouan female professionals—one an anthropologist and the other an artist—who provided emotional support to one another during their sojourns in New York City. Although they did not express this culture conflict, the two sisters may be viewed as two professional Native women who faced the dilemma of choosing between careers in both white and Native worlds. Indeed, during Ella's lifetime I noticed subtle changes in her attitudes toward Dakota identity. In the cultural context of the early twentieth century, she had remarked of her cousin, "Poor Anna, she married a full-blood." However, years later, when one of her nephews married a full-blood, she seemed inexplicably pleased.

In many ways, Ella Deloria stood within and outside her own culture. Insiders are those persons who are socialized from an early age as participants in a particular culture, as Deloria was. Many Native ethnographers of her era and earlier, such as Francis and Bright Eyes LaFlesche of the Omaha, were primarily viewed as informants or assistants to ethnographers from outside the culture. These ethnographers may be professionally trained or amateur, are usually male and Caucasian, and, as "friends of Indians," believe themselves "experts." They are sometimes inclined to think that they know more about Indians than the Indians themselves know. In developing her writing and analytical skills to interpret the insider's perspective—the emic voice (Medicine 1980)—Deloria did not experience alienation from her Dakota identity, as do some Native people who become professional ethnographers through university training.

While *Dakota Grammar* is significant for researchers in Native American linguistics and bilingual education, *Dakota Texts* and *Speaking of Indians* are valuable to students of ethnic literature. *Dakota Texts,* a scholarly work, contains folktales recorded directly from storytellers. These are accompanied by free and literal translations as well as commentaries on Dakota grammar and customs.

Deloria's valuable footnotes to the stories have made literary analysis of old texts accessible to modern scholars (Medicine 1980).

Speaking of Indians, intended for a primarily white readership, examines both traditional and contemporary Indian life through Ella's devoutly Christian perspective. Yet she retains reverence for traditional Dakota spiritual concerns such as the Sun Dance and the Vision Quest. The book is divided into three sections. The first part rejects stereotyped portrayals of Indians and discusses them as people with "a scheme of life that worked," after a line in Stephen Vincent Benét's poem "Western Star." With the coming of European settlers, Deloria found, Indian tribal societies were forced to cope with rapid social change toward assimilation and were further damaged by the European tendency to view all tribes as the same.

The second part of the book delineates the importance of kinship obligations among the Sioux, especially the contrast between the white culture's emphasis on acquiring possessions and the Sioux culture's value of sharing as expressed through give-aways (Picotte and Pavich 1983). In this section Deloria also mentions the egalitarian nature of Sioux society: "Outsiders seeing women keep to themselves have frequently expressed a snap judgment that they were regarded as inferior to the noble male. The simple fact is that woman had her own place and man his; they were not the same and neither inferior nor superior" (1944b [1979]:39).

The third part of *Speaking of Indians* examines the obstacles facing the Sioux after they were relocated to reservations following the decimation of the buffalo herds and the loss of the nomadic way of life. She asserts that, based on their notions of kinship, "Indians believed that the mighty leaders in Washington would indeed care for their Indian children" (Picotte and Pavich 1983:xvii). Although the tone of the book is sometimes viewed as "conciliatory," it concludes with a call for justice and basic human rights for American Indians (Picotte and Pavich 1983:xviii).

During her sixties and seventies, Deloria continued her field research, with brief interludes of full-time work as the director of St. Elizabeth's School (1955–58) and briefly at the Sioux Indian Museum in Rapid City and the W. H. Over Museum at the University of South Dakota (Vermillion). She also supported herself through small research grants, lecturing, writing, and consulting, but her limited income greatly handicapped her literary output. Columbia University transferred her notes and manuscripts to the American Philosophical Society in Philadelphia, which also holds the Deloria-Boas correspondence, and she was never able to work with these materials again. Her later materials are stored at the University of South Dakota. Her last concentrated writing endeavor occurred while she was living in a motel in Vermillion. After suffering a stroke in 1970, she died the following year.

Deloria's body of work remains among the fullest accounts of Dakota culture in the Native language. It is unique as a Native woman's perspective, which had previously been lacking in writing on the Lakota/Dakota/Nakota people, and as an interpretation of Dakota reality to other people. Although she was acknowledged by her colleagues Margaret Mead, Jeanette Mirsky, and Esther Goldfrank for having collected this body of information, many contemporary Siouan scholars also recognize her influence as a full-fledged ethnographer. She produced a definitive dictionary and grammar, provided thorough descriptions of traditional social organization and religious life, edited and translated texts dictated by various storytellers, and composed commentaries and annotations to these texts. At the same time, she honored her family obligations as a Dakota woman and left a lasting legacy for scholars and for the culture that had sustained her.

Ella Cara Deloria: Early Lakota Ethnologist (Newly Discovered Novelist)

My views on Ella Deloria have not changed significantly since I wrote brief biographical notes about her (Medicine 1980, 1989). I practice what I teach—return your writing to your constituents for comments. The 1980 publication was approved by Vine Deloria, Sr., who said, "When Vine [Deloria, Jr.] wrote about anthropologists, he didn't mean you or your Aunt Ella. He meant others." Vine Junior stated, "It sounds like her."

In this essay, I wish to present Aunt Ella as a Native woman and contextualize her life within Lakota cultural contours that shaped her life and work. She strongly identifies with the "Standing Rock people." She once told me, "I know more about them than the Dakota. I grew up in Wakpala [South Dakota]." Although she knew her band affiliation and her enrollment, her identity was firmly embedded as a Lakota.[8] The Deloria family was accepted in the Wakpala community. Although Ella and her sister Susie were summer visitors, their sustained visits evidenced their interest in community life and allowed Ella's linguistic interpretations.

Ella Deloria attended St. Elizabeth's Mission in Wakpala, where her father, the Rev. Philip Deloria, was the first Native Episcopal missionary. She continued at All Saints School in Sioux Falls, and Oberlin College, receiving a B.S. in 1915 from Columbia University Teachers' College. Ella spent several years as director of the St. Elizabeth's Episcopal Boarding School in the 1950s. She and Susie were committed to the Christian education of a segment of the Lakota population. As the students attended the public school in Wakpala, her job was mainly administrative and church-related. Although Ella was committed to higher education, few of the high school graduates pursued this avenue.

She taught in Bureau of Indian Affairs schools and at Haskell Institute, also working for the YWCA in New York City. She began to do fieldwork around 1927, resigning from Haskell to devote time to Dakota research and to publish scholarly works with Boas until his death in 1942. She also contributed much to the work of others. Boas said of Ella's work: "She has a thorough grasp of the grammar and spirit of the language. We have written together a grammar of the Dakota, of the Teton, Yankton, and Assiniboine dialects, and she is thoroughly conversant not only with the forms but also with the very intricate psychological background" (Deloria 1944b [1979]). Ella's letters to Boas reflected the conflict between her professional commitments and deeply felt kinship obligations. She cared for her father during his long illness and helped to support her sister Susie.

My assessment of Ella Deloria's role as a Native intellectual is that she has not been appreciated by Lakota/Dakota people teaching in the tribally controlled colleges. At Standing Rock, one Lakota teacher of the Lakota language felt that *Dakota Grammar* was "too technical." *Speaking of Indians* was used in her Lakota culture class. A non-Lakota teaching an education class was contemplating using *Waterlily* (Deloria 1988). Two male Lakota instructors at Sinte Gleska University (Rosebud, South Dakota) appreciated the explication of the tiospaye concept and the social-life aspect in *Speaking of Indians*.[9]

Although a process of reconstruction of Lakota culture seems underway at each college, there seems to be continued disenchantment with ethnological work, although Frances Densmore's work on Lakota music is being used in some recordings of contemporary Lakota music and in the revitalization of Sun Dance songs. Thus, I was interested to read the book of Robert Warrior (an Osage English professor) and his comments on Ella Deloria. After stating that literary production changed after Matthews and McNickle's work, Warrior writes that "literary production by Natives declined rapidly and was done primarily by anthropologists and historians. The most well known is Ella Cara Deloria, the aunt of Vine Deloria, Jr., whose posthumously published historical novel, *Waterlily*, and anthropological texts have been important in the recovery of Native intellectual traditions" (1995:24). He also refers to "Ella Deloria's liberal ethnographic work" (42).

In assessing Ella's writings, one must place her in space and time and in her religious orientation—as well as her keen interest in her Lakota heritage. *Speaking of Indians* demonstrates this commitment. Her motivation appears to be to act as a culture broker. She wished to convey the human character of Lakota life to a non-Native audience. Her information was collected when Lakota people spoke of a glorious Lakota past, of which she heard through family histories, war exploits, orality, and pantomime and song. *Dakota Texts* reflects this tradition and the morality and ethical behavior that were transmitted orally. Her informants (and she used that term) were Patrick Shields and Joseph White Plume of Standing Rock, whose lives were oriented toward the proper functioning of kinship, which they saw as the bedrock of Lakota culture. Mrs. Andrew Little Moon, mother of Sammy Red Eagle, and other persons in the Women's Auxiliary to the Brothers of Christian Unity (BCU) of the Episcopal Church also appeared to be eager informants. After all, who could refuse to answer questions posed by the eldest daughter of the Reverend Deloria?

Ella's constant interest was in writing ethnographic materials. This knowledge, however, was not presented to the people themselves. When I ask community people about her writings, they are unable to name them. Indeed, her brother, Vine Deloria, Sr., although a good informant to Ray DeMallie and others, did not know the bulk of her work. When pressed, he told me that much of her collections were lost when she could not pay storage fees while she and Susie lived in New Jersey. I was told by a Native literature instructor at the University of Minnesota that Sam Deloria (Ella's nephew) did not know that she had written a novel. In 1970 she told me, "I have written a novel. It is not an ethnography so I don't want you to read it. I don't want it published." This is a clue as to her view of her work. It was ethnographic and reflective of a part of her life that she cherished.

It may be that most anthropologists are unaware of Ella Deloria's ethnographic work.[10] Siouan specialists have utilized it. Ernest Schusky has lauded her work on the dynamics of kinship that demonstrates the nuances of kin relations and called it "the best work on kinship!" Others, DeMallie, for example, have used her as an informant (now termed "consultant"). Her linguistic texts are excellent. Julian Rice's appropriations (Deloria 1994) are finding a niche in Native American literature courses.

Ella Deloria's work as an ethnographer and an indigenous linguist was not fully recognized until the long-delayed publication of her novel *Waterlily* in 1988. It is ironic that although she did not want it published it has superseded her ethnographic contributions. It is now on bibliographies of courses on Native women and Indian literature and is read like an ethnographic text—which would have displeased her, I am sure. Although seen as "sugary" and "idealistic" by one Native professor teaching American Indian literature, it nonetheless is important in delineating the kinship dimension in dyadic interaction between members of the tiospaye. Morality, ethical behavior, and the unifying theme of reciprocity are manifested from a feminine perspective. The articulation of male and female relationships is significant. It may be the emphasis on gender complementarity that causes some modern feminists to object to the novel.

In his assessment of *Waterlily,* anthropologist John Prater writes, "Perhaps she did not look critically at her Christian beliefs, and the image of the Sioux she creates in *Waterlily* is not Sioux at all but a Christian image super-imposed on Sioux characters" (1995:46). He traces their form "from Ella Deloria's own 'life myth.'" He attributes her "multi-cultural heritage" as a position to understand a "context of varied intercourse." To my knowledge, her heritage was definitely Lakota, not Dakota. She, like all aboriginal people, was subjected to Christianization and cultural imperialism. She mediated adaptive strategies that allowed her to function adequately in two social systems. These strategies fostered her effectiveness as she described herself—a Lakota woman and an ethnographer. I believe that we can anticipate more literary speculations and anthropological analyses (e.g., Finn 1995) of her personhood and her contributions through *Waterlily.* Her ethnographic oeuvre, however, may be her lasting contribution to the Americanist tradition.

Perhaps the most telling thing about Finn's article is her "writing against the *in*grained" respect for "personal dignity" (1995:344, emphasis in the original), which typifies Ella Deloria. This overriding sense of personal autonomy confronts Finn, who feels a sense of complicity. This is perhaps the major difference in writing about another culture and the intrusive quality of "others" writing about us. Perhaps I, too, have fallen into this anthropological trap in this essay. Lakota women, then and now, do not separate the "personal and political," because we must deal with issues that involve our communities. However, within the community context we are allowed to maintain our own dignity and idiosyncrasies. This was recognized by Aunt Ella, and it allowed her intellectual freedom and honor for her achievements. I hope I have portrayed this quality.

Ella Deloria "mentored" many scholars. Now called a "consultant," she was used as an informant, as was her brother, Vine Senior. I wonder how many helped her in her impoverished years in Vermillion, South Dakota? When I drove to her motel to take her to lunch, she would scan the motel room, humming and looking for something to give to me. There was little but stained coffee cups, a picture of Franz Boas, a typewriter, and several boxes. Her humor and her pleasure at "going out to lunch" were sufficient.

Only one scholar, to my knowledge, aided Aunt Ella in her scholarly research. Robert Hall, while at the University of South Dakota in the late 1960s, obtained a grant for her to accomplish her greatest desire—as she said, "to do a proper Lakota dictionary with the psychological meanings of the words and ideas." In this effort, she clearly shows the influence of Ruth Benedict and Margaret Mead. Mead once told me that "Ella was an asset at Columbia."

Esther Goldfrank clearly articulated her indebtedness to Aunt Ella in her work on Sioux personality. She also stated that after Ella presented linguistic data, she turned to Franz Boas to ask, "Is that alright, Dr. Boas?" Further, Goldfrank stated, "Ella was the main source for Jeanette Mirsky's work on the Lakota." Therefore, I maintain that Ella Deloria was an "ethnographic informant, par excellence." She, however, had an abiding interest in Lakota culture and language, and this interest sustained her through the trying times of her life. Current reference to her as a "consultant" diminishes her intellectual and communicative skills—both in Lakota and in English.

My data on Ella Deloria are the result of almost daily contact with her from 1969 to 1970, when we both lived in Vermillion, South Dakota. I was directing an oral-history project at the University of South Dakota. Because I became an "anthro," many people feel that Ella was a role model for me. Notions of cultural difference were part of my early socialization. As a child, I only knew that she "lived in the East, and talked about Indians," according to my mother. When Aunt Ella visited our home, she asked a lot of questions about Lakota life and language. When I graduated from college in 1945, she gave me her book *Speaking of Indians* and said, "I'm proud of you!"

Upon my return to Wakpala as a retiree in 1989, I had the opportunity to contextualize her life in the community and the community view of her. I interviewed individuals who had worked with her while she managed St. Elizabeth's Mission from 1955 to 1958. The general statement was "lela ta yan Lakcol wo glake" (she spoke Lakota very well). They noted that she "went away to give speeches." Students who attended the public school during this period liked her but had no knowledge of her published work or her work as an ethnographer.

After I left Vermillion, in an undated letter, she wrote, "There are two very nice Sisters in college and one drives so I have been going with them, once to Mission, and the other day I took them to the New Year's dinner and party at St. Mary's and we had a great time, they enjoyed it. One is Theresa Martin and the other is Sister Michael (Many Wounds) of Pine Ridge.[11] Both full bloods and very smart girls." Her attitudes about "blooded-ness" and her concern for reciprocity are evident.

Non-Native people in surrounding border towns very seldom state overt assessments of Lakota people, but when I asked a *wasicu* (white) woman and active member of the Episcopal church if she remembered Ella Deloria, she said, "We thought she was a wonderful woman. I wish she were here to help us decide what to do with St. Elizabeth's Mission." The Lakota pastor of the parish said, "She was a good woman."

Ella told me of her invitation to a Sun Dance on Pine Ridge reservation. First, she asked a female cousin and her husband (from Wakpala) to accompany her and Susie (her constant companion in the field). This was proper decorum. During the performance of the Heyoka (Contrary) Ceremony, the Heyoka removes, with bare hands, the parts of the ceremonial puppy from the boiling water in the pot. She was given the head—a great honor. She said, "I ate this without any fuss."

Her Lakota appetite was embedded in her cravings for certain, in Lakota terms, delicacies. She often asked my mother for prairie dogs—which father shot and the *women* ate with appreciation. In our home in Vermillion, where she ate dinner almost every day, she often said, "*To'win* (niece), is there anything else?" I would bring out raw kidney on a wooden cutting board. (My son would say, "This is where I leave you." He preferred his kidneys cooked!) Later, after smiling with satisfaction, she would say, "Is that all?" This was a signal to bring out Kahlua, which she dearly loved. This ritual was not a daily one. These examples show clearly her true bicultural adaptations. She was equally at home at formal receptions and in poor Lakota homes, although she never mastered the household arts of Lakota food preservation and preparation, which was expected of every "full-blood" woman.

Ella Deloria's presentation of self also heralded her mixed-blood status. She was always properly dressed—in white woman's style. She delighted in recounting the many times Lakota people spoke Lakota in her presence. She could answer them in Lakota and say, "Maaah, I am Lakota, too." Her informants were mainly Episcopalians, or *shina ska* (white robes). Because of the separation of churches, she seldom interviewed Catholics, who were mainly from the Sihasapa (Blackfoot) band. In interviewing older Lakota, she would listen attentively, record the data in her car, and question them or another about some obscure point at a later time.

When one considers the time of Ella Deloria's work, and the space in which she operated—the old car she shared with her sister and the apartment in Palisades, New Jersey—one wonders at her production. *Dakota Texts* and her work on the Sun Dance and legends and folktales were marvels of translation and interpretation. Seeing herself as an interpreter of Lakota culture and language, she chose a career that was, perhaps, happenstance. As an ethnologist/informant, she lived a precarious life in a strange culture, constantly on the economic fringes. Marriage seemed out of the question for her. As the eldest daughter of an Episcopalian minister, her marriage options were nil. Her sense of superiority and attitudes toward the ubiquitous "full-bloods" were limiting factors. But she once told me, "If I had met a man like [your son] Ted's father, I might have gotten married."

This attitude was clearly articulated to me, when on one occasion she stated, "Poor Anna, she married a full-blood." Angered, I said, "But he fed your relatives." (Many of her female cousins had married wasicu men who arrived as bums on the railroad.) Her attitudes seemed apparent in the non-marriage of her younger sister, who often told my mother, "I could have married any man I wanted," or "I envy you for your children." My father often left the room when the Deloria girls arrived. He never did enter into the jovial joking relationship with Ella as he did with Susie.[12] He was well aware of not only full-blood/half-breed dimensions but also religious affiliation. Mother converted to Catholicism when she married my father. I relate these poignant instances to indicate the difficult cultural choices that women in the Lakota culture of my mother's generation faced.

It appears that Ella was quite aware of the "blooded" distinction. I remember postcards from Palisades, one from Aunt Ella saying, "I may be more closely related to Martin than you" after she had discovered a Sihasapa ancestor. Yet the full-blood, Martin Medicine (Sitting Crow was his Lakota name) was often a source for her linguistic work. She would tell Mother, "Ask Martin what this word means and tell me."

Ella's letters to Boas reveal the ubiquitous tension between these potential distinctions (even factions), especially in Pine Ridge. She once told me that some older men were speaking about her in Lakota as a *wasicu-winyan* (white woman). She answered them: "Ee, tu wale, mishyama Lakota ki!" (Unbelievable! I'm a Lakota, too). I asked, "What did they do then?" She said, "They stood up and shook my hand." She was an *eyeska* (translator) or *ah oze* (yellow armpit), as the mixed-blood students at St. Elizabeth's were labeled.[13]

My association with Ella Deloria was framed within a Lakota kinship nexus. She and Susie visited us each summer. Susie and my mother, Anna Gabe, were inseparable, fun-loving culprits at St. Elizabeth's Mission when all were students. Tipi Sapa (the Reverend Deloria) claimed relationship to my mother's father, Baptiste Gabe, whose father was a Frenchman from Louisiana and whose mother was a Miniconjou woman. The Deloria girls and Mother said they were cousins. Mother was the same age as Susan, three years younger than Ella. Susie was a pretty, fun-loving person. Ella, being the elder, was the authoritative figure. She was viewed as a "kill-joy"—according to Mother. She was upset when Susie and Mother chewed buttons off their blouses to throw into the collection plate instead of the nickel coin each Protestant child received every Sunday to put in the plate. Contributing to the church was ingrained early in Christian enculturation.

When I asked my mother, "What kind of person was Aunt Ella?" she replied, "She was very vain." Subsequent experiences with her while living in Vermillion revealed this tendency. She never forgot (and did not let you forget) her mixed-blood origins. That badge of blood-lines was predominant in her relationships with the Lakota people of Standing Rock Reservation, which she considered her home. She often told my eldest sister Marguerite, "Bea and I put Wakpala on the map."

Recently, Nora Hawk, a Lakota "elderly" (as we are called) told me about an incident that occurred when she worked for Ella in 1955. Christmas was apparently a time of joy and caroling for the students at St. Elizabeth's Mission, and Ella was part of this Christian time of holiness. The dining room was decorated with streamers of green and red tissue paper, still a tradition at festive events in Wakpala. After dinner, in the "Big Girls' Dormitory," Ella said to a younger girl, *"Cepansi* (female cousin), eyaya na, minexuasa jikala makauy ye" (go and tear a small piece of the red streamer and bring it to me). (Aunt Ella was always precise in using Lakota kin terms, and a Lakota could not refuse any request made in the name of kinship.) "Taku ye?" (Why?), asked the minion. "T'osa wani yakin kte" (You'll see), said Ella. When the younger girl gave the scrap of red tissue paper to Ella, she moistened it with saliva and daubed it on her cheeks to add color, smiling as she did so.

This vanity persisted into her later years. When I sponsored a fashion show to establish the Ella Deloria Scholarship for Indian Women at the University of South Dakota in 1969, I took her to a beauty shop for a shampoo and set. She said, "They took me way in back where no one could see me. How nice!" *Amerindian* ("New Scholarship" 1969:4) described Ella Deloria as a graduate of Columbia University who had been "associated with the University in the field of research and with the W. H. Over Museum." She came "from a famous Dakota family . . . and [was] famous in her own right as author and anthropologist. . . .

Miss Bea Medicine, also a Dakota [*sic*] and an anthropologist, . . . wrote and delivered the commentary for the performance, the first of its kind ever held at the University." The national television coverage must have pleased Ella Deloria! Patricia Albers and I have donated my royalties from *The Hidden Half* to this scholarship, and Pat's to a scholarship for Indian women at the University of North Dakota.

Notes

1. *Editor's note [from the original publication]*: The diacritical markings used in this article are only approximations, because our focus is on the literary contribution of Deloria rather than her linguistic achievement.

2. After the death of her mother, Ella Deloria devoted much of her life to the care of her younger sister and brother, Susan Mable and Vine Victor Deloria. Her nephew, Vine Deloria, Jr., is the author of *Custer Died for Your Sins, We Talk, You Listen, Behind the Trail of Broken Treaties,* and *Metaphysics of Modern Existence.* The essay was sent to her brother, Vine Deloria, Sr., for comment and is published with his recommendation.

3. She did much of her research on Standing Rock, Pine Ridge, and Rosebud reservations. These Western Teton groups spoke Lakota, but Deloria uses the general term *Dakota,* covering all dialects.

4. Margaret Mead (1973) referred to Deloria as a "colleague." See also Mirsky (1937) and Goldfrank (1943). Ella Deloria was also involved in the 1967 Chicago conference that resulted in *The Modern Sioux* (Nurge 1970).

5. A third publication is Ella Deloria's, *Dakota Texts* (Deloria 1932), hereafter referred to as *Texts.* References to *Speaking of Indians* will be cited as *Speaking,* and citations will be given from the 1979 edition, the pagination of which differs from the original edition (Deloria 1944b).

6. When my son was ten or eleven, he wrote an account of the ceremony in which he was given his family name (Garner 1970).

7. My family and I lived in Vermillion, South Dakota (1968–69), where Aunt Ella became a part of the household—coming almost every day for dinner and visiting. Much of my contribution is based upon that interaction.

8. Once, in Vine Junior's presence, my mother said, "Bea wants to know how the Delorias were enrolled on Standing Rock." Vine, Sr. replied, "You know, your father [Baptiste Gabe] and your uncle, Charlie Gabe, worked to get me enrolled." I had asked my father, who had replied, "Ask your mother." Even in those days, as today, tensions regarding tribal enrollment were obvious.

9. These young men and the white instructor of culture do not like Julian Rice's interpretations of Ella's work. They use the four texts in *Ella Deloria's The Buffalo People* (Deloria 1994) and nothing else.

10. Ray DeMallie presented a paper about her at the Ethnohistory Conference in November 1996. I have heard the paper but have not read it.

11. Theresa Martin was the Lakota language teacher at Standing Rock, now Sitting Bull College, for eleven years.

12. Sadly, Aunt Ella related Susie's last days, which were spent removing the beads from a pair of old moccasins. "But Susie was not right when she got older," she said. Did she remember that we placed new moccasins on the deceased to travel the Spirit Trail?

13. I asked my mother, "So, what did you do when they called you *ah oze?*" She said, "We'd raise our arms and say, 'We don't have yellow armpits.'"

References

Albers, Patricia, and Beatrice Medicine. 1983. *The Hidden Half: Studies of Plains Indian Women.* Washington: University Press of America.

Boas, Franz, and Ella Deloria. 1941. *Dakota Grammar.* Memoirs of the National Academy of Sciences, vol. 23. Washington: Government Printing Office.

Deloria, Ella C. 1929. "The Sun Dance of the Oglala Sioux." *Journal of American Folklore* 42(166): 354–413.

———. 1932. *Dakota Texts.* New York: G. E. Stechert.

———. 1944a. "Dakota Treatment of Murderers." *Proceedings of the American Philosophical Society* 88(5): 368–71.

———. 1944b [1979]. *Speaking of Indians.* New York: Friendship Press. Reprint, with introduction by Agnes Picotte and Paul N. Pavich. Vermillion: Dakota Press.

———. 1973. Review of *The Modern Sioux. Journal of Ethnic Studies* 1(1): 87–97.

———. 1988. *Waterlily.* Lincoln: University of Nebraska Press.

———. 1994. *Ella Deloria's The Buffalo People.* Edited by Julian Rice. Albuquerque: University of New Mexico Press.

Deloria, Ella C., and Franz Boas. 1933. "Notes on the Dakota, Teton Dialect." *International Journal of American Linguistics* 7(3–4): 97–121.

Finn, Janet L. 1995. "Ella Cara Deloria and Mourning Dove: Writing for Cultures, Writing against the Grain." In *Women Writing Culture,* ed. Ruth Behar and Deborah Gordon, 335–50. Berkeley: University of California Press.

Garner, Edward. 1970. "The Day I Became 'Sitting Crow.'" *The Bay Leaf* 4(8): 3–4.

Goldfrank, Esther S. 1943. "Historic Change and Social Character: A Study of the Teton Dakota." *American Anthropologist* 45(1): 67–83.

Jahner, Elaine A., ed. 1983. "Introduction." In James R. Walker, *Lakota Myth.* Lincoln: University of Nebraska Press.

Medicine, Beatrice. 1978. "Learning to Be an Anthropologist and Remaining 'Native.'" In *Applied Anthropology in America,* ed. Elizabeth M. Eddy and William L. Partridge, 182–96. New York: Columbia University Press.

———. 1980. "Ella C. Deloria, the Emic Voice." *MELUS* [*Multi-Ethnic Literature in the U.S.*] 7(4): 23–30.

———. 1989. "Ella Cara Deloria." In *Women Anthropologists: A Biographical Dictionary,* ed. Ute Gacs et al., 45–50. New York: Greenwood Press.

Mead, Margaret. 1937. *Cooperation and Competition among Primitive Peoples.* New York: McGraw-Hill.

———. 1973. "The American Indian as a Significant Determinant of Anthropological Style." In *Anthropology and the American Indian: A Symposium,* ed. Jeannette Henry, 68–74. San Francisco: Indian Historian Press.

Mirsky, Jeanette. 1937. "The Dakota." In Margaret Mead, *Cooperation and Competition among Primitive Peoples.* New York: McGraw-Hill.

Murray, Janette K. 1974. "Ella Deloria: A Biographical Sketch and Literary Analysis." Ph.D. diss., University of North Dakota.

"New Scholarship Named for Ella Deloria." 1969. *Amerindian* 17(6): 4.

Nurge, Ethel, ed. 1970. *The Modern Sioux: Social Systems and Reservation Culture.* Lincoln: University of Nebraska Press.

Picotte, Agnes, and Paul N. Pavich. 1983. "Introductory Notes." In *Speaking of Indians.* Vermillion: State Publishing Co.

Prater, John. 1995. "Ella Deloria: Varied Intercourse." *Wicazo Sa Review: A Journal of Native American Studies* 11(2): 40–46.

Warrior, Robert Allen. 1995. *Tribal Secrets: Recovering American Indian Intellectual Traditions.* Minneapolis: University of Minnesota Press.

CHAPTER 26

Anthropology as the
Indian's Image-Maker

Anthropologists as reporters of "exotic" and "primitive" people of the world have, by the very nature of their data, been portrait painters of indigenous people and purveyors of images of these human beings. This projection of image is done through standard ethnography courses, area courses, people-of-the-world courses, and through comparative, cross-cultural data stemming principally from the life-styles of these non-Western people. The European background of most investigators has inevitably presented an overlay of a "manifest destiny" quality implicit in the investigative role. The material for the ethnographies deriving from the anthropological axiom of fieldwork, and specialization in competency based upon that method of collecting data, is an important part of the rite of passage into becoming an anthropologist.

North American Indians, or "Amerindians," or "Indian-Americans," and, more recently, "Native Americans," have been the subject of much anthropological theorizing, interrogation, and analytical interpretations of these creatures' life-ways. Indians are seen as creatures, as experimental objects, as givens! The people of the Americas have been variously known by the above designations and other names. Tribal designations or names in their native language for "the people" are preferred by the native Indians. However, the white terminology has reflected a certain color and orientation to the Indians' examination. This has ranged from the "vanishing American" syndrome to the present-day activist and articulate Native American who poses a problem for contemporary anthropologists.

Most students in Native American studies programs categorically reject anthropological reporting on their tribes. Indeed, some subtle pressure is applied to those few Indians entering anthropology, which causes much soul-searching and thinking about the discipline in relation to the "Indian world" or the "Indian movement." Some anthropologists are seen as patronizing, some as of the "bleeding heart" variety, and some as still romanticizing.

The image of the Indian as internalized by the anthropologist has had great implication in the implementation of his research. We have learned in history of anthropology courses of the need to collect data, items of material culture to enhance museums, "memory" cultures from the aged Indians that predominated during the time of Boas and his students. Much of this early data-collecting was fostered in an atmosphere of Indian preoccupation with the "good old golden days." The data are of an extremely variable quality, depending upon the skills of the anthropological fieldworkers.

A major influence in Native communities was the training of Indians to collect Native texts, folktales, and genealogies. Such Indian people as Ella Deloria, Henry Hunt, S. Cranmer, Francis LaFlesche, and others have provided an awareness of anthropology and a legacy of Native Indians entering the discipline. The works of these individuals have seldom been utilized by equally ethnocentric American Indian college students.

However, it is the casting of American Indian life-styles onto the printed page that has lent a certain unchallenged expertise and validity to anthropologists as image-makers for Indians. The printed word, so important in academia as *the* documentable source, has resulted in the corrupting concept of an ethnographic present, which has posed the Native American in a stilted, static stance and had great repercussions in the image-molding perspective of American anthropology.

A contemporary Indian author, D'Arcy McNickle, has put into print some observations on American Indians: "Tribes were seen as components of 'culture areas,' frozen in the days of Boas, Wissler, and Lowie" (McNickle 1970:6). This image has led credence to that of contemporary mass media and feedback into the curricula of social science studies at all levels of the education system. The stolid, stupid image is imputed in such terms as the "Digger ecological domains and social systems." McNickle describes exceedingly well the general tenor of the courses offered in anthropology departments:

> Such studies recorded impressively long lists of behavioral practices, technologies, and material artifacts which seemed to describe a tribe exhaustively, and yet said nothing about it at all. Usually, it was not clear whether the traits described were still practiced or were long defunct. In instances where it was clearly shown that the traits were non-existent, the tribe was pronounced dead or dying. At the other extreme, tribes that had disappeared as living societies were described in the literature as possessing the attributes of a contemporary community. The traits themselves—their origins, their cognate forms in neighbor-

ing areas—became so central to the exercise that association with a tribal name was added almost as an afterthought. (1970:6)

We pay deference to the printed word.

It is within this realm that we choose to explore this implication. There is currently a great importance assigned (with corresponding funding) to obtaining tribal histories from the "Indian point of view." This view shall predominate and place us in a vulnerable position, with cries of "subjectivity" and "ethnocentrism" from anthropological colleagues. This can also be heard in shouts of "emotionality" and designations of "tertiary sources" by many so-called ethno-historians.

Most of the audience who are, or profess to be, American Indians have had some acquaintance with the word *anthropologist*. However, for many of us, the generic phrase *white man* has greater implications. It encompasses the "bogey man" of our childhood and by extension can be applied to the unpredictable decision-maker in the institutions of the dominant society of our adulthood.

Although anthropologists have not held decision-making posts in institutions making policy decisions for the welfare of most Indians, their reports are usually consulted and given credence. The sacrosanct soundness of their printed observations casts credibility that is seldom questioned. More damaging perhaps is the utilization of anthropologists' oral testimony in action-oriented policy, with complete disregard for this assessment in the activation of programs affecting Native American life. However, because anthropologists, as experts on indigenous life, are "consulted," "primitive" aboriginal life is preserved.

Fieldwork, being a requirement for becoming an anthropologist, predicated studying a group of most accessible Indians. Generally, permission to enter a reservation was obtained from a white decision-maker—the agent of the agency. Seldom were Indians consulted. They were available. It is astonishing that the rules of hospitality and graciousness extended to ethnologists in the Wissler and Lowie periods are still prevalent in many areas.

Generally, fieldwork was oriented to collecting, displaying, and storing material objects in museums. This was the direct outgrowth of the culture-area concept, which categorized tribal entities, especially in the Plains, into static units bolstered by traits collected by the "laundry list" method. In the eagerness to trace diffusion of material goods, parfleche designs, moccasin types, and medicine bundles assumed more dynamic qualities than people did. Many Indians were seen as living museum-pieces. The recording of music and language grossly obscured the dynamics of Indian interaction and laid the foundations for the "apathetic, defeated Indian." The over-riding conviction of the disappearing Native hastened the collection of a record that has formed a congealed ethnographic present impervious to change. The image of Plains Indians generally remained fixed in the mind of the public.

This model has had pervasive and predominant consequences for the American Indian, as in Wissler (1946 [1967]: 175–76), whose description of the Dakota depicts the Plains Indian model that persists to the present:

Early anthropological fieldworkers tended to be well-meaning scholars and men of good will, or so this is what many Indians on the Plains say. The flavor of this favorable interaction is predominant in Lowie's "My Crow Interpreter" (1960:428–37). This delicate, dyadic relationship seems the exception rather than the rule however.

The Dakota were the heroes of the original Wild West shows, Longfellow's Minnehaha belonged to the family, and such fine musical compositions as "The Waters of Minnetonka," or "Red Wing," immortalized Dakota music; and finally, the Dakota is the ideal of the artists. Tall, slender, with small hands and feet but sinewy body, strong features, high cheekbones and beaked nose—the Indian of the nickel—all these characteristics may be seen in the Dakota or some of their hybrids. We expect all Indians to wear the Dakota costume, so that no matter what tribe, all modern Indians appear in it. It is the conventional formal dress of the contemporary Indian, but was devised by members of the Siouan Family and popularized by the Dakota. When a new president is inaugurated in Washington, a few Indians ride in the procession wearing the traditional costume of the Dakota. The painter or the illustrator knows that if he presents a conventionalized figure in the Dakota style of dress, man or woman, it will spell Indian. It is a kind of picture writing. This is why we see paintings of the Pilgrims landing at the famous rock greeted by Indians dressed like Dakota, or again Indians receiving Henry Hudson at Manhattan in the same kind of clothes, or Pocahantas in the wedding dress of a Dakota bride. All absurdities, except that we understand this to be art's way of telling us that Indians are being depicted.

Buffalo Bill was a great showman, the first to capitalize the popularity of the Indian. He chose his Indians from the Dakota and, both in America and Europe, persistently spread their fame, with drooping eagle-feather headdress and sharp features, so that young and old rarely imagine there are any other kind of Indians. Therefore, it behooves us to look a little deeper into the history of the Siouan Family of which they are a part.

The "our Indians" approach was well established as a tradition with the publication of Clark Wissler's *Indians of the United States*. By this time, the overriding image of *the* Plains Indian added much to the impression of a stolid, taciturn, stoic with no sense of humor and only grunts and groans to indicate human communication. Otherwise, what was the function of sign language? This "our Indians" orientation has relevance to the "my people" approach of anthropologists who study Indians in California. To quote Wissler, "in contrast to the Hopi and Zuni Pueblos, and even an Iroquois Village, they fall well below par" (1946 [1967]:204–5).

It is exceedingly difficult to focus the viewpoints of Indians and coalesce upon *one* anthropologist. Each group reacts from its own particular perspective. We have not, however, heard any Native Americans using the term *our anthropologist*. Anthropologists may have accepted Indians as they were, labeling them "non-technological," "primitive," and, more recently, "tribal" or "folk." This has predicated a comparative approach with its anthropological vantage point situated comfortably in a European-based, highly technologically developed society.

Despite this essentially value-laden view as seen by many Native Americans, anthropologists have contributed significantly to the diversity of cultures in Native North America. This has had great influence in the presentation of differences in language, physical type, and ways of life. Life-styles are seen as essentially unique adaptation to ecological areas. Only within the subject matter of anthropology has it been possible to convey this richness of culture. The generalized picture of thematic styles—stoicism, lack of humor, underlying savageness in males and a corresponding gentleness in females, and a tremendous tendency toward (but an inability to hold) firewater—posited by the pioneers of American anthropology presents an image of American Indians that is difficult to dispel.

It has been, it seems, exceedingly impossible for anthropologists to present the external changes superimposed by the dominant society upon indigenous social systems. In many cases, treaties, governmental policies, and effects of educational and religious superstructures have seldom been within the province of anthropological exploration. This has often led to an investigative leap into "acculturation" studies, which were seen in unilineal developmental schemes. Thus, residual remembrances formed before-and-after episodes of American Indian life. Social disorganizational reports prevailed. Conceptual schemes of Indians showed greater or lesser degrees of acculturation to an implicitly superior life-way. These adjustments could be rated on scales and anchored in polar types. Adjustmental categories of orientation emerged—"Native-to-white"—and Indians of all tribes could possibly be placed in this new heuristic model. These categories often replaced such all-encompassing terms as *Dyonisian* and *Appolonian*.

In gross terms, the *Image of the Indian* has been presented as a picturesque person, a noble savage, and as "shrewd, far shrewder than any of the beasts around them," (Wissler 1946 [1967]: 157) but still fumbling for acceptance and appreciation of a superior white society. The words of a song by Floyd Westerman, a Sisseton folksinger, are pertinent (1969). Encapsulated on reservations, American Indians still remain target populations for "the anthros, coming like death and taxes to our land."

References

Lowie, Robert H. 1960. "My Crow Interpreter." In *In the Company of Man: Twenty Portraits by Anthropologists,* ed. J. B. Casagrande, 428–37. New York: Harper and Row.

McNickle, D'Arcy. 1970. "American Indians Who Never Were." *Indian Historian* 3(3): 4–7.

Westerman, Floyd. 1969. "Here Come the Anthros." On *Custer Died for Your Sins* (PLP-5 Perception).

Wissler, Clark. 1946 [1967]. *Indians of the United States.* Garden City: Doubleday. Revised by Lucy W. Kluckhohn. Garden City: Doubleday.

CHAPTER 27

The Native American

The term commonly used to designate the Native American—
"American Indian"—is a highly deceptive one. It is a name imposed by foreigners and covers a multitude of distinct tribal aggregates that comprise the aboriginal inhabitants of North America who have been, at one time or another it is estimated, between one and ten million in number (Dobyns 1966; Oswalt 1966). This initial uncertainty about the Native American laid a basis for confusion that continues to the present day. The Native American is possibly the least understood ethnic minority in contemporary American society. The rich and varied cultural and linguistic backgrounds of the approximately three hundred Indian tribes currently in existence in the United States are, and have been, severely distorted by historical documents written by non-Indians and blurred by images presented by the mass media.

In 1970, for the first time in the history of the census, the census questionnaire included a section that allowed Native Americans to identify themselves according to tribal affiliation. Although much of this data is not yet tabulated, the available information reflects the growth of a group of Native Americans—urban Indians—who are outcasts of two social systems: their Native communities on reservations scattered throughout the United States and the urban areas that present an unfamiliar setting. It is on the urban group of Native Americans that we shall focus in this chapter.

The increase in the population of Indians in the four southwestern states of California, Colorado, Utah, and Oklahoma has been considerable and reflects the movement of Native Americans into urban areas. In these four states, the number of Native Americans increased from 134,952 in 1960 to 208,777 in 1970 (an increase of 54 percent). By contrast, the increase in the total population of these states increased only 24 percent. The contrasting increases for Native Americans and total population by state during this ten-year period were as follows: Colorado, 106 percent versus 26 percent; Utah, 62 percent versus 19 percent; California, 54 percent versus 27 percent; and Oklahoma, 51 percent versus 10 percent.[1]

Essentially, the definition of "who is an Indian" is fraught with legal and sociological hazards. Generally, social scientists—especially anthropologists who focus on Native Americans—see reservation enclaves of people who are distinct culturally as the only "true" Indians. Similar designations relying upon biological characteristics (black hair, brown skin, almond-shaped eyes) and viable cultural manifestations (utilizing Native language, practicing a Native religion, or wearing "traditional" clothing) are often criteria employed by other social scientists—sociologists, psychologists, and many historians. The concern for research dealing with the urban Indian is relatively recent.

The Bureau of Indian Affairs (BIA), which has been assigned the care of Indians, defines them in this fashion: "To be designated as an Indian eligible for basic Bureau of Indian Affairs services, an individual must live on or near a reservation or on or near trust land or restricted land under the jurisdiction of the Bureau, be a member of a tribe, band, or group of Indians recognized by the Federal Government, and, for some purposes, be of one-fourth or more Indian descent" (Bureau of Indian Affairs 1970:6).

To further confuse Indian identification, the mass media of television, films, and popular writing have persistently presented the Plains Indian as the generalized prototype and stereotype of the contemporary Indian. This image has generally remained fixed in the mind of the public. Wissler explains the process:

> The Dakota were the heroes of the original Wild West shows, Longfellow's Minnehaha belonged to the family, and such fine musical compositions as "The Waters of Minnetonka," or "Red Wing," immortalized Dakota music; and finally, the Dakota is the ideal of the artists. Tall, slender, with small hands and feet but sinewy body, strong features, high cheekbones and a beaked nose— the Indian of the nickel—all those characteristics may be seen in the Dakota or some of their hybrids. We expect all Indians to wear the Dakota costume, so that no matter what tribe, all modern Indians appear in it. It is the conventional formal dress of the contemporary Indian, but it was devised by members of the Siouan Family and popularized by the Dakota. When a new president is inaugurated in Washington, a few Indians ride in the procession wearing the traditional costume of the Dakota. The painter or the illustrator knows that if he presents a conventionalized figure in the Dakota style of dress, man or woman, it will spell Indian. It is a kind of picture writing. This is why we see paintings of the Pilgrims landing at the famous rock greeted by Indians dressed like Dakota, or again Indians receiving Henry Hudson at Manhattan in the same kind of clothes, or Pocahontas in the wedding dress of a Dakota bride. All absurdities, except that we understand this to be art's way of telling us that Indians are being depicted.

Buffalo Bill . . . chose his Indians from the Dakota and, both in America and Europe, persistently spread their fame, with drooping eagle-feather headdress and sharp features, so that young and old rarely imagine there are any other kinds of Indians. (1946 [1967]: 175–76)

This perception has undoubtedly formed the basis for Indian-white interaction in present-day society. Most Native Americans are constantly expected to respond to such utterances as "How," "Ugh," "Chief," "Sitting Bull," "Hiawatha," and, in some instances, "Princess" (as in "Princess Rainwater"). The reprehensible term *squaw* is also the rule. Of Algonkian origin, it is highly objectionable to most Indian women. These terms are white articulations that have been developed for dealing with an out-group but are often seen as normative by the members of the dominant society.

To fully appreciate the marginal character of American Indians in their native land, consider the startling fact that not until the passage of a congressional act in 1924 was full citizenship conferred upon all Native Americans. Previous to this action, most Natives were wards of the federal government. Exceptions were those Indian combatants in World War I, who became citizens in 1920.

The Dilemma of the Native American

The Problem of Identification

Most "first" Americans have been conditioned to accept the umbrella term *Indian*. However, the Native American defines himself in quite another manner—according to tribal affiliation. Most Native Americans prefer to be called by their tribal name; for example, the people most call "Navajo" call themselves Din'e (which in their Athabaskan language means "people"). The "Dakota" prefer to be called Dakota, Lakota, or Nakota, according to the three different dialectical divisions of this Siouan language group. The Dakota are not keen about their designation "Sioux" commonly found in history books. This is because "Sioux" is a French corruption of a term of the Chippewa (traditional enemies of the Dakota), *naduwessioux*, which can be translated to mean "enemies" or "snakes." The village-dwelling (Pueblo) Indians of the Southwest prefer to be called by the specific name of their pueblo—for example, Santa Clara Pueblo. The Pueblo Indians represent at least three different language stocks or phyla (Dozier 1970), thus the Native name is different for each pueblo.

These few examples of the total number of ongoing aboriginal cultures represent but a small segment of Native American societies from which urban Indians have been recruited. Throughout the long history of contact with non-Natives, the various Indian tribes have been labeled "Aborigines," "Indians," "Natives," "North American Indians," "Amerinds," "Red Indians," "Amerindians," "Indian-Americans," and, most recently, "Native Americans." The most meaningful and persisting self-perception has been in terms of tribal affiliation and reservation enrollment. Therefore, it is not uncommon to hear the phrase "Standing Rock Sioux." This designates a Sioux (Dakota) who may be of the Hunkpapa, Blackfeet (Sihasapa), or other band from the Standing Rock Reservation in North and South Dakota. Increasingly, as a result of intertribal marriage, many hyphenated tribal affiliations are prevalent. Thus, it is possible to designate one's tribal background as Kiowa-Navajo-Cheyenne-Arapaho, although the place where such as individual is enrolled on the tribal reservation rolls is important. This usually gives the tribal affiliation (as, for example, Navajo) where such a multi-tribal person is enrolled. This would be his "reservation" or his agency.

The Problem of Identity

More critical, how a Native American feels about his tribal ancestry is particularly significant. It is difficult to convey this "feeling" or affective aspect of Native American identity. There are many individuals who are biologically of only one-eighth Indian blood. Thus, they are not Indian according to BIA definition. However, their identity and loyalty may be stronger to their Native American heritage than their physical appearance indicates. John Rainer, from Taos Pueblo, once defined an Indian as "anyone who needs to be an Indian." Generally, the role of the Native American mother is critical in such a situation. Children of white mothers and Native American fathers tend to be socialized in a non-Indian milieu. Moreover, because many Native Americans may be products of federal or parochial boarding schools, a pan-Indian orientation centering upon the Plains Indian motif tends to predominate.

A development since 1934, when the Indian Reorganization Act was passed, has been the assumption of more decision-making powers by tribal governments. Such matters as controlling enrollment of individuals born in urban areas have been within the jurisdiction of tribal councils. This poses a problem when one reexamines BIA's definition of an Indian. It further complicates the identity of Indians, because enrollment of a child born outside the reservation rests upon the decisions of the tribal councils. The following example illustrates some possible problems. One Oglala family (Sioux from Pine Ridge Reservation) has six children. One child is not enrolled and is thus not an Indian. This child was born while the parents were living off the reservation, resulting in a judgment that reflects a capricious decision at the reservation level. This situation is one which many Native Americans living in urban areas face.

The American Indian is seemingly a myth in the mind of non-Indians. The myth is often a composite of images portrayed by the mass media, which rarely, if ever, considers tribal and linguistic differences.

Assimilation through Work and Education

Whence came the urban Indian who represents such a polyglot of tribes? Throughout the "civilization" of the country and the growth of cities, Native Americans have participated in sporadic and unique transactions with the dominant society. These interactions have included attendance at non-reservation boarding schools such as Carlisle in Pennsylvania (founded in 1859) and Haskell Institute (now Haskell Junior College) in Lawrence, Kansas. These off-reservation boarding schools often fostered "outing" programs. Indeed, one scholar writes in reference to Carlisle that "a basic element of . . . policy was the 'outing' system, which might today be considered the first individual Indian 'relocation' program" (Waddel and Watson 1971:35). The "outing" system featured the assignment of Native American youths to work for families in the white community. Most often the job involved farming or housework. This policy of acquainting Indian youth with the workaday world of the dominant society persisted until the 1960s. It also provided free labor for the white community.

Many students attending these schools did not return to their reservation homes. However, the incomplete record-keeping of the BIA provides insufficient data to determine precise off-reservation residence. Implicitly, the thrust of early educational programs was to propel Indians toward assimilation into the superordinant society. Intermarriage with non-Indians was another contributing factor. Again, demographic data are lacking. However, the result was that a nucleus of non-reservation Indians was formed.

Division and Assignment of Tribal Lands

Concurrent with the trend to educate Native Americans away from tribal life was the Dawes Act passed by Congress in 1887. This legislation formed the basis for much of the subsequent administered human relationships that have characterized the lives of Native Americans. It presented the notion of "competency" in the control and utilization of the 160 acres that were given to each male adult. Competency was determined by the white administrators. According to the Native Flathead anthropologist D'Arcy McNickle:

> The essential features of the legislation were: (a) The President was authorized to divide tribal lands and assign or allot 160 acres to each family head, eighty acres to single persons over eighteen and orphans under eighteen, and forty acres to each other single person under eighteen. (b) Each Indian would make his own selection, but if he failed or refused, a Government Agent would make the selection. (c) Title to the land was placed in trust for twenty-five years, or longer, at the President's discretion. (d) Citizenship was conferred upon all allottees and upon other Indians who abandoned their tribes and adopted "the habits of civilized life." (e) Surplus tribal lands remaining after allotment might be sold to the United States. (1962:48–49)

In essence, the Dawes Act and subsequent amendments allowed for land to pass out of Indian hands. Most of the land was sold. The problem of inheritance rights concerning such land has presented unbelievable and unforeseen complications. In some cases, the 160 acres of the original allotment may have several dozen heirs. The allotment system also allowed for the so-called checkerboard settlement pattern on many reservations. White purchasers bought land on Indian reservations. The selling or leasing of allotted land and the "undeveloped" reservation economy forced many Indians toward off-reservation residence (Deloria 1969, 1970).

Prejudice, Fear, Stereotyping, and Buck-passing

Coupled with the foregoing, the prejudice toward, and fear of, Native Americans by local whites resulted in general non-employment of Native Americans (Braroe 1965; White 1970). The stereotyping of Indians as "lazy, drunken, and undependable" very often left no alternative except urban migration.

No attempt at delineating the reservation Indian from the non-reservation Indian resident was made. The "Meriam report" (Meriam 1928) mentions the "migrated Indian" as those Native individuals who left the reservation. Significantly, this report focused on reservations with few economic resources and opportunities and implied programs for "relocation." The image of the Indian as a ward of a benevolent federal government caring for his health, education, and welfare poses many continuing problems for urban life. This picture also is a hindrance to being understood by non-Indians. Native Americans experience great difficulty in obtaining aid from non-federal agencies. The belief that Native Americans are the responsibility of their non-reservation municipalities is still operative in federal policy. Bouncing between such agencies in the private and public sector of urban life often seems an extension of the "buck-passing" so characteristic of Indian life on reservations, where an individual is sent from office to office with nothing settled. The resulting sense of utter frustration of Indians is difficult to convey.

Further, most Native Americans have been subjected to various legal actions (as the result of treaties) specific to their tribe. The tribe's sovereign status has in many instances set policy for continued relations with the federal government.

Traditional Approaches to Resolving the Dilemma of the Native American

It is necessary that we examine the social milieu and legal precedents that have predicated the situation of the contemporary urban Indian from a specific tribal group in order to have a framework for understanding.

Murray Wax reflects the bias of many sociologists in expressing the need for precision in the specification of demographic data on urban Indians. His presentation pinpoints the overriding problem of "who is an Indian or what kind of Indian" (Wax 1971; see also Blumenfeld 1966; Dowling 1968; Hodge 1969; Kelly and Cramer 1966), which typifies the dilemma of the urban Indian. Wilfred Pelletier (Odawa from Ontario), basing his statement upon long experience with Canadian cities and Natives, states, "There is just no use trying to keep a list of Indian people in the city" (Pelletier et al. 1971:16).

Wax (1971), however, presents the case of the Iroquois in the North Gowanus area of Brooklyn, who have long served as a model of Native Americans well adjusted to urban living. More tellingly, it demonstrates the attitude of Iroquois (from Caughnawaga Reserve near Montreal, Quebec) toward the arbitrary dividing boundaries in North America and their apparent ability to successfully compartmentalize Native and urban life—not only in economic terms but also in sociocultural terms. Most members of this matrilineal society have successfully maintained Iroquois as a mother tongue and Iroquois child-training practices as a modus operandi for successful urban adjustment. A personal view of adjustment in another tribal group is expressed by Dunn and Redbird (Dunn 1971).

During World War II, many Native Americans of all tribes enlisted in the Armed Services. Many others migrated to Los Angeles, San Francisco, Chicago, and other urban areas where war-related industries provided a livelihood. Some returned to their Native communities after the war. Some remained to contribute to the growing urban Indian population.

In 1953, congressional opinion favored federal withdrawal from Indian affairs. "Termination," "relocation," and attempts by state and local communities to assume law enforcement on reservations were seen by many Indians as a neatly tied package attempt to further destroy their Native life-styles and heritages. The relocation program initially concentrated on finding employment for Navajo and Hopi Indians in off-reservation jobs. In the 1950s, however, placement officers were hired by the BIA to recruit Native Americans in other parts of the country to seek employment outside reservations.

Enticement of Native Americans to migrate to cities predominated in this new government program. Correlated with this was the 1953 decision, written into law by President Eisenhower, which allowed Indians to legally consume alcoholic beverages. This new freedom for Indians saw the demise of white bootleggers who had operated in off-reservation towns. The new license temporarily intensified reservation drinking. Many tribal law officials "harassed" relocation officers to transport "problem Indians" to urban areas. Whatever the pressures, it seems apparent that any new federal program must present favorable statistics in order to ensure future funding. This rationale has been basic in policy decisions regarding the program, which has been renamed "Field Employment Assistance." The following from an in-house memo of the BIA's Oakland–San Francisco Field Employment Assistance Office presents a recent summation:

During the years of 1960 through 1967, there have been 3,958 single and family units of Indian origin that have been relocated to the Bay Area from reservations in Indian country. These units represent a total of 6,489 persons and comprise tribal groups from all over the continental United States. The majority of clients, however, have come to us from the Northern Plains and the Southwest. The Sioux and the Navajo are most representative of those areas and make up about fifty percent of our total annual intake.

Since the employment assistance program is a voluntary one, clients choosing to come to the Bay Area have been motivated by a desire to improve their conditions through the better employment and educational opportunities existing in an urban setting. The Oakland–San Francisco Field Employment Assistance Office is only one of seven similar offices that are situated throughout the United States serving American Indians.

Waddell and Watson (1971) present data on the Navajo that are based primarily upon Din'e adaptation in Denver. Again, this concentration upon one tribal group typifies the anthropological research concerns for "my people." There appears to be more data for the Dakota than for most groups (Ablon 1964; Hurt 1962).

The foregoing does not exclude those Native Americans who looked to "relocation" as a means of providing a more satisfying and stable life for themselves and their families. The "adventure" aspect of relocatees does present another variable for consideration, but that has not been investigated.

In another area, the beginnings of a powerless, undereducated, unqualified, and unsure group of Native Americans were shunted to urban areas—mainly Chicago, Minneapolis, Los Angeles, Dallas, and the San Francisco Bay area. Those individuals who made the transition found themselves in what were, to many, unresolvable dilemmas. Technological devices alone—gas and electric stoves, indoor plumbing, streetcars and buses, elevators, and other aspects of urban living—demanded immediate adjustments. Completely new interpersonal relationships had to be absorbed and internalized into a meaningful and cogent frame of reference. Old kinship patterns became nonfunctional as families began urban life as nuclear units. Generally, many families were placed in apartments in inner cities or in housing developments. Housing in low-income areas and training for jobs at paraprofessional levels posed new sets of transactions with blacks, Chicanos, and other disadvantaged groups equally low on the socioeconomic scale.

Subgroups of Indians apparently coalesced along tribal lines. Commonality was based on adjusting to a new urban life-style. The diverse cultural groups could be contrasted to those groups of Native Americans who had remained in the cities after World War II or who elected individually to migrate to metropolitan centers. The Native Americans were apparently adapting to a white middle-class existence, with homes in the suburbs or at least away from the city center. This aggregate of individuals represents a demographic unknown. Thus, it is only recently, since the "invasion" of Alcatraz, that many of these people have reidentified as Native Americans. The occupation of Alcatraz Island by a group of Native American students from San Francisco State College presented a daring symbolic act that initiated a series of Native land grabs. The impetus for identity as Native Americans seemed hopeful. Apparently, the trend to reaffirm "Indianness" began in the early 1960s with the large influx of relocatees. In addition, an undetermined number of skid-row inhabitants are part of Native urban life.

Indians, on or off reservations, are poverty-stricken groups with little means of controlling their aims, their aspirations, or the consequences of their actions. Political astuteness has not characterized these groups. Most Native Americans are historically and presently seen as conquered and vanquished people. Ambivalent feelings toward Native Americans prevail. Rousseau's noble savage finds a counterpart in the present "man of nature" who knows ecological secrets and has such appeal to the counterculture. Concurrently, the image of the drunken, worthless Indian persists. Most significantly for the Indian, the scapegoat has been the federal government. The population of the dominant society often operates under the false assumption that the needs of the Indian are cared for by a benevolent government.

Social scientists often attempt to relate the subordinate position of the Indian to an acculturation model, with gradients ranging from so-called traditional (residues of tribal life-ways) to orientation to white standards. Seldom is the latter standard specified. Often this scheme is the yardstick for measuring Native adjustment and acceptance in the larger society. Being "more Indian" is a term often used to indicate ongoing heritage.

Generally, the Native American subset has blamed "them" for their difficulties. "They" might variously mean the federal government or its myriad departments—the Department of the Interior, Bureau of Indian Affairs, U.S. Public Health Service (responsible for Indian health since 1957), Department of Health, Education, and Welfare, Office of Economic Opportunity, Housing and Urban Development, and many others. Within the past five years, it has become increasingly popular for other federal agencies—for example, the Departments of Labor, Justice, and Agriculture—to establish "Indian desks" to deal with Native Americans. State governments have also established Commissions on Indian Affairs (e.g., Montana, New Mexico, and North and South Dakota). Thus, "they" for most Native Americans tends to become extremely diffuse, distant, and frustrating. Indeed, the greater proportion of Indians have never heard of these bureaucratic structures. The alphabetizing of federal agencies, HEW, HUD, and others, has further confused this group of people.

Barriers to the resolution of the "Indian problem" are great and cumbersome. Individual motivation and education have varied extremely. Education for Indians has both tended to alienate Indians from their Native communities and failed to prepare them efficiently for participation in white society (Aurbach,

Fuchs, and MacGregor 1970; Medicine 1971). Motivation and commitment to problem-solving is also individually perceived and acted upon. Thus, no one Indian can speak for the whole population of diverse tribes, much less for his own tribe.

The subordinate status of Indian groups in the larger society, plus their political manipulation by vested interest groups, has perpetrated the puppet status of most Indian groups. This is seen on all levels—municipal, state, and federal. A great part of these pressures emanate from such groups as farmers, ranchers, fishermen, oilmen, and others. Groups who have special interests in water, land, timber, oil, and other natural resources obviously do not condone Native Americans obtaining power or status. However the general policy affecting Indians is construed, it has an ultimate effect upon the urban Indian group.

Most tribal governments insist that urban Indians (now called "urbs") may not vote in tribal elections. (Reservation residents apparently fear that urbs may foster land sales and ultimately opt for termination of the reservations.) Furthermore, returnees must reside on their home reservations for a year before voting for tribal officers or seeking office themselves. (The returned relocatee is greatly handicapped. Much the same legal restrictions inhibit urban Indian participation in municipal and state elections. Welfare requirements also tend to be discriminatory to city Indians.)

Most Native American students in ethnic studies departments in colleges and universities apparently view the urban transition as a travail, as indicated by such courses as "The Urban Dilemma" or "The Native American Experience" or "The Indian in Contemporary Society," which usually deal with the urbanization process and its further destruction of traditional life.

Recent Approaches to Resolving the Dilemma of the Native American

Various church organizations have entered the "Indian center" movement in an attempt to provide smoother adaptations for migrant Indians to city life. For example, the Episcopal Church operates the St. Augustine Center in Chicago. Although primarily a casework agency, this center has recently sponsored research and published the results. Support from social scientists for a multi-tribal urban Indian component has been negligible. Since the early 1950s, anthropologists have provided impetus and guidance in the establishment of the American Indian Center in Chicago, which still operates effectively. Liaisons with other urban organizations such as the Welfare Council, Social Service Exchange, and Red Feather Service indicate a different level of integration at various times in the history of this center. Research aimed at its own needs also appears to be characteristic. In the autumn of 1971, experimental elementary and high schools were established. Relevant curricula are aimed specifically at Native American students, and attempts are made to deal with their needs in education. By contrast, sociologists in Minneapolis have generally used urban Indian people and their organizations as research conglomerates. Publication of their data has, it seems, established these white investigators as self-ascribed "experts" in Indian affairs. Indian-oriented research often establishes the basis and funds for the development and continuation of such "white Indian experts."

Initiated by an anthropologist, the Seattle Indian Center has an Indian board of directors and is operated by the American Indian Women's Service League. This group has engendered criticism because it seemed that Native American men were excluded, but in actuality they have been much involved. After a period of militant activism, the center has now entered a larger Native coalition, although its future direction is difficult to predict. However, it has allowed for the assumption of powerful roles by newly emergent Indians.

The Oakland Inter-Tribal Friendship House was originally sponsored by the American Friends Service Committee and continues to operate. In 1970 another Native-run center was established in Oakland. The endeavor was short-lived, however. The San Francisco Indian Center originally sponsored by the Society of St. Vincent de Paul was taken over by an all-Indian organization in 1963 (when the society withdrew its support) and is still in operation.

As might be expected, each center reflects its uniqueness in an urban setting, and policies and practices also reflect the power plays and struggles of migrant indigenous tribes. The current input from college and university students attempting community involvement and change is variable and transitory at best.

Urban Indian centers have great potential for self-help, self-study, and problem alleviation. Some have initiated alcoholism prevention programs, tutoring services for elementary and high school students, and personal and family counseling. The more prevalent pattern, however, involves monthly powwows (Indian social dancing of a pan-Indian character) (Howard 1955). Classes in art, beadwork, and dance permeate the programs and increasingly contribute to a generalized pan-Indian urban group. It is not uncommon to see, for example, a Navajo Indian dressed in Plains-type costume and dancing to Plains Indian music. This is, in a sense, a response to what an Indian is supposed to be.

A singular attempt was recently made to coalesce urban Indians on a national scale. In 1967 an organization was started in Seattle by a pan-Indian group of individuals experienced in off-reservation affairs and whose main concern was the plight of Native Americans living in urban areas. Funded by a Ford Foundation grant, American Indians–United was formed in Chicago in 1968. Its demise occurred in 1970. Inept and inexperienced leadership, petty jealousies, and "ego trips" dissipated the structure. Vested interests representing various urban areas were also a factor. Much time, energy, money, and ability was used in trying to establish a viable structure involving widely dispersed and culturally different people from various urban environments—such as Pampas, Texas, and Fairbanks, Alaska. Technical assistance, economic development, center programming, fund raising, educational concerns, and media surveillance were some of the ambitious aims that occupied the embryonic and essentially disorganized staff. The Church Federation of Greater Chicago served as custodian of funds and unofficial consultant to this Chicago-based national group. Since 1970 nothing else has evolved to unite the entire urban Indian scene in the United States.

The longer-established Indian centers (in Oakland and San Francisco) and the newly emerging centers in the San Francisco Bay area (such as San Jose and the Santa Clara Valley group) are reacting to the recently formed Bay Area Native American Council, which is viewed by its organizers as the umbrella organization and conduit for funds that are still negotiable. One might see these as attempts at self-determination and may be tied to a speech of President Nixon on July 8, 1970. In referring to urban Indians, he stated: "Lost in the anonymity of the city, often cut off from family and friends, many urban Indians are slow to establish new community ties. Many drift from neighborhood to neighborhood; many shuttle back and forth between reservation and urban areas. Cultural differences compound these problems. As a result, programs designed to help such persons often miss the most deprived and least understood segment of the urban poverty population." This so-called historic speech stressed Indian self-determination and raised the hopes of Native Americans throughout the country.

In December 1970, a meeting of urban Indian groups in Virginia ended in turmoil and destruction of property by some urban Indian militants. Little was accomplished to deal with the salient problems of city Indians. The meeting, sponsored by the National Council of Indian Opportunity, seemingly reflected the lack of understanding and awareness of the dynamics of urban Indian organization. Unfortunately, it also served to reinforce tribal stereotypes of urban Indian militancy and "marching and burning." This seemed to further alienate the "urbans" from funding sources and tribal people.

The urban Indian center movement in Canada had beginnings with the establishment of the Toronto and Winnipeg centers in the late 1950s. Since then, centers have been established in Edmonton, Vancouver, Calgary, and Regina. The Native "problem" in Canada is a dual one. Presently, there is much concern for the métis (mixed Indian and non-Indian people) (Lagasse 1959). According to law, if a Native woman marries a non-Native man, she loses her status as an Indian. However, if a Native man marries a non-Native woman, the woman becomes a "treaty Indian." This matrimonial inequity has recently been challenged in court by a Native woman married to a non-Indian. The métis are not "treaty" and are enfranchised.[2] The Indian-Eskimo Association, composed primarily of non-Indians, has been involved in Native American work. Recent intertribal organizations such as the Alberta Indian Association, the Native Indian Brotherhood, and various métis organizations are showing vigor and insight in dealing with their own affairs. The métis in particular are becoming quite assertive.

Since 1970, attempts have been made in Los Angeles to coordinate all existing Indian organizations in the area into one major group. The same attempt was successful in Denver, with the opening of an Indian center in January 1971. There is a growing tendency to establish Indian centers in most urban areas to meet the specialized needs of the migrant Indians. An underlying premise is that Native American needs are unique and that interaction in exclusively Indian centers often gives esprit de corps and maintains Indian identity.

The success of the centers, given sufficient funds and community support, rests almost entirely upon the commitment and ability of directors and staff. Successes and failures of center programs are seen differently by members of various tribes, the public, and professionals. Vine Deloria, Jr., writes incisively of the different perceptions involving tribal leadership at all levels (Deloria 1969, 1970). Generally, the image of an inarticulate, incompetent savage who would be utterly destroyed save for his work colors the views of most non-Indians involved in "Indian work." Although anthropologists, sociologists, governmental policymakers, missionaries, and others have made mistakes in interfering in Indian lives, mistakes made by Native people are usually not forgotten and are pointed to with "we told you so" implications.

Indian academicians and federally employed Indians met to discuss issues in Indian affairs in January 1971. Further meetings of a smaller group led to the Conference for Indian Self-Determination held in Kansas City in March. The meeting showed the growing gulf between the reservation-based Indians and the urbs. Indirectly, the conference aimed at securing federal commitment to "Indian self-determination" and emphasizing the need for tribal involvement in controlling Indian destiny. The conference pushed for a reassessment of the National Congress of American Indians, the National Indian Press Association, the National Council of Indian Opportunity, and the Americans for Indian Opportunity.

Interestingly, by non-endorsement, a new organization called the National Tribal Chairman's Organization was formed in 1971. Clearly, there were indications that urban Indians were not the concern of the Bureau of Indian Affairs. Urban Indians were seen as equivalent with militants and competitors for "Indian funds" and definitely a threat to land-based reservation groups. In some instances, this trend seemed to by fostered by career men in the Bureau of Indian Affairs. Obviously, city-dwelling Indians gained little from the meeting.

Since 1970 a coalition of federal agencies has been considering the needs of urban Indians (referred to as "racially isolated urban Indians"). This has resulted in the projected establishment of four "model" urban Indian centers located in Gallup (New Mexico), Minneapolis, Los Angeles, and Fairbanks (Alaska). At this time, funding has not materialized, and it appears that a stalemate exists. This new attempt to deal with the well-being of the urbans has been principally dealt with by an Indian board in conjunction with representatives from federal agencies. Funding for this endeavor is also being sought from the private sector and possibly could undercut any attempts for local self-determination. The New York

City–based Association of American Indian Affairs will act as sponsor and fund conduit. Autumn 1971 saw urban Indian health-care centers being formed in San Francisco–Oakland. Seattle utilizes the U.S. Public Health Service hospital with an Indian health board. There is an arena of great need and inadequacy in meeting the health needs of Indians.

The increasingly prevalent attitude that Native Americans must have advocacy is apparent in such proliferating organizations as California Indian Legal Services, Native American Rights Fund, Americans for Indian Opportunity, and other sprouting Indian-oriented groups. Generally, these are geared to the betterment of life for the reservation Indians. Most of these organizations have Indians on their boards of directors. However, all but one—Americans for Indian Opportunity—have non-Indian directors. The effectiveness of these boards is a moot point. Not only are the Indians often predominantly "token," but it also might seem that they are in the peculiar position of being "taken" (i.e., collected) to create more "white Indian experts."

The continuing attitude of many social scientists that North American Indians are captive groups for their examination still predominates in the contemporary situation. The current cry for Indian control of their lives and for self-determination is usually given lip service by most "change agents," whose role as "mentor" and "protector" often negates independent indigenous action.

Native Americans do not have an effective lobbying group in Washington. The National Congress of American Indians has not fulfilled this duty since the late 1960s. The white-controlled Association of American Indian Affairs is perhaps the most involved lobbying group at the present time, and its input into federal programs concerning Indians seems considerable. A newly incorporated firm, Indian conceived and operated, the Institute for the Development of Indian Law, Inc., opens an interesting and hopeful avenue for social change based upon the realities of present-day Indian life.

Most Native Americans feel that they have been unbearably researched. A degree of Native control of research appears to be much needed. Many local, state, and federal agencies directly concerned with Indians have seldom consulted the multitudinous research results and existing monographs. Although there is little published material specifically based on urban Indian life-styles, ethnographic monographs on various tribes do have relevance to many groups. Increasingly, as reservations are closed to white researchers, urban Indian populations will undoubtedly be utilized, made possible by the relative powerlessness of Indian groups and the tight control on tribal and urban Indian enclaves by those involved in political chicanery.

Allied to this despairing notion is the belief underlying ethnic relations in the United States. It is a general assumption that Indians must be taught to be leaders. Thus, leadership training workshops, Upward Bound Programs, and other "mainstream propelling" projects abound during the summer months. Little is done to present power politics in a vernacular comprehensible to Native American students and adults (Deloria 1970).

In the area of education for understanding Native people, the weight of explanation and the crossing of cultural barriers are most often placed upon the shoulders of an Indian from any tribe. The reality of cultural diversity is seldom comprehended, for the melting-pot myth is a sacred value of too many white Americans. As a corollary, the "pulling oneself up by the bootstraps" syndrome nullifies any attempt to understand the unique positions of the varieties of Native Americans—both as groups and individuals.

Such militant organizations as the American Indian Movement, which originated in Minneapolis and now has chapters in Denver, Sioux City (Iowa), Rapid City (South Dakota), and Cincinnati, portend to effectuate change and act effectively as support for urban Indians. The Urban Indian Development Association (UIDA) in Los Angeles also promises intelligent, concerted action to improve the lot of Indians in that city. UIDA has recently taken over the housing segment of the BIA Employment Assistance Program (formerly its "relocation program").

Prospects for the Native American

When urban Indian centers and organizations are strengthened by relevant and realistic programs, assured of adequate and constant funding, controlled by competent Indian boards and directors, and truly made up of all segments of the urban Indian "community," the plight of the Indian city-dwellers should improve.

At the present time, a definition of an urban Indian and his rights, and of the clear-cut responsibilities of local, state, and federal agencies, would greatly help in removing this disadvantaged group from the limbo of uncertainty.

It is inevitable that due to the disappearing land base of the reservations (for example, thirty-two thousand acres of Indian land were offered for sale on Standing Rock Reservation in July 1970) Native Americans will remain a part of the larger, worldwide urbanization process. It may be that the situation of this essentially disenfranchised and polarized group cannot be remedied until certain basic policy decisions affecting their life chances are established.

At the present time, a coalition with other pigmented ethnic groups (e.g., Asians, blacks, and Chicanos) seems unrealistic to most Indians. The view that each Indian tribe has of its own uniqueness and historical past also diminishes an effective national organization dealing with urban Indian dilemmas and disasters.

The continuing administered human-relationships aspect of Native life-ways will not greatly improve until the predominantly white or white-oriented bulwark of the many bureaucracies that control the indigenous way of living is circumvented. Dependency has been built into Indian-white relationships, and a symbiotic system still persists. Only when Native Americans have equal access to political power, decision making, and socioeconomic advantages will there be any hope of equality for them in their homeland. Until then, many Native Americans—urban and reservation—are as strangers in their own land.

Notes

1. I wish to thank R. H. Isaacson, acting director, BIA Employment Assistance Office, Alameda, California (personal communication, July 14, 1971), and Joseph E. Trimble (Lakota), social psychologist, Oklahoma City University, who provided the Oklahoma data.

2. The complex nature of the Canadian Native situation is well treated in several references (Dunn 1971; Nagler 1970; Pelletier et al. 1971; Waubageshig 1970).

References

Ablon, J. 1964. "Relocated American Indians in the San Francisco Bay Area." *Human Organization* 23(4): 296–304.

Ames, David W., and Burton R. Fisher. 1959. "The Menominee Termination Crisis: Barriers in the Way of Rapid Cultural Transition." *Human Organization* 18(3): 101–11.

Aurbach, H. A., E. Fuchs, and G. MacGregor. 1970. *The Status of American Indian Education.* University Park: Pennsylvania State University.

Blumenfeld, Ruth. 1965. "Mohawks: Round Trip to the High Steel." *Trans-Action* 3(1): 19–21.

Braroe, Niels W. 1965. "Reciprocal Exploitation in an Indian-White Community." *Southwestern Journal of Anthropology* 21(2): 166–78.

Bureau of Indian Affairs. 1970. *Answers to Your Questions about American Indians.* Washington: Government Printing Office.

Deloria, V., Jr. 1969. *Custer Died for Your Sins.* New York: Macmillan.

———. 1970. *We Talk, You Listen.* New York: Macmillan.

Dobyns, H. F. 1966. "Estimating Aboriginal American Population: An appraisal of Techniques with a New Hemispheric Estimate." *Current Anthropology* 7(4): 395–416.

Dowling, J. H. 1968. "A 'Rural' Indian Community in an Urban Setting." *Human Organization* 27(3): 236–40.

Dozier, E. P. 1970. *The Pueblo Indians of North America.* New York: Holt, Rinehart and Winston.

Dunn, M. 1971. *Red on White: The Biography of Duke Redbird.* Toronto: New Press.

Gold, D. 1967. "Psychological Changes Associated with Acculturation of Saskatchewan Indians." *Journal of Social Psychology* 71(2d half): 177–84.

Hodge, W. H. 1969. *The Albuquerque Navahos.* Tucson: University of Arizona Press.

Howard, J. H. 1955. "The Pan-Indian Culture of Oklahoma." *Scientific Monthly* 81(5): 215–20.

Hurt, W. R., Jr. 1962. "The Urbanization of the Yankton Indians." *Human Organization* 20(4): 226–31.

Kelly, R. E., and J. O. Cramer. 1966. *American Indians in Small Cities: A Survey of Urban Acculturation in Two Northern Arizona Communities.* Flagstaff: Department of Rehabilitation, Northern Arizona University.

Lagasse, J. H. 1959. *A Study of the Population of Indian Ancestry Living in Manitoba.* Vols. 1, 2. Winnipeg: Department of Agriculture and Immigration.

Levine, S., and N. O. Lurie, eds. 1968. *The American Indian Today.* Deland: Everett Edwards.

McNickle, D. A. 1962. *The Indian Tribes of the United States: Ethnic and Cultural Survival.* New York: Oxford University Press.

Medicine, B. 1971. "The Anthropologist and American Indian Studies Programs." *Indian Historian* 4(1): 15–18, 63.

Meriam, L., ed. 1928. *The Problem of Indian Administration: Summary of Findings and Recommendations.* Baltimore: Johns Hopkins University Press.

Nagler, M. 1970. *Indians in the City: A Study of the Urbanization of Indians in Toronto.* Ottawa: Saint Paul University, Canadian Research Center for Anthropology.

Oswalt, W. H. 1966. *This Land Was Theirs: A Study of the North American Indian.* New York: John Wiley.

Pelletier, W., D. G. Poole, J. A. Mackenzie, R. K. Thomas, and F. C. Toombs. 1971. *For Every North American Indian Who Begins to Disappear, I Also Begin to Disappear.* Toronto: Neewin Publishing.

Price, J. A. 1968. "The Migration and Adaptation of American Indians in Los Angeles." *Human Organization* 27(2): 168–75.

Waddel, J. O., and O. M. Watson. 1971. *The American Indian in Urban Society.* Boston: Little, Brown.

Waubageshig (Harvey McCue). 1970. *The Only Good Indian: Essays by Canadian Indians.* Chicago: New Press.

Wax, M. 1971. *Indian Americans: Unity and Diversity.* Englewood Cliffs: Prentice-Hall.

White, R. J. 1970. "The Lower-class 'Culture and Excitement' among Contemporary Sioux." In *The Modern Sioux: Social Systems and Reservation Culture,* ed. Ethel Nurge, 175–97. Lincoln: University of Nebraska Press.

Wissler, C. 1946 [1967]. *Indians of the United States.* Garden City: Doubleday. Revised by Lucy W. Kluckhohn. Garden City: Doubleday.

Oral History as Truth:
Validity in Recent Court Cases
Involving Native Americans

The focus of this essay is upon the use and acceptance of oral traditions in law cases dealing with Native American protest and consequences
based upon treaties. The admission of oral history as statements of veracity
removes such utterances above the level of hearsay evidence, which often clouds
testimony in cases being tried in the American judicial system.

In the murky area of definitional discussions surrounding the field of "eth-
no-history," this aspect fits one of the three categories suggested by William C.
Sturtevant in *Introduction to Cultural Anthropology* (1968:454). The use of traditions, either oral or written, as a primary source for data is important to this
presentation. It is obvious that the Native American tribal bands involved in this
litigation were non-literate at the time of treaty-making. The reliance and evaluation of oral tradition assumes great significance, and the utilization of folk
viewpoints regarding history is salient.

Moreover, a plea for Indian history from Native viewpoints is recognized by
Eleanor Leacock in *North American Indians in Historical Perspective* (1971:14),
who states that faddist counter-culture groups often obscure "the relevant historical fact that out of their particular experience, Indians (as well as other so-
called backward people of the heretofore colonial world) would have an important statement to make." It is the unique perspective of Indian tribes involved
in law cases that allows a reassessment of statements made by Native Americans.

Presenting history from the "Indian point of view" was a directive in the oral
history projects that were handsomely funded by the Doris Duke Foundation
in several institutions (i.e., the Universities of California, Los Angeles; Illinois
at Urbana-Champaign; New Mexico; South Dakota; and Utah, among others).

Besides allowing for a number of theses and dissertations, this funding led to the emergence of white "experts" on Indians, for example, Joseph Cash, and the production of books such as *To Be an Indian* in 1971 (Cash and Hoover, eds. 1971).

Most important, the validity of Indians writing their own historical experiences may be seen in the following histories: *Noon nee me poo (We, the Nez Perces): Culture and History of the Nez Perces* (Slickpoo and Walker 1972); *Nu mee poom tit wah tit (Nez Perce Legends)* (Slickpoo 1973); *The Southern Utes: A Tribal History* (Jefferson, Delaney, and Thompson 1972); and *Ute People: An Historical Study* (Lyman 1970). These publications have raised the concern and critical appraisal of certain non-Native historians who are obviously tied to the use of documents and thus question the methodology of Native writing and interpretation (Washburn 1975:288). This stance might be expected in a literate society, and the aforementioned tribal histories are courageous and much-needed attempts to provide alternative analyses of events that have direct influences on the life-styles and life chances of Natives in North America.

The fact is, indigenous cultures of North America and elsewhere have had, as part of their heritages, strong emphases on oral history and traditions. These have persisted despite strong efforts directed toward acculturation to the dominant society via educational endeavors and language and religious suppression.

A newer interpretation of this emphasis is seen in Nancy Lurie's writing: "Without denying the contributory influences of the reservation system, racism, and educational and material deprivation, I believe that the fundamental reasons for articulation lie in the essential differences in white and Indian traditions and in the historical conditions of contact" (1971:421). Although Lurie is undoubtedly coalescing certain tendencies of articulation that might lead to action, there is no denying that oratory and oral history have always been factors in the traditions of the Native American tribes. Both Lurie in *North American Indians in Historical Perspective* and Sturtevant in *Introduction to Cultural Anthropology* appear anticipatory in their analyses of the use of historical tradition in the adaptive strategies of Native Americans.

The use of oral history seems to have assumed a new directive in its utilization since the beginning of the Indian land claims.

Anthropologists have had a long and continued involvement in legal cases centering upon the Indian Claims Commission Act of 1946. In response to a paper regarding this issue, Ken Martin (Assiniboine) makes a strong statement regarding oral history: "There are many, many qualified and literate Indian people and why do we have a discipline (Anthropology) in our educational system in this country defining what we mean as Indian people? Why can't the government understand that we can talk? We can tell them how it is, based on our oral history, based on our traditions. We can tell where we were. Our people know where we came from. We should not have to depend on another segment of Society to tell us where we lived" (1973:51).

Many such statements are often dismissed as subjective, ethnocentric, and unscientific. Therefore, it is refreshing to read this excerpt from Leopold Pospisil, for the reference is to Plains tribes where chieftainships were critical:

> In the anthropological literature, the formal tribal authority is usually called *chief*. Because of the publicity and explicitness of his decision-making activity, his role and function are well remembered and may be accurately resurrected by a skilled anthropologist from old informants' memories. The quality of formality is the reason that the accounts of Cheyenne and Comanche Indians are so accurate and specific and therefore so valuable. In contrast, the accounts of the informal and later "pacified" and supposedly leaderless and lawless tribal bands are frustratingly inadequate and disappointing. (1978:20)

Pospisil is commenting on *The Cheyenne Way* by Karl Llewellyn and Adamson Hoebel (1941), which is a landmark study of "primitive law." Further, Pospisil comments that these persons—a lawyer and an anthropologist—formulated law by examining explicit rules that pertained to the content of legal codes. In the case of the Cheyenne, these were well remembered. Thus, a model for casuistic discussions of nonliterate societies was well established in anthropology.

It is, therefore, in the arena of action that the historical precedents have relevance. More specifically, the "take-over" and occupancy of Wounded Knee hamlet on the Pine Ridge (Oglala Sioux) Reservation, South Dakota, by members of the American Indian Movement (AIM) in spring 1973 precipitated the court action now under consideration.

The legal action known as the "Consolidated Wounded Knee Cases" was intended to dismiss charges against those persons involved under the rubric of "non-leadership" categories. The motion to dismiss was based upon the lack of jurisdiction under the Sioux Nation–United States Treaty of April 29, 1868 (the Fort Laramie Treaty). Evidence was presented before and heard by District Judge Warren K. Urbom of the Eighth Circuit Court of the United States in Lincoln, Nebraska, from December 16, 1974, until January 2, 1975. Lawyers for the appellants were John E. Thorne and Vine Deloria, Jr.

The main interpretation was based upon the 1868 Treaty and what those Lakota (Western Teton division) who signed this treaty comprehended the context of that agreement to be at that time. It was in this context that the aspects of oral history and its verbal transmission assumed great importance. Approximately thirty-eight Native Americans of Siouan heritage testified regarding their history, which they had obtained via verbal communication in their socialization processes as Lakota people. Many of the Lakota had ancestors who actually had placed X's (their marks) on the treaty agreement. Many of the Lakota elders spoke in their native tongue for greater accuracy and ease of expression. At his request, I translated the statements made in Lakota by Paul High Bear into English.

Surprisingly, two of the forty Native Americans who were of Siouan ancestry evolved as expert witnesses (Jacobs 1975:598). The four expert witnesses of
Native American descent were Vine Deloria, Jr. (Sioux), Kirke Kickingbird (Kiowa), Roxanne Dunbar (Cheyenne-Nez Percé), and I (a Sioux).

A quotation from the legal brief indicates the significance of this law case: "As
previously stated, this is the first time such evidence has ever been presented in
a Court, and it stands undisputed, the single government witness agreeing with
the evidence, and the government itself having stated in chambers that its own
investigation revealed that oral history as given was accurate" (Throne and
Deloria n.d.:3). Thus, the oral testimony regarding their tribal history by these
Native Americans was accepted, and it "stands undisputed and established that
the Lakota who signed the 1868 Treaty understood the agreement to be that on
their homeland, the Sioux retained full criminal jurisdiction over anyone com-
mitting any alleged crime within their homeland established under the Treaty"
(Thorne and Deloria n.d.:7). Further, Thorne and Deloria state:

> No witnesses were produced by the government to dispute the aforementioned
> oral history. No witnesses who were members of any Indian Nation or tribe,

Wešlekapi Teca ©1998 by
Ted Garner (oiled maple and
cherry; 23 by 11 by 3 inches).
(Courtesy of Ted Garner)

let alone the Sioux, were called by the government, their one witness being an historian, Mr. Joseph Cash. He testified that if an oral history was passed down by the whites, he would expect the oral history of the Lakota to be more accurate. . . . Interestingly, this witness also testified that he had seen and looked at a nonexistent history book and author, and identified yet another nonexistent history book and author as one he had not read. (8)

In addition, in the same legal brief, Wilbur Jacobs indicated that if both an oral and a written history existed centering on the 1868 Treaty, the oral history would be more precise if there was a variation between it and the written version. He writes, "Again and again the relevant Indian oral history added a new dimension to legal deliberations" (1975:596). Therefore, by presenting this data, it must be concluded that the oral history accounts of Native Americans have established a precedent in legal cases.

References

Cash, Joseph H., and Herbert T. Hoover, eds. 1971. *To Be an Indian: An Oral History.* New York: Holt, Rinehart and Winston.

Jacobs, Wilbur R. 1975. "Native American History: How It Illuminates Our Past." *American Historical Review* 80: 598.

Jefferson, James, Robert W. Delaney, and Gregory C. Thompson. 1972. *The Southern Utes: A Tribal History,* ed. Floyd O'Neill. Ignacio, Utah: Southern Ute Tribe.

Leacock, Eleanor B. 1971. "Introduction." In *North American Indians in Historical Perspective,* ed. Eleanor Burke Leacock and Nancy O. Lurie. New York: Random House.

Llewellyn, Karl N., and E. Adamson Hoebel. 1941. *The Cheyenne Way: Conflict and Case Law in Primitive Jurisprudence.* Norman: University of Oklahoma Press.

Lurie, Nancy O. 1971. "The Contemporary American Indian Scene." In *North American Indians in Historical Perspective,* ed. Eleanor Burke Leacock and Nancy O. Lurie. New York: Random House.

Lyman, June. 1970. *Ute People: An Historical Study.* Salt Lake City: Unitah School District and the Western History Center, University of Utah.

Martin, Ken. 1973. "Response." In Symposium on Anthropology and the American Indian, *A Report.* San Francisco: Indian Historian Press.

Pospisil, Leopold. 1978. *The Ethnology of Law.* Menlo Park, Calif.: Cummings, 1978.

Slickpoo, Allen P., Sr. 1973. *Nu mee poom tit wah tit (Nez Perce Legends).* (Lapwai, Idaho: Nez Perce Tribe of Idaho.

Slickpoo, Allen P., Sr., and Deward E Walker, Jr. 1972. *Noon nee me poo (We, the Nez Perces): Culture and History of the Nez Perces.* Lapwai, Idaho: Nez Perce Tribe of Idaho, 1972.

Sturtevant, William C. 1968. "Anthropology, History, and Ethnohistory." In *Introduction to Cultural Anthropology: Essays in the Scope and Methods of the Science of Man,* ed. James A. Clifton. Boston: Houghton Mifflin.

Throne, John E., and Vine Deloria, Jr. 1974. "Appellants' Opening Brief in the United States Court of Appeals for the Eighth Circuit." *United States vs. Consolidated Wounded Knee Cases* (389 F Supp 235).

Washburn, Wilcomb E. 1975. *The Indian in America.* New York: Harper and Row.

CHAPTER 29

Finders Keepers

There are many dangers inherent in a discussion of the role and function of museums, the place of artifact and "artifake," and the ethics and ethos of museum personnel, for there are as many divergent views as there are contemporary Native American individuals, tribes, and related organizations. The orientation toward allowing various ethnic groups to voice their concerns seems important at this time, a challenge born out of current concessions to cultural pluralism, factors of self-determination, community control of schools, and the cybernetic effect of ethnic studies in higher education.

I do not wish to speak authoritatively for *all* Native Americans, for we have many "experts on Indians" to do this. This essay is an effort to coalesce various articulations that have been made by Native Americans regarding museums. The following compilation of sentiments and resolutions seems necessary in order to establish a link for understanding Native viewpoints.

Divergent Individual, Group, and Organizational Views

Myriad images abound about the functions of gatherers of facts (historians, anthropologists, archaeologists) and gatherers of objects (museum workers, collectors, primitive art buffs) from the experiences that Native Americans have had with them. The basis of interaction between these gatherers and Native people includes coercion to trade items such as basketry for food, pressure to sell personal items such as amulets and sacred tribal items (wampum belts, medicine bundles, and holy pipes), or statements such as, "We would like to write the history of your people so your grandchildren will know about their culture." Many of us recall experiences within our kin groups when family heirlooms were sold to provide food for our families. In other instances, Native Americans may be engaged in selling cultural items that have been stolen from other tribal members or dug from ancestral graves. Thus, the individual Native American's experiential stance is extremely variable, idiosyncratic, and difficult to generalize.

The intention of museums as seen by Native communities (a term that seems to achieve more relevance in contemporary Indian life) also seems to reflect divergencies. Many community views are diffuse, reflecting tribal council, conservative, progressive, and other indigenous factors. In addition, there are statements by many white-dominated organizations involved with Indian affairs and the welfare of Native people (for example, the Indian Arts and Crafts Board aligned with the Bureau of Indian Affairs). However, this group has not, to my knowledge, issued a statement on their perception of museums and their collections with respect to tribes and communities. And there are also non-reservation communities and urban groups that are becoming more assertive.

What Are the Official Views?

Contact was made with the influential National Congress of American Indians (NCAI) this fall [1973] to obtain a statement based on resolutions that represent a consensus of its views. Unfortunately, the effort met with no response from the new NCAI officials. However, in November 1972 the National Indian Education Association (NIEA) met and heard the following resolution:

> WHEREAS, the Northwest Indian Education Conference Committee recognizes that social science and educational researchers have not developed a stringent code of ethics and guidelines governing their collection and use of material gathered from Indian people and Alaskan natives,
>
> NOW THEREFORE BE IT RESOLVED, that the professional organizations whose members conduct such research should develop guidelines pertaining to the collection and use of materials in relation to:
>
> 1. Questions of ownership of materials,
> 2. Compensation for time and materials,
> 3. Training of Native Language specialists, with relevant social science and language art skills,
> 4. Reproduction and publication rights.
>
> BE IT FURTHER RESOLVED, that tribes determine what subjects are to be researched and that researchers be accountable and comply to the needs assessments of such tribes.

The resolution was adopted unanimously by the NIEA. This significant and cogent statement is purposefully generalized to extend to all aspects of research collections among Indian groups. Of importance is its base in a local group (the

Makah Tribal Council) and in a regional organization and acceptance by a national intertribal body.

At another level of pan-tribal interaction, a resolution presented by the steering committee of the first Indian Ecumenical Conference (held at Crow Agency, Montana, in August 1970) reads:

> BE IT RESOLVED: The Convention go on record as opposing the indiscriminate desecration of our historic and religious monuments, our burial grounds, our pictographs, etc., by such outside institutions as universities, park service, the Army Corps of Engineers, Highway Departments, etc. We would strongly recommend that the Indian religious leaders of the tribes involved be consulted before any excavations of these sacred places take place.
>
> Further, that the sacred relics which are now in museums and which were collected by quasi-legal and immoral methods be returned on request to the tribe involved. Moreover, those sacred relics acquired legitimately by museums should be on loan for such periods as they are needed by Indian tribes. Further, museums should hire Indians qualified to care for such sacred objects now in their possession.

Reaffirmation of all the resolutions passed at this conference was expressed at the second meeting in Alberta, Canada. The second resolution indicates that no response was made by the agencies mentioned in the 1970 resolution, thus it directs the steering committee to seek legal aid in implementing the above statement.

Views in Print

Other possible indications of Native sentiment may be found in publications written by Native Americans (table 29.1). *Indian Voices* (Scholder 1970:206) made specific reference to museums. One unidentified speaker noted that many museums "take 20 percent off the top" of the purchase price of articles made by craftspeople.

In the same publication, Buffy Sainte-Marie stated, "I think eventually we should consider the role of the museums in Indian arts, because I don't think except for a few exceptions, the museums have title to most of what they have. Not that I am against them displaying certain objects and things, but I think that eventually we should, as Indians and as artists, make a claim on things that really don't belong to the museums" (216). This statement was amplified by Jeanette Henry (1970:17). Responding to the Committee on Anthropological Research in Museums (CARM), Henry describes museums as "those mausoleums of various and sundry collections of what is known as 'artifacts,' or 'evidences of ancient cultures.' There is gross hoarding of artifacts and art materials in the great museums. In many, many cases, our most priceless pieces of

Table 29.1. Museum-Native Group Discord

Museum or Institution Involved	Native Group Involved	Rationale for Protest or Discontent	Resulting Action or Statement by Museum Personnel
A. University			
Anthropology lab	American Indian Movement (AIM) local urban chapter	Return "remains and possessions to our people to be put back in to Sacred Mother Earth"	Dean suggests AIM take action if it thinks University has its property
Geology	Native American Student Association	Return remains of Indian woman on display	Bones returned and reburied on reservation with tribal elder officiating
Archaeology	Tribal group from urban Indian center	"Diggings are wrong" "Start studying yourself"	To stop would "set a precedent" re study in U.S.
B. City			
Natural history	Native group led by native lecturer	"Violation of sacred burial grounds; racist display"	Reburial on Indian land; give-away and rites paid for by museum
C. Governmental			
Provincial[a]	Native educator speaks	Museums "are not good places if they take things . . . needed by peoples . . . to rediscover who they were, and who they will become"	None reported
Military	Uncertain in report	"Nature of display of braids of 'Wandering Spirit'"	"Responsibility of museum to preserve and conserve all artifacts"
County historical			
I.	AIM chapter	"It is wrong to put the bones of Indians on public display"	Bones have significant educational value— "clues to early Indian culture "
II.	Tribal group	Return of chief's remains; asks for supportive letters	None reported
III.	Local Indians do not wish involvement	Complaints from visitors regarding display of Fox chief	Curator "change in social patterns"; reburial planned

a. Canadian.

antiquity are ill-cared-for, hidden in steel caskets, treated like mummified objects of savagery." After discussing treatment of antiquities at various famous museums and stating that "concerned museum directors" ask what will become of these items, she concludes:

> A simple answer is to share these objects with native tribes and groups which have a moral right to them, to help them create living museums of their own. We who are the LIVING descendants of native American culture say with utmost sincerity: We want your help to reconstitute our own culture, to reconstruct, in the best sense, our true history. We want the true story of our people known. We who are Indian scholars, Native historians, traditional speakers, medicine men, diagnosticians . . . we are the best interpreters of our people. Certainly there are some frauds and ignoramuses among us. But if you are intelligent, as it is generally believed, the sheep would not be difficult to separate from the wolves.

Beyond Words to Activism

But what of the numerous confrontations by Native Americans with museums across the land? To assess their impact, I examined *Akwesasne Notes* from last year. This publication was possibly the most influential and comprehensive newspaper of its kind at the time because it pertained to Native people in both the United States and Canada. *Akwesasne Notes* reaches reservation, non-reservation, and urban enclaves and is extremely popular in colleges and universities. It also has direct influence by providing news to Natives in prison (the input is evident in the letters to the publication's editor).

An examination of the chart printed in this article [table 29.1] gives evidence of reported actions in *Notes* and indicates that the greatest activity is directed toward the recovery and reburial of Indian skeletal remains displayed in various museums. (Most often, the Native groups involved tend to be militant, urban, and university-based.) If more data were available, the rationale for this activism (which began in the late 1960s) would focus on the burial of bones back into the Sacred Mother Earth. As is evident from the chart, the response from administrators of museums has ranged from none to going beyond the demands of the dissidents.

Another interesting trend noted in the late winter 1972 edition of *Notes* is the emergence of Indian-operated museums, in this case the Six Nations Indian Museum in Onchiota, New York. This move is coupled with the revival of older craft techniques and the establishment of arts and crafts shops. Increased Native American sophistication in utilizing legal avenues in their relationships with institutions, "cultural enrichment" programs on many reservations, and community-controlled institutions offers new dimensions for consideration by museum personnel.

An inscription located inside the new, Indian-operated Arapahoe Culture

Museum in Ethete, Wyoming, describes, I believe, the sentiments and beliefs of most Natives throughout America: "They tried to rub out our old beliefs, our way of life. They put us in jail if we did our ceremonies. They burned our medicine bundles, threw our pipes into the fire. Many of our sacred things were lost forever. It's coming back now. They took everything from us, but as long as we still have our Pipe, our drums, our songs, our language, our old faith, we will remain Arapaho."

References

Akwesasne Notes. 1971–72. Early and late autumn. Rooseveltown, N.Y.: Cornwell Island Reserve.

Henry, Jeanette. 1970. "A Rebuttal to the Five Anthropologists on the Issue of Wampum Return." *Indian Historian* 3(2): 15–17.

Sainte-Marie, Buffy. 1970. Response to Fritz Scholder, "Native Arts in America." In First Convocation of American Indian Scholars, *Indian Voices.* San Francisco: Indian Historian Press.

Scholder, Fritz. 1970. "Native Arts in America." In First Convocation of American Indian Scholars, *Indian Voices,* 191–218. San Francisco: Indian Historian Press.

CHAPTER 30

American Indians and Anthropologists: Issues of History, Empowerment, and Application

Mitakuyepi oyasin chante waste ya nape chiyusa pe.[1] This Lakota greeting is heard at the beginning of each speech in any community gathering on the Standing Rock Reservation. I translate: "All my kinpersons with a good heart, I shake your hand." This salutation contains anthropological concepts: kinship; holism of a circle, which is basic to Lakota ethos; rapport; and, in some cases, friendship with all. This utterance has sustained me both in my life as a Lakota woman and as an anthropologist in the often hostile worlds of graduate school and departments of anthropology.

I thank you for honoring me with the Malinowski Award. But I, too, have read his journals! This has been troublesome for me. However, at my age, the thought of what may happen to my field notes and correspondence poses problems that we all must consider at some time.

I have written about my experiences in "Learning to be an Anthropologist and Remaining 'Native'" (Medicine 1978). This was published before the age of reflexivity and the "othering" of indigenous people. Writing in such a personal manner was an effort to honor my first professor of anthropology, Solon T. Kimball, who taught me the value of applying anthropological analyses to everyday life. This has been a directive for me.

I have chosen to discuss the interface of American Indians and anthropologists—not in the disparaging manner of writers as Vine Deloria in his book *Custer Died for Your Sins* (1969) and the more recent book *Red Earth, White Lies* (1996). To assess the thrust of anthropologists into the lives of American Indians and Alaska Natives seems necessary at this time. After all, as applied anthropologists and as change agents, this is what we do. I prefer not to use "Native American," for it is too fraught with inclusivity. In the world of government

ABOVE: Ground-breaking for the new Wakpala, South Dakota, Public School, August 2000. Left to right: Susan Smith, Ron Brownotter, Vern Iron Cloud, Robert Tiger, Milo Cadotte, Pat Hawk, and Beatrice Medicine, a member of the school board. (Courtesy of Robert Tiger)

LEFT: March 2000. (Courtesy of Charlie Soap)

agencies for funding purposes, this term includes Native Hawaiians and Pacific Islanders. I use the labeling accepted by the advocacy group, the National Congress of American Indians, which is American Indian and Alaska Native.

Most Natives prefer a linguistically appropriate name for themselves, as Lakota for Sioux, or Anishinabe for Chippewa, and so on. Further, in university settings, students often checked the "Native American" category, indicating "I was born here, so I am Native American." Moreover, now that affirmative action is so contentious, perhaps fewer faculty will claim indigenous North American heritage. Many have done so to meet quota requests. The use of perduring terms—such as Lakota—may be disarming to anthropologists and others, but it is indicative of enhanced efforts at self-determination for indigenous nations. Moreover, the idea of nationhood is basic to anti-Indian "red-neck" groups in "Indian Country." This current backlash and issues of repatriation and intellectual property rights may be an added burden to research. Surely, for "anthropological adoptee," which complicates our kinship structures, adoption is not so lauded by "anthros" these days. Labeling is still a significant feature in contemporary Native communities and the cause of much ire among Indians. That is evidenced by the names of sports teams—which is now a legal issue.

Perhaps it may be of interest to note that, at last count, there were eighty-six "Native" anthropologists with advanced degrees in the discipline. Dr. Jo Allyn Archambault, a Lakota anthropologist at the Smithsonian Institution and also from Standing Rock, continues the work we began in the little-read publication *The Minority Experience in Anthropology* (1973). Such applied anthropologists as Delmos Jones, Tom Weaver, Jim Gibbs, and others began this venture of assessing minority input into the discipline. Unfortunately, the Project Committee of Anthropologists in Primarily Minority Institutions (CAPMI), which placed retired professors in primarily minority institutions and was begun in the AAA while "Skip" Rappaport was president, has not continued. Subsequent presidents showed no interest in this venture. Certainly, tribally controlled colleges would benefit from being introduced to cross-cultural experiences that might circumvent the tribal ethnocentrism that seems to be increasing along with homophobia as HIV-AIDS rates rise in Native communities.

The disenchantment with anthropology as a discipline and the anthropologist as "officious meddler" is still a part of the fabric of research in reservation and urban communities. This disdain may increase as issues of repatriation and intellectual property rights escalate—for example, Kennewick Man.

The history of applied anthropology in "Native" U.S. and "aboriginal" Canadian contexts should be updated. The need to examine our "imperialistic" navels seems propitious. Perhaps the residue of previous applied programs has not been as efficacious as we thought. I feel, however, that we have learned a great deal by early experiments. Because the theme of this conference [in 1996] is globalization, I call attention to a video that we, a Lithuanian colleague and I, made in Russia. We call it *Seeking the Spirit—"Plains Indians" in Russia*. This Slavic version of a powwow features tipis, feathers, and Plains Indian music and dance. The phenomenon is widespread in Europe and indicates the tenaciousness of *the* Indian image and determined cultural appropriation.

Because I come from a culture in which the spoken word and oral history are the mainstays of cultural continuity, perhaps my written speech might be more concretized with anthropological jargon. This "anthro speak" has been a challenge to me in interpreting research results to Native people in North America, Australia, and New Zealand. There, aboriginal people look to North American Natives in an interaction that begs for research in a globalization based upon common colonialist histories.

As some of you know, I dropped my membership in this society [the Society for Applied Anthropology], for I did not find much useful published data on *"us."* I do not, however, recommend dropping your membership to get an award! I am encouraged by what seems a new commitment to American Indian and Alaskan Native and Canadian aboriginal issues. It seems a conscious effort of such scholars as Tony Paredes, Murray Wax, Don Stull, Sally Robinson, and others that a new Committee on Indian Concerns has been formed in this association. I am sorry to have missed the formative meetings. I was stuck in a snowbank west of Mission, South Dakota, on my way here [Baltimore]. Interacting in a "home/community" culture and in anthropology may underlay constant segmentalization of dual lives that may be the lot of "anthros of color." It has been a survival strategy for me. In my time, doctoral degrees were seen as alienating from our societies.

But referring to the historic record—printed, that is—we find that Vine Deloria's (1969) diatribe against the "tribe" of anthropologists caused some to no longer refer to us as *"my"* Indians. Some no longer flaunted their "adoption" by "their Indian family." However, some of us "Native" anthropologists were put in a triple bind—other than being Native and an anthropologist—the third being the diverse cultures of "Indian Country" and the question "who speaks for the Indians?" The new posture of defending our discipline and livelihood seemed a "white burden" to me. It was not too comforting when Vine Deloria, Sr., said, "When Vine wrote that book, he was not talking about you or Aunt Ella. He meant other anthropologists." He was referring to his sister, Ella Deloria, a Boasian linguist informant/collaborator who produced the elegant *Dakota Grammar* (1941). Her novel *Waterlily* is now used as ethnographic text in Native literature and women's studies courses. She, in 1969, did not want me to read it. "It's not an ethnography," she said. "It is only a novel."

Appraisals of indigenous women are revealing. Kamala Visweswaran, writes: "Many works, including Zora Neal Hurston's *Tell My Horse* (1938), which explores cross-cultural experiences of womanhood in the United States and Caribbean, or Ella Deloria's *Waterlily* (1988), a novel about coming into womanhood in the Dakota Sioux society, reveal the use of a form of gender standpoint to explore the impact of race upon the authors and those they write about, but disturb the coherence of identification between author, subject and reader by generating multiple positionings in their texts" (1997:604). This is the type of anthropological analysis many indigenous women distrust, especially after their death. Ella Deloria was writing in the "ethnographic present." She wrote ethnography!

I mention Ella Deloria, for she came from a generation of "informants"— now soothingly called "consultants"—who added much fine material in the early years of collecting data from the "vanishing North American Indians." Now, many anthropologists may say, "Who reads ethnography?" or decline offers of books by retired anthropologists. I was surprised by *no* response when I offered my books to Standing Rock College, now called Sitting Bull College.

Some books, such as Joseph Casagrande's *In the Company of Man: Twenty Portraits by Anthropologists* (1960), produced sketches of Natives in the genre of "my favorite informant." The sketches are revealing of the interface of both and would be interesting contrastive data with the more reflexive works of today. This book includes an interesting contribution by Nancy Lurie. Her work with the Winnebago provides, in my view, a good model of anthropological involvement with Native groups.

Kimball and Watson's edited book *Crossing Cultural Boundaries* (1972) is also significant in the similar history of anthropology approach. The frankness of these works possibly heralds the current rage of reflexive texts and the baring of anthropological souls. It is unfortunate that more contemporary Native anthropologists such as Edward P. Dozier, the respected Santa Clara Pueblo anthropologist, have not left impressions on the discipline.

Dozier, in true understanding of Lakota culture, acted as a protecting "cousin" in my graduate work in New Mexico. Kimball worked in the Collier administration (the New Deal for Indians). Both were well aware of the work of D'Arcy McNickle in the Bureau of Indian Affairs (BIA) and in the Society for Applied Anthropology, plus his establishment of the National Congress of American Indians as the leading tribal advocacy group, which persists to the present day. It was Native intellectuals such as McNickle and Dozier who initially supported Indian concerns in this association. It seems to me that this tradition of concern in the association has not persisted in the applied field by indigenous anthropologists. Taking stock of this direction might be revealing.

Some anthropology programs have included Native participants. In 1973 the annual "tribal rites" of the American Anthropological Association featured a symposium on "Anthropology and the American Indian," which subsequently was published in 1974 by the now-defunct Indian Historian Press. It included such persons as Al Ortiz, Roger Buffalohead, Ken Martin, me, and the adversarial Vine Deloria, Jr. The house was packed. This symposium might be viewed as a nod in the direction of ethnic studies, which grew out of the 1960s' protests and housed many American Indian programs. The most memorable event, however, was the "take-over" of the AAA executive suite for an evening party.

From that period, the contributions of "people of color"—the then-trendy term used to include all minorities—have not been a strong feature in a sociology of knowledge in approaching our discipline, especially in the applied field. For example, there is an American Indian/Alaska Native Professors' Association that meets yearly and has more than a thousand aspiring-for-tenure, tenured, and retired members. The membership includes faculty from the nineteen tribally controlled colleges in the U.S. and Canada and encompasses all disciplines. This association meets the needs of the diverse cultural base of the members and presents a more egalitarian and supportive atmosphere than do their individual academic associations.

Many Native professionals castigate anthropologists but use the products of their research in classes. But the image of Vine Deloria's portrayal still is relevant to many. Because the 1980 U.S. Census contained a "self-ascribed" category for Native identification, many persons—black and white—claimed Indian ancestry. Of course, all had a "Cherokee princess" for a grandmother, as Vine Deloria said in 1969! This latter group, called "wannabes" (among other terms), played havoc with affirmative action policies and admissions standards in institutions of higher education, especially in California. They seemed to be an incipient "elite" group.

Often the latter were either products of an urban experience or of such universities as Harvard or Stanford, which were seen as more prestigious than the state universities that many of us attended. Subsequent research has indicated that growing numbers of Native professionals are rising from the ranks of bureaucrats—from those Indians employed in the Bureau of Indian Affairs, the Indian Health Service, and other government agencies. More recently, children of this new professional class are crowding elite prep schools in the East. Other "elites" are newly emerged Indians. Self-ascription in the next census will also be significant. Many "emergent Indians" may be seen as "amateur Indians." Self-serving enters here. Indian identification almost guarantees the funding of proposals—usually written by white persons in an "equity" apportionment.

Some Native people indicate that one must almost become an "amateur anthropologist" to maintain the cultural integrity of indigenous life-styles and knowledge about their history and events. This need is based upon colonialist teachings and education away from their cultures. In the present revitalization of belief systems and traditional rituals, many "traditionalists" have consulted early Bureau of American Ethnology (BAE) reports. With such groups as the ailing American Indian Movement (AIM), the rhetoric against anthropologists has been chronic and rabid. Venom especially centers upon archaeological excavations, burial remains, and sacred object removal. Repatriation offices have been established in many reservation bureaucracies and, as long as funding is available, supply much-needed jobs. This area, plus gaming, needs investigation. Generally, I think that there is little knowledge of what an applied anthropologist does. People seem to expect advocacy from any anthropologist.

Therefore, when attempting to confront disaffection with our work, one must be fully cognizant of where this discontent originates. One must consider the whole—and wide—range of Native social groupings. As the federal recognition section of the BIA indicates, there are more Native groups clamoring for federal recognition (American Indian Policy Review Commission 1977–78). This section of the BIA has also been a source of employment for anthropologists as well as historians who do research and testify for these forgotten groups and enduring enclaves of Native people. This direction is often seen as detrimental to reservation (or treaty) Indians, for it is believed that a potential abuse may ensue—that is, "more Indians, less funds."

This new endeavor is reminiscent of the Indian Claims Commission of the 1950s, which pitted anthropologists against each other in court cases. As always, federal Indian policy decisions have historically provided work for anthropologists and historians, yet it seems clear that such labor is not seen as applied by many of these researchers. The new enterprise of federal recognition poses new perspectives on "who is an Indian?" Many of these emerging groups are often racially mixed. Some have clearly African American characteristics and minimize cultural ways, such as language, expressive elements of culture-rituals, ceremonies, music, and dance. Others exhibit Euro-American characteristics and also lack cultural manifestations of "Indian-ness." These social indices often lead to growing tribal ethnocentrism in many reservations. In tandem with a growing exclusion of "urban Indians" seen on many reservations, this is a factor in the distrust of multiculturalism in some areas. Serving as "consultants" to such a wide range of Native groups has implications for what our function as applied anthropologists might be. This will color our perceptions of "advocacy" versus livelihood in an era of academic entrenchment and the realistic training of our students.

Of the million Native population in the United States, 63 percent are urbanized or off-reservation in border towns contiguous to reservations. This fact is important for applied research. Given that attitudes of reservation residents are often unsympathetic to urban groups, the needs of urban kin are overlooked, and urban adjustment often includes homelessness and resentment when city residents return home. After a preponderance of the "culture of poverty" and urban migrant studies in the 1960s, this aspect of contemporary Native life is now neglected. It seems that studies of physical disabilities, HIV-AIDS, and diabetes research are evident, just as alcoholism studies predominated in the 1960s. The effects of alcoholism are seen in Fetal Alcohol Syndrome/Fetal Alcohol Effects research.

Often, it is implicit that our research "empowers" people. To me, empowering people—especially "people of color"—means teaching and researching issues of race, class, gender, and power relations in ways that can be understood and utilized by "target populations." Moreover, as applied anthropologists, we should do more participatory research and not use Native people as consultants but as co-directors of research projects. Thus, they can learn research techniques and initiate and implement their own "needs assessments" and application strategies to improve the quality of life in their own communities.

The generations-old complaints by Native people still ring true: "We never see the books or paper you write about us," or, "Are you writing a book about us to make a lot of money?" I wish the latter was true for all of us—red, white, or black. My meager royalties go to the Ella Deloria Scholarship for Indian Women in South Dakota.

Native expectation is that the finished product will be at least shown to them. This expectation is the source of the greatest disaffection in Native groups. The question is, How many people on the reservations or in the urban enclaves read these reports? How are these reports incorporated into improving the quality of life on the local level, where the manifestations of the ever-invoked litany of Native dysfunctions form the basis of daily life? But many anthropologists have not had the opportunity to know or attempt to know if their reports have been read or utilized by Native people.

I note, however, that more book reviews are being written by Native people and appear more frequently in the literature. This may be the result of such publications as *The American Indian Culture and Research Journal,* published at UCLA, or the Indian studies journal *Wicazo Sa,* published at the University of Minnesota. Both are edited by Indian persons. Some of us have insisted that books be reviewed by those groups who have been the target of investigations. I quote from one review of Marla K. Powers's book *Oglala Women: Myth, Ritual, and Reality* (1986). The Lakota writer Debra White Plume ends an astute evaluation with this statement: "The author courageously attempts to get the buffalo, but all she has gotten is the fly on the buffalo's back" (Mack and White Plume 1988:78). Perhaps we as anthropologists should prepare ourselves for more critical evaluations of our work and think of ways of integrating criticism into our future work.

The impact of ethnographic and anthropological writings upon contemporary revitalization of Native belief systems begs for investigation, as does contemporary socialization, clarification of "Indian values," and cultural transmission in reservation and urban communities. The results of medical anthropological and applied programs in alcohol prevention are needed to assess the utilization of Native curing modalities in alcohol treatment programs based upon Native traditions, although this is occurring in many places. In some reservations, residents know the treaties upon which their sovereignty is based. This interest is heightened by the "backlash" occurring in non-Native communities. Anti-Indian associations are forming in many places. Many of these present the worst racist attitudes of people surrounding the reservations.

Environmental impact statements and needs assessments in preparation for grant-writing are happening. However, studies of communities in these circumstances are not forthcoming. Many Indian people feel that comprehension of these aspects of contemporary life is basic to their survival as distinct cultural groups. I have noted that the more "traditional" groups (whatever the term *traditional* means in today's Indian world) tend to be more tolerant, helpful, and intellectually interested in our tasks and results.

Some of my best insights into what we might label "ethno-histories" or "ethno-methodologies" have originated from hunches that my kin and friends have offered me. In my community, upon our return visits we were expected to give summaries of our activities in research or teaching. This is a tradition of long standing. My mother and her cousins were expected to make reports. One of my aunts was to do this. She apparently stood for ten minutes in silence. Then she said, "Henala epikte" (that is all I'm going to say). She had obviously been translating English into Lakota—but silently. Amid peals of laughter, the "herald" said, "Lela pila oyampe" (you have honored us). Obtaining indigenous critique from my elderly kin is still important to me. I read my writings to them. These ideas, perhaps, could be more fully acknowledged in our writings.

Recently, reflexivity (and I do not mean postmodern nonsense) has occurred in some sections of our discipline. Perhaps feminist perspectives have also had some influence. The National Association for the Practice of Anthropology and the journal *Practicing Anthropology* indicate more usable treatises for the subaltern population. The SfAA [Society for Applied Anthropology], I note, has a group to create an "institutional history." I sincerely hope that "herstory" and the impact of indigenous people as research constituencies are included in such a compilation. In closing, I quote from Irving Hallowell, an anthropologist whom I greatly admired in my graduate training:

> Finally, it seems to me that among these more recent influences, the impact of the Indian on modern anthropology should not be omitted. The social sciences as they have developed in the United States during the past half-century have attained an unusual prominence in American culture. Among these[,] anthropology in its modern form was just getting underway about the time the frontier closed. It was in the 1890s that Franz Boas began to teach at Columbia University and to train students in fieldwork. Boas was a specialist in studies of the American Indian and a majority of his early students followed in his footsteps. Indeed, practically all the chief authorities on North American Indian ethnology, archaeology, and linguistics have been American. A historical accident? Of course, but that is the point. It is only recently among the younger generation that more attention is being devoted to people in the South Seas, Africa, and Asia. But it was the study of the Indians, and the problems that emerged from the investigation of the Indian as a subject, that gave American anthropology a distinctive coloring as compared with British, French, and German anthropology. (1957:254–55)

I have tried, in my academic career, to respect the insights of my anthropological elders. Thus, I am hopeful that the charming and fascinating accounts of our own applied anthropologists—via the President's Advisory Council—may produce a lively and useful history of the Society for Applied Anthropology.

Note

1. *Note at the beginning of the original essay:* This article—originally presented as the Bronislaw Malinowki Award lecture at the 1996 SfAA annual meeting in Baltimore—attempts to describe relations between anthropologists and Natives of North America. Tensions and directions of research concerning these indigenous people are outlined. This is a strictly individual appraisal with suggested research possibilities.

References

American Indian Policy Review Commission. 1977–78. *Meetings of the American Indian Policy Review Commission.* Washington: Government Printing Office.

Boas, Franz, and Ella Deloria. 1941. *Dakota Grammar.* Memoirs of the National Academy of Sciences, vol. 23. Washington: Government Printing Office.

Casagrande, Joseph B. 1960. *In the Company of Man: Twenty Portraits by Anthropologists.* New York: Harper and Row.

Deloria, Ella. 1988. *Waterlilly.* Lincoln: University of Nebraska Press.

Deloria, Vine, Jr. 1969. *Custer Died for Your Sins.* New York: Macmillan.

———. *Red Earth, White Lies: Native Americans and the Myth of Scientific Fact.* 1995. New York: Scribner.

Hallowell, A. Irving. 1957. "The Backwash of the Frontier: The Impact of the Indian on American Culture." In *The Frontier in Perspective,* ed. Walker Wyman and Clifton Kroeber, 229–58. Madison: University of Wisconsin Press.

Hill, Ruth Beebe. 1979. *Hanta Yo.* Garden City: Doubleday.

Kimball, Solon, and James V. Watson. 1972. *Crossing Cultural Boundries: The Anthropological Experience.* San Francisco: Chandler Publishers.

Mack, Dorothy, and Debra White Plume. 1988. "Review of Marla N. Powers, Oglala Women: Myth, Ritual, and Reality." *American Indian Quarterly* 12(1): 76–78.

Medicine, Beatrice. 1978. "Learning to be an Anthropologist and Remaining 'Native.'" In *Applied Anthropology in America: Past Contributions and Future Directions,* ed. Elizabeth Eddy and William Partridge, 182–96. New York: Columbia University Press.

Powers, Marla N. 1986. *Oglala Women: Myth, Ritual, and Reality.* Chicago: University of Chicago Press.

Visweswaran, Kamala. 1997. "History of Feminist Ethnography." *Annual Review of Anthropology* 26: 591–621.

Appendix:
Curriculum Vitae

Beatrice Medicine

PERSONAL DATA

Associate Professor of Anthropology Emeritus
(Retired August 1, 1988)
Department of Anthropology
California State University, Northridge
Northridge, California

EDUCATIONAL BACKGROUND

Ph.D. 1983, University of Wisconsin–Madison, Cultural Anthropology
M.A. 1954, Michigan State University, Sociology and Anthropology
B.S. 1945, South Dakota State University Brookings, Education, Art, and History

PROFESSIONAL EXPERIENCE

1999–present	Visiting Professor, Brandon University, Brandon, Manitoba
1998	Stanley Knowles Distinguished Professor, Brandon University, Brandon, Manitoba
1996	Buckman Professor, Department of Human Ecology, University of Minnesota, Twin Cities
1995–present	Adjunct Professor, Department of Educational Foundations, University of Alberta, Edmonton
1995	Scholar in Residence, Minnesota Historical Society, St. Paul
1995	Visiting Scholar, Museum of Anthropology, University of British Columbia, Vancouver
1993	Visiting Professor, Rural Sociology, South Dakota State University, Brookings
1993–94	Research Coordinator, Women's Perspectives, Royal Commission on Aboriginal Peoples, Ottawa, Ontario, Canada

1992	Visiting Distinguished Professor, Women's Studies, University of Toronto
1991	Visiting Professor, Saskatchewan Indian Fed. College, Regina, Saskatchewan
1991	Visiting Professor, Colorado College
1991	Visiting Professor, Anthropology, Humboldt State University, California
1989	Standing Rock College, Fort Yates, N.D.
1988	Retired August 1, 1988
1985–88	Professor, Department of Anthropology, and Director, Native Centre, University of Calgary, Alberta, Canada
1982–85	Associate Professor of Anthropology, Coordinator, Interdisciplinary Program in American Indian Studies, California State University, Northridge
1978–82	Advanced Opportunity Fellow, Department of Anthropology, University of Wisconsin–Madison
1981 (Spring)	Visiting Professor, Graduate School of Public Affairs, University of Washington, Seattle
1979 (Summer)	Visiting Professor, Department of Education Policy Sciences, University of Wisconsin–Madison
1976 (Summer)	Visiting Professor, Educational Anthropology, University of New Brunswick, Fredericton, New Brunswick, Canada
1975–76	Visiting Associate Professor, Anthropology, Stanford University, Stanford, Calif.
1974–75	Visiting Professor, Anthropology, Colorado College, Colorado Springs
1973–74	Visiting Professor, Anthropology, Native American Studies Program, Dartmouth College, Hanover, N.H.
1972–73	Fellow, Center for the History of American Indians, Newberry Library, Chicago
1971–73	Pre-Doctoral Lecturer, Anthropology, University of Washington, Seattle
1970–71	Associate Professor, Anthropology, San Francisco State University, San Francisco, Calif.
1969–1970	Assistant Professor, San Francisco State University, San Francisco, Calif.
1969 (Summer)	Assistant Professor, Teacher Corps, University of Nebraska, Omaha
1968–69	Director, American Indian Research, Oral History Project, and Assistant Professor of Anthropology, University of South Dakota, Vermillion
1967–68	Lecturer, Sociology and Anthropology, University of Montana, Missoula

1966	Psychiatric Social Worker, Provincial Guidance Centre, Calgary, Alberta, Canada
1965	Lecturer, Social Science, Michigan State University, East Lansing
1963–64	Lecturer, Sociology, Mount Royal College, and Teacher/Counselor, Indian Affairs Branch, Calgary, Alberta, Canada
1960–63	Lecturer, Anthropology, University of British Columbia, Vancouver, British Columbia, Canada
1955–58	Teaching and Research Assistant, University of Washington, Seattle
1951–54	Research Assistant, Sociology and Anthropology, Michigan State University, East Lansing
1950–51	Teacher, Home Economics, Flandreau Indian School, Flandreau, S.D.
1949–50	Teacher, Navajo Adult Beginner's Program, Albuquerque Indian School, Albuquerque, N.M.
1948–49	Teacher, Santo Domingo Pueblo, United Pueblos Agency, Albuquerque, N.M.
1947–48	Health Education Lecturer, Michigan Tuberculosis Association, Lansing
1945–46	Teacher, Home Economics, Haskell Indian Institute (B.I.A.), Lawrence, Kan.

PROFESSIONAL MEMBERSHIP

1. American Anthropological Association
   a. Committee on Minorities in Anthropology, 1973–76
   b. Member, Steering Committee, Council of Anthropology and Education, 1975–77
   c. Nominations Committee, 1980
   d. Alcohol and Drug Study Group
   e. Ethics Committee
2. American Ethnological Society
3. American Ethno-historical Society
4. Society of Applied Anthropology, Fellow
5. Canadian Society for Sociology and Anthropology
6. National Indian Education Association
7. American Indian Historical Society
   a. Editorial Board, 1969–75
   b. Native American Scholars Board, Steering and Selection, 1971
8. Northwest Indian Scholars
9. Southwest Anthropological Association, Executive Board, 1983–86
10. Advisory Board of National Research for Handicapped Native Americans, Northern Arizona University, Flagstaff, 1984

PROFESSIONAL SERVICE

1. Editorial Board, *Journal of Canadian Indian Languages,* Centre for the Study
   and Teaching of Canadian Native Languages, London, University of Western
   Ontario
2. Ethnic Associations—Involvement
   a. National Congress of American Indians (Education Issues), 1966–present
   b. North American Indian Women's Association
   c. World Council of Indigenous Peoples (Observer)
   d. Organization of American States, First Congress of Indigenous Women,
      Chiapas, Mexico, 1973
   e. Assembly of California Indian Women (President, 1982)
3. Pardon Board, Standing Rock Reservation (Lakota Nation), Ft. Yates, N.D.
4. School Board, Wakpala Public School, Wakpala, S.D.

EDITORIAL BOARDS

Journal of Canadian Native Languages, University of Western Ontario, London
Associate Editor: *Wicazo Sa: Indian Studies Journal,* Eastern Washington University, Cheney
National Women's Studies Association Journal, Ohio State University, Columbus

PROFESSIONAL COMMITTEES

Society for Applied Anthropology: Malinowski Awards, 1985–89; Indian Issues
   Committee
American Anthropological Association: Concerns for Minority Education Committee; Board; Ethics Committee
Council on Education and Anthropology

INVITED PAPERS READ

1986	Canberra, Australia—Australia, New Zealand, and Canada Studies Association—"Native Canadian Women: An Assessment"
1988	Zagreb, Yugoslavia—International Union of Anthropologists and Ethnologists Conference—"Siouan Sobriety: An Emerging Enterprise"
1990	Lisbon, Portugal—International Union of Anthropologists and Ethnologists Conference—Commentator on papers of Minority Anthropologists
1991	Amsterdam, The Netherlands—International Law and Society Association—"The Legal Status of North American Indigenous Women" and "The Status of American Indians in Historical and Health Research"
1993	Moscow, Russia—International Hunting and Gathering Societies—Plenary Address—"Empowerment of Native Women Through Organizations"

| 1994 | Gaborone, Botswana, Africa—International Congress on Women's Health Issues—Keynote Address—"Health Issues Affecting American Indian Women"; elected to Board of Directors |
| 1996 | Saskatoon, Saskatchewan—International Congress on Women's Health Issues—Keynote Address; selected for Ethics Board |

SERVICE TO CALIFORNIA STATE UNIVERSITY

1982–85	Coordinator, Interdisciplinary Program in American Indian Studies
1982–83	Anthropology Department Curriculum Committee
1982 (Fall)	School of Social and Behavioral Science Academic Planning
1983–84	Student Affirmative Action Coordinating Council
1984	Scholarly Publications Award Selection Committee
1984–85	Participant, Chancellor's Office Grant to "Cross-Cultural Perspectives in the Social Sciences"

SERVICE TO THE UNIVERSITY OF CALGARY

- Tenure Committee, Search Committee, and Native Education Committee—Faculty of Education
- Ethics Committee, Department of Anthropology
- TUCFA—Status of Women Committee
- Tri-University Native Education Committee
- Board of Directors, Nechi Drug and Treatment Centre, Edmonton
- Advisory Board, Native Studies Review, University of Saskatchewan, Saskatoon
- Glenbow Museum, Olympic Advisory Committee
- Board: Urban Aboriginal Affairs Council, City of Calgary
- Board: Canadian Native Arts Association
- Film: *Native Higher Education* for Native Outreach
- Tenure and Promotion Committee, Department of Anthropology
- Board: Metis Association of Alberta
- Advisory Board: Native Education Centre, Vancouver, British Columbia
- Committee to Study Canadian Values: The Faculty of Education
- Instructional Development Committee of the General Faculties Council

COMMUNITY AND CIVIC INVOLVEMENT

1999–present	Member of pardon board for the Standing Rock Indian Nation
1985–86	Board of directors, life tenure, Nechi Institute on Alcohol and Drug Education
1983–86	Governing board, Common Cause
	Expert witness at:
	1973 Yvonne Wanro trial, Spokane, Wash.
	1974 Wounded Knee trial, Lincoln, Neb.
	1976 Topsky Eagle Feathers trial, Pocatello, Idaho

1977	Greybull grandchildren custody case, Portland, Ore.
1983	Fortunate Eagle trial, Reno, Nev.
1973	Consultant, Human Services Department, Sinte Gleska Community College, Rosebud, S.D.
1972	Curriculum advisor, Lakota Higher Education Center, Pine Ridge, S.D.
1971–73	Consultant, American Indian Heritage Program, Seattle, Wash.
1968–70 and	
1977–80	Education consultant, National Congress of American Indians, Washington, D.C.
1970	Planning Committee, Indian Alcoholism and Drug Use
1970–71	Mayor's Committee on the Status of Women, San Francisco, Calif.
1970	Steering Committee member, Indian Ecumenical Convocation of North America
1968–70	Consultant, Textbook Evaluation Committee, American Indians United
1968	Teaching "Cultural Enrichment Program," Standing Rock Reservation, S.D., summer
1960–64	Board of directors, Native Urban Indian Centers in Vancouver, British Columbia, and Calgary, Alberta
1954	American Indian Women's Service League, Seattle, Wash., charter member

HONORS, AWARDS, FELLOWSHIPS

1996	Malinowski Award, Society for Applied Anthropology
1995	Ohana Award, Multi-Cultural Counseling Excellence, American Association of Counselors
1993	Distinguished Native American Alumna Award, South Dakota State University
1993	Distinguished Service Award, American Anthropological Association, Annual Meeting, Chicago
1993	Honorary doctorate of humane letters, Michigan State University
1990	Illinois State Board of Education, Chicago, Citation for "Outstanding Contributions for the Promotion of Sex Equity in Education"
1990	Outstanding Lakota Woman, Standing Rock College
1989	(Second) Martin Luther King, Jr. and Rosa Parks Outstanding Minority Professor Visiting Professor, Anthropology, Wayne State University, Detroit
1987	(First) Martin Luther King, Jr. and Rosa Parks Outstanding Minority Professor Visiting Professor, Anthropology, University of Michigan

1984	Faculty Award for Meritorious Service, California State University, Northridge
1983	Outstanding Minority Researcher, American Educational Research Association
1983	Outstanding Woman of Color, National Institute of Women of Color, Washington, D.C. (for anthropological contributions)
1980	Biographic Sketch in *Native American Indian Personalities: Historical and Contemporary* (Dansville, N.Y.: Instructor Publications, Inc.)
1979	Honorary Doctorate of Humane Letters, Northern Michigan University, Aug. 1979
1978	Cited in *The Directory of Significant Twentieth-Century American Minority Women* (Gaylord Professional Publications)
1978	Biographic sketch in *Moving Forward* of the Bookmark Reading Program, 3d ed.
1977	Sacred Pipe Woman, Sun Dance at Standing Rock Reservation
1977	American Indian Representative to the World Conference on Indigenous People, Geneva, Switzerland
1977	Outstanding Alumna, South Dakota State University
1976	Panelist at White House Conference on Ethnic Studies, Washington, D.C.
1975	Biographic Sketch in *American Indian Contributions of American Life* (Benefic Press)
1972	Honored in "Potlatch" ceremony by Makah Tribal People at National Indian Education Conference for Contributions to Indian Education
1972	American Council of Learned Societies Travel Grant, Americanist Annual Meeting, Rome, Italy
1968	Cited in "The Role of Racial Minorities in the United States," Seattle, Washington
1967	Ethnological Research Grant, National Museum of Canada
1960 and 1970	Who's Who among American Indians Alpha Kappa Delta, Sociology Honorary Phi Upsilon Omicron, Home Economic Honorary
1966–67	Career Development Grant, National Institute of Mental Health
1963–64	American Council of Learned Societies Research Grant
1956	Outstanding Alumna, South Dakota State University
1954	American Council of Learned Societies Fellowship
1953–54	John Hay Whitney Foundation Fellowship
1950–54	Illinois Federation of Women's Clubs Fellowships
1941–45	South Dakota State University, Laverne Noyes Fellowship

PUBLICATIONS

Books

2001   *Learning to Be an Anthropologist and Remaining "Native."* Urbana: University of Illinois Press.

1983   "An Ethnography of Drinking and Sobriety among the Lakota Sioux." Ph.D. diss. Madison: University of Wisconsin.

1983   with Patricia Albers, eds. *The Hidden Half: Studies of Plains Indian Women.* Washington, D.C.: University Press of America. (Selected as *Choice* Significant Academic Book, 1983).

1978   *Native American Women: A Perspective.* Austin, Tex.: National Education Laboratory Publishers, Inc.

Articles and Chapters in Books

1999   "Reconciliation: Indians and Whites in South Dakota," in *Re-considering Reconciliation.* Calgary: Institute of the Humanities. 27–54.

1999   "Ella C. Deloria: Ethnographic Informant and Newly Discovered Novelist," in *Theorizing the Americanist Tradition,* Lisa Valentine and Regna Darnell, eds. Toronto: University of Toronto Press. 259–67.

1998   "Alcohol and Aborigines: The North American Perspective," *A/B/M/R/F: Journal of the Alcoholic Beverage Medical Research Foundation* (Baltimore). 7–11.

1998   "American Indians and Anthropologists: Issues of History, Empowerment, and Appreciation," *Journal of the Society for Applied Anthropology* 57(3):253–57.

1998   "Native American Religions" (403–5) and "Great Plains" (411–12) in *The Reader's Companion to U.S. Women's History,* Wilma Mankiller et al., eds. New York: Houghton Mifflin.

1997   "Searching for the Bishop," in *Reinventing the Enemy's Language,* Joy Harjo and Gloria Bird, editors. New York: W. W. Norton. 208–11.

1997   "Changing Native American Roles in an Urban Context *and* Changing Native American Sex Roles in an Urban Context," in *Two-Spirit People,* Sue-Ellen Jacobs, Wesley Thomas, and Sabine Lang, editors. Urbana: University of Illinois Press. 145–73.

1997   "Lakota Star Quilts: Commodity, Ceremony, and Economic Development," in *To Honor and Comfort: Native Quilting Traditions,* Marsha L McDowell and C. Kurt Dewhurst, editors. Santa Fe: Museum of New Mexico Press and Michigan State University Museum. 111–17.

1996   "Families" (pp. 71–72), "Gender" (pp. 216–18), and "Women" (pp. 685–89), in *Encyclopedia of North American Indians,* Frederick E. Hoxie, editor. Boston: Houghton-Mifflin.

                "Border Town" poem in *Indigenous Woman* 11(14): 38–39.

1994   "Families" (pp. 193–95) and "Gender" (pp. 207–8), in *Native America in the Twentieth Century: An Encyclopedia,* Mary B. Davis, editor. New York: Garland Publishing.

1993   "American Indian Women: Mental Health Issues which Relate to Drug Abuse." *Wicazo Sa Review* 9(2): 85–90.

1993   with Joseph E. Trimble. "Diversification of American Indians: Forming an Indigenous Perspective," in *Indigenous Psychologies: Research and Experience in Cultural Context,* Nichol Kim and John W. Barry, editors. Newbury Park: Sage Publications. 133–51.

1993   "North American Indigenous Women and Cultural Domination," *American Indian Culture and Research Journal* 17(2): 121–30; reprinted in *Cultural Survival Quarterly* (Winter 1994): 66–69.

1990   "Carrying the Culture: American Indian and Alaska Native Women Workers," in *Risks and Challenges: Women, Work, and the Future.* Washington, D.C.: Wider Opportunities for Women, Inc.

1989   "Indian Identity within Communities and Externally Imposed Policies." *Ethnicity* (Moscow, Russia) Institute of Ethnography Publications: 119–30.

1988   "Ella Cara Deloria," in *Women Anthropologists: A Biographical Dictionary,* Uta Gracs, Aisha Khan, Jerrie McIntyre, and Ruth Weinberg, editors. New York: Greenwood Press. 45–50.

1988   "Native American (Indian) Women: A Call for Research." *Anthropology and Education Quarterly* 19(2): 86–92.

1987   "The Role of American Indian Women in Cultural Continuity and Transition," in *Women and Language in Transition,* Joyce Penfield, editor. SUNY Press. 159–66.

1987   "Indian Women and the Renaissance of Traditional Religion," in *Sioux Indian Religion,* Raymond J. DeMallie and Douglas R. Parks, editors. Norman: University of Oklahoma Press. 159–71.

1987   "The Role of Elders in Native Education," in *Indian Education in Canada,* vol. 2: *The Challenge,* Jean Barman, Yvonne Hebert, and Don McCaskill, editors. Vancouver, B.C.: University of British Columbia Press. 152–52.

1987   "Understanding the Native Community." *Multicultural Education Journal* 5 (April): 21–26. Alberta Teachers Association, Edmonton. "The Cultural Background of American Indian Art," in *New Directions Northwest* [museum catalog]. Portland, Ore.: Art Museum and Evergreen State College. 1–10.

1986   "Beyond Compare and Contrast . . . Perspectives from Anthropology," in *Unmasking Culture: Cross-Cultural Perspectives in the Social and Behavioral Sciences,* Luicija Baskauskas, editor. N.p.: Chandler and Sharp. 107–18. "Contemporary Cultural Revitalization: Bilingual and Bicultural Education," in *Wicazo Sa Review: Indian Studies Journal* 2 (Spring): 31–35.

1984   with Trimble, Manson, and Dinges. "American Indian Concepts of Mental Health Reflections and Directions," in *Mental Health Services: The Cross-Cultural Context,* Paul B. Pedersen, editor. Beverly Hills: Sage Publications. 199–220.

1983   "Ina," in *Sinister Wisdom* (Amherst, Mass.) 22/23. Reprinted in *A Gathering of Spirit*. 1984.
"Indian Women: Tribal Identity as Status Quo," in *Woman's Nature: Rationalizations of Inequality*, Marian Lowe and Ruth Hubbard, editors. New York: Pergamon Press. 63–73.

1982   "New Roads to Coping: Siouan Sobriety," in *New Directions in Prevention among American Indian and Alaskan Native Communities*, Spero M. Manson, editor. Portland, Ore.: Health Sciences University. 189–213.
"Native American Women Look at Mental Health," in *Plainswoman* (University of North Dakota) 6(4): 7.

1981   "Contemporary Literature on Indian Women: A Review Essay," in *Frontiers: A Journal of Women's Studies* (University of Colorado, Boulder) 6(3): 122–25.

1981   "Wakan: Thoughts on Sacredness," in *Anthropology Resource Center Newsletter* 5(4): 7.

1981   "Native American Resistance to Integration: Contemporary Confrontations and Religious Revitalization," in *Plains Anthropologist* 26(94), pt. 1: 277–86.

1981   "The Interaction of Culture and Sex Roles in the Schools," in *Integrateducation* 20(1–2): 28–37.

1981   "'Speaking Indian': Parameters of Language Use among American Indians," in *Focus* (National Clearing House for Bilingual Education, Washington, D.C.) (March 1981): 107.

1981   "American Indian Family: Cultural Change and Adaptive Strategies," in *Journal of Ethnic Studies* 8 (Winter): 13–23.

1980   with Spero Manson and Wally Funmaker, "Training of American Indians and Alaskan Natives in Mental Health," in *Practical Anthropology* 2(1): 4–5, 22–24.

1980   "Ella C. Deloria: The Emic Voice," in *Journal of the Society for the Study of Multi-Ethnic Literature of the United States* 7 (Winter):23–30.

1980   "The Interaction of Culture and Sex Roles in the Schools," in *Proceedings of the Conference of the Educational and Occupational Needs of American Indian Women* (National Institute of Education, Washington, D.C.) 1980: 121–58.

1980   "American Indian Women: Spirituality and Status," in *Bread and Roses* (Madison, Wis.) 2 (Autumn): 15–18.
with Patricia Albers, "Star Quilts," in *Native Arts/West* (Santa Fe, N.M.) July: 9–15.

1980   "Searching for the Bishop," in *Plainswoman* (Grand Forks, N.D.) 3 (March–April): 9–19. Reprinted in *Reinventing the Enemy's Language*, Joy Harjo et al., eds. New York: W. W. Norton, 1997. 207–11.

1979   "Native Americans Communication Patterns: The Case of the Lakota Speakers," in *Handbook of Transcultural Communication*. Beverly Hills: Sage Publications. 378–81.

1979   "Bilingual Education and Public Policy: The Case of the American Indians," in *Bilingual Education and Public Policy in the United States,* Raymond Padilla, editor. Ypsilanti: Eastern Michigan University. 395–407.

1979   "Hanta Yo: A New Phenomenon," in *The Indian Historian* 12(2): 2–5. Reprinted in *Kainai News* 5(5): 2.

1978   "Learning to Be an Anthropologist and Remaining 'Native,'" in *Applied Anthropology in America: Past Contributions and Future Directions,* Elizabeth Eddy and William Partridge, editors. New York: Columbia University Press. 182–96.

1978   *Native American Women: A Perspective.* Austin, Tex.: National Educational Laboratory Publishers, Inc.
        "Kunshiki—Grandmothers," in *Plainswomen* (Grand Forks, N.D.) 1 (July-Aug.): 11–12.

1978   "Higher Education: A Threshold for Native Americans," in *Thresholds in Education* (DeKalb, Ill.) 4 (May): 22–25.

1978   "We Talk of Mental Health," in *Newsletter of the National Center for American Indian and Alaskan Native Health* 2 (Spring): 5.

1977   "NIEA, NCAI, NIYC Revisited" (poem), in *Wassaja* (Dec.), n.p.

1976   "The Schooling Process—Some Lakota (Sioux) Views," in *Anthropological Study of Education,* Craig Calhoun and Francis A. J. Ianni, editors. The Hague: Mouton Publishers. N.p.

1976   "Oral History as Truth: Validity of Recent Court Cases Involving Native Americans," *Folklore Forum* (Bibliographic and Special Series) 9(15): 1–5.

1976   with Joseph Trimble. "Development of Models and Levels of Interpretation in Mental Health," in *Anthropology and Mental Health,* Joseph Westermeyer, editor. The Hague: Mouton Publishers. N.p.

1975   "The Role of Women in Native American Societies: A Bibliography," in *Indian Historian* 8(3): 50–54.

1975   "Spotted Tail," "Gall," "Sitting Bull," "Ely S. Parker," "Sioux Indians," and "American Indian Movement," in *World Book Encyclopedia.* Chicago (originally published in 1975 and republished in all editions to the present).

1975   "Self-Direction in Sioux Education," in *Integrateducation* 78 (Nov.–Dec.): 15–17.

1974   "Religion and Philosophy," in *Encyclopedia of Americas,* n.p. Scholarly Press, Inc. 166–78.

1973   "The Big Foot Trail to Wounded Knee" (poem), in *Indian Historian* 6(4): 23–35.

1973   "The Native American," in *The Outsiders,* D. Spiegel and P. K. Spiegel, editors. San Francisco: Rinehart Press. 391–407.

1973   "Finders Keepers," in *Museum News* 51 (March): 20–26.

1971   "The Anthropologist as the Indian's Image-Maker," in *Indian Historian* 4(3): 27–29.

1970   "Red Power, Real or Potential," in *Indian Voices: The First Convocation of American Indian Scholars*. San Francisco: Indian Historian Press. 299–307. Excerpted in *The American Indian: A Rising Ethnic Force*, Herbert L. Marx, editor. *The Reference Shelf* 45(5): 41–45. New York: H. W. Wilson, 1973.

1969   "The American Indian in Modern Society," in *South Dakota Review* (Vermillion): 189–91.

"The Changing Dakota Family," *Pine Ridge Research Bulletin* 9: n.p.

1968   "The Use of Magic among the Stoney Indians," in *Thirty-eighth Internationalen Amerikanistenkongresses* (1968): 283–92.

1950   with Florence Hawley. "Changing Foods and Food Habits," in *El Palacio* 57(10): 324–31.

Book Reviews

1988   Review of E. Jane Gay, *With the Nez Perces: Alice Fletcher in the Field, 1889–1892*, Lincoln: University of Nebraska Press, 1981, in *American Indian Quarterly* 12 (Winter): 78–79.

1987   Review of Marla N. Powers, *Oglala Women: Myth, Ritual and Reality*, in *American Anthropologist* 89(4): 975–76.

1986   Review of Ohoyo Makachi, "Words of Today's American Women," in *American Indian Quarterly* 5: 246–47.

1983   Review of Mary Lee Stearns, *Culture in Custody: The Masset Band in Culture*, in *Journal of Canadian Ethnology Society* 3(2): 77–78.

1981   Review of Ernest L. Schusky, editor, *Political Organization of Native North Americans*, Washington, D.C.: University Press of America, 1980, in *American Ethnologist* 8(2): 403–4.

1980   Review of Ruth Beebe Hill, *Hanta Yo*, Garden City: Doubleday, 1979, in *ASAIL Newsletter* 3 (Winter): 50–55.

1979   Review of Adolph Hungry Wolf, *The Blood People: A Division of the Blackfoot Confederacy*, in *Journal of Ethnic Studies* 7 (Summer): 117–19.

1973   Review of Ethel Nurge, *The Modern Sioux*, in *Journal of Ethnic Studies* 1(1): 87–89.

Review of A. D. Coleman and T. C. McLuhan, *Portraits from North American Indian Life*, in *Pacific Search* (April): 16.

1972   Review of James McLaughlin, *My Friend the Indian*, in *American Anthropologist* 74(1–2): 171–72.

PAPERS PRESENTED AT PROFESSIONAL MEETINGS (SELECTED)

1999   "Ella Deloria—Lakota Ethnographer." American Anthropological Association. Chicago.

1999   "Lakota Views on Art." Native American Art Studies Association Bienniel Meet, Victoria, B.C.

1999   Invited Paper. International Conference on Reconciliation. Calgary, Alberta.

1996   Malinowski Award Address. Society for Applied Anthropology

1985 (Nov.)	Invited Speaker at the Conference on "The Native American: His Arts, His Culture, and His History." West Virginia State College
1984	Invited Sessions: American Anthropological Association, Annual Meeting a. Field Work Methods: "Ties That Bind," Committee on the Status of Women in Anthropology b. "Career Patterns of American Indian Women," Council of Education and Anthropology "Ethnicity, Identity, and the Future of American Indians." Society for Applied Anthropology, Annual Meeting
1982	"Policy Decisions: Federal Regulations and American Indian Identity Issues." American Anthropological Association, Annual Meeting
1981	Invited Session Discussant on "Linguistically Marginated: The Transformation of Dominated Speech Varieties." American Anthropological Association
1979 (Aug.)	"The Dakota Indian Memorial Feast: Reservation and Urban Manifestations." International Congress of Americanists, Lima, Peru
1978 (Aug.)	"Issues in the Professionalization of Native American Women." American Psychological Association, Annual Meeting, Toronto, Canada
1974	"Indian Women's Roles: Traditional and Contemporary." American Psychological Association, Annual Meeting, Chicago, Illinois
1973	"Self-Direction in Sioux Education." American Anthropological Association, Mexico City, Mexico "North American Native Women: The Aspirations and Their Associations." Presented as a Delegate to the Inter-American Commission on Indigenous Women, Chiapas, Mexico
1972 (Nov.)	"Native Americans in the Modern World." Southwest Minnesota State College, Marshall
1972 (Aug.)	"Warrior Women of the Plains." International Congress of Americanists, Rome, Italy
1972 (June)	Chair Native American Studies Symposium, International Congress of Americanists, Mexico
1972 (April)	"Racism and Ethnic Relations." Chair, conference entitled "Racism and Ethnic Relations" for the Society for Applied Anthropology, Montreal, Canada
1972 (March)	"Warrior Women Societies." Solicited and presented at Northwest Anthropological Conference, Portland, Ore.
1971 (May)	"Ethnic Studies and Native Americans." National Education Association, Washington, D.C.

1970 (Nov.)	American Anthropological Association, Annual Meeting, San Diego, Calif. a. "The Anthropologists as the Indian's Image Maker" b. "The Anthropologist and Ethnic Studies Programs" (both presented)
1970 (Oct.)	"The Ethnographic Study of Indian Women." Solicited and presented at American Ethnohistorical Society, Annual Convention, Missoula, Mont.
1970 (Aug.)	"The Role of the White Indian Expert." 2d Annual Conference, National Indian Education Association, Minneapolis, Minn.
1969	"The Indian in Institutions of Higher Learning" and "American Indian Women." Solicited and presented at 1st Annual Conference, National Indian Education Association, Minneapolis, Minn.
1969 (Dec.)	"The Native American in Modern Society." Northwestern State College, Orange City, Iowa
1969 (Sept.)	"The Red Man Yesterday." Solicited by the Governor's Interstate Indian Council, Wichita, Kan.
1968 (Aug.)	"Magic among the Stoney Indians" and "The Dynamics of a Dakota Indian Giveaway." International Congress of Americanists, Stuttgart, Germany
1968 (June)	"Magic among the Stoney Indians." Canadian Sociology and Anthropological Association, Calgary, Alberta
1968 (May)	"Patterns and Periphery of Plains Indian Pow-Wows." Central States Anthropological Society, Milwaukee, Wis.
1968 (March)	"The Pow-Wow as a Social Factor in the Northern Plains Ceremonialism." Montana Academy of Sciences, Helena

Ongoing Research

1. Mental Health Issues among American Indians.
2. Women's Issues—Professionalization, Sterilization, Socialization, Aging.
3. Bilingual Education—American and Canadian Indians.
4. Alcohol and Drug Use and Abuse among American Indians.
5. Ethno-methodologies and Research Needs of American Indians.
6. Socialization of Children and Identity Issues.

INDEX

Page numbers for photographs and artwork are in italics.

can Indian and Alaskan Native; Native American
Indians of the United States, 292
Indian Self-Determination Act (1977), 46, 55
Indian studies programs. *See* American Indian studies programs
Indian Voices, 319, 320
indigenous: bureaucracy, 180; people/societies, 13–14, 28, 51, 75, 94, 109, 137, 161, 289, 291, 293, 326; viewpoints, 138, 139, 186, 293, 326
individual autonomy. *See* personal autonomy
infant mortality rates. *See* death, infant rates of
infertility, 6
informants, 5, 7, 187, 277, 281, 282; Boasian (linguistic), 269, 326–27; Natives as, 29, 92–93, 135n, 187, 277, 326–27; role of, 4, 92; women as, 92, 282, 326–27
inheritance rights, 159–60, 249, 300
inipi. See sweats
Institute for the Development of Indian Law, Inc., 308
intermarriage. *See* marriage, interracial; marriage, intertribal
International Conference of the Indigenous Women in the New World, 93
International Congress of Americanists, 135n
International Women's Year, 93
Interstate Congress for Equal Rights and Responsibilities (1976), 89, 181
Intertribal Friendship House, 37
intoxication: arrests for, 9. *See also* drunkeness
Introduction to Cultural Anthropology, 312, 313
Iroquois, 92, 108–9, 154, 256, 257, 292, 301; Iroquoian-speakers, 45, 55, 192, 301
isnati (lives alone or apart), 118, 141, 193–94
ito mani k'tca (supreme or ultimate drunks), 217
ito mani sni (sober), 215
Iya, 274

Jacobs, Wilbur, 315, 316
Jahner, Elaine, 277
James, William, 135n
Jefferson, James, 313
Jesuits, 101
Joe, Jennie, 259
Johnson, C. A., 220–21
Johnson, D. L., 220–21
Johnson-O'Malley Funds (1934), 27, 44, 53, 63
Jones, David E., 200
Jones, Delmos, 325

Jones, William, 4, 123
Jorgensen, Joseph G., 88–89, 185, 186, 223–24, 259–60
Jules-Rosette, B., 215

Kashaya Pomo, 30
Kaska Indians, 131
Katz, Jane B., 200
Katz, Jonathan, 124–25
Kehoe, Alice B., 154
Kelly, R. E., 301
Kemnitzer, L. S., 208, 210, 215, 224
Kennewick Man, 325
KEPLV theory. *See* Southall, Aidan
Keresan, 24, 45
Kickingbird, Kirke, 315
Kidwell, Clara Sue, 110, 112
Kimball, Solon T., 323, 327
kin/kinship, 9, 14, 24, 60, 74, 76, 84, 92, 96, 117, 129, 134, 149, 163, 203, 217, 249, 250, 270; bilateral, 96, 143, 148–49, 251, 257; circle/group, 6, 10, 60, 76, 96, 110, 117, 143, 151, 180, 241, 250, 254, 255, 259–62, 264, 317–18, 323; devaluation of, 260, 263; European model of, 149, 154, 157; expectations, 97, 150, 157, 212, 252; fictive, 105, 203, 252; loyalties, 7, 272, 277, 280; matrilineal, 94–95, 105, 108–9, 213, 254, 257; patrilineal, 94, 105, 1009, 143, 154, 155, 257; patterns of, 51, 68, 105, 153, 204–5, 254, 255, 257, 271, 281, 302, 325; proper behavior, 60, 132, 247–48, 251, 278; studies, 6, 120, 252, 256–57, 281; terminology, 148–49, 156, 250, 251–53, 272–73, 285; ties, 12, 143, 168, 216, 251, 256. *See also tiospaye*
Kiowa, 108, 118, 161, 234, 257, 260, 298, 315
Knack, Martha, 24
Knapp, Frances, 128, 135n
kola (friend), 97; *kola*-hood (traditional friend group), 212, 213, 223
Kopytoff, Igor, 185
koshkalaka (young man, youth), 118
koshkalaka winyan ("lesbian-woman"), 118
Koster, John, 180, 182, 186
Kunitz, Stephen J., 197, 207, 216, 230, 232
Kutenai (Kootnai), 123, 126n, 128, 199
Kuttner, R. E., 209, 214–14
Kwakiutl, 91, 92

labor, division of, 98; sexual, 38, 98, 142
lactation, 194, 247
LaFlesche, Francis, 4, 21, 47–48, 92, 277, 290
Laguna, 259
Lakota (Sioux), 5, 6, 7, 8, 10, 23, 28, 30, 32, 46,

Index

367

Southall, Aiden, 120, 122
South Dakota Department of Public Instruction, 63
Southern Utes: A Tribal History, 313
Speaking of Indians, 167, 270–71, 275, 277, 278, 280, 283, 286n
Spindler, Louise, 198–99, 200
spiritual: needs, 181–82; roles of men, 192
spiritual culture areas, 271
spirituality: of Native peoples, 181, 191, 278; Native women and, 191–95
Spradley, James, 209
Stack, Carol B., 254
Standing Bear, Luther, 21, 41–42, 97, 100, 195
Standing Rock: Community College, 66, 327, *see also* Sitting Bull College; Sioux and, 55, 217, 279, 298, *see also* Sioux Nation; Standing Rock Reservation, 6, 7, 10, 50, 55, 58–59, 60, 96, 105, 144, 151, 160, 164, 207, 210, 211, 239, 275, 280, 285, 286n, 298, 309, 323, 325; tribal council, 39
Stanford University, 30, 328; powwow, 37
star quilts: ceremonial use of, 168, 169, 170, *172–73;* for children, 168, 171; commercial manufacture of, 170–71; commodificiation of, 168, 170; display of, 169; distinct value places on, 168; giving as a gift, 168, 171, 250; introduction of, 167; miniature, 168; non-Native interest in, 170–71, 250; *wichapi shina* (star robes), 168
State University of New York (SUNY)–Albany, 30
Steinmetz, Fr. Paul B., S. J., 177–78
St. Elizabeth's Mission (Wakpala, S.D.), 269, 275, 278, 279, 283–84
stereotypes, 124, 210, 228, 231, 233–34, 248, 278, 289, 290, 296, 307; in art, 292, 296; about Native women, 101, 108–9; prejudice and fear caused by, 300; of urban Indian militancy, 306, 307
sterilization of Native women, 145, 157, 202, 203
Stevens, Don, 181
Stevens, Jane, 181
Stewart, Irene, 142–43
Stoney Indians, 30
Stull, Don, 326
Sturtevant, William C., 312, 313
substance abuse. *See* alcohol and drugs, abuse
suicide, 92, 124, 256; rates, 108, 162
Sully, Mary, 277
Sully, Thomas, 275
Sun Dance, 22, 28, 87, 96, 99, 141–42, 144, 170, 177–78, 182–86, 193, 194, 195, 221, 223–24,

255, 260, 275, 278, 280, 283; to combat addiction to alcohol/drugs, 185, 223–24; committees, 184; at Green Grass, 183–84, 185; honorary positions in, 132, 193, 223–24; international, 28, 183; intertribal, 28, 182, 183–84, 185–86, 191, 195, 224; leaders, 184; as political statement, 186; as problem-solving agent, 185–86, 223–24; prohibition of, 22, 124, 143, 155, 182, 183, 191–92; studies of, 187, 223–24; Sun Dance Woman, 131–32, 144; tree as sacred symbol of, 99, 142, 144, 193; use of to cope with social and economic deprivations, 185–86; virgin maidens of, 142, 144, 193, 194
support systems: in sobriety, *see* sobriety, support systems and; for urban Indians, 125, 309
surrogate parents. *See* parental surrogates
sweats (*inipi*), 3, 183
Sword, George, 276–77
Szasz, Margaret, 50

taboo(s): incest, 258, 274; mother-in-law, 99; sexual, 98, 140–41, 194
Takes the Gun, Laura, *140*
Talbot, Steve, 180
Taos Pueblo, 298
target population(s), 11, 13, 88, 293, 329
task force(s): educational, 36
teachers, 22, 25, 61–62, 63; aides, 23, 55, 62; role of Native, 9, 29; role of non-Native, 76; training, 31, 54, 69; U.S. Indian Service, 51. *See also* educators
Tell My Horse, 326
Ten Fingers, 276
Teton (Sioux). *See* Sioux Nation, Teton (Western)
textbooks: on Native culture(s), 5; in the vernacular, 21
Thomas Duggan's Journal (1973), 128, 135n
Thomas, Robert (Cherokee), 38
Thompson, George C., 313
Thorne, John E., 314–16
Thornton, Russell, 87, 89
Tiger, Robert, 324
tiole (looking for a home, homeless), 245
tiospaye (*tiyospaye*, extended kinship group), 6, 10, 60, 96, 97, 143, 150, 163, 168, 169, 193, 194, 211, 212, 239–40, 242, 256, 257, 258–61, 271, 280, 281; Native definitions of, 258–59, 260; political, 169. *See also* kin, kinship
tipi, 96, 141, 167, 193, 271–72, 326
Title I of the Elementary and Secondary Act (1965), 25, 53

urban Indian centers, 31, 183, 304–8, 309, 320; as liaisons with other urban agencies, 304
Urban Indian Development Association (UIDA), 309
urbanization (of Native Americans), 120, 198, 295–310; as further destruction of traditional life, 304; increased alcohol consumption and, 120, 209; process, 122, 125, 304, 309; research, 117–19, 120, 122–26
Urbom, Warren K., 314. *See also* Wounded Knee, trials
U.S. Census of Population Report, 120; for 1970, 105, 295–96; for 1980, 161–62
U.S. Commission on Civil Rights, 162, 164–65, 260
U.S. Congress, 3, 53, 54, 153–54, 157, 170, 181, 234, 299; confering of full citizenship on Native Americans, 297; congressional hearings, 26, 36, 139; halt of treaty-making, 36; role in governing Indian policy/laws, 153–54, 301
U.S. Constitution, 40
U.S. Department of Commerce, 216
U.S. Department of Health, Education, and Welfare (HEW), 69, 83, 303
U.S. Department of the Interior (previously, Department of War), 100, 162, 303
U.S. Department of Labor: 164; *Handbook of Women Workers*, 164, 165
U.S. Indian Health Service, 234
U.S. Indian Service, 51; Education Division of, 51
U.S. Office of Education, 44
U.S. Public Health Service, 11, 68, 158, 303, 308
U.S. Senate: 1969 Committee Report, 43
U.S. Supreme Court, 156, 159–60
Ute, 186, 223
Ute People: An Historical Study, 313

value: constructs (Native), 98, 187, 259, 271; of males, 213; placed on creative powers of women, 137–40, 154, 192–94; placed on speaking a Native language, 23, 152; systems (norms), 22, 50–51, 61, 76, 80, 95, 96, 97, 105, 124, 139, 144–45, 147, 149, 156, 163, 177, 187, 252, 258, 263, 264, 271, 274, 330; tribal ethics and, 86, 87, 139, 263, 274
vanishing American, 4, 91, 327; syndrome, 92–3, 289
Van Kirk, Sylvia, 154
venereal disease, 242
vernacular(s), 23, 25, 40, 46; boarding school-type, 22; English, and Christianity, 22; En-

glish, instruction in, 22; English, translation of research into, 11; Indian-English, 42; intertribal (urban), 122; reservation, 28, 68
veterans, Native American, 250; ceremonies for, 250; Vietnam, 169–70
Vietnam Veterans' Association, 169–70
vision quests, 187, 192, 193, 214, 275, 278; unproductive, 129
Visweswaran, Kamala, 326–27
vocational testing, 62
vocational training, 103–4
vocation(s), 62. *See also* occupations

Wabaunsee, A. John, 26
wacantognaka (understanding on a high level), 69
wacunza (to cause harm), 219
Waddell, J. O., 207, 231, 302
Wahpeton, 133, 170
Wahrhaftig, Albert, 38
wakan (power), 124, 184–85, 192–95, 214, 222; of women, 141–42, 192–95
Wakan Tanka (Great Sacredness), 182, 193, 224
wakan yesa (sacred being), 168
Wakinya (Thunder Beings), 131
Walker, Deward E., Jr., 313
Walker, James R., 178, 276–77
Wallace, Anthony F. C., 178, 185
wampum belts, 317
Wanagi Omani (Spirit Road/Milky Way), 169
wanagi yuhapi (keeping the spirit of the deceased), 169
wana yat k'e sni (does not drink), 217–18
Wandrow case (1971), 158
wa pi ya (curer). *See* medicine men; medicine women
warfare, 177; prestige and glory from, 133–34; women in, 129, 133–35
Warren, Pearl (Makah), 41
Warren, William (Ojibwa/Anishinabe), 92
warrior: society, 39, 95, 96, 97, 108, 140, 150–51, 154–55, 193, 194, 231, 250; syndrome, 213; woman, 118, 128–35
Warrior, Robert, 280
warrior role(s), 99–100, 128–35, 141; destruction of by dominant society, 143, 151, 216; rejection of, 99, 12, 129;
"Warrior Women of the Plains," 118
Washburn, Wilcomb, 313
wasicu (white persons), 61–62, 122, 243, 283
wasicup/wasicukipi, 65
wasicu wicoyake, 64, 68
wasiglapi (affronted), 169

BEATRICE MEDICINE is professor emeritus from California State University-Northridge. She currently lives in Wakpala, S.D. She is coauthor, with Pat Albers, of *The Hidden Half: Studies of Plains Indian Women* and has published numerous articles in anthropology and American Indian studies journals.

SUE-ELLEN JACOBS is professor of women's studies at the University of Washington-Seattle. She is coeditor, with Wesley Thomas and Sabine Lang, of *Two-Spirit People: Native American Gender Identity, Sexuality, and Spirituality.* She is also the coauthor, with Charlene Allison and Mary Porter, of *Winds of Change: Women in Pacific Northwest Commercial Fishing.* She is a feminist and applied anthropologist whose articles and papers have been published in many diverse journals and books.

TED GARNER is Bea Medicine's son and a sculptor living in Chicago. He has exhibited in many places.

FAYE V. HARRISON is a professor of anthropology at the University of Tennessee in Knoxville. She is the editor of *Decolonizing Anthropology: Moving Further toward an Anthropology for Liberation* and coeditor (with Ira E. Harrison) of *African-American Pioneers in Anthropology.* She has also published in anthropology, feminist, and American ethnic studies journals.

Composed in 10.5/12.5 Minion
with Minion display
by Jim Proefrock
at the University of Illinois Press
Manufactured by Thomson-Shore, Inc.

University of Illinois Press
1325 South Oak Street
Champaign, IL 61820-6903
www.press.uillinois.edu

DATE DUE

JAN 2 0 2004			
	APR 0 4 2006		

Demco, Inc. 38-293